China's Outward Foreign Investment

A Political Perspective

Xiaofei Li

University Press of America,® Inc.
Lanham · Boulder · New York · Toronto · Plymouth, UK

University Press of America,® Inc.
4501 Forbes Boulevard
Suite 200
Lanham, Maryland 20706
UPA Acquisitions Department (301) 459-3366

Estover Road
Plymouth PL6 7PY
United Kingdom

Printed in the United States of America
British Library Cataloging in Publication Information Available

Library of Congress Control Number: 2010930462
ISBN: 978-0-7618-5263-6 (paperback : alk. paper)
eISBN: 978-0-7618-5264-3

™The paper used in this publication meets the minimum requirements of American National Standard for Information Sciences—Permanence of Paper for Printed Library Materials, ANSI Z39.48-1992

DEDICATION

I wish to thank my three graduate school mentors, Dr. William Heaton, Dr. James P. O'Leary, and Dr. Joan B. Urban, who worked with me very closely in bringing this text to fruition and to whom this work is dedicated. They not only constantly encouraged me in my academic progress, but also cared about me as an overseas student far away from home. More importantly, they have become role models for my future growth and development both as a person and as a scholar. This book is a token of my gratitude for their efforts. I also wish to thank Dr. Hannah Marks for her continual support that made this project possible. I also wish to thank Dr. Joseph G. Leichter for his constant support and encouragement of my studies.

TABLE OF CONTENTS

		Page
	Introduction	vii
I	Exposition of China's Outward FDI	1
II	Merchant-State Dualism in China's History	49
III	Current Illustrations of Dualism in China's FDI	81
IV	Decision-Making and Political Give-and-Take in FDI	117
V	Case Study One – The Iron and Steel Industry	131
VI	Case Study Two – The Oil and Gas Industry	155
VII	Case Study Three – The Electrical Appliances Industry	197
VIII	Conclusion	235
IX	Bibliography	243

INTRODUCTION

Like a band of travelers who see a footprint in a desert, they now realize they are not alone and are left to wonder what this imprint portends. This is how the West feels about the recent emergence of China as a significant player on the global economic stage. China is not only a well-publicized recipient of investments from other nations; but as the number of their foreign bids shows, the Chinese are rapidly growing as investors abroad as well. In particular, Chinese foreign direct investment (FDI) outflows have increased about twenty-fold since 2000.[1] About half of Chinese FDI is in the natural resource industries, in such regions as Africa, South America, and the Middle East. At the same time, the larger Chinese services and manufacturing multinationals have become active players in international mergers and investment. China is now the third largest source of FDI in Asia behind only Japan and Hong Kong, according to UNCTAD's figures from 2006.[2] However, it is uncertain whether or not the recent attention-getting bids by Chinese companies for stakes in Western firms are early indicators of the future of global economic relations.

This book attempts to assess this momentum, and, by peeking through the window of Chinese overseas FDI, to look inside contemporary Chinese government-business relations. From the perspective of political economy, China itself presents a most intriguing case since it has a market economy running atop a stagnant communist regime. Various models have been proposed to explain Chinese government-business relationships, including pluralism, state corporatism, clientelism, socialist corporatism and East Asian statism. However, the complex situation in China renders any of the above models of government-business relations ineffective. In response to this complexity, I propose the model of "merchant-state dualism," which is a hybrid relationship between the state and society that maintains state control over merchants, while giving them some autonomy.[3] My research, by exploring the characteristics of China's outward foreign investment, its motivation, its sector distribution, and its geographical distribution, examines such a dualistic relationship as it manifests itself in China' overseas foreign direct investment.

The concept of merchant-state dualism was originated by Margaret Pearson. I have adopted and examined it from a different perspective. Pearson, along with many previous scholars, by following the traditional civil society approach and examining the roles and functions of Chinese merchant associations, has begun and ended her investigations with a measurement of the degree to which such associations are autonomous from the state. However, I believe that such associations are historically weak in China and that the influence of business is not dependent upon only strong associations. Therefore, merchant associations do not serve as a powerful instrument to examine China's political and economic context. I thus attempt to establish merchant-state dualism as an appropriate model for explaining contemporary government-business relations by examining China's decision-making mechanism, Chinese companies' manifold paths of influence on public policy, the direct interaction and interplay between business and government, as well as the central leadership's overall political thinking—all with a view to China's outward FDI.

Hypothesis and Research Questions:

By an exposition and analysis of China's overseas investment, my research illustrates the current pattern of merchant-state dualism in China. In doing so, the following questions are raised: Do businesses serve as instruments of state control, and also lobby on behalf of the merchants? Does the state, at the same time, deploy a corporatist strategy to control these business groups? These two questions are the basic subject of my research.

Merchant-state dualism was a dominant pattern of operation from the late Qing dynasty through the Nationalist period and up to the Communist revolution. This dualism was replaced by a state-dominated singular structure, when the capitalist class was eliminated in the Maoist era. China's current economic reforms, however, are restoring merchant dynamism in post-Mao China. My investigation of the interactions between business and government elites in determining Chinese outward foreign direct investment illustrates that the current government recognizes the functional importance of merchant groups. When government interests do not coincide with the corporate interests of enterprises, a calculation of benefits and costs, and a political give and take between state leaders and industrial leaders, takes place. The book explores this give and take, which in turn highlights the dualistic role of businesses, as well as the hybrid relations between the two, that is, merchant-state dualism.

Significance of Economic and Political Factors

As long as the current modernizing leadership of China intends to integrate the country's economy with that of the world by running the Chinese economy largely according to market principles, the economic characteristics of the Chinese firms themselves will dominate these firms' interactions with the state. The most recent examples of a flood of overseas investments by cash-rich Chinese banks, insurers, and pension funds all demonstrate that the Chinese government has continued to give merchants a significant degree of autonomy. Moreover, other economic factors have an impact on any individual Chinese company's behavior in dealing with the Chinese government. These factors include ownership form, company size, production methods and organization, trade patterns, the competitiveness of markets, and price elasticity.[4]

On the other hand, a large body of evidence shows that economics do not always dominate the political behavior of a given actor. Such behavior is also influenced by ideology, cultural norms, and political institutions.[5] As for Chinese state-business relations, China's political institutions have seemingly conditioned its bureaucrats and businessmen to behave in a common fashion.[6] This political control is reflected in the Chinese government's ability to select, rethink and limit inward FDI to the high-tech sector and specially needed industries, as well as in the government's economic nationalism. Another aspect of the significance of politics on Chinese economic development is that the Chinese Communist Party (CCP) sees itself differently from the way most outsiders see it. In spite of acknowledged problems of discipline and corruption, the CCP does not view itself as a moribund, demoralized, and anachronistic organization. Rather, the Party sees itself as a highly organized, well-oiled and dedicated group of politician-technocrats who are faced with problems at the lower levels of the organization.[7] Whether this self-confident and optimistic view of the Party and of China is accurate is yet to be determined. However, the Party will very likely be acting on the basis of such a positive self-image.

A closer analysis of government-business relations, however, reveals that what is most likely is that no one factor is completely dominant in determining the relations between the Chinese government and Chinese businesses. That is, both economic and political circumstances seem to shape government-business relations. Those studies which take into account only economic factors to explain these relations overstate their case.[8] Economic characteristics do not by themselves consistently induce a certain type of behavior. As for the government side of the business-government equation, states are not passive agents. They are constantly trying to shape their societies, though they do not always do so in a productive or successful manner.[9] Thus, both economic and political factors should be taken into account in analyzing China's political economy.

China as an Exemplary Case

China serves as an exemplary case for two reasons. First, knowledge of the situation being contemporary China can enrich our understanding of the broader theoretical issues. Such an understanding can lead to greater overall comprehension of the relative importance of economic and political factors in shaping government-business relations in general. Second, and perhaps more important, is that the timing is significant. The twentieth century saw the emergence of Japan as a major force in the world economy. The twenty-first century is witnessing the nascent emergence of China in the same economic arena. After entering the World Trade Organization, China's blistering domestic economic growth accelerated its outward FDI. This acceleration was in no small part driven by the search for natural resources with which to feed China's economic boom. The expansion of Chinese outward FDI is in turn driving up prices in many sectors of the international markets—some to record highs. Ever increasing market prices themselves shape Chinese international behavior and foreign policy. For these reasons, this study can serve as a baseline from which to compare future circumstances. Such future comparisons can both enrich our understanding of China and facilitate future analysis of relevant political theories.[10]

The case of China is even further distinguished from previous ones by the role of the country's economic history and current political institutions. For over three decades, China had a centrally planned economy which was virtually impervious to the impact of market forces. China has been gradually shifting from a centrally planned economy to a capitalist economy since the late 1970s. The country has been attempting to reform and revitalize its state-owned enterprises. This is in sharp contrast to the European post-Communist states, which quickly instituted privatization schemes. While the Chinese government is encouraging the formation of private enterprises, state-owned enterprises still account for a significant portion of Chinese industrial output. At the same time, China has maintained an authoritarian regime that formally reserves to itself the right to make policy.[11]

Research Methods

The research incorporates three case studies of Chinese foreign direct investment to provide an empirical basis for the hypothesis. These cases include examples from three economically distinct industrial sectors—the iron and steel industry (Baosteel and the Capital Iron and Steel Group); the oil and gas industry (CNPC, Sinopec and CNOOC) and the electrical appliance industry (TCL and Haier). The three industries differ in several ways, including their economies of scale, capital intensiveness, the proportion of state-owned to private enterprises, and the degree of sector domination by the constituent companies.

The decision making process of the central leadership in China forms links between the economic and political spheres. In order to examine these links, firms engaging in overseas FDI from three economically distinct sectors have been chosen for examination. The consumer electrical appliances industry tends to be fairly knowledge intensive, and requires fairly educated professionals. In addition, its smaller economies of scale result in a tendency for firms involved in this industry to be relatively small. By contrast, the steel, oil and gas industries are capital and labor intensive. Their high economies of scale tend to result in firms that are quite large. The production of steel and oil in China is more concentrated than is the production of consumer electronics. Also, a higher proportion of steel, oil and gas enterprises are state-owned than are electrical appliance enterprises.

The three selected industries, aside from being in relatively distinct economic sectors that engage in FDI, produce what are, for the most part, economic necessities. What is more, the steel industry has consistently been central to the PRC's drive for the economy. Although the industry lags behind global standards of quality, China has been one of the world's largest steel producers since 1996. The consumer electrical appliance industry has also been growing fast to meet the demands of China's expanding urban and rural populations, as well as the demands of overseas markets.[12] As for oil and gas—the bedrock, as it were, of any modern industrial economy—before 1993, China was self-sufficient in production. As of 2003, China was the world's second largest consumer of oil.[13]

Outline of the Book

The book is composed of nine chapters. The first is an introduction to the research questions and hypotheses, and the project's overall research design. It also outlines the process that led to this study's research strategy and substantive conclusions. The second chapter is an exposition of China's outward foreign direct investment, focusing on its characteristics, its motivations, its sector and geographical distributions. The chapter also examines the evolution of Chinese outward FDI, and compares it to the FDI experiences in other countries in the region.

The third chapter is an introduction to the concept of merchant-state dualism, and an examination of this dualism throughout China's history. The chapter begins with a critical examination of the current range of patterns of government-business relations that have existed in countries around the world. This examination sets the stage for considering where China should be situated in these frameworks of government-business relations. I then argue that earlier scholarship has persuasively shown that government-business relations in China do not fit into any of these existing patterns. The research then proposes the model of merchant-state dualism for government-business relations in China. The chapter compares and contrasts the current pattern of merchant-state dualism with the historical ones. It does so by examining the operation of merchant-state dualism in Chinese history from the late Qing dynasty, through the Nationalist period and up until the Communist revolution. The chapter explains how merchant-state dualism can be understood in the post-Mao era of the 1980s and 1990s, by taking into account the role of economic factors in shaping government-business relations in the Chinese policy process, as well as the state role of maintaining its control over the business groups.

Chapter four illustrates the continued existence of this dualistic relationship by presenting many current empirical examples in support of merchant-state dualism, examples that show the coexistence, the interplay, and the merger of both merchant autonomy and state control. Chapter five also illustrates this dualistic relationship between businesses and government from the perspective of the political give and take in China's overseas FDI. By exploring the reasons for selecting certain foreign investments in light of internal economic and political concerns and in light of the external effects of investing in politically sensitive countries, the research highlights the political underpinnings and calculations of China's foreign investment as it relates to merchant-state dualism.

Chapters six, seven and eight incorporate three case studies of Chinese foreign direct investment to provide an empirical basis for the hypothesis. These cases include examples from three economically distinct industrial sectors—the iron and steel industry (Baosteel and the Capital Iron and Steel Group, China's most important state-owned steelmakers); the oil and gas industry (CNPC, Sinopec and CNOOC, China's three largest state-owned oil companies) and the electrical appliance industry (TCL and Haier, China's newly-founded largest home appliance manufacturers).

The concluding chapter synthesizes the findings derived from the empirical cases. It concludes that merchant-state dualism is the most suitable model for explaining contemporary Chinese government-business relations. The chapter also addresses the implications of this study's conclusions for understanding China, including its state-society relations, policy-making process, and chances for democratization. Thus, the study speaks both to the transformation of politics caused by the introduction of markets as well as to the consequences of politics for economic development.[14]

Notes

1. PPI Trade Fact of the Week, "Chinese Direct Investment Abroad Has Grown Twenty-Fold since 2000," Progressive Policy Institute, October 24, 2007.

2. United Nations Conference on Trade and Development (UNCTAD), *World Investment Report 2007,* p. 44.

3. This definition is given by author herself, a definition which is, however, based upon the central theme of Margaret M. Pearson, *China's New Business Elite,* Berkeley and Los Angeles, California: University of California Press, 1997; as well as upon Gordon White, "Prospect for Civil Society in China: A Case Study of Xiaoshan City," *The Australian Journal of Chinese Affairs,* No. 29, January 1993, p. 63-87.

4. Jeffrey A. Frieden, *Debt, Development, and Democracy: Modern Political Economy and Latin America, 1965-1985,* Princeton, NJ: Princeton University Press, 1991; Ronald Rogowski, *Commerce and Coalition: How Trade Affects Domestic Political Alignments,* Princeton, NJ: Princeton University Press, 1989.

5. Donald P. Green and Ian Shapiro, *Pathologies of Rational Choice Theory: A Critique of Applications in Political Science,* New Haven, Conn.: Yale University Press, 1994; Elinor Ostrom, "A Behavioral Approach to the Rational Choice Theory of Collective Action: Presidential Address, American Political Science Association, 1997," *American Political Science Review,* Vol. 92, No.1, March 1998, p. 1-22.

6. Scott Kennedy, *The Business of Lobbying in China,* Cambridge, Massachusetts: Harvard University Press, 2005, p. 17.

7. Andrew J. Nathan and Bruce Gilley, *China's New Rulers: The Secret Files,* New York: The New York Review of Books, Inc., 2003, p. 260-263.

8. Kennedy, 2005, p. 17.

9. Bruce J. Dickson, *Red Capitalists in China: The Party, Private Entrepreneurs, and Prospects for Political Change,* Cambridge: Cambridge University Press, 2003, p. 22.

10. Kennedy, 2005, p. 20.

11. Ibid., p. 19.

12. Ibid., p. 21.

13. Erica Downs, "The Brookings Foreign Policy Studies Energy Security Series: China," The Brookings Institution, December 2006, p. 1, 6, and 9.

14. Kennedy, 2005, p. 24.

CHAPTER I EXPOSITION OF CHINA'S OUTWARD FDI

In order to examine and assess the success, or lack thereof, of China's outward foreign direct investment (FDI), this section will explore the overall scale of China's outward FDI, paying particular attention to its geographical and sector distribution, its motivations, and its benefits and challenges. This section has the following organization: First, I will introduce the general characteristics of China's outward FDI. I will then discuss the progression of Chinese outward FDI. Afterwards, I will examine China's motives for encouraging and supporting overseas FDI. I will then analyze its sector distribution, scales of operation and geographical pattern. After that, I will assess the overall rewards and the major challenges facing Chinese FDI. Finally, I will compare and contrast the experiences and lessons of Japanese and Korean FDI outflows, and conclude by summarizing this section's major findings.

The Characteristics of China's Outward Foreign Direct Investment:

Characteristic 1: The first characteristic is the diversified ownership of a investing company where the state has a controlling share. In the present pattern of China's foreign direct investment outflows, although the dominant position is held by large and medium scale state-owned enterprises, four types of investing companies have arisen: [1]

The first type is the financial transnational group, represented by the China International Trust Investment Company (CITIC). CITIC takes funds and makes diverse investments in finance, trade, production, technology, aviation, and information technology. It has established more than 30 overseas branches, whose total value is US $376 million. CITIC has, thus, become a large scale and comprehensive international financial group. [2]

The second type of investing company is the trading transnational group, represented by the China National Chemical Import and Export Corporation (CNCIEC). Since 1988, this company has contracted with the Chinese State Council, and has engaged in the process of internationalization. The CNCIEC focuses its business primarily on the international trade, and also conducts foreign direct investment. Its overseas business volume presently surpasses US $3.7 billion. More than one quarter of the corporation's capital, sales volume, total output, profits and number of employees is overseas.[3] This company qualifies as a multinational corporation by many standards.

The third type of investing company is the industrial group, represented by the Capital Iron and Steel Corporation (CISC). Its investment abroad is centered upon industries related to iron and steel, both upstream and downstream in the chain of production. It has established 18 joint capital enterprises overseas, whose present value is approximately US $150 million. Over fifty percent of its overseas investments are in the iron and steel industry. For example, the CISC has spent US $120 million to purchase a Peruvian iron ore company. The Peruvian company provides the CISC with vast amounts of inexpensive high-grade raw material. The CISC also controls fifty-one percent of the Hong Kong Dongrong company, by which CISC controls 1/3 of Hong Kong's market in iron products.[4] These actions of these large state-owned conglomerates reflect the visions of economic growth promoted by the conservatives in the then Chinese leadership. This conservative leadership included Wu Bangguo, chairman of the Standing Committee of the National People's Congress, who spent his entire career in the state-owned industrial sector, as well as then Executive Vice Premier, Huang Ju, who was in charge of fiscal and financial matters. Above all, this merger of state firms to create large "national leaders" was also promoted by then Premier Zhu Rongji.[5]

The fourth type of investing company is the technological transnational group, represented by the Lenovo and Stone companies. These companies base their business on high-tech and unique technologies. They use their technological superiority in conducting foreign investment and in expanding their market. That is, they capitalize on their technological know-how to react both to changes in market conditions, as well as changes in consumer demand.

In addition, as the Chinese domestic economy further develops, privately owned enterprises arise and gain strength. As a result of these enterprises, clearly defined property rights, their flexible management system, and their own initiatives to adapt to the overseas market environment, privately owned enterprises have been achieving success. For instance, the Wanxiang automobile spare parts manufacturer in Zhejiang province has infiltrated the American market, and supplies spare parts for the world's top automobile giants like Ford. Other examples of privately owned companies that have achieved success include Shenzhen Huawei and Chuangwei, both of which have established many specialized markets in the world.[6]

Characteristic 2: The second characteristic of China's outward FDI is the diversification of investment in various market sectors concentrating on resources development.

The sectors of Chinese foreign direct investment are widespread. These sectors include industrial manufacturing, farming and animal husbandry, resource development, transportation, dining, tourism, consulting services, general trade, finance, and real estate. Among the above industries, Chinese companies are most likely to invest in sectors in which they possess a certain technical superiority, like textiles, clothing manufacture, shoe making, furniture, and jewelry manufacturing. These industries do not require much investment and they usually produce quick profits. This feature of Chinese FDI is in keeping with that of most developing countries. That is, most developing nations tend to put their FDI into low end technology. They also tend to concentrate their FDI in the traditional manufacturing industry.

More and more of Chinese FDI is being put into resource development. In fact, it is the sector that is experiencing the most growth in Chinese FDI. Although the number of resource development projects is relatively small, the scale of the investments they receive from Chinese companies is large. In fact, resource development sector is becoming the focal point of Chinese foreign direct investment. By the end of 1990, investment in resource development accounted for 1/3 of the total of China's foreign direct investment. For example, the $180 million investment in the Channar Mine in Australia by the China Metallurgical Import & Export Corporation (CMIEC), the CITIC and China National Non-Ferrous Metal Industrial Corporation's $120 million investment in the Portland Aluminum Smelter in Australia, the Capital Iron and Steel Corporation (CISC)'s acquisition of Hierro Peru Mining Ltd, China Petroleum and National Gas Corporation's investment in the exploration and exploitation of oil in Papua New Guinea, etc.[7] These are all large FDI projects in resource development. This foreign investment focusing on resource exploration reveals the overall strategy of Hu Jintao, General Secretary of Chinese Communist Party, and Chinese Premier Wen Jiabao. This strategy was set forth in Hu's report delivered at the 17th National Congress of the Communist Party of China on October 15, 2007: "Adhering to the basic state policy of opening up, we will better integrate our 'bring in' and 'go global' strategies, …"[8] That is, by establishing numerous overseas bases for the supply of resources, they hope that China can fully use these markets, and provide a long-term stable supply of resources for its economy.[9]

Characteristic 3: The third characteristic of China's outward FDI is that the majority of FDI organizations are primarily middle-and-small-scale projects, with few being large-scale. Since China is a third world country and has begun only recently to engage in international direct investment, Chinese companies do not have an abundance of capital to invest. In addition, the management personnel of Chinese enterprises have limited international management experience. Moreover, the overwhelming number of FDI projects is of a small scale, with a limited number of large scale FDI projects. According to recent statistics, among the 10,673 Chinese FDI projects, the average investment is only US $3.57 million. These statistics include a small number of huge resource development projects. Thus, the vast majority of foreign investments amount to only several hundred thousand US dollars. This average Chinese investment is lower than the average FDI of the developed nations—which is approximately US $6 million—but higher than that of various nations of the former Soviet Union and Eastern Europe—which is approximately US $1.4 million. Actually, the average amount of Chinese FDI per project is slightly higher than the amount per project spent by other developing nations, which averages approximately US $2.6 million per project.[10] China's relatively small amount of FDI per project is in keeping with it status as a developing nation. That is, the money it uses for FDI does not stem so much from surplus capital as it does in the developed nations. China's scale of FDI is therefore correspondingly smaller.

Characteristic 4: The fourth characteristic of China's outward FDI is that its distribution is wide, but it is concentrated in relatively few geographical areas. The geographical distribution of Chinese FDI is at present quite wide spread, covering 160 of the world's countries. Nonetheless, China's investments are not evenly distributed in every country and region, but are centered in certain nations.

CHART 1.1

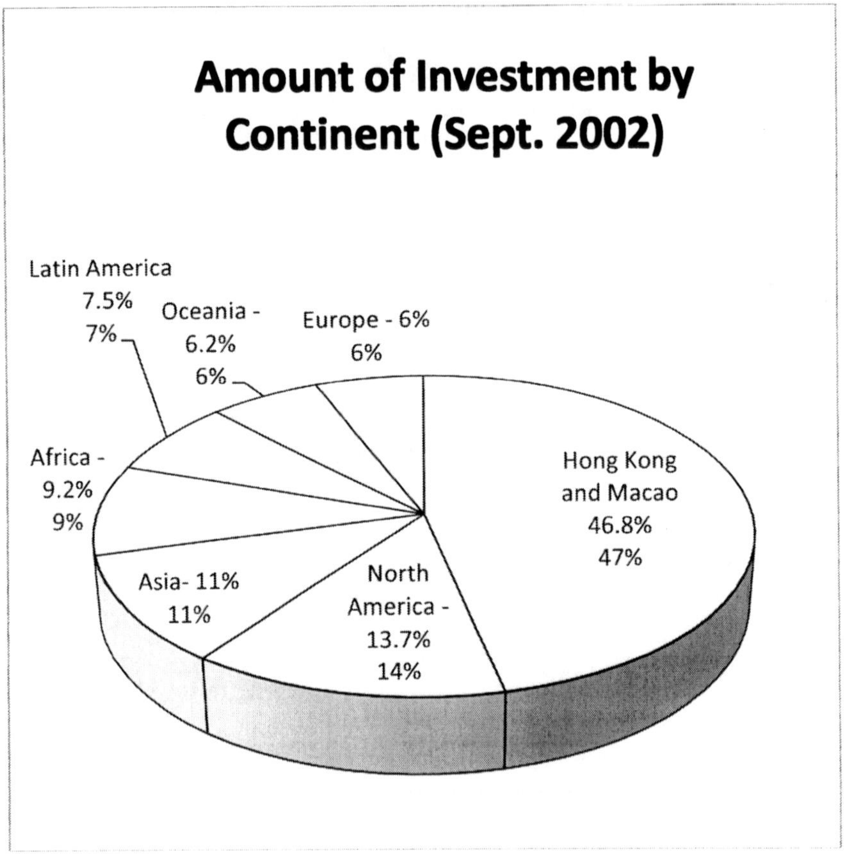

CHART 1.2

Amount of Investment by Country in Billions (USD) (Sept. 2002) Total - US $7.2 Billion

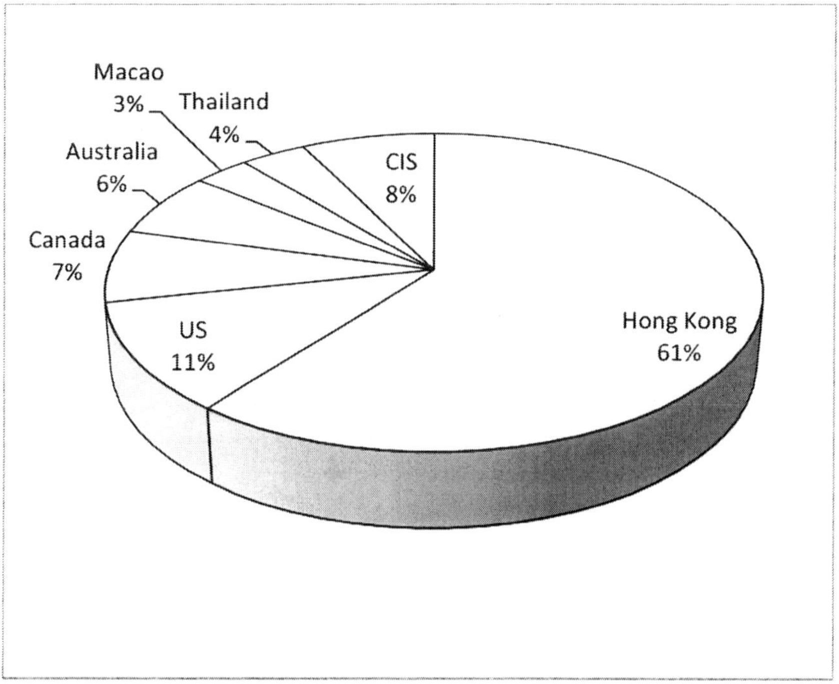

Data provided by Jiang Qunying, *Research on the Current Situation and Countermeasures of Foreign Direct Investment of Chinese Enterprises,* Doctoral Dissertation, Fu Dan University, April 30, 2003.

All these data indicate that Chinese investment is quite concentrated in its regional distribution. China's concentration of the regional distribution of its FDI is characteristic of developing nations. That is, its transnational investments are relatively low. The degree of transnational investment can be measured by the Outward FDI Performance Index, which shows the world share of an economy's outward FDI as a ratio of its share in world GDP. The average Outward FDI Performance Index values are higher for developed than for developing countries. For example, from 2003 to 2005, Norway and Luxembourg had the highest Outward FDI Performance Index of 5.80 and 4.99, respectively. However, the Outward FDI Performance Index of China during the same period was only 0.09.[11]

However, the regional distribution of Chinese investment has been becoming more dispersed. At the same time, however, the sectors of industry, into which China is putting its FDI, is becoming more concentrated. Chinese FDI in the development of natural resources (including oil and gas, forestry, minerals, and fisheries), is mainly distributed in the countries of Russia, Canada, Australia, Indonesia, and Peru. Chinese FDI in agriculture and trade (including farming, animal husbandry, the retail industry, and hotel and dining industry) is mainly distributed in the Commonwealth of Independent States (CIS), some Eastern European countries, Asia, and Africa. Chinese FDI in the manufacturing industry (including textiles, clothing, food, electric appliances, small machinery, motorcycles, and hardware and tools) is distributed quite widely. Chinese FDI in the high-tech industry (including communications, photo-electric technology, software development, and research and development for electrical appliances) is mainly concentrated in the U.S., Britain, Australia, Japan, Singapore, and South Korea.[12]

Characteristic 5: The fifth characteristic of China's outward FDI is that it is financed primarily by joint capital—the methods for which are increasing in number. Chinese enterprises' own funds for FDI are limited. The Chinese government has also adopted very strict policies to control foreign exchange. Thus, the majority of Chinese overseas investments take the form of joint capital ventures. During the period from 1979 through 1998, the most a Chinese company contributed to a joint venture was 73% of the total amount invested with the rest of the funding for the project provided by joint capital. For most of these years, Chinese companies were contributing between 40% and 60% of the total worth of the joint ventures.[13] Since 2000, the average Chinese share of equity invested in these joint ventures has increased to over 65%.[14] In order to make up for shortfalls of funds, Chinese enterprises would often sell trademark rights, permits, technology stocks, equipment stocks, and commodity stocks. Some Chinese enterprises would employ creative financing methods, such as overseas loans, international bonds, and international financing rental. For example, in 1990, the Shanghai Electric Cable Research Institute established the Malaysia-China Electric Cable Company in Malaysia. The Chinese investors provided all the necessary equipment and technology as their share of the investment. One of CITIC's subsidiary companies formed a joint venture with a Canadian company to build up pulp mill. Large banks in Canada provided CITIC's subsidiary with necessary funding. CITIC's total investment in the CITIC-Australia Portland Aluminum Factory was provided by international financing rental.[15]

From the economic perspective, the current phase of China's foreign investment is the second stage of the investment development cycle. (This will be explained in greater detail later on). China's overall investment condition conforms to this stage. Apart from the characteristics that are shared and common to the FDI of developing nations, China's FDI also has its own characteristics. In particular, China's system of FDI is a product of the governmental policy of "Going Global." "Going Global" is a significant policy decision essentially made by the Chinese Communist Party (CCP) at the turn of the century on the basis of a comprehensive survey of domestic and international economic developments. In March 2001, the "Going Global" strategy was written into The Tenth Five-Year Plan (2001-2005) for National Economy and Social Development.[16] It was later on raised in the November 2002 16th Party Congress and the March 2003 National People's Congress, respectively.[17] The Chinese leadership most recently reiterated this at the October 15, 2007 17th Party Congress. This report from this congress states: "We will make innovations in our way of overseas investment and cooperation, support domestic enterprises in carrying out international operations of R&D, production and marketing, and accelerate the growth of Chinese multinational corporations and Chinese brand names in the world market. We will vigorously carry out mutually beneficial international cooperation in energy and resources."[18]

Evolution of China's Outward FDI

The growth of China's outward FDI has experienced four stages during the past two and a half decades. We will call the first stage, from 1979 to 1983, the Preliminary stage; the second stage, from 1984 to 1991, will be called the Experimental stage; the third stage, from 1992 to 2001, will be called the Expansion and Consolidation stage; and the fourth stage, from 2001 until the present, will be called the Gradual Globalization stage.[19]

1. First stage (1979-1983): The Preliminary Stage

This stage was just the beginning of China's economic restructuring and opening up to foreign countries. Therefore, no domestic policies were in place nor was there any domestic economic theory to guide the Chinese in their outward foreign direct investment. Therefore, Chinese foreign direct investment during this period had only a preliminary nature.

Chinese enterprises set up 76 projects during this time, projects that included both wholly owned and joint venture companies. The amount invested by China in this preliminary stage was only US$50 million. Although these projects were set up in 23 separate countries, they were of a relatively small scale.[20] A small number of industries including Chinese restaurants, trading, contracting, marine transportation, and consultation services, garnered the lion's share of the total investments.[21]

State-owned foreign trading companies at the central and regional government levels, and the international economic and technical collaboration companies at the provincial and city government levels were the first Chinese enterprises to engage in transnational operations.[22]

Chinese policy objectives were the driving force for FDI at the preliminary stage. FDI at this time was only intended to facilitate cooperation with foreign nations, initiate trade relations, and increase China's economic and political influence on the world's stage, rather than to maximize profits. Some enterprises were set up hastily and badly managed due to a lack of Chinese experience in international operations. These enterprises were continually in the red.[23]

The Shanghai Machinery Export Company, the China Petrochemical Import-Export Corporation and the China Wukuang Import-Export Company, all of them well-known domestically, engaged in FDI during the preliminary stage.

Their major projects at this time included joint-venture companies, contracting projects, and trading companies.[24]

2. Second stage (1984-1991): The Experimental Stage

Chinese FDI entered into an experimental stage as the pace of Chinese economic reform increased. During this stage, the Chinese made tremendous advances in both technical and managerial standards. As a result, Chinese companies began to engage in FDI on a larger scale. At this time, Chinese enterprises began to participate more fully in international economic competition.

China's exports greatly increased, as did foreign exchange reserves from 1990 on. Unfortunately, a shortage of resources at this time hindered Chinese economic development. Moreover, China had to transfer mature technologies and industries overseas to make the necessary adjustments to the industrial structure. At this point, China decided to increasingly encourage outward FDI. As one would expect, the profit motive began to play a more dominant role in Chinese outward FDI.

Capital Iron and Steel, China International Investment and Trust Corporation, Shenzhen Saige Ltd., and large and medium scale manufacturers began to follow the ever increasing crowd of Chinese enterprises engaging in outward FDI.[25] Simultaneously, China dramatically increased the scale of its outward FDI during this Experimental stage. Although large enterprises accounted for only 8% of the total number of enterprises established overseas, these companies accounted for 76% of the total amount invested.[26]

The Experimental stage, therefore, has three chief features: (a) investment expanded to include the areas of resource development, agricultural and industrial production, and other service industries, (b) the rate of FDI rapidly increased, (c) the motivation for FDI changed from the policy objectives of the central, provincial and city governments to the desire to increase profits, as well as the influence of China on world political and economic events.[27]

3. Third stage (1992 to 2001): The Expansion and Consolidation Stage

The so-called 1992 Deng Xiaoping's Southern Tour Speech and the ensuing determination to establish a socialist market economy caused Chinese economic reform to advance rapidly. At the beginning of 1992, Deng Xiaoping toured Southern China and gave his famous speech. In May of that same year, he inspected the Capital Iron and Steel Corporation (CISC) in Beijing. After the inspection, the Chinese State Council gave the CISC expanded rights to engage in FDI.[28] This indicated that international investments by Chinese companies were entering a new phase of development. During this stage, China's FDI spread 120 countries, and in particular to the countries of the former Soviet Union.

An overall rise in prices in 1993 indicated that China's economy may have been overheating. Clearly at this time the large and medium-sized state enterprises were operating at less than optimal efficiency. This led to the Chinese government implementing an economic restructuring. Among other things, this restructuring called for a period of adjustment for overseas investment. Sources of funding for FDI began to dry up as China tightened its control over the economy, reducing the money supply in order to rein in inflation. The Chinese government also began to scrutinize overseas investment projects much more carefully. It tightened up review processes implemented by the relevant government agencies, and required registration of already established overseas enterprises. Consequently, the number of overseas investment enterprises that were registered, as well as those in the process of gaining registration, fell precipitously.

The number of overseas investment projects did not start to rise again until 1995. In 1996, the number of Chinese FDI projects fell compared with 1995; however, the total amount of money invested over the previous year almost doubled. This indicates that the scale of Chinese overseas FDI in 1996 was relatively large. In 1997, the scale of overseas FDI fell. In 1998, the scale of investment per enterprise fell again, although both the number of enterprises set up overseas and the total amount of money invested had increased.[29]

4. Fourth Stage (2001, when China Joined WTO, to the Present): The Gradually Globalization and Going Out Stage

The following groups in China began to engage in outward FDI during this time: large and middle scale production enterprises, enterprise groups, international investment trust companies, and scientific research institutions. The sectors involved in FDI extended to over 20 industries, including resources development, manufacturing, commercial services and transportation.[30] In this stage, the Chinese leadership proposed the policy of "Going Global," and the government vigorously implemented this strategy, as well as formulated economic reform and a strategy of opening up in the new context of globalization. During this stage, the technical content in overseas FDI is continuously increasing. Large-sized key state enterprises and highly performing private enterprises take the lead in overseas investment. Overseas mergers and acquisitions, mainly in telecommunications, automobile and resource development, have become the major method of FDI.

In 1999, China took overseas investments with overseas processing trade as its new starting point.[31] In 2000, for the first time, the government formally implemented the strategy of "Going Global."[32] In 2001, the focus of investment gradually shifted from Hong Kong, Macao and North America to Asia, the Pacific, Europe, Africa and Latin America. Thus, the geographical distribution of FDI became more balanced.[33] In 2002, overseas projects in natural resources, including oil and gas, minerals, forestry and fishery gradually started to show economic benefits. In addition, remarkable results were achieved in exploring the markets of Latin America.[34] In 2003, resource exploitation, processing and manufacturing, and the service trades became the three backbone fields of China's overseas investment.[35] In 2004, areas of overseas investment were becoming increasingly diversified. In terms of industry distribution, China's foreign direct investment mainly flowed to the mining industry (52.8%), the commercial service industry (26.5%), the manufacturing industry (13.5%), and the wholesale and retail industry (3%).[36] In 2005, overseas direct investment increased rapidly, while overseas mergers and acquisitions became the major method of outward FDI. Overseas mergers and acquisitions, mainly in telecommunications, automobile and resource development, accounted for 56.5% of the total overseas direct investment. At the same time, the establishment of factories and business, mainly in such manufacturing industries as textile and garments, machinery, medicines, electronics and food processing, accounted for 43.5% of the total overseas direct investment.[37] The year 2006 was the first year of the "11th Five-year Plan" and saw a 32% increase in China's outflows to US $16 billion.[38] Mergers and acquisitions of foreign companies were vibrant, accounting for 36.7% of the total amount of overseas direct investments.[39] Considerable investment in the other developing and transitional economies accounted for a large part of this overseas expansion.[40] Moreover, the construction of overseas economic and trade cooperation zones was started up, and the first group of cooperation zones were determined in November, 2006. In addition, the Chinese Ministry of Commerce formally concluded inter-governmental framework agreements with Pakistan, Vietnam and seven other countries, determined the bilateral economic cooperation mechanisms with these countries, and created a good external environment for Chinese enterprises to "Go Global."[41]

If one observes the amount of FDI flows from China to rest of world, one can see that these flows have increased almost thirty-fold during the period 2000 until 2006. About fifty percent of China's FDI is in industries related to natural resources. This FDI is then directed through tax havens and sent along to Africa, South America and the Middle East. Other Chinese participants in international mergers and cross border investments are large Chinese service and manufacturing multinationals. China is now the third largest source of outward FDI in Asia, according to UNCTAD's 2006 figures, second only to Japan and Hong Kong.[42]

In general, in reviewing the past two and a half decades of China's reform and process of opening up, one may see the correlation between China's domestic political economy and its outward FDI. From 1979 to the first half of the 1980s, because the government was just starting to implement the policies of reform and opening up, Chinese domestic enterprises were just beginnings to make preliminary contact with and to understand the outside world. Thus, the process of outward FDI was moving slowly and steadily. After the mid-1980s, process started to speed up. In 1987, the number of Chinese FDI projects broke 100. This trend continued into the 1990s. Based on the statistical data, clearly in the early 1990s, the increase in outward Chinese FDI was tremendous. In 1992, for example, the number of overseas non-trade FDI projects reached 1,360.[43] However, for several years after 1993, the Chinese domestic economy began to over-heat. In reaction to this, Chinese government decided to implement an economic structural adjustment, and to reduce the money supply. During these years, the Chinese economy was in a period of adjustment and recovery. As for overseas FDI, the Chinese State Council began to strictly examine such investments and their approval procedures. Accordingly, the development of overseas FDI was slow at this time. In the late 1990s, the Chinese government carried out an economic "soft landing" policy. As a result, Chinese domestic enterprises gained strength, competition between them intensified and many enterprises saw their domestic market share reduced, and the profit rates on their domestic investments generally drop. This unfavorable domestic situation fueled Chinese enterprises' desires to develop overseas markets. This in turn initiated a new round of foreign direct investment. Starting from 1999, the Chinese government encouraged domestic enterprises to invest overseas, and to shift their mature technologies overseas as well. Therefore, Chinese outward foreign direct investment once again entered a period of acceleration. This upsurge was a direct result of the "Going Global" policy proposed by then president, Jiang Zemin.[44] The government branches have vigorously implemented this strategy since then. This strategy has been continued and aggressively pursued by the current Hu Jintao-Wen Jiabao administration, and, as a result, foreign direct investment has grown by leaps and bounds. The most prominent area of FDI is resource exploitation, which is used to fuel the current rapid domestic growth.

The Motivation for Chinese FDI

Competition, cost factors and product characteristics usually provide the motivation for transferring production plants overseas as well as for foreign FDI. The inflow and outflow of FDI can also be influenced by the host nation's investment environment, such as tax incentives, tariffs and trade barriers. Thus, the motivation for foreign direct investment can usually be characterized as either expansive or defensive.[45] Expansive FDI takes place when a company looks for overseas bases from which it can either develop overseas markets or obtain necessary raw materials. In the case of defense FDI, changes in the investment environment in the home nation, such as fierce competition, provide the primary reason for moving production overseas. In the case of China, these economic reasons are mixed with political ones.

With China, provincial and city level international economic and technical collaboration companies were the first to engage in FDI during the early period of economic reform. These included the Shanghai Overseas Economic and Technical Collaboration Company and the Fujian Overseas Economic and Technical Collaboration Company. These companies used their experience in foreign assistance and support *to undertake labor collaboration and contracting, and to establish joint venture companies in developing countries*. China's government opened the country to foreign investment in the late 1980s, hoping to gain management experience, technology and foreign capital. It also encouraged Chinese businesses to engage in overseas FDI, as well as transnational operations. As a result, one of China's main strategies for economic development and for *domestic industrial structural adjustment and overall institutional change* became overseas FDI. This gradual increase in FDI is in line with the reformist vision of economic growth that was articulated by Deng Xiaoping, who launched China's pragmatic, market-oriented reforms, and who from 1987 to 1997 exercised behind-the-scenes veto power over major decisions. This strategy of gradually increasing FDI was presided over by Party General Secretaries Hu Yaobang (1980-1987) and Zhao Ziyang (1987-1989). In the 1990s, private enterprises, following the government's lead, began to conduct feasibility studies of overseas FDI, and began the actual expansion of such investment.[46] Their motivation tended to be more *trade-related, with the desire to increase exports, develop new markets, exploit local conditions to their advantage, and obtain resources or commercial benefits*.[47]

In the 1990s, Chinese enterprises had the following motivations for outward FDI: (a) accomplishment of the enterprises' overall strategic objectives; (b) promotion of exports; (c) obtaining profits on their overseas investments; and

(d) expanding the enterprise, as well as its markets, etc.[48] This approach demonstrates the then Chinese president Jiang Zemin's and premier Zhu Rongji's overall commitment to continuing reform and encouragement of the growth of various types of companies. The Chinese government maintains tight control of the operations of its state-owned enterprises which are involved in transnational operations. This is different from the situation in other nations. This reveals a more cautious side of Jiang Zemin's policy. That is, he insisted that many state-owned enterprises must and can be saved, and that public ownership must be retained as a dominant force in the Chinese economy.[49] *Diplomatic and political concerns, nevertheless, are still important factors in Chinese outward FDI.* Thus China clearly hopes to advance its international economic and political influence through the use of overseas FDI.

An example of this is Chinese FDI in Hong Kong. Economically, many Chinese transnational corporations use Hong Kong as their original headquarters or launching pads for their larger strategic goals of their internationalization. These companies include Guangdong Enterprise (Holdings) Ltd., China Resources, and Fujian Enterprise (Holdings) Ltd., all of which have used their Hong Kong offices to establish foreign affiliates in other countries.[50] Other Chinese companies use Hong Kong to observe world market trends and improve their information channels. Hong Kong is important to Chinese companies because of its geographic and cultural proximity to China, as well as for economic considerations.

Political considerations always play a major role in any analysis of Chinese outward FDI. China has invested heavily in the Hong Kong economy to build trust in its intention to maintain its present political and economic policy towards that city. These numerous high profile investments include China Merchants Holdings Ltd.'s acquisition of Union Bank; CITIC's acquisition of the Ka Wah Bank; the second harbor tunnel ($390 million); the Bank of China Building ($130 million), and CITIC's partial take-over of Cathay Pacific Airways (a 12.5 percent stake for $260 million).[51] Sectors like housing and telecommunications have also been the target of investments of Chinese transnational corporations, as well as services from waste disposal to power plants. Consequently, more than 1800 Chinese companies have invested in Hong Kong.[52] These investments by Chinese corporations are somewhat like hostages given to Hong Kong, in that the payoff of these investments depends upon a functioning Hong Kong economy. These heavy investments in Hong Kong increase the incentives for the Chinese to keep their promises to Hong Kong.[53] This engagement of Chinese investors in Hong Kong has had a significant effect on Beijing's strategy of avoiding negative economic and political effects both before and after Britain's return of Hong Kong to China.

Since the 16th Party Congress in 2002, the current leadership of Hu Jintao and Wen Jiabao have vigorously implemented and continued the "Going Global" strategy. The Chinese strategy of "Going Global" was conceived in the mid-1990's and formally promulgated in 2000. As of now, the strategy of "Going Global" is an important part of China's push towards economic openness, as stated the in report of the 17th Party Congress, "Solid steps were taken in implementing the 'go global' strategy, and the open economy entered a new stage of development."[54] The report continues by stating: "Adhering to the basic state policy of opening up, we will better integrate our 'bring in' and 'go global' strategies. . . . "[55] The expansion of outward FDI from China has been driven primarily by the *"Going Global."* This strategy is considered by some to be the second most important driving force behind Chinese outward FDI today.[56]

The economic motivations for China's current outward FDI are many, in addition to the motivation of the aforementioned government policy engineering. First, several Chinese TNCs have *expanded their markets* tremendously through FDI and have grown into global players. This has taken place in a wide variety of industries, such as white goods and personal computers—Haier in the industry of white goods, and Lenovo in the industry of personal computers. Both companies are latecomers to their industries. Since 2000, their cross-border M&As have contributed significantly to their market growth in developed countries.[57] Second, Chinese TNCs in primary industries have recently increased *natural-resource-seeking* FDI. Chinese TNCs gain access to resources outside their national borders—and even on a global scale—through outward FDI. Outward FDI is also an efficient way for Chinese TNCs to expand their production and reserves and sustain competitiveness in the oil, gas and other mining industries.[58] Third, a portion of outward FDI from China is connected to *strategic-asset-seeking* activities by Chinese TNCs in the developed countries of the world. Chinese TNCs can increase their rates of production of high value products and services (and so enhance their competitiveness) through the acquisition of assets such as technologies, skills, R&D facilities, brand names and distribution networks. This helps them establish a reputation in the international markets by moving them up the value chain—from manufacturing to R&D, branding and distribution.[59] Fourth, Chinese TNCs were found to have more *profitable* foreign operations than domestic ones, according to a recent survey of Chinese TNCs. For example, the profitability of one of the largest Chinese TNCs, China State Construction Engineering Corporation, is much lower at home than abroad.[60]

To sum up, outward FDI can help companies realize various strategic objectives, such as market expansion, increase in efficiency and acquisition of natural resources and strategic assets. It also creates conduits through which firms can realize higher positions on the value chain, begin higher value added activities, and enhance their competitive edge. On the other hand, outward FDI is subject to various difficulties and risks, which can bring with them unforeseen costs. Thus solid corporate strategies and experienced managerial staffs are essential for companies to maximize their total benefits from "Going Global." Government policy can help create an environment that leads to investment. Such an environment can help firms seize opportunities for globalization and improve their competitiveness on the global stage.

Sector Distribution of Chinese Overseas Investment

Chinese companies put their overseas investment into three major sectors. This is shown in Table 1.1.

TABLE 1.1
Sector Distribution of Chinese Outward FDI Flows, 1984-1987 (Million Yuan)

Sector and Industry	Outward Investment Value			
	1984	1985	1986	1987
1. Primary Sector	142.5	10.9	14	281.4
Agriculture	141.0	7.9	13.1	13.5
Mining and quarrying	0.2	-	-	145.5
2. Secondary Sector	12.5	59.5	156.8	237.4
Food, beverages and tobacco	-	5.4	9.6	4.3
Textiles, leather and clothing	5.7	9.3	34.7	28.2
Paper	0.9	10.3	-	-
Chemicals	-	3.4	12.9	4.1
Coal and petroleum products	-	0.3	-	2.8
Rubber products	-	4.7	20.7	4.7
Non-metallic mineral product	-	-	2.3	4.9
Metals	1.9	3.3	5.2	198.7
Mechanical equipment	0.1	2	0.7	-
Electrical equipment	2.9	3.9	52.6	9.3
Motor vehicles	-	-	-	0.7
Other transport equipment	0.4	-	-	15.4
Other manufacturing	0.4	0.2	2.6	30.4
3. Tertiary Sector	24.6	71.1	90.4	232.3
Construction	3.9	15.6	10.7	9.4
Distributive trade	3.8	19.4	20	32.8
Transport and storage	2.6	2.8	11.2	10.3
Finance and insurance	-	0.1	17.3	-
Other services	14.1	13.1	25.3	78.7
Total	179.6	141.5	261.2	1051.1

Source: United Nations, *World Investment Directory 1992, Vol.1, Asia and the Pacific,* p. 70.

Three trends in the 1980s are clear from this table. First, while investment in mining rose; the amount of investment in agriculture fell. This is in keeping with the trend towards emphasizing resource development, which began in the late 1980s.

Second, the proportion of outward FDI in secondary and tertiary industries has gradually risen. In 1984, secondary and tertiary industries accounted for only 7.0% and 13.7% respectively of total outward FDI, while investment in primary industries accounted for 79.3% of the total. However, by the end of the 1987, FDI in secondary and tertiary industries had risen to 55.1% and 22.1% of the total respectively, while FDI in primary industries had fallen to 26.8%.[61]

Third, FDI in metals manufacturing experienced the most rapid growth in the secondary industrial. Textiles and electrical equipment manufacturing also experienced a rapid growth in investment.

TABLE 1.2
Distribution of Chinese Outward Trade and Non-Trade FDI Flows, 1993-1995 (US$ Million)

	1993	1994	1995	Average Size (1995)
1. Number of Projects	380	145	197	
Trade	85	39	78	
Manufact. & agricultural Sector	175	81	73	
Contracting projects	14	9	15	
Resources exploration	4	4	5	
Others	102	12	26	
2. Signed outward FDI Cont. value	119.75	80.39	130.98	
Trade	23.71	9.77	24.55	0.3147
Manufact. & agricultural sector	59.55	58.10	64.34	0.881
Contracting projects	7.56	3.33	4.99	0.3326
Resources exploration	1.38	1.43	14.86	2.972
Others	27.55	7.76	22.24	0.8553

Source: Lin Wulang, *Inflow and Outward FDI of China,* Taipei, Mainland Affairs Council, 1997.

If one compares trade and non-trade investment in the 1990s, Table 1.2 clearly shows that the agricultural sector and the industrial manufacturing had the largest share of Chinese overseas FDI, followed by trade. The highest number of investment enterprises established overseas has consistently been in the industrial manufacturing and agricultural sectors. The number of overseas investment enterprises in these sectors was greater than 50% of the total in both 1993 and 1994.[62] Not until 1995 did the number of trade enterprises established overseas exceed those in the industrial manufacturing and agricultural sectors, and then only slightly.

Rather than merely throwing money at these projects, Chinese overseas FDI in the industrial manufacturing sector at this stage consisted mainly of the participation in operational management and technical guidance, and the provision of technology and equipment.

Resource development has undergone a significant growth in Chinese outward FDI, as an analysis of the total amount of investment shows. From 1993 until 1995, the proportion of total FDI in resource development increased from 1.1% to 11.1%.[63] This was due to a low per capita level of resources in China, given its large population.

The consumption of resources has been fueling China's recent rapid economic growth. This has resulted a shortage of certain resources. In order to solve this problem, China has had to collaborate with other countries on resource development. Such collaboration has taken the form of establishing paper, pulp and logging plants in countries and areas, such as Africa, the South Pacific, South America, and North America—all of which have expansive reserves of timber. In addition, China is cooperating with over 20 developing nations in the mining of iron ore and precious metals, and the development of fishery resources. The purchase of a Peruvian iron-mining company by China's Capital Iron and Steel is one prominent example. Mining equipment and production costs are high for iron ore in China, since very little of the ore is usable. In fact, given the current rate of extraction and consumption, the supply of iron ore in China is only expected to last 20 years. Although these reserves might last as much as 40 years, if mining technology is greatly improved, it is still far lower than the global average of 150 years. In light of this, on November 5, 1992 China's Capital Iron and Steel purchased the Peruvian iron mining company. That is, it did so in order to make full use of that country's plentiful supply of high-quality iron ore in the development of the Chinese iron and steel industry.[64]

CHART 1.3

Economic Sector Distribution of China's Overseas FDI in 2003 & 2004

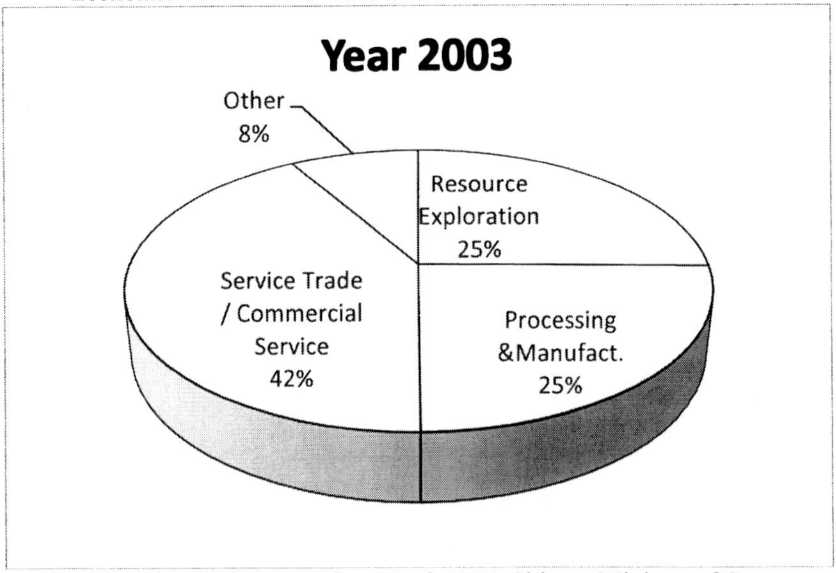

Source: *China Commerce Year Book 2004,* Chinese Ministry of Commerce

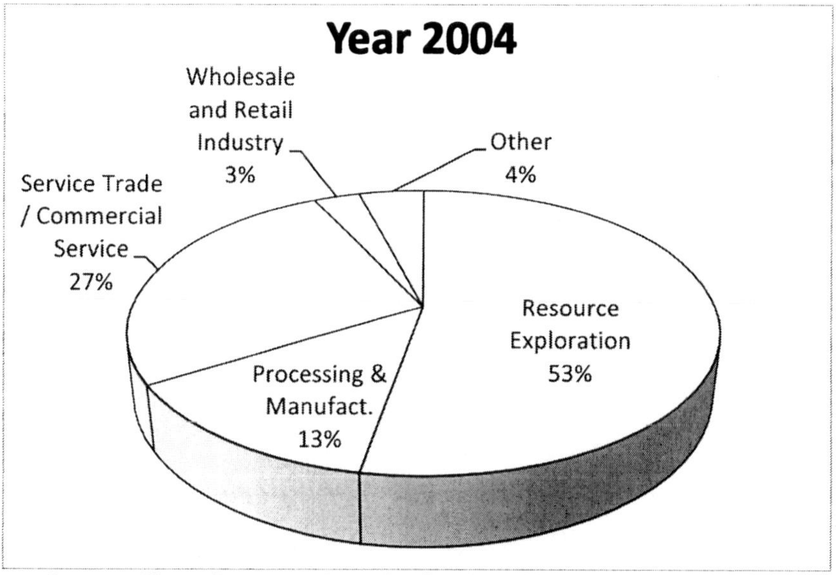

Source: *China Commerce Year Book 2005,* Chinese Ministry of Commerce

Chart 1.3 gives us the flavor of Chinese FDI outflows in 2000s. Chart 1.3 shows that in 2003, resource exploitation, processing and manufacturing and service trade became the three backbone fields of China's overseas investment. The trade commercial service industry mainly includes trade distribution, transportation, research and development, traveling, etc. The industry distribution of 2004 shows a similar pattern, that is, China's non-financial foreign direct investment mainly flowed to the mining industry, the commercial service industry, the manufacturing industry and the wholesale and retail industry.

China's FDI outflows surged in 2005, reaching US $11 billion, driven mainly by some mega M&As in manufacturing and natural resources.[65] The statistics from 2005 show that the establishment of factories and businesses in that year were mainly in such manufacturing industries as textile and garments, machinery, medicines, electronics and food processing, all of which occupied 43.5% of the total overseas direct investment.[66] For instance, Shanghai Automotive Industry Corporation Group acquired Ssangyong Motor (Republic of Korea) for US $531 million, and Nanjing Automobile Group acquired MG Rover (United Kingdom) for US $122 million.[67] In addition, China has intensified its efforts to acquire oil assets. Following the failure of CNOOC in its bid for Unocal in the United States, Chinese oil companies have been successful elsewhere: China National Petroleum Corporation (CNPC) won the bid for PetroKazakhstan, headquartered in Canada, in August 2005; and CNPC and Sinopec jointly purchased EnCana's (Canada) oil assets in the Akpo offshore oilfield, owned by South Atlantic Petroleum Ltd. (Nigeria), in January 2006.[68]

2006 exhibits a very similar pattern of sector distribution. By industrial sector, overseas investments were mainly made in the mining industry, the commercial services industry and the manufacturing industry. Large overseas direct investment projects consistently took the form of mergers and acquisitions, which amounted to US $4.74 billion, accounting for 36.7% of the total amount of overseas direct investments.[69] In 2006, China and Russia made breakthroughs regarding cooperation on the issue of petroleum and natural gas. Sinopec invested US $3.61 billion to acquire the Russian Udmurtija Petroleum Company. China's CNOOC spent US $2.268 billion to acquire 45% of the equity in the marine petroleum exploitation license of Nigeria, which is China's largest acquisition project in Africa to date.[70] Moreover, Chinese and Indian oil companies have also begun to cooperate in bidding for foreign oil assets. In addition, China is also actively investing in mining. In 2006, Chalco (China) won a bid for a project in Australia, and Minmetals (China) established a joint venture in cooperation with Codelco (Chile).[71]

TABLE 1.4

Outward FDI Flows from China

	Number of Business (1)	Chinese Inves. Value ($ million) (2)	Average Chinese Invest. Value ($ million) (3)=(2)/(1)	Total Invest. Value ($ million) (4)	Chinese Equity Share (5) =[(2)/(4)] × 100 %
1979	4	0.53	0.13	1.2	44
1980	13	31.87	2.45	68	47
1981	13	2.6	0.20	6.8	38
1982	13	2	0.15	6	33
1983	33	13	0.39	10	130
1984	37	100	2.70	118	85
1985	76	47	0.62	88	53
1986	88	33	0.38	109	30
1987	108	410	3.80	1373	30
1988	141	75	0.53	118	64
1989	119	236	1.98	325	73
1990	156	77	0.49	167	46
1991	207	367	1.77	759	48
1992	355	195	0.55	351	56
1993	294	96	0.33	187	51
1994	106	71	0.67	124	57
1995	119	106	0.89	200	53
1996	103	294	2.85	494	59
1997	158	196	1.24	325	60
1998	266	259	0.97	-	-
1999	207	561	2.71	-	-
2000	243	551	1.94	822	67
2001	232	707	2.52	1040	68
2002	350	982.68	2.81	1446	68
2003	510	2087	4.11	-	-
2004	829	3620	4.5	-	-

2005	1067	6920	6.49	-	-
2006	1307	16130	12.34	-	-
Total	10673	38097	3.57	-	-

Source: *Almanac of China Foreign Economic Relations and Trade,* 1991- 2001; *Yearbook of China's Foreign Economic Relations and Trade*, 2002 - 2003; and *China Commerce Yearbook,* 2004 - 2007.

Organization and Scale of Operations

The scale of China's overseas investment projects tends to be somewhat small compared with the scale of FDI projects of other developed countries. The data in Table 1.4 indicates that the average amount of Chinese outward FDI per project was between US $320,000 and US $2,850,000 in the 1980s and the 1990s. This average has increased to between US $4 million and US $6.5 million over the years 2003 to 2005. In 2006, some substantial overseas investments made by large Chinese State-owned companies brought the average to US $12.34 million. The table also shows that in 1997 less than 1% of all Chinese overseas FDI projects involved an investment of over US $5 million. Only 30 non-trade related Chinese FDI projects involved a sum of over US $5 million.[72] In 2000, 13 projects received over US $10 million from China. In 2001, 14 Chinese investment projects were over US $10 million. The investment by China in these projects took up 38% of China's total investment that year.[73]

TABLE 1.5
Distribution of Chinese Outward Trade and Non-Trade FDI Flows, 1993-1995 (US $ Million)

	1993	1994	1995	Average Size (1995)
1. Number of Projects	380	145	197	
Trade	85	39	78	
Manufact. & agricultural Sector	175	81	73	
Contracting projects	14	9	15	
Resources exploration	4	4	5	
Others	102	12	26	
2. Signed outward FDI value	119.75	80.39	130.98	
Trade	23.71	9.77	24.55	0.3147
Manufact. & agricultural sector	59.55	58.10	64.34	0.881
Contracting projects	7.56	3.33	4.99	0.3326
Resources exploration	1.38	1.43	14.86	2.972
Others	27.55	7.76	22.24	0.8553

Source: Lin Wulang, *Inflow and Outward FDI of China,* Taipei, Mainland Affairs Council, 1997.

An examination of the scale of operations in the different investment categories is worthwhile. The data for 1995 from Table 1.5 show that the resource development sector had a relatively large scale of investments. The industrial manufacturing and agricultural sector came next. Investments in overseas trade and contracting projects received the least amount of money.

The forms of organization used by Chinese overseas investment enterprises fall into the following five categories: equity-type joint-venture companies; contract-type joint-venture companies; wholly-owned enterprises; branch offices; and acquisition of local enterprises (in part or in whole). The joint-venture enterprise is the most common form of overseas investment, accounting for two-thirds of all Chinese overseas investment.[74] This phenomenon stems from the Chinese desire to share risk and dominate the market. Money is not the only form of Chinese investment in joint ventures. They also contribute equipment, machinery, tools, raw materials, vehicles, etc. Chinese companies are also given incentives by their government to invest with other non-monetary means. These incentives are a result of China's control on foreign exchange. When a Chinese enterprise decides to invest in cash, it obtains the necessary finance from local banks in the host country, the international capital markets, or international organizations.

Chinese investment may take different forms in developed and developing countries. In the developed nations, Chinese investment usually takes the form of cash or international financing. This tends to be the case with large and medium-sized resource development or production projects, since the host country's economic and technical levels tend to be relatively high. In the developing nations, Chinese overseas investment in production-related projects tends to be in the form of machinery, raw materials, technology or labor. Chinese investment is usually in the form of cash for trade projects. In general, physical objects and technology account for two thirds of Chinese outward FDI. The cash form of investment accounts for one-third of the total. [75]

For most Chinese investment companies other than State-owned enterprises, less than 10% of the cash used for Chinese outward FDI originates in the Chinese government's foreign exchange. In other words, 90% of the cash used for FDI for those non-State-owned companies comes from the international capital markets, as well as from other overseas sources.[76] The Chinese use various methods for obtaining financing for foreign FDI. These include overseas enterprise loans, secured loans, and international financing rental. When the Chinese enterprises first ventured into transnational investment, they used relatively little foreign capital. This was because of Chinese unfamiliarity with the international capital markets. However, Chinese enterprises began to use foreign capital on a larger scale, once they gained experience in international finance.

Geographical Distribution of China's Outward Foreign Direct Investment

-Geographical Distribution by Continent-

By 2005 China had undertaken FDI in over 160 countries worldwide.[77] If we explore the geographical distribution of these overseas investments, we can see from Table 1.6 that the regions with the largest number of Chinese overseas investment projects by the end of 2004 are, in order, Asia, Europe and North America. These three regions have also received the largest monetary amounts of Chinese overseas FDI. However, this pattern is changing somewhat. The most recent tendencies are exhibited in Table 1.6.

TABLE 1.6
Chinese Outward FDI by Region, Accumulative until End of 2004
($ million and %)

	Number of Projects (Share)	Chinese Investment (Share) US$	Average Chinese Investment Value
Asia	4237 (51.05%)	8216.9224 (54.28%)	1.9393
Africa	715 (8.62%)	1357.4924 (8.97%)	1.8986
Europe	1473 (17.75%)	1765.7224 (11.66%)	1.1987
Oceania	353 (4.25%)	820.2135 (5.42%)	2.3236
North America	1056 (12.72%)	1556.522 (10.28%)	1.4738
Latin America	465 (5.60%)	1421.862 (9.39%)	3.0578
Total	8299 (100%)	15138.7355 (100%)	1.8242

Source: *China Commerce Yearbook 2005* (Note: the author can only compare the cumulative effects until the end of the year 2004, because the *China Commerce Yearbook* stopped giving out statistical data based on numbers of projects or enterprises in 2005).

Owing to its geographical proximity, Asia has become the largest market for Chinese overseas investment, with the total amount invested standing at US $8216.92 million, accounting for 54.28% of the total Chinese FDI. The main reason for the heavy investment in Asia because the Chinese government encouraged investments in Hong Kong and Macao. The next largest Chinese foreign investments were in Europe and North America, amounting to US $1765.72 million and US $1556.52 million respectively, and accounting for 11.66% and 10.28% of the total. These large amounts were due to the superior investment environment of these locations. Latin America and Africa have attracted a significant proportion of Chinese capital because of their extensive pool of resources. In terms of the numbers of Chinese FDI projects, Asia has the largest number, with 4237, accounting for 51.05% of the total. This is followed by Europe and North America, with 1473 and 1056 respectively, accounting for 17.75% and 12.72% of the total. The average amount of money invested per project is highest in Latin America, where it stands at approximately US $3.058 million, which is 2.55 times the average figure for Europe and 2.07 times the average figure for North America.[78]

TABLE 1.7
Chinese Outward FDI by Region—Tendencies in 2005 & 2006

Chinese Investment Value (US $ Million) (Share %)				
	2005	2006	Total	Percentage
Asia	2172 (31%)	7663 (30%)	9835	40%
Latin America	3350.8 (48.2%)	8468.7 (60%)	11820	48.1%
Europe	734 (10.6%)	597.7 (4.8%)	1332	5.4%
Africa	345.6 (5%)	520 (2.8%)	866	3.5%
North America	266.3 (3.8%)	258 (1.2%)	524	2.1%
Oceania	84.3 (1.2%)	126.4 (0.7%)	211	0.86%
Total	6953 (100%)	17634 (100%)	24587	100%

Source: *China Commerce Yearbook 2006* and *2007.*

Although China stopped giving out statistical data based upon numbers of projects or enterprises in 2005, we can still glean the most recent tendencies in light of the 2005 and 2006 figures. The lion's share of Chinese overseas FDI tends to be taken up by Latin America and Asia, with each region taking 48% and 40% respectively (See above Table 1.7). The amount of FDI in Europe and North America declined quickly during the past two years. This tendency is confirmed by the most recent available data for the year 2006. According to the statistics of the *China Commerce Yearbook 2007*, Chinese overseas investments for the year 2006 were chiefly sent to Latin America (mainly the Cayman Islands and the British Virgin Islands), as well as to Asia (mainly Hong Kong, Singapore, Vietnam and Mongolia).[79] Chinese FDI in Europe and North America once again dropped tremendously. Therefore, in the next few years, Latin America will likely surpass Europe and North America in the regional distribution of Chinese outward FDI.

Nevertheless, one should note here that huge amounts of outflows are routed through Hong Kong, the Cayman Islands and the British Virgin Island. This surge outflows to Latin America is actually the result of "round-tripping"—a phenomenon by which PRC funds are sent out of China only to return disguised as inward FDI. These routed funds are then eligible for preferential policies by the PRC, which are available only to foreign investors.[80] This explains why there are a huge amount of outflows to and inflows from these three tax havens simultaneously. The Chinese Ministry of Commerce, the State Administration of Foreign Exchange, and the State Administration of Taxation have been watching this issue closely. If the Chinese government reduces tax incentives for foreign investors, and imposes tighter regulations on such offshore activities, one could see a decrease in the amount of flows to and from these regions.[81]

-Geographical Distribution of FDI by Country-

Table 1.8 provides details of the 10 host nations with the largest amount of Chinese overseas investment by the end of 2006, through an analysis of the geographical distribution of Chinese overseas investment enterprises by country. We can see that during the 1990s, the most important countries for Chinese overseas investment were the U.S., Canada and Australia, accounting for 42.32% of the total. While at the end of 2006 the most important region for Chinese overseas investment was Hong Kong, accounting for 35.88% of the total.[82]

One of the main objectives of China's overseas FDI is to obtain resources. That is why the largest share of Chinese FDI in the 1990s was in the developed countries, since these nations are rich in resources. In addition, most of these regions and countries have sound financial and consumer markets, offer favorable investment environment, have a superior infrastructure, highly developed technology and advanced management methods. China can use overseas FDI to learn advanced management techniques, and to acquire necessary advanced technology. This is consistent with the policy aims that brought the Chinese government to encourage overseas FDI at first.[83] Interestingly enough, since 2000, the same goal of resource seeking and exploitation has navigated the course of China's FDI, leading it this time to the Latin American countries, specifically, Peru, Venezuela, Brazil and Mexico at first, and Cayman Islands and Virgin Islands more recently. They are the fastest growing recipients of Chinese overseas investment.

The data in Table 1.8 also show us that Hong Kong, the U.S. and Russia have consistently been major recipients of Chinese investment. It also shows us that investment in these three economies has grown steadily and significantly during the 1990s and 2000s. Table 1.8 also indicates that a significant proportion of Chinese investment has also been attracted by South Korea, along with other countries including, Denmark, Thailand, South Africa and Brazil. Comparison of the levels of Chinese overseas investment in 1990, 1998 and 2006 shows that the proportion of investment going to Canada and Australia has fallen. Given that the total amount of Chinese FDI has increased during this period, this may indicate that Chinese investment is gradually becoming more widely distributed.

The table also shows that the fastest growing targets for Chinese investment in the 1990s were Peru and South Africa. The figures from 1990 to 1998 indicate that these two countries experienced the fastest growth in Chinese FDI. From 1979 until 1990, China had invested a total amount in Peru of US $710,000. From 1979 until 1998, the cumulative amount that China had invested

TABLE 1.8

Chinese Outward FDI by Country, 1990, 1998 and 2006 ($ Million and %)

	As of 1990		As of 1998		As of 2006		Growth Rate 1998-2006	
	Num. of Project	Chinese Invest. Value	Num. of Projects	Chinese Invest. Value	Num. of Projects (2004)	Chinese Invest. Value	Num. of Projects (%)	Chinese Invest. Value (Fold)
Hong Kong	116	98.8973	189	230.5003	2258	13668.427	1095%	58
Cayman Is.	-	-	6	2.1	40	9528.1406	567%	4536
Virgin Is.	-	-	16	1.57	78	1982.2891	388%	1262
U.S.A.	112	288.6887	274	401.0400	883	1502.7701	222%	2.8
Russia	33	26.8249	259	99.5777	575	1429.1214	122%	13.4
Rep. Korea	-	-	19	9.9640	91	949.6272	379%	94
Bermuda	-	-	8	13.598	15	809.86	88%	58.6
Australia	48	309.2268	96	329.2100	256	820.8278	167%	1.5
Canada	36	52.9984	82	376.4509	173	553.144	111%	0.47
Denmark	0	0	2	0.3490	4	463.4134	100%	1157
Thailand	61	34.4485	136	67.2345	262	379.8491	93%	4.7
South Africa	0	0	50	54.2100	120	293.5751	140%	4.4
Sudan	-	-	8	11.575	20	291.9563	150%	24
Macao	24	15.8822	49	57.4102	248	194.799	406%	2.4
Peru	1	0.7178	9	120.7198	23	207.7835	156%	0.72
Brazil	7	9.9580	23	42.0497	77	160.9922	235%	2.8

Source: *Almanac of China Foreign Economic Relations and Trade,* 1991 – 2001; *Yearbook of China's Foreign Economic Relations and Trade*, 2002 – 2003; and *China Commerce Yearbook*, 2004 – 2007.

in Peru came to US $120,719,800, a 167-fold increase over the earlier figure. Actually, most of this US $120 million increase in investment came from the Chinese CISC's purchase of a Peruvian iron mining company in November 1992.[84]

The Chinese did not invest in South Africa before 1990, because there was no official diplomatic relationship between the two countries. One of the reasons the Chinese government encouraged economic and trade relationships with South Africa was to help pave the way for diplomatic relations between the two countries. Chinese capital began to flow into South Africa in 1996, followed by a rapid increase in the number of Chinese enterprises investing in this country. By 1998, 50 Chinese enterprises had set up business there with the total amount invested reaching US $54.21 million. However, the size of the average investment was still comparatively small.[85]

Since 2000, thc important new targets for Chinese investment have been the Republic of Korea, Denmark and the Sudan. It can be seen from Table 1.8 that prior to 2000, Chinese investment in the Republic of Korea was only US $9.964 million. However, by the end of 2006, that amount had increased to US $949.6 million, a 94-fold increase. Part of this increase was due to the BOE Technology Group Corporation's purchase in 2003 of liquid crystal display technology from the Hyundai Company in the Republic of Korea. This investment by BOE came to US $190 million. Also, China's investment in Denmark during the period from 1998 to 2006 increased from US $0.349 million to US $463.41 million. In reality, most of this increase came from a single deal. In 2003, the China National Chemical Import and Export Company purchased Atlantis Oil in Norway, for a price of US $460 million.[86]

In addition to the Republic of Korea, Denmark and the Sudan, Chinese investments in other countries have tended to increase as well. For most other countries, with the exception of Peru, the dollar amount of Chinese investment increased by at least 100%. These countries include Russia, Macao, Thailand, South Africa, the Sudan, and Brazil, as well as the region of Hong Kong. The rate of growth of Chinese investment in the developed nations, however, has tended to be lower. In Canada, for example, Chinese investment grew by only 47% over the 8-year period, 1998—2006. Chinese investment in Australia during the same period only grew by 150%. The United States is the only developed nation in this period, in which Chinese investment at least doubled.[87]

If one analyzes the number of Chinese overseas investment projects, one can see from the table that prior to 1991 the three host regions with the largest number of Chinese projects were Hong Kong, the U.S. and Thailand. By 1998, the top three host areas in the number of Chinese projects were the U.S., Russia and Hong Kong. By 2004, the top three host areas, according to the same criteria, were Hong Kong, the U.S. and Russia. Overall, the regions with a relatively large number of Chinese projects include Hong Kong, Thailand, and Macao, as well as developed nations, such as the U.S., Australia, Canada, Russia and South Africa.

The table also shows the rate of growth in the number of Chinese overseas projects. In addition to Hong Kong, where the number of such projects increased from 189 in 1998 to 2258 in 2004, regions where the number more than tripled include Macao, where it rose from 49 to 248, a 406% increase; the Republic of Korea, where the number rose from 19 to 91, an increase of approximately 379%; the Cayman Islands, where the number increased five-fold from 6 to 40; and the Virgin Islands, where the number increased nearly 4-fold from 17 to 78. The number of Chinese projects in the U.S., Russia, Australia, Canada, South Africa, and Brazil also more than doubled from 1998 to 2004. Prior to 1991, Thailand used to be one of the largest hosts to Chinese projects by number. However, the increase in the number of Chinese projects in Thailand from 1998 to 2004 was only 93%, the lowest increase for any of the major recipients of Chinese investment.[88]

-Chinese Direct Investment in Russia-

China and Russia have collaborated in various economic areas for many years. This is mainly due to the complementary nature of their economies, as well as their geographical proximity. Ever since the Russian Federation became an independent nation on December 15, 1991, China has been working aggressively to encourage different forms of economic and trade collaboration with Russia in order to develop economic ties between the two nations. China has hoped not only to foster ties in the form of bilateral trade with Russia, but also to establish various forms of technical and economic cooperation.

At present, Russia is China's eighth largest trading partner, and China is Russia's fourth largest trading partner. In 2005, the total value of Sino-Russian trade was about US $29.1 billion. The majority of Chinese exports to Russia are textiles and food products. The main products exported from Russia to China are steel, chemical fertilizers and timber. These products still dominate these two nations' import-export structure.[89]

TABLE 1.9
Chinese Outward FDI in Russia

	Number of Projects	Chinese Investment Value ($ Million)
Until 1990, cumulative	33	26.8249
1991	66	21.8018
1992	86	40.106
1993	35	6.453
1994	5	0.57
1995	1	0.05
1996	1	0.08
1997	7	1.192
1998	25	2.5
1999	12	3.8
2000	14	13.87
2001	12	12.41
2002	27	35.45

2003	41	339.29
2004	52	110.79
2005	-	320
2006	-	452.11

Source: *Almanac of China Foreign Economic Relations and Trade,* 1991 – 2001; *Yearbook of China's Foreign Economic Relations and Trade,* 2002 – 2003; and *China Commerce Yearbook,* 2004 – 2007.

Table 1.9 reviews Chinese FDI in Russia in the 1990s and 2000s, both in terms of the number of projects and the total amount invested. The table shows that during the period 1991 to 1993, Chinese enterprises invested a considerable amount in Russia. The Chinese invested somewhat less in Russia from 1994 to 1997. However, it began to increase again in 1998. The political and economic situation in Russia, as well as the overall international situation was most likely the cause for this variation in the amount of Chinese investment. The wave of direct investment from 1992 to 1993 was partly due to optimistic expectations for economic growth in Russia, and partly due to encouragement by the Chinese government. Many other countries also began to increase their investments in Russia during this time because of Russia's endowment of natural resources, extensive energy supplies, and well-developed industrial infrastructure, as well as Russia's 'shock therapy' approach to economic reforms in 1992.[90]

The problems of inflation and unemployment became increasingly serious in Russia at this time, and excessively rapid reform in that country led to a dramatic fall in capital investment and a sharp reduction in output. Therefore, during the period of 1994 to 1997, the rate of increase of Chinese FDI in Russia was drastically lower than in the preceding years. However, in 1998 Chinese enterprises began once again to invest in Russia. During the period of 2000 until 2006, quite a few large-scale Chinese investment projects took place in Russia related to resource exploration and oil and gas pipelines. These investments made Russia one of the top recipients of Chinese overseas FDI.[91]

By 2006, Chinese investment in Russia exceeded US $1.429 billion, with a total of over 575 Chinese enterprises having invested there. The main business areas in which these Chinese companies were involved included import-export trade, microelectronics, communications, garment processing, home appliance assembly, restaurant operation, timber processing, resource development and agriculture.[92]

The Overall Benefits and Major Problems of Chinese FDI

-Benefits to China of its Overseas Investments-

The following is a list of benefits that China receives from its outward FDI:

1. The use of foreign resources to compensate for domestic resources that are in short supply. This benefit indicates the successful implementation of the Chinese leadership's decision for "Going Global." In 2003, at the Chinese Communist Party's Central Committee Meeting on Population, Resources and

the Environment, Party General Hu Jintao emphasized the strengthening and promotion of Chinese enterprises' overseas operations for resource exploitation. In November of that same year, at the Central Financial and Economic Affairs Meeting, Hu again stressed this point. In October 2004, at the 4th Plenary meeting of the 16th Party's Congress, Premier Wen Jiabao reiterated this same goal of encouraging Chinese enterprises to "Going Global" in order to obtain natural resources.[93] On October 15, 2007, Party chief Hu Jintao in his report delivered at the 17th National Congress of the CCP stated that: "Solid steps were taken in implementing the 'go global' strategy . . . We will vigorously carry out mutually beneficial international cooperation in energy and resources."[94]

Chinese enterprises have established several dozen joint ventures and wholly-owned fishery companies in more than 20 nations and regions to make up for a shortage of domestic fishery resources in China. These investments have significantly increased the supply of fish products in China. These companies have operations in the Indian, Pacific and Atlantic Oceans. Since 1985, a number of Chinese TNCs have been able to supply China with hundreds of thousands of fishing products. They have been able to do so by establishing either joint ventures or wholly Chinese-owned fishing affiliates in such countries as Morocco, Senegal, Sierra Leone, Gabon, Nigeria, Iran, the United States, Argentina, CIS countries and Indonesia.[95] For example, the scope of the Shanghai Aquatic Product Group's deep-sea fishing operation has expanded from Russia's Bering Strait, West Africa's Mauritania, and Morocco's Sahara open sea area to now include the entire northern and southern Pacific Ocean, and the Atlantic and Indian Oceans. Moreover, in 2003, Shanghai Aquatic planned to establish and to invest in new fishery bases in Australia, Bangladesh and India. According to the statistics, in 2002, Shanghai Aquatic's deep-sea fishing output amounted to 70,000 tons annually. In 2007, the newspaper *Jiefang Ribao* estimated this amount to increase progressively to 120,000 tons.[96]

Chinese transnational corporations have also invested actively in North America, Latin America, Africa and the South Pacific to compensate for China's lack of adequate forestry resources. For instance, Xi-lin Ltd., a wholly-owned subsidiary established by China Investment and Trust in the U.S., has shipped over 700,000 cubic meters of timber back to China within a 5-year period.[97] Domestic Chinese enterprises have succeeded in setting up overseas enterprises in Russia to develop Russia's Far East forest resources, and simultaneously, bring considerable profits to both China and Russia.

In addition, the China Iron Mining Company run by the China Metallurgical Import & Export Corporation (CMIEC) ships a large quantity of high-quality iron ore, in collaboration with Brazil and Australia. They also provide a ready supply of raw materials for China's iron and steel industry by shipping copper and aluminum to China in addition to iron ore. The CMIEC cooperated with Australia in the management of the Channar iron ore project. China invested US $250 million in this project, accounting for 40% of the total investment. During the 30 year period of cooperation, this project is expected to bring 200 million tons of high quality iron ore to China. In addition, China has developed copper mines in Zambia, and zinc mines in Mongolia to make up for its domestic insufficiency in these minerals. Overall, China has invested the most money in natural resource projects. The average scale and cost of these projects are the largest, and they tend to be most efficient at meeting China's needs.[98]

2. Access to advanced foreign technology and management experience.

As stated earlier, some large Chinese companies have been able to acquire technology through mergers with or acquisitions of foreign corporations. Smaller Chinese enterprises usually purchase machinery overseas, and bring the new technology back to China. Chinese TNCs are also acquiring marketing skills from abroad, in the form of managerial expertise and skill, through outward FDI. Outward FDI can also positively impact domestic managerial practices and employment composition, by increasing the number of management jobs and reducing that of blue-collar jobs.[99] For example, the Shanghai Meilin Food Company purchased advanced equipment for its Canadian plant and then brought it back to China. This equipment included precise measuring tools and instruments which were able to significantly improve the efficiency of production of Shanghai Meilin Food's plants in China.[100]

China Deep-Sea Fisheries is another example. They learned how to design and manufacture their own fishing equipment by purchasing large fishing vessels overseas. These two are the best examples of Chinese companies obtaining new technology by using overseas investment.[101]

3. Making increased use of overseas funding.

As indicated earlier, Chinese overseas investments are 33% cash, but only a tenth of this amount is remitted out of China. The international capital markets supply the remaining 90% of Chinese funds used for overseas FDI. Enterprises which are short of capital compensate for this by getting their funding from the international markets. This has led China increasingly to use foreign capital. The benefits of using overseas funding obtained in this way are the same as if they had been obtained within China itself. For example, CITIC was able to garner a profit of tens of millions of US dollars in a 2-year period by using funding obtained from international sources to acquire a share in Australia's Portland Aluminum Refinery.[102]

4. Developing and expanding export markets.

Hi-tech business groups, such as Lian Xiang and Stone, have helped to promote exports of their products by overseas investment. In addition, companies such as China Chemical Engineering and China Construction, have helped increase exports of their construction equipment, facilities, materials, technology and labor through their transnational operations.[103]

5. Promoting the reform of Chinese industrial structure.

Dongbei Pharmaceuticals is a good example of reform of industrial structure. This company adopted an overseas investment strategy for two reasons. First, its production capacity was far greater than domestic demand for its products. Second, pharmaceutical exports were being affected by high tariff barriers. Through such a strategy, it was able to absorb the surplus capacity in the domestic market by transferring some production capacity overseas. In the hi-tech sector, the Saige Group has been combining trade and investment to export mature products and technologies to less developed nations and regions. It has also been aggressively developing new technologies and products. All of this has helped the enterprise transform itself rapidly.[104]

6. Securing foreign exchange.

Estimates indicate that 28% of China's overseas investments are breaking even, 17% are operating at a loss, while 55% are turning a profit.[105] The companies that are making profits on their foreign investments can help with the flow of foreign exchange into China. For example, the bicycle and tire factories established in Ghana and Brazil by the Shanghai bicycle manufacturers, Yongjiu and Fenghuang, have earned profits of over US $100 million by means of exports to neighboring countries. Huan Yu Electronics established a joint venture in London with a Hong Kong company to manufacture 14-inch color television sets. Huan Yu was able to recoup its original investment within 60 days. China's international balance of payments is clearly helped by the profits made by these overseas investment enterprises.[106]

Overall, these benefits are precisely in line with the objectives of the Chinese government's policy of "Going Global." According to the *Yearbook of China's Foreign Economic Relations and Trade 2001,* by "Going Global" an enterprise can invest and set up factories overseas, better utilize domestic and foreign markets and resources, further expand the export of equipment, materials and labor services and create new opportunities for exports. Thus, by "Going Global," enterprises can participate in international competition and cooperation, improve their competitive edge and develop into transnational companies.[107]

-Problems concerning China's Overseas FDI-[108]

China's overseas FDI enterprises are beset with several major problems. First, Chinese overseas FDI enterprises generally operate on a small scale. They are usually less than capable in their competitiveness and ability to develop overseas markets.[109] Their inability to compete effectively also indicates that China's FDI is the product of a governmental policy of "Going Global," rather than of a natural economic process. This also helps to explain the next problem of China's FDI.

The development of overseas enterprises is sometimes hindered by several blind spots. For example, many Chinese companies decide to engage in FDI while they are still unsure about the reasons why they should do so. They also make such overseas investments, when they are undecided about the prospective locations of their overseas factories, when they are unsure as how they can develop their overseas markets and so on. In particular, China's policy of transforming various medium and large sized state enterprises into business groups, and demanding that the group so formed establish itself as a world class enterprise within a short span of time, has forced some enterprises to blunder into FDI in order to reach the mandated goal of internationalization as quickly as possible. This often results in abject failure.[110]

Third, the level of managerial competence is low among Chinese overseas enterprises. When some Chinese companies establish their overseas enterprises, they use the same style of management as in their domestic enterprises. They make little effort to learn from the management styles of the advanced countries. This often results in the overseas subsidiary being poorly managed, causing it to operate at a loss. In the more severe cases, the financial difficulties of an overseas subsidiary can have an extremely adverse impact on the financial structure of the parent company.[111]

Fourth, Chinese FDI causes "capital flight". Overseas investments can protect against Chinese domestic inflation and exchange rate depreciation, because equity markets in China are still relatively small and are subject to government intervention. This gives China's enterprises the incentive to set up subsidiaries overseas to achieve a more balanced portfolio, and to avoid foreign exchange and other restrictions with which they are hampered at home. This phenomenon is generally referred to as capital flight. That is, overseas development is a possible destination for capital flight for Chinese enterprises.[112] The current large scale of such capital flight has caused a large quantity of China's state-owned assets to head overseas.

Finally, since Chinese domestic business is usually less complex than overseas FDI, it requires personnel with much broader knowledge and international management skills than can usually be found in domestic companies. China is sorely lacking in personnel with international management skills and sufficient knowledge about the market conditions of host countries. China desperately needs managers who are skilled in the language, business culture, competition policy, knowledge of suppliers, and distribution networks in the host country. China also needs managers who have a good understanding of international legal frameworks, international finance, taxation, communications, customs regulations and so forth.[113] What is more, selection of personnel by merit for Chinese foreign affiliates is rarely used in China—nepotism is widespread and pervasive.[114]

Future Suggestions

(1) The Choice of Investment Sectors.

First, China has extensive labor resources. This condition is suitable for the development of both labor-intensive industries and resource exploration industries. These industries include construction contracting and the export of labor services. Next, China has gradually created for itself an advantage in traditional industries and small scale manufacturing technology. For example, such technologies and products as small scale batch manufacturing technology, multipurpose electromechanical devices, and labor-intensive production technology tend to be standardized and are the sunset industries in the developed countries. However, to those countries whose technological skill is equal to or less than that of China's, the aforementioned technology is useful. In the international markets, these sunset utilitarian industries are mainly textiles, machine processing, and the manufacture of toys. All of these are suitable arenas for China's mid- and small-scale enterprises to compete in. In addition, the traditional Chinese industries which draw on its national culture are advantageous for Chinese enterprises. These industries include Chinese herbal medicine, Chinese food, and Chinese arts and crafts. Moreover, some of China's industries have advanced technology even when compared to those of the developed countries. These include the space industry, the materials industry, bio-engineering, and architecture. These Chinese industries are all world class, and, thus, have the ability to invest in the global market.[115]

Therefore, with respect to industrial sectors, it might be better for China to direct its outward FDI to resource development, to labor-intensive small scale manufacturing industries, as well as to technological development. However, concerning China's future FDI strategy, China would perhaps be benefited if it enlarged its investments in the manufacturing and service industry, while simultaneously maintaining its investments in the industrial sector. In the manufacturing industry, it would be to China's advantage to increase the proportion of its investments in the high-tech industry, through speeding up investment in the developed countries in order to obtain necessary core technology. As for service industries, China would be well served by increasing its investments in the professional services industries, including information services and financial services. This kind of investment can not only bring great profits, but can also provide the supporting services for Chinese overseas industrial manufacturing companies.[116]

(2) Choice of Geographical Regions for China's FDI.[117]

China's foreign direct investment strategy might consider a diverse geographic distribution. In the developed countries of Europe and the U.S., market capacity is large, purchasing power is strong, the infrastructure is highly developed, science and technology are extremely advanced, the societies are highly open, labor costs are high, supply of funding is sufficient, enterprises' competition is intense, and the barriers to enter their markets are high. Therefore, according to Wang Yan, China's investments in these markets should be in the high-tech industries and those industries in which China has traditionally had superiority. Investment in high-tech industries may help China to obtain the latest technology. Chinese investments in traditional manufacturing industries in these markets can help China establish sales organizations and assembly plants in the developed countries. China could supply the components and parts for these plants from the developing countries, where labor costs are low, and assemble the products in the developed countries, Europe and the U.S. In this way, Chinese companies may bypass the high wage barrier in these regions.

In East Asia, South Asia and China's neighboring countries, market potential is great because these areas have large populations. Countries in this region are also vigorously trying to develop their national economies and give preferential treatment to foreign companies in hopes of gaining foreign investments. While their technical level is quite close to that of China's, their market growth is not mature, and the demand for high quality products is small. Therefore, Lang Fukuan and Wang Hong maintain that in these markets China should invest in the traditional manufacturing industries. In addition, since these areas have a great demand for utilitarian technology, Chinese FDI in these regions may also take the form of equipment and technology.

Because the Middle East oil producing countries have huge income from petroleum, these countries are among the world's wealthiest and greatest consumers. However, the scale of their commodity markets is limited since their general economic level is not high. These countries in the Middle East are engaged in massive social welfare projects, and infrastructure construction. They are also the world's most important contracting service markets. Therefore, in this region, according to Wang Wenju and Xulin, China should engage in project contracting and the export of labor services as its most important investment goal.

In the markets of Africa, the economic development of most countries is low, their technologies are not advanced and the average income per person is trivial. However, the governments of the African countries usually have policies that give preference to foreign companies; therefore, Chinese investments in this region might be in the labor intensive industries, as well as resource development.[118]

In Latin America, economic activity is vigorous, the average per capita income is higher than that of the other developing nations, the investment environment has improvcd significantly, and the area is rich in resources. Therefore, in this market, Chinese might consider directing its FID towards the traditional manufacturing industries, and resource development.[119]

Since the economies of the Central and Eastern European markets have started to recover, entry conditions into these markets are good, and it is fast becoming the world's new hot spot for investment. Therefore, in this market, China could be benefited by investing in industries that Central and Eastern Europe are not known for, such as light industry, spinning and weaving, clothing manufacturing, toy making, and food processing.[120]

(3) China's potential use of a multi-channel financing strategy for FDI could be beneficial. Such a strategy seeks funds both domestically and from the international capital markets.[121]

China is relatively short of funds. In foreign direct investment, China could find it favorable to consider employing both domestic and international financing methods. The international capital markets provide many ways for financing Chinese FDI. These include the international bond market, the international stock market and the international medium and long-term credit market between banks. China could strengthen its understanding of the rules of international financing, as well as its understanding of financial tools, and their process of operation. China can also consider diversifying its sources of financing as much as possible in order to correspondingly diversify the risk. China could get its financing from multiple sources, and avoid concentrating its sources in any one individual country or area.

According to Zhu Wenming, China should integrate production and finance such as the way U.S. automobile manufacturers have integrated both production of cars and financing. China has been integrating production and finance for only the past 20 years. In l987, the Dongfeng Automobile Financing Company and the China Trust Industrial Bank opened an era of Chinese integration of production and finance. From 1987 to the present, the number of integrated finance and production companies has increased to 70. During the same time, the number of enterprise owned commercial banks increased from 1 to 4. These four are the China Trust Industrial Bank, the Guangda Bank, the Zhaoshang

Bank and the Sino bank.[122] The scale and service of these banks are gradually moving towards maturity, along with China's economic and monetary reforms.

China in Comparison with Other Global Investors

Foreign direct investment can be traced all the way back to the beginning of capitalism. In 1600, the establishment of the East India Company by England was a successful example of a European state's implementation of foreign direct investment. However, only after World War II, was there a large scale world-wide growth of foreign direct investment. In particular, after 1960, the world's political and economic environment experienced a huge change with the fall of colonialism. In addition, enhanced international production levels and advanced technology enabled the developed countries, led by the United States, to engage in rapid development of FDI. (FDI developed more rapidly at the end of the 1970s and the beginning of the 1980s.)[123]

When the European Economic Community was first being established in the mid-1950s, the America-led developed countries started to make large-scale investments in Europe. At the same time, the European multinational corporations were also enlarging their direct investments in the U.S. The driving force for outward investment in this period arose from a liberalized FDI policy in many countries, as well as from the worldwide spread of trade protectionism. Most outward FDI made during this time came from the multinational corporations of the developed nations. At this same time, Japan's economy was developing rapidly, and increasing its amount of foreign direct investment. In the late 1980s, Japanese enterprises led the world in foreign direct investment. At this time, the developing nations and regions also began to participate in foreign direct investment.

The 1997 Asian Financial Crisis had a serious adverse effect on global foreign direct investment, especially on the investments of various newly emerging countries in East Asia. This Financial Crisis also weakened economies of other Asian nations and, as a result, their FDI decreased as well. This crisis, however, did not have a devastating effect on the FDI of all the developed countries. After several years of recovery, the level of global foreign direct investment reached a new high. FDI reached its peak in 2000, when it amounted to a total of US $14.9 trillion. In 2001, however, FDI outflows receded to US $7.35 trillion.[124]

Foreign direct investment is the major way for enterprises to transfer elements of production around the world, and is also a driving force for economic globalization. Multi-national corporations spurred on the development of FDI, as well as sped up the international flow of the elements of production, thereby advancing economic globalization. However, the more economic globalization increased, the more foreign direct investment increased. Thus, FDI and globalization are mutually encouraging. In other words, FDI is the propelling force and the catalyst for the creation and development for economic globalization. This same economic globalization in turn impels the scale of FDI to become greater and greater.

-The Experience and Success of Japan's FDI-

An analysis of the various phases of Japan's post-War economic development might be helpful in understanding its progress in FDI. Japan's economy can be divided into four stages: 1. the major importation stage (1945 ~1955); 2. the major exportation stage (1956 ~1965); 3. the major manufacturing stage (1966 ~1973); and 4. the major overseas investment stage (1974 ~ present). The development of Japan's foreign direct investment has the following characteristics: (1) its foreign direct investment is a result of a higher stage of economic development; (2) the export trade developed first, and FDI was a direct result of this; (3) Japan's import-export growth rate is faster than its economic growth rate, and its foreign direct investment growth rate is faster than its import-export growth rate.[125] Moreover, Japan's foreign direct investment has had a tremendous influence on its international division of labor and on the optimization of its industrial structure.

The fast growth of Japan's FDI is a result of its promotion by the Japanese government. On September 30, 1969, Japan implemented a policy of liberalization of foreign investment. In September of 1970, it started a second round of liberalization of foreign investment. Between July 1971 and June 1972, the Japanese government implemented three more rounds of liberalization of its foreign investment policy. All of this reform basically removed any restrictions on outward Japanese FDI. In addition to the reforms, Japan has adopted a series of preferential policies for its companies that engage in outward FDI. These policies consist of preferential treatment in both tax and finance.[126]

Just as its Japanese counterpart has done, the Chinese government has also achieved considerable progress in its promotion of overseas foreign investment, especially from 2000 to the present. Examples of this promotion include the governmental increase in security in general, laws and regulations, and administrative systems for implementing the strategy of "Going Global." The Chinese government has also gradually been establishing mechanisms for coordinating and implementing outward foreign investment. It also increased the number of fairs, exhibitions and seminars dealing with FDI. These measures will be discussed in detail at another point.

In addition, the government has adopted a selective policy to encourage outward FDI. The NDRC and the Export-Import Bank of China issued a statement in October 2004, to promote the following: (i) projects for the exploration of resources to alleviate the domestic shortage of natural resources, (ii) projects that encourage exportation of domestic technologies, products, equipment and labor, (iii) the promotion of overseas R&D centers to make use of advanced technologies from around the globe, as well as international managerial skills and professionals, and (iv) mergers and acquisitions that can increase the competitive edge of Chinese enterprises in the international markets and promote their entry into such markets.[127] The Government offers preferred credit terms and other incentives to promote these four types of FDI. The Export-Import Bank of China provides special types of loans for overseas investments by its credit plan for exports and streamlines the process of screening such projects. The NDRC, as well as other agencies, is working to bring about a better mechanism for the control of the risks inherent in these overseas investments. One of the improvements made so far is the provision of insurance especially for such investments.[128]

If we compare China's economic situation with Japan's, we will find that the phase of China's economic development that took place between 1981 and 1989 is like the phase that Japan experienced between 1945 and 1955. This is so because during both these times, Chin and Japan were major importers. China's economy in the period of 1990 to 1998 is similar to Japan's economy in 1956 to 1965, since during these times, both nations were major producers. China's phase from 1999 to 2002 is like Japan's phase from 1966 to 1975. At these times, both countries were in the process of transitioning from being a producer to being an exporter. Just as outward FDI played a positive role in Japan's economy; it has also had a significant positive effect on Chinese economic development.[129]

-The Experience and Success of South Korea's Outward FDI-

The South Korean government has played a huge role in promoting outward FDI. Since the mid-1980s, the South Korean government has realized the importance of outward FDI in promoting its country's exports, as well as in strengthening its companies' competitive advantage. Therefore, the South Korean government has started to relax its restrictions on outward FDI, and has adopted various kinds of economic measures to encourage South Korean Companies to engage in outward FDI. The government has set up institutions and organizations to provide service and support for its companies that invest overseas. For example, the South Korean Import-Export Bank funds up to 80% of an outward FDI project. The South Korean Export Insurance Company also provides an enterprise with various types of insurance, including insurance against war, political and non-commercial risk. This insurance covers 90% of a company's investment in outward FDI. In 1988, the government also established the Overseas Investment Information Center for the purpose of providing economic information for small businesses. The South Korean government also gives preferential tax treatment to companies that engage in outward FDI. If a South Korean company has to pay taxes to a host country, it need not pay additional taxes to the South Korean government. This avoids the problem of double taxation.[130]

Just as the Korean government has done, the Chinese government has adopted favorable fiscal policies on overseas investment. In 2003, the Ministry of Commerce, the Ministry of Finance, the People's Bank of China and the State Administration of Foreign Exchange issued the *Complementary Notice on Relevant Issues on Discount of Foreign Exchange Loans and Medium- and Long-term RMB Loans to Overseas Processing Trade Enterprise.* This reinforced the central government's support for foreign trade development funds for overseas processing trade projects. In 2004, China began to permit firms engaging in outward FDI to keep all of the foreign exchange earned in the first five years of the firms' existence. After that, these firms are subject to an income tax, and must submit 20% of their stipulated foreign exchange quota.[131] In late 2005, after consultation with the Ministry of Land and Resources, the Ministry of Commerce established the *Specialty Fund for Overseas Prospecting and Exploitation of Mine Resources*. The Ministry of Commerce also formulated and issued policies and measures on promoting resource exploitation in Africa, under the framework of the Sino-Africa Cooperation Forum.[132]

South Korean companies usually establish a sound infrastructure and other ancillary facilities in the host countries, before actually setting up manufacturing plants overseas. South Korean companies prefer sole ownership rights as opposed to joint ventures. In the initial investment stage, South Korean enterprises often acquire the purchased enterprise's trademark rights through merger and acquisition. They may also try to strengthen their property rights in their foreign assets through sublets, or through subsidiary companies. For example, Samsung Electrical Appliances purchased the American AST research institute. LG purchased its trade name and marketing channels. Zenith was one of America's last producers of television sets.[133]

To sum up, China might be benefited by learning from South Korea's example of a government policy that supports outward FDI by its nation's companies. Moreover, China could also learn from South Korea's companies the steps and methods of setting up overseas enterprises. In fact, many Chinese companies have already started to follow South Korea's example by adopting sublets and acquisitions to carry on overseas investments. For example, a large number of high-profiled M&As took place in the first decade of this century. First, in 2004, the Chinese electronics conglomerate TCL merged its television business with that of France-based Thomson, parent of the RCA brand. In early 2005, Chinese computer maker Lenovo purchased the personal computer wing of IBM, which produces the Thinkpad series of computers. In June 2005, the Chinese appliance giant Haier made an unsuccessful bid for its US counterpart Maytag. In August 2005, CNOOC's failed bid for Unocal came at the end of a string of attempts by Chinese companies to acquire Western companies. In 2006, the automobile firm Chery, based in Anhui province, bought Britain's defunct MG brand. In 2007, Chinese financial services firms bought stakes in the investment banks Bear Stearns, Barclay's and the Blackstone Group.[134]

-Japan and South Korea's Transnational Management Modes-

Currently, there are two kinds of modes of international management. The first one is the western management model employed by the European and American countries. In this model, the large manufacturing enterprises are responsible for most of the outward FDI. The strength of these manufacturing enterprises is usually related to their monopoly on high technology and their scale of production. The other international management model is the one employed by the multinational corporations of Japan and South Korea. In this model, the companies that conduct the bulk of the outward FDI are the Japanese *sogo shosha* and Korean *chaebol*. The biggest strength of these companies lie in their accumulated market experience and management skills acquired from their long term involvement in international trade. These skills include information development, market development, the raising of funds, and risk avoidance. These companies are varied in size and their management control is flexible.[135]

The development of Japan and South Korea's *sogo shosha* also indicates the importance of governmental support. The Chinese government might be benefited by advancing these corporate models, given their success. The Chinese government still exerts a great influence on the economy and economic development, and could easily take effective measures to impel the creation and development of Chinese-style *sogo shosha*. The Chinese government has apparently already started to experiment with the *soga shosa* model. In 1994, the Chinese State Council officially authorized the CNCIEC to experiment with the *sogo shosha* style of corporation. The Chinese State Council has also planned to set up a total of 10 to 15 experimental *sogo shosha* -type companies in Shanghai, Suzhou, and Dalian.[136]

The foundation of this strategy is the promotion of the international operations of suitable Chinese firms. The transnational corporations of China (TNCs) came into existence later than their foreign counterparts in the newly industrialized economies (NIEs). The first generation of Chinese TNCs was for the most part large State-owned enterprises, which operated as monopolies in such industries as financial services, shipping, international trading and natural resources. Many of these TNCs began overseas operations after China started its "open-door" policy in the late 1970s. CITIC is a diversified financial and industrial conglomerate, which is now one of the top 100 TNCs in the world. CITIC was founded by the Chinese national government in 1979. In the early stages of its "open-door" policy, the Chinese government has established several similar companies whose focus is on international business. These companies include China Resources and China Merchants. Other Chinese State-owned TNCs at the forefront of their respective sectors include COSCO, China State Construction Engineering Corporation, CNPC, Sinochem, CNOOC, China Minmetals and COFCO. The first stop along the path of the internationalization of these first-generation Chinese TNCs is Hong Kong. This city is still the major location for "overseas" operations of these companies.[137]

After the early 1990s, the second generation of major Chinese TNCs emerged. These companies were involved in competitive manufacturing industries, in particular those related to electronics and information and communication technologies. FDI from this generation of Chinese TNCs has mostly been fueled by the international expansion of Chinese firms in their desire to gain such assets as brands and technologies. In addition, supportive government policies, along with positive effects from inward FDI, contributed to the development of these electronics companies in China. Some of these Chinese companies are rapidly moving towards internationalization through aggressive acquisitions. Companies such as Haier and TCL now have major roles in consumer electronics on the world stage; Lenovo, following its purchase of IBM's PC business, is now the third largest personal computer manufacturer in the world; as for the market for global telecom equipment, Huawei Technologies and ZTE are in strong competition with TNCs in the developed countries. Even somewhat small Chinese companies are now extremely internationalized over a wide range of industries. Examples of these smaller industries include Glanz, Pearl River Piano Corporation and Zhenhua Harbor Equipment. The second generation of Chinese TNCs have many different ownership structures, including private ownership, local government ownership and foreign involvement.[138]

Conclusion

China's overseas FDI has taken a different form from that of the U.S., Japan, Europe, and the other advanced countries. The latter have shaped their FDI according to the advantages of their domestic industries, using overseas FDI to create a worldwide industrial system. However, China's FDI is chiefly the result of governmental engineering, especially China's strategy of "Going Global". The foundation of this strategy is the promotion of the international operations of suitable Chinese firms, with a view towards the improvement of resource allocation and the enhancement of their international competitiveness. The responsibility for the implementation and coordination has been given to the Ministry of Commerce. The National Development and Reform Commission (NDRC) is another central Government agency involved in the implementation of the strategy. Overseas investment has become the focal point of the "Going Global" strategy. In the past few years, the Chinese government has increasingly encouraged outward FDI by providing information about foreign locations, by granting incentives to corporations engaged in FDI and by gradually relaxing foreign exchange controls. The Chinese leadership is also setting up a supporting mechanism for outward FDI, with the participation of various departments of the central Government. The Government is also actively participating in various bilateral and multilateral initiatives in order to facilitate and protect overseas investments of Chinese firms.[139]

The speed at which China's overseas FDI has developed over the past 25 years is quite impressive, especially when compared with that of the other developing nations. In the past quarter century, China has established 10,673 overseas investment projects around the globe. An important characteristic of China's overseas FDI is that it is dominated by small and medium scale companies with an average overseas investment of US $3.57 million.[140] The majority of companies engaging in overseas FDI make investments between several hundred thousand and several million US dollars. The majority of companies that engage in overseas FDI tend to form joint ventures with host nation enterprises.

The scale of China's overseas investment companies has slowly grown from small-scale trading companies and agricultural enterprises to medium-size and large-scale industrial enterprises and resource development companies. The type of China's outward FDI has gradually moved from government-directed investment to profit-oriented investment directed by the enterprises themselves, as a result of Chinese economic liberalization, In spite of this, the majority of enterprises engaging in overseas FDI are still state-owned business groups at both national and regional levels. On the one hand, the increase in corporate involvement in FDI is in keeping with the Chinese government's commitment to economic reform and its determination to modernize the Chinese economy and integrated with that of the rest of the world. On the other hand, that the Chinese government still plays an important role in FDI via state-owned enterprises reveals the government's cautiousness, as well as its desire to retain a dominant role in guiding the economy.

Political considerations in Chinese outward FDI are still apparent. For example, Chinese transnational corporations are for the most part state-run, and are subjected to the foreign policies of the central government. However, economic considerations are evidently now the motivating factors for Chinese outward FDI. This also reveals the current leaders' more pragmatic and technocratic thinking. In particular, the following major economic factors can be seen in Chinese outward FDI. First, many Chinese transnational corporations invest abroad to expand, maintain or seek markets for export, to undergo a process of upward mobility in their economic development, as well as a process of structural change. What is more, increasing protectionism in other countries, as well as growing competition in China, has forced many Chinese companies to establish factories overseas. In addition, Chinese foreign affiliates play a very important role in collecting current information on the international market. In sum, the growth of China's overseas FDI is fueled by market seeking, by political motivation, by the availability and price of natural resources, and by the desire to take advantage of lower labor costs.

Moreover, the macroeconomic situation and institutional structure, and the physical and human infrastructure of the host country also play important roles in China's outward FDI. China's overseas FDI is concentrated in a small group of economically developed countries and regions, although it is spread over 160 different countries. M&As have become a major mode of entry by Chinese companies for these developed countries. In recent years, Chinese TNCs have undertaken an increasing number of mega deals in the United States and Europe.

China's outward FDI in the natural resources sector is concentrated in a few resource-rich countries in Latin America, Africa, and North America. Its outward FDI in the services sector is primarily in the developed countries. Chinese FDI in neighboring countries is due to cultural similarity, low costs, and greater familiarity with business conditions in the region.

Chinese overseas investment is concentrated in the U.S., Canada and Australia, because of their first-rate infrastructure, high technology, advanced management methods, superior investment environment and developed financial and consumer markets. China has directed its outward FDI to other countries in the Asia Pacific region, because of their geographical and cultural proximity. Thus, China has gradually increased the rate of its investment in the region over the past few years. In particular, it has rapidly increased its investments in Malaysia, Singapore and Thailand, as well as in other countries of the Association of Southeast Asian Nations (ASEAN). The Chinese have also begun to direct their investment toward the Commonwealth of Independent States and Eastern Europe following the collapse of the Soviet Union. China has also been expanding its technical and economic collaboration with these countries because of their extensive resource endowment.

The pattern of Chinese outward FDI reflects the existing structure of the Chinese domestic political economy: a) Chinese outward FDI in the natural resources is small in number but large in scale, and is primarily in minerals and forestry in the western hemisphere and Australia, and ocean fisheries in Latin America and Africa. The increasing percentage of Chinese outward FDI in the natural resources sector is a result of the country's rapid economic development. This rapid development requires resource consumption that domestic supplies cannot satisfy, and is in keeping with the reformist vision of maintaining rapid economic growth. b) The large percentage of China's FDI in the trading sector shows that Chinese outward FDI is significantly used to promote and serve the export of commodities.[141] This is an integral part of the government's policy of "Going Global."

China's comparative advantage is also reflected by its pattern of outward FDI. A relatively small share of Chinese outward FDI is directed towards the manufacturing sector. These investments are cheaply made in Asia, Africa and the Pacific. Chinese investment in this sector has several characteristics: relatively small-scale projects; the production of undifferentiated and low-value-added goods; relatively simple and adapted technologies; and labor-intensive production techniques and processes. Chinese companies have a competitive advantage in industries, such as the manufacture of textile and clothing, footwear, bicycles, simple electrical appliances, and electronic products. The low percentage of Chinese outward FDI in the manufacturing sector shows clearly the current developmental stage of the Chinese economy, which is not yet in a position to export technologically-oriented capital.[142]

One of the uses of Chinese outward FDI is to acquire a stable supply of resources, primarily in mining, fisheries, and forestry. China has now become a net resources importing rather than an exporting country, because of its rapid economic development. Thus, Chinese outward FDI in the resources sector plays a growing role in compensating for the shortages of raw materials in China. Chinese resource seeking FDI has mostly taken the form of mergers and acquisitions involving oil and gas companies from China. These State-owned companies—by actively investing abroad—are at the lead of their government's efforts to secure overseas energy sources.

Secondly, some Chinese transnational corporations use outward FDI as an effective channel to obtain foreign technology and management skills. The Chinese foreign affiliates are very important since they can collect up-to-date information on overseas technological development. However, Chinese transnational corporations have less incentive in their outward FDI for efficiency-seeking in supply of low-cost, productive labor and inexpensive land, since these are plentiful in China.

Thirdly, other companies use outward FDI to raise capital for domestic use. They do this primarily by seeking public listing of their shares on the Hong Kong Stock Exchange. Some of the funds raised there are used to support investment projects in China. This establishes a direct link between outward and inward FDI.[143] In these cases, outward FDI is a means for Chinese transnational corporations to overcome the domestic scarcity of capital.

In sum, manifold economic and political forces set off the internationalization of TNCs or result in their further expansion overseas. These forces which are driving internationalization often include a small domestic market, competitive pressures and government policies which encourage foreign expansion. These drivers are likely to have different impacts on different companies, depending on the firm's competitive stance, motivations and choices.[144] In addition, the growth of outward FDI from China has been accelerated by the rise in its foreign currency reserves. Japan experienced a surge in outward FDI during the 1980s because of a rapid accumulation of foreign currency reserves. China could have a similar experience in the coming years.[145] Indeed, the promotion of outward FDI has become an imperative for the Chinese Government because of the pressure from the large and ever-increasing amounts of foreign reserves in China. These foreign reserves have led the Chinese government to adopt a "Going Global" strategy, as well as to take concrete steps to foster the internationalization of Chinese companies.

John Dunning maintains that countries tend to go through five stages in their path of investment development. Generally, China is now in Stage 2. Its inward FDI is starting to increase because of advantageous conditions. These advantages include inexpensive land, an improved infrastructure, huge market size and potential, increasingly liberal governmental policies, and a low-cost but well-educated and well-trained labor force. China's outward FDI is growing as a result of advantages produced by an increasingly strong political commitment on the part of the Chinese government to further liberalize its economic system and to integrate more with the global and regional economy. Without doubt, China will soon pass Dunning's Stage 3. In this stage, the rate of inward FDI gradually decreases and the rate of outward FDI correspondingly increases. This substantially improves the country's net outward investment position.[146] This increase in the rate of outward FDI, as predicted by Dunning's Stage 3, will be enhanced and furthered by the "Going Global" policy initiated by the Chinese Communist Party and implemented by the Chinese government and its agencies.

Notes

1. This section is referred to two articles: Wang Zongkeng, "Discuss the Current Conditions, Trends and Strategies of Chinese Multinational Corporations (qiantan woguo kuaguogongsi de fazhanxianzhuang, qushi yu duice," *Productivity Studies* (shengchanli yangyu), No. 10, 2004; and Zuo Xiaoshun, "Theoretical Thoughts on the Foreign Direct Investment of Our Country (woguo duiwaizhijietouzi de lilunsikao)," *Investment Research* (touzi yanju), No. 6, 1998.

2. Qiao Jinmin, "Chinese Enterprises' Overseas Investment (zhongguo qiye duiwazhijietouzi yanjiu)," *Investment Research* (touzi yanju), No. 2, 1996, p. 16.

3. Ibid.

4. Ibid., p. 16-17.

5. Andrew J. Nathan and Bruce Gilley, *China's New Rulers: The Secret Files*, New York Review of Books, Inc. 2003, p. 200.

6. Jiang Qunying, *Research on the Current Situation and Countermeasures of Foreign Direct Investment of Chinese Enterprises* (zhongguo qiye duiwai zhijietouzi de xianzhuang he duice yanjiu), Doctoral Dissertation, Fu Dan University, April 30, 2003, p. 60-61.

7. Zhan Xiaoning, "Transnational and Outward Investment: the Case of Chinese Firms (kuaguo yu duiwaitouzi: zhongguo gongsi anli)," *Transnational Corporations* (kuaguo gongsi), Vol. 4, No. 3, December 1995, p. 75-76.

8. Hu Jintao, "Hold High the Great Banner of Socialism with Chinese Characteristics and Strive for New Victories in Building a Moderately Prosperous Society in all Respects," Report to the Seventeenth National Congress of the Communist Party of China on October 15, 2007, *Beijing Review,* No. 45, November 8, 2007, at http://www.bjreview.com.cn/document/txt/2007-11/20/content_86325.htm.

9. Lian Changyun, Liu Dawen, Qiu Ruizhao and Yuan Chunhua, "Thoughts on the Global Mineral Resources Strategy Adopted by China (guanyu zhongguo quanqiu kuangchanziyuan zhanlue de zikao)," *Geological Bulletin of China* (dizhi tongbao),Vol. 24, No. 9, Sept. 2005, p. 796.

10. Data are based on *Almanac of China's Foreign Economic Relations and Trade*, 1991 – 2001, *Yearbook of China's Foreign Economic Relations and Trade*, 2002 – 2003, and *China Commerce Yearbook*, 2004 – 2006; as well as Qiao Jinmin, "Chinese Enterprises' Overseas Investment (zhongguo qiye duiwazhijietouzi yanjiu)," *Investment Research* (touzi yanjiu), No. 2, 1996.

11. United Nations Conference on Trade and Development (UNCTAD), *World Investment Report 2006,* p. 114.

12. Wang Yan, *Testifying Analysis of China's Outward Foreign Direct Investment* (zhongguo duiwai zhijietouzi de shizhengfenyi), Master Thesis, Foreign Economic Trade University (tuiwai jingjimaoyi daxue), China, April, 2006, p. 5.

13. Data was gained from *Almanac* 1991 – 2001.

14. See Table 4 of this chapter.

15. Zhu Wenming, *China's Foreign Direct Investment Studies—Based on the Economic Globalization's Analysis and Strategy* (zhongguo duiwai zhijietouzi yanjiu—jingji quanqiuhua fenxi he zhanlue), Doctoral Dissertation, China's Academy of Social Science (zhongguo shehui kexueyuan), May 2001, p. 101-102.

16. "The Tenth Five-year Plan of National Economic and Social Development for People's Republic of China (zhonghua renmin gongheguo guominjingji he shehuifazhan dishige wunian jihua gangyao)," *Economy Daily* (jingji ribao), March 18, 2001.

17. Wang Zhigang and Zhang Jiayi, "Policy Study of 'Going Global' on Mineral Resources (kuangchanziyuan "zouchuqu" zhengceyanjiu)," *Journal of China National Land Resources Economic Study Institute* (zhongguo guotuziyuan jingjiyanjiusuo qikan), Vol. 2, No. 7, 2003, p. 272.

18. Hu Jintao, *Report,* October 15, 2007.

19. Zhu, 2001, p. 23.

20. Data was calculated from *Almanac*, 1984.

21. Zhu, 2001, p. 23-24.

22. Jiang, 2003, p. 56.

23. Kevin G. Cai, "Outward Foreign Direct Investment: A Novel Dimension of China's Integration into the Regional and Global Economy," *The China Quarterly,* No. 160, Dec. 1999, p. 859.

24. Hsiu-Ling Wu, Chien-Hsun Chen, "An Assessment of Outward Foreign Direct Investment from China's Transitional Economy," *Europe-Asia Studies,* Vol. 53, No. 8, Dec. 2001, p. 1238.

25. Zhu, 2001, p. 24.

26. Hsiu-Ling Wu, *et al.*, 2001, p. 1239.

27. Ibid.

28. Zhu, 2001, p. 25.

29. Hsiu-Ling Wu, *et al.*, 2001, p. 1240.

30. Zhu, 2001, p. 25.

31. Zhao Chuang, "Developing Overseas Investments with Overseas Processing Trade as the New Starting Point," *Almanac of China's Foreign Economic Relations and Trade 2000,* p. 45. Zhao Chuang was deputy director of the Trade Development Department in the Ministry of Foreign Trade and Economic Cooperation.

32. Wang Hui, "Implementing Vigorously the Opening Strategy of 'Going Global'," *Almanac of China's Foreign Economic Relations and Trade 2001,* Chinese Ministry of Foreign Trade and Economic Cooperation (MOFTEC), p. 94. Wang Hui was Director General of Department of Foreign Trade, MOFTEC.

33. Chen Jian, "The Strategy of 'Going Global' Carried through Effectively and Foreign Economic Cooperation Developed Continuously and Steadily," *Yearbook of China's Foreign Economic Relations and Trade 2002,* MOFTEC, p. 136-137. Chen Jian was Director General of Department of Foreign Economic Cooperation, MOFTEC.

34. Wu Xilin, "The 'Going Global' Strategy of China Made New Progress in 2002," *Yearbook of China's Foreign Economic Relations and Trade 2003,* MOFTEC, p. 51-53. Wu was Deputy Director General of the Department of Foreign Economic Cooperation, MOFTEC.

35. Wu Xilin, "The 'Going Global' Strategy of China Made Great Achievements in 2003," *China Commerce Yearbook 2004,* Chinese Ministry of Commerce, p. 73-74.

36. Wu Xilin, "General Situation of the Implementation of 'Going Global' Strategy in 2004," *China Commerce Yearbook 2005,* Chinese Ministry of Commerce, p. 107.

37. Wu Xilin, "General Situation of the Implementation of 'Going Global' Strategy in 2005," *China Commerce Yearbook 2006,* Chinese Ministry of Commerce, p. 441-443.

38. UNCTAD, *World Investment Report 2007,* p. 44.

39. Wu Xilin, "Implementation of the Strategy of 'Going Global' in China in 2006," *China Commerce Yearbook 2007,* Chinese Ministry of Commerce, p. 418.

40. UNCTAD, *World Investment Report 2007*, p. 44-47.

41. Wu, *China Commerce Yearbook 2007,* p. 419-420.

42. PPI Trade Fact of the Week, "Chinese Direct Investment Abroad Has Grown Twenty-Fold since 2000," Progressive Policy Institute, October 24, 2007.

43. Jiang, 2003, p. 62.

44. Ibid., p. 66.

45. Hsiu-Ling Wu, *et al.*, 2001, p. 1236.

46. Hou Jianping, "Industry Opinions for Chinese Direct Investment Overseas (woguoqiye haiwai zhijietouzi de chanyexuanze)," *International Trade Journal* (guojimaoyi wenti), No. 8, 1998, p. 24-28.

47. This section is summarized from Cai, 1999, p. 867-868; and from Hsiu-Ling Wu, *et al.*, 2001, p. 1236-1237.

48. Liu Yan, *Multinational Corporation and Internationalization of Chinese Enterprises* (kuaguogongsi he zhongguo qiye de guojihua), Beijing, China Trust Press, 1992.

49. Nathan and Gilley, 2003, p. 205-206.

50. United Nations Conference on Trade and Development (UNCTAD), *World Investment Report 1995,* p. 56-57.

51. Ibid., p. 330.

52. *China Economic Times,* May 22, 1997, p. 1.

53. Brigitte Bacher, Oliver Lorz and Ludger Schuknecht, "Chinese Investments—'Hostages' for Hong Kong?" *Journal of Institutional and Theoretical Economics (JITE),* Vol. 148, 1992, p. 645-654.

54. Hu Jintao, *Report,* October 15, 2007.

55. Ibid.

56. UNCTAD, *World Investment Report 2006,* p. 210.

57. Ibid., p. 170-172.

58. Ibid., p. 172-173; and UNCTAD, *World Investment Report 2007,* p. 100-153.

59. UNCTAD, *World Investment Report 2006,* p. 173.

60. Ibid., p. 174-175.

61. These percentages are calculated by the author based upon the data provided by the United Nations' *World Investment Directory 1992,* introduced from Hsiu-Ling Wu, *et al.*, 2001, p. 1240-1241.

62. This percentage is calculated by the author based upon the data provided by Lin Wulang, *Inflow and Outward FDI of China,* Taipei, Mainland Affairs Council, 1997, introduced from Hsiu-Ling Wu, *et al.*, 2001, p. 1242.

63. Ibid.

64. The information of these examples is referred to Hsiu-Ling Wu, *et al.*, 2001, p. 1242.

65. UNCTAD, *World Investment Report 2006,* p. 54.

66. All these data are provided by *China Commerce Yearbook*, 2004 – 2006, Chinese Ministry of Commerce.

67. UNCTAD, *World Investment Report 2006,* p. 95.

68. Ibid., p. 58.

69. Wu, *China Commerce Yearbook 2007,* p. 418.

70. Ibid.

71. UNCTAD, *World Investment Report 2006*, p. 58.

72. Hsiu-Ling Wu, *et al.*, 2001, p. 1243.

73. *Yearbook of China's Foreign Economic Relations and Trade 2002,* Ministry of Foreign Trade and Economic Cooperation (MOFTEC), p. 137.

74. Zhao Minyuan, "Promoting Internationalization and Virtualization (dali tuijin neibuhua he xunihua)," *Investment Research* (touzi yanjiu), No. 1, 1998, p. 41-44.

75. Ma Quanjun, Ju Jialiang, "The Comparison of Foreign Capital Utilization and Foreign Investment of Our Country (woguo liyong waizi yu duiwai touzi de duibi fenxi)," *Investment Research* (touzi yanjiu), No. 12, 1998, p. 37.

76. Ibid.

77. *China Commerce Yearbook 2005,* Chinese Ministry of Commerce, p. 107.

78. All the data and percentage are calculated by the author based upon the statistics provided by *China Commerce Yearbook*, 2004 – 2005, Chinese Ministry of Commerce.

79. *China Commerce Yearbook 2007,* p. 418.

80. The US-China Business Council, "Foreign Investment in China," February 2007, at http://www.uschina.org/info/forecast/2007/foreign-investment.html.

81. Ibid.

82. All the figures in this section are calculated by the author based upon the statistics of 1990 and 1998 provided by Hsiu-Ling Wu, *et al.*, 2001, p. 1246, as well as upon the data from 2000 to 2005 provided by the *Almanac* 2001, *Yearbook*, 2002 – 2003, and *China Commerce Yearbook*, 2004 – 2006.

83. Ma Xiuyan, Li Jianjun, "Location Decision of Chinese Outward FDI (zhongguo haiwai zhijie touzi de quwei xuanze)," *Investment Research* (touzi yanjiu), No. 6, 1995, p. 47-49.

84. Hsiu-Ling Wu, *et al.*, 2001, p. 1247.

85. Ibid.

86. *Commerce Yearbook 2004*, Chinese Ministry of Commerce, p. 73.

87. All the figures in this section are calculated by the author herself.

88. All the percentages in this section are calculated by the author herself.

89. "Sino-Russian bilateral trade registers a 40% increase", *People's Daily,* January 25, 2007.

90. Hsiu-Ling *et al.*, 2001, p. 1248-1249.

91. Ibid.

92. This figure is added by author based on the accumulative figure in *Commerce Yearbook 2004*, and *Commerce Yearbook* 2005-2006, Chinese Ministry of Commerce.

93. Lian Changyun, *et al.*, 2005, p. 796.

94. Hu Jintao, *Report,* October 15, 2007.

95. Jiang Guoping, Liu An, and Ye Xiangling, "The Conditions and Functions of the Chinese Multinational Corporation's Overseas FDI (zhongguo kuaguo gongsi haiwai zhijie touzi xianzhuang yu zuoyong)," *International Economy and Trade* (guoji jingmao), No. 5, 2003, p. 34.

96. Song Pengxia, "Wider Scope of Blue Oceanic Industry (tuokuan haiyang gongye)," *Liberation Daily* (jiefang ribao), February 27, 2003.

97. Jiang Guoping, *et al.*, 2003, p. 35.

98. Jiang, 2003, p. 97.

99. UNCTAD, *World Investment Report 2006,* p. 177.

100. Yin Ziqing, *Twenty Years of Reforms of Chinese Foreign Economy and Trade* (zhongguo duiwai jingjimaoyi gaige ershinian), Henan, Zhengzhou Press, 1998.

101. Ibid.

102. Pan Ye, *The Strategies for China to Develop Outward FDI* (zhongguo fazhan duiwai zhijie touzi de zhanlue), Beijing, Economic Science Press, 1998.

103. Li Yiling, Cao Fengqi, *Multinational Operation of Chinese Enterprises* (zhongguo qiye kuakuo jingying), Beijing, China Planning Press, 1996.

104. Ibid.

105. Shi Lei, "China's Foreign Investment: the Problems and the Legal Countermoves (woguo haiwai touzizhong chunzai de wenti ji duice)," *Investment Research* (touzi yanjiu), No. 5, 1998, p. 34.

106. Li Yiling, *et al,* 1996.

107. Wang Hui, "Implementing Vigorously the Opening Strategy of 'Going Global'," *Almanac of China's Foreign Economic Relations and Trade 2001,* Chinese Ministry of Foreign Trade and Economic Cooperation (MOFTEC), p. 94 - 95.

108. This section is referred to Li Xingong, "The Development and Trouble of Chinese Enterprise's Overseas Investment (woguo qiye haiwaitouzi de fazhan yu kunrao)," *Reference News* (cankao xiaoxi), October 25, 1996, p. 42-44.

109. Wang Wenju, Xu Lin, "The Problems and Countermeasures of Chinese Outward FDI (shilun woguo duiwai zhijie touzi de zhuyao wenti he duice)," *Finance and Trade Research* (caimao yanjiu), No. 2, 2000, p. 51.

110. Lin Ye, "Chinese Enterprises are Facing a New Challenge to Adjust their Strategies in Transnational Operation (zhongguo qiye kuaguo jingying de zhanluexing tiaozheng)," *International Economic Cooperation* (guoji xingji hezuo), No. 10, 1998, p. 37-38; and Cai, 1999, p. 877.

111. Li Ji, Li Lin, "Prerequisite to Transnational Chinese Enterprises: Reformation of Administrative System (zhongguo qiye kuaguo touzi de qianti: zhili jizhi gaizhao)," *Reform* (gaige), No. 2, 2000, p. 49-55.

112. Gunter, F.R., "Capital Flight from the People's Republic of China: 1984-1994," *China Economic Review,* No. 7, 1996, p. 77-96; and Song Wenbing, "A Study of China's Capital Outflow: 1987-1997 (1987 – 1997 zhongguo ziben waitao yanjiu)," *Economic Research Journal* (jingji yanjiu qikan), No. 5, 1999, p. 39-48.

113. Cai, 1999, p. 874.

114. Jiang Bolong, Zou Zhenfang, *Foreign Investment of Chinese Enterprises* (zhongguo qiye duiwai touzi), Beijing, Economic Science Press, 1996, p. 16-18.

115. This section is referred to Lang Fukuan, Wang Hong, "Discuss China's Multinational Corporation's Development and Strategy (lun woguo kuaguo gongsi de fazhan zhanlue)," *Economic Outlook the Bohai Sea* (huan bohai jingji liaowang), No. 3, 2002, p. 3-4; Zhang Yatao, "Choice of Entry for Chinese TNCs' outward FDI (zhongguo kuaguo gongsi duiwai zhijietaouzi fangshi de xuanze), *Jiangsu Social Science,* No. 3, 1996, p. 25; Wang, 2006, p. 13-14; Wang and Xu, 2000, p 53; and Hou, 1998, p. 24-28.

116. Ibid.

117. This section is referred to Wang, 2006, p. 12; and Lang Fukuan, *et al.*, 2002, p. 2-3; Ma and Li, 1995, p. 49; and Wang and Xu, 2000, p 54.

118. Referred to Wang and Xu, 2000, p. 54; and Ma and Li, 1995, p. 49.

119. Referred to Wang, 2006, p. 5; and Lang Fukuan, *et al.*, 2002, p. 2-3.

120. Referred to Lang Fukuan, *et al.*, 2002, p. 2-3; and Wang and Xu, 2000, p 54.

121. This section summarized the opinions of Zhu Xiaoliang, Zhu Jun, "Strategic Thinking on China's Multinational Corporation's Development (fazhan woguo kuaguo gongsi de zhanlue sikao)," *Journal of Chinese Agricultural Bank Wuhan Management Cadres College* (zhongguo nongyeyinhang wuhan ganbu kuanli xueyuan xuebao), No. 73, April 1999, p. 25-26; Shi, 1998, p. 35-36; Hou, 1998, p. 25; and Wang and Xu, 2000, p 54.

122. Zhu, 2001, p. 104-105.

123. Jiang, 2003, p. 43.

124. UNCTAD, *World Investment Report 2002* at website: http://www.unctad.org

125. Jiang, 2003, p. 102-103.

126. Ibid., p. 104.

127. UNCTAD, *World Investment Report 2007,* p. 210.

128. Ibid.

129. Jiang, 2003, p. 120.

130. Su Dongsui, *International Management and Operations Forum and Collection* (guoji kuanli yu yunxing lunji), Shanghai, World Economic Literature Publishing House, 2000.

131. Axèle Giroud, "Chinese Outward Foreign Direct Investment," paper prepared for the UNCTAD expert meeting on enhancing the productive capacity of developing country firms through internationalization, Geneva, December 5-7, 2005, p. 25; and UNCTAD, *World Investment Report 2006,* p. 212.

132. Wu Xilin, "The 'Going Global' Strategy of China Made Great Achievements in 2003," *China Commerce Yearbook 2004,* Chinese Ministry of Commerce, p. 74.

133. Jiang, p. 121.

134. PPI Trade Fact of the Week, October 24, 2007.

135. Zhu and Zhu, 1999, p. 25.

136. Liu Shenhe, Song Shengzhou, "Chinese Multinational Corporation's Models (zhongguo de kuaguo gongsi moshi)," *Enterprise Economy* (qiye jingji), No. 7, 1995, p. 18.

137. UNCTAD, *World Investment Report 2006,* p. 130.

138. Ibid.

139. Ibid., p. 210.

140. Information is obtained from Table 3.

141. Cai, 1999, p. 865.

142. Ibid., p. 866.

143. UNCTAD, *World Investment Report 1995,* p. 56-57.
144. UNCTAD, *World Investment Report 2006,* p. 142.
145. Ibid., p. 54-55.
146. Cai, 1999, p. 878-880.

CHAPTER II MERCHANT-STATE DUALISM IN CHINA'S HISTORY

Various Models of Merchant-State Relations

Introduction:

China provides an interesting case for the study of the relations between government and society. Three models of state-society relations have arisen from China's economic reforms: pluralism, state corporatism, and clientelism.

During the 1950s, 1960s, and 1970s, scholars applied the totalitarian model to the Chinese state on the assumption that China did not allow societal actors any autonomy. This model assumes that the ruling party fundamentally penetrates society, i.e., that virtually no boundary exists between societal groups and the state.[1]

Many social and economic elements in China were aroused by the early stages of economic reform that took place in the late 1970s and 1980s. The new phenomenon cannot adequately be explained by the term totalitarianism. The pluralist model of China, however, underemphasizes the authority of the state, as well as its interests. This model focuses on the group as the essential unit of society to the exclusion of other factors.[2] Thus, the 1980s saw the rise of neo-traditionalism as a theoretical construction to explain changes in China that were not adequately addressed by either totalitarianism or pluralism. Oi and Walder's view of neo-traditionalism provides a good understanding of the politics of Chinese communism during the early reform era.[3] It concluded that neo-traditionalism could be applied to a non-market system in a Leninist state where the government has denied societal actors substantial autonomy.

Following upon the reforms, autonomy of societal actors from the Party-state has increased. The authority of the Party system is still in place at the level of the factory, even though the strength of organized dependence has been reduced.[4] The model of democratization (civil society) and the model of state corporatism have recently been brought to bear in examinations of China.

The model of democratization is highly problematic in the post-Mao context, appealing as it may be. Compared with this model, a much closer framework is provided by the model of state corporatism for explaining the type of state-society relations that has come about from the Chinese economic reforms.[5]

Deficiency of the Civil Society Model

The three models of pluralism, civil society, and democratization, all envision the principle that the political system is easily accessible and that an abundant amount of participants of society are willing to work together to defend their interests.[6]

A few elements of business-government relations in China do point towards pluralism. For example, one can identify various contact points (both direct and indirect) between the business community and the state itself. These two entities do cooperate to work on issues such as policy on a regular basis before policies become established.[7] However, three areas prevent the Chinese business sector and other members of society from fully protecting their interests. These are restrictions on the independence of Chinese associations; the fact that policy making is not completely transparent; and the fact that a norm exists to foster co-operation and non-transparency in business-government relationships.[8] These three factors tell us that China cannot be labeled as pluralist from a macro perspective.

The lack of direct and simple causal links between economic reforms and democratization also show the impossibility of considering post-Mao China in the light of the models of democratization or civil society. Market reforms may well bring up new groups who can operate with more autonomy and with more opportunities for change from a political perspective. The market may even be viewed as embracing "an economic environment more propitious for the maintenance of poly-archal elements." It may even "reduce the area of political authority and hence [provide] greater independence for the individual" as well as for the group.[9] But none of this will necessarily result in a definite change towards the creation of civil society in the country. The important consideration here is that the state can still shape the process at both a central and local level and can also have an effect on the independent operation of new economic factors. To this end the "transitions" literature would seem to suggest the unlikelihood that democratization will come to China based purely on economic reforms.[10]

The Theory of Corporatism

One variation of corporatism—state corporatism—appears to be a better potential fit for China than does the civil society model. This is especially true when one considers the insights that state corporatism gives in the relationships between the state and society in China after Mao.

State corporatism recognizes the existence of economic and societal interests in addition to the state. In states such as these, economies were re-structured by the state with a view towards corporatism—this was done to try to convince society to support economic development.[11] For example, Poland created a corporatist solution that brought the Catholic Church and then the Solidarity movement into the equation. This led to economic, religious/social independence which ultimately went on to undermine the traditional authority of the

Party-state.[12] Romania, on the other hand, needed to create a system of national construction and so, in the late 1970s, established a corporatist structure that encompassed industry and agriculture.[13] A form of corporatism is also evident in Brezhnev's Soviet Union where significant functional interests were incorporated into the policy process while maintaining the authority of the Soviet Communist Party.[14]

In China, as reforms have become more widespread, interests external to the Party have been legitimized, as well as the interests over and above those of the peasants and workers. These have been ratified at high levels—for example, at the 13th Party Congress Party General Secretary Zhao Ziyang tried to gain approval for a far broader and more diverse interest range than would have been permitted under Mao.[15] At the same time, state corporatism shows consistency with the post-Mao reformers' emphasis on coordinating and harmonizing the legitimate interests of society with the goals of the state.[16] Additionally, the primary goal of state corporatism is to balance society's interests with rapid economic development on a national basis—in China the primary goal of the state is rapid industrialization. Finally, state corporatism (unlike civil society) does not overlook the fundamental hierarchy of power between society and the state as it takes a strong state as its core.[17]

The Missing Organizational Components of Corporatism

Scholars may have seen a lot of parallels with corporatism in China in its Reform era, but China does not show all of the organizational components associated with corporatism. Although the issue of limited autonomy is a key facet of state corporatism, it is not the only facet to be considered in this system.

Three other components are less prominent in China. These involve associations which should be compulsory, have a hierarchical order and have jurisdictional monopolies.[18] In China, associations are voluntary in law—in fact, most of them are, in practice, voluntary as well. Most Chinese associations have little autonomy. In addition, the government does not simply interact with business via associations only. The country has a range of other routes including direct interaction and other kinds of intermediaries. Therefore, classifying China as having either state or societal corporatism in place is not appropriate, no matter from the perspective of businesses or from the perspective of associations. Additionally, the restricted autonomy of associations in the business sector is based on the government's role in creating them, they have connections with government agencies and they often employ government officials in their organizations. This merger of business and state cannot be found in a state corporatism model.[19]

If Schmitter did not expect that state corporatism could be applied to socialist states that were in a process of transition, Margaret Pearson defines a link between state corporatism and the socialist structure. She termed this link "socialist corporatism."[20] This is a strategy that the state uses to co-opt those social elements that could potentially work autonomously from the state. This pattern of state-society relations will probably endure on the basis that it suits the interests of both business leaders and of the central and local governments. Socialist corporatism can help illustrate how a socialist state evolves from a Party-dominated Leninist system where the state highly penetrates into the society to one where the state allows the business sector some independence. This independence is given on the consideration that industrialization requires economic drivers that are external to the structure of the Party-state. At the same time, the state also looks to hinder the autonomous organization of societal groups with the potential to undermine the state. Therefore, the model of socialist corporatism allows for a thorough understanding of the rationale, and helps capture the devolution of power, and the institutional structure that socialist reformers need to create an autonomous society; however, at the same time, the model also describes the development and range of this autonomy.[21]

Socialist corporatism and state corporatism differ significantly. First, Schmitter envisages the origin of state corporatism to be in the context of the "rapid, highly visible demise of nascent pluralism." That is, this occurs in a capitalist state where the state, as a substitute for a weak business class, tries to suppress demands of subordinate classes to maintain social peace.[22] However, for a socialist state in a process of reform, socialist corporatism is attempting to prevent new autonomous groups of society from emerging and asserting themselves, rather than to capture the groups that already exist.[23] Second, Schmitter's theory of state corporatism, as can be seen in Brazil and Portugal, for example, is to consolidate and coordinate social forces to improve the country's position in the global economy.[24] Socialist reform, however, shows a tendency to devolve bureaucratic power from a structure that has been in existence for decades. Therefore, socialist corporatism puts an emphasis on dispersing power to extra-state bodies, even if the state itself has helped to create these bodies in the first place. Third, this model also fits the Leninist background in China that espouses an expansive state and a large, planning bureaucratic system, as well as its historical legacy of having weak societal institutions. These historical factors will all influence the new corporatist institutions that are born from reform, some of which were formed by the state in the first place, but were given much more autonomy later on.[25]

Clientelism is a kind of mutually beneficial relationship. This positive-sum and symbiotic element gives it apparent stability. Scholars have mixed opinions towards whether clientelism applies to China's state-society relations. Some scholars agree with Pearson that clientelism is a feasible and important strategy in post-Mao China. From her perspective, this informal relationship between political and business realms will remain, as long as the official channels between business and government are inadequately institutionalized. When it comes to China's case, given that the policy interests of the fairly independent economic elite groups are increasing, while they still have no significant impact on the country's political institutions, personal connections in relationships with officials will probably stay positive.[26]

Other scholars, such as Scott Kennedy, contend that the clientistic model does not apply to business-government relationships at the level of national policymaking. This may come as a surprise as the general belief is that corruption is so far-reaching in China because of governmental interference in regulating the economy.[27] According to Kennedy's argument, local patronage cannot be easily transposed to fit the way that national economic policymaking works. This patronage, commonly observed in local settings, includes business licenses, permits, bank loans and investment approval, as well as access to land and resources, obtaining favorable court case verdicts, the sale of certain products and the reduction of tax payments.[28]

This point of Kennedy has been further confirmed and verified by Nathan and Gilley in their book, *China's New Rulers: The Secret Files.* There they state that "an investigative report is unlikely to contain allegations of corruption, since someone officially suspected of corruption will not have risen far enough to be a candidate for Politburo standing."[29] From another perspective, Kennedy argues that this use of connections is not only applicable to clientelism but also to pluralist or corporatist frameworks. This includes businesses that—without giving a material incentive—build new relationships to gain the trust of regulators, gain knowledge of governmental policies and promote their own agendas.[30]

The East Asian statist model argues that the economic co-ordination by the state caused the outstanding growth in the emerging industrialized countries of the region. This statist model is designed to explain economic performance rather than the relationship between state and society. The conventional East Asian statist model describes how independent states, through intelligent and non-corrupt bureaucracies, were able to astutely manipulate their economies via methods such as screening foreign investment and promoting exports. This strategy enabled them to shape their market forces to meet the state's goals—i.e. the quick development of industrialization. Associations and large business conglomerates coordinate the relationships between business and government. The business associations in this context are strongly guided by or chosen by the state. Thus, some comparisons between China and East Asian statism are appropriate. However, the legacy of socialism in China means that corporatist institutions are less strong than in the rest of East Asia. Yet these corporatist institutions would normally help coordinate business-government relationships and facilitate effective policymaking. Therefore, the situation in China has too many differences to be a complete match with the East Asian statist model.[31]

Merchant-State Dualism in History

"Merchant-state dualism" is a hybrid relationship between the state and society that maintains state control over merchants, while giving them some autonomy. The dual roles of the new businesses are to serve as instruments of state control, and to lobby on behalf of the business elite. At the same time, the state deploys a corporatist strategy to control these new business groups.[32]

The traditional relationship between merchants and the state at both the national and local levels is long lasting. In this tradition, the merchant elite is neither completely dominated by the state nor is it completely autonomous, but is situated between the state and its society. The merchant elite may even sometimes mix socially with the official class and undertake 'public' works. In Chinese history, the precise nature of merchant-state relations varied over time, depending on the specific historical context. This dualistic relationship continued except in two extreme conditions. These were the effects of the fall of the Qing government on the one hand, which saw an almost complete collapse of centralized authority, and the effects of the Maoist era on the other, where the state tried to eliminate private business as a whole.[33]

Merchant Life in Qing China:

According to the official Confucian doctrine, merchants (known as *shang* 商) were considered to be one of the lowest social orders. This doctrine stressed their negative elements. They were ranked after scholar-officials (known as *shi* 仕), peasants (known as *nong* 农) and artisans (known as *gong* 公). This reflects the view that agriculture, not trade, was considered to be the foundation of a strong economy. This perspective was fostered by the traditional idea that trading led to private gain (known as s*i* 私), which was considered to be both selfish and illegitimate, and by the idea that a private society could not subsist autonomously from the state.[34] Despite this disdain, the state tolerated a prosperous private economy and extensive rural local markets—these were, in fact, a key factor in the well-being of the imperial state.[35] Trading guilds also prospered and served as intermediaries between merchants and state officials. The guilds started out small and grew into larger networks by the eighteenth and nineteenth centuries. These included regionally based guilds (known as *huiguan* 会馆) and trade or professional guilds and associations (known as *hanghui* 行会, *gongsuo* 公所 and *fatuan* 法团). These guilds were organized around the specific production or processing of a commodity such as salt or tea. These guilds/associations may have started around local areas or clans, and developed into larger community based organizations with various complex functions.[36]

Therefore, the coexistence of doctrinal disdain of economic activity and a flouring merchant and guild life meant that the role of merchants was fraught with complexity. In essence, merchants had a dual position comprised of both autonomy and elements of state control.[37]

Late-Qing Merchants and Guilds from 1840 to 1911

The circumstances of merchants in China saw improvements in the late-Qing period from the mid-nineteenth century until 1911 when the Qing Empire fell. Qing authority was weakened by the interference of foreign military forces and rebellion on domestic fronts. This also saw an increase in the authority of merchants and merchant organizations. Even though merchant power was increasing, the government still tried to retain control of private business.[38]

The Qing army suffered many military losses in this period which resulted in a growth in foreign economic presence in the country's Treaty Ports. This led to a new merchant group known as the comprador bourgeoisie (*maiban zibenjia* 买办资本家).[39] The members of this group had begun life as clerks and purveyors in the previous Cohong (*gonghang* 工行) system, and now began to accumulate significant private wealth. Compradors and other prominent merchants in China at the time were also responsible for the introduction of a more cosmopolitan lifestyle in urban areas on the coast. Shanghai based compradors, for example, tended to live in the International Settlement. Their blue silk floor length gowns were changed for Western-style jackets and suits and they chose to live in Western-style houses. They spoke English and adopted Christian ways with many converting to Christianity.[40] The late Qing period also saw a rise in prominence for business guilds and an increase in their political activity. During the Taiping Rebellion of the 1850s, for example, guilds helped keep social order and took on municipal government power. As Qing rule went into decline, merchants' contact with Sun Yat-sen's Revolutionary Alliance (*Tongmenghui* 同盟会) increased. Moreover, many merchants and compradors became participants in the new municipal governments during their short appearance after the 1911 revolution.[41]

Given the declining strength of the Qing Empire and the subsequent rise in merchant authority, government reformers in the late nineteenth century had to re-assess China's economic strategy and the merchant role therein.[42] They deduced that China would need the assistance of industrialists and commercial experts if it were to industrialize. An imperial law was passed in 1903 which created the Ministry of Commerce with a view to limiting the influence of the state over merchants and the accrual of wealth.

Some state officials turned industrialists, gave up their positions in government, and successfully set up businesses—this development resonates with similar occurrences in post-Mao China. These new industrialists were able to use their government connections to play a bigger role in their businesses. The social distinctions between the official and merchant ranks were further blurred by these changes and—by the early 1900s—a new local leadership class was created known as gentry-merchants (*shenshang* 绅商).[43]

Therefore, during the late Qing, industrialization and the foreign threat generated a more sophisticated role for merchants and the creation of new institutions to guide industrialization. Despite this fact, the essence of the old dual pattern—state supervision mixed with limited merchant autonomy, and the social blending of official and merchant groups—remained.[44]

A Push toward Merchant Autonomy: The "Golden Age" of 1911-1927

Following the fall of the Qing Empire in 1911, merchants and related associations made strides towards achieving autonomy and activism. This was a golden age for them. According to Marie-Claire Bergere, this period in Shanghai "saw the emergence of an autonomous society in Chinese history—an urban society dominated by the united front of business circles, well structured and inspired by a modernist and pro-Western intelligentsia."[45] Following the start of World War I, Chinese entrepreneurs—especially on the coast around the Treaty Port of Shanghai—appeared in the wake of the increased demand for imported goods. The post-war wave of industrialization had an emphasis on producing consumer goods such as food, textiles, cigarettes, and confectionaries. This also gave merchants in the booming coastal cities a range of new opportunities.[46] As a result, the business class in China got wealthier and became more professional.

These changes caused political turmoil and social unrest. Several types of political activism were born from the immediate aftermath of the May Fourth movement with merchants, students, intellectuals and workers joining together to protest against the May, 1919 announcement that the government had agreed to transfer German rights in Shandong Province to Japan. The Beijing government was publicly criticized by trade groups who began promoting so-called patriotic products.[47] Many of these merchant initiatives proved successful. In 1923, the president of the Republic was removed by a military coup in Beijing. At this point, the Shanghai Chamber of Commerce declared independence and intended to set up a merchant government (*shangren zhengfu* 商人政府), even though it had no territorial basis or military forces. This dramatic move failed.[48]

Nationalist Suppression and the Return to Dualism:

The ascendancy to power in 1927 of the Nationalists unfortunately put an end to this so-called golden age for the business elite. The government of Chiang Kai-shek brought back the merchant dualism model.[49] Nationalization of key industries by the government in Nanjing, however, was slow, as Chiang had needed the political and financial support of Shanghai's influential capitalists to rise to power. Personal ties, such as those with Finance Minister, T.V. Song (a member of one of the most well-known capitalist families in Shanghai), were used by the capitalists to influence governmental decisions.[50] With a swing towards conservatism in the 1930s, many members of the bourgeoisie depended on Chiang to restore social order and to reduce overseas economic competition. The Nationalist government, however, ultimately adopted an opposing stance towards merchant autonomy. Pressures such as anti-Japanese conflicts and the ensuing civil war, along with Nationalist policies that were becoming more restrictive, led to the emigration of many of the merchant elite to Hong Kong and other locations outside China.[51]

The Nationalist government left the merchant organizations intact, but it removed much of the ability of the associations to act in the vigorous, self-interested manner of the previous years. The state pre-empted the further emergence of competing, autonomous organizations and demobilized what previously had been a politically active constituency.[52]

The Fate of China's Business Elite during the Maoist Years:

The constraints that the business class had to endure under the Nationalists were merely a small indication of its fate in the upcoming years. As the communist regime came to power in 1949, the balance between the business elite and the state shifted to the polar opposite of that which existed in the golden age. Marxist ideology on commerce deepened the Confucian tenet that private interests were to be subordinate to the interests of the state. Under Maoism some individual interests were acknowledged, but the Communist system denied that separate interests could exist.[53] The party tried to change the ideology of the comprador bourgeoisie resulting in the Wufan (literally, "Five-Anti" "五反") campaign of 1951-1952.[54] The so-called 'bad' bourgeois classes were subjected to struggle and self criticism sessions by Party cadres. Many of the biggest capitalist families had their assets confiscated in the first half of the 1950s during the 'transformation to socialism'. The broader business class, as a result, was effectively reduced to next to nothing.[55]

Corporatist Co-optation during the Post-Mao State:

A remarkable structure of autonomy and independent opinions is widespread among the new business elite in China in the post-Mao period. However, China has not seen its new business elite develop into a strong, autonomous, politically active and democratizing influence. Rather, the state has initiated a strategy of organizing the business elite in order to avoid independent societal pressure. [56] This culminated in then Present Jiang Zemin's "The Three Represents," which called upon the Party to represent "the interests of the vast majority of the population" as well as "advanced productive forces" and "advanced cultural forces." [57] "The Three Represents" saw a shift in Party ideology towards increasing its base by incorporating the growing middle class. This fundamental revision of Party ideology was announced in 2000 and was written into the Party's constitution in 2002.[58]

Comparison and Contrast:

When examining the relationships between merchants and the state from the later Qing period to the era of Mao, it becomes clear that the political role played by merchants and associations was neither simple nor identical. In fact, these relationships have historically been variable and complex.

First, the typical pattern is dualism. In this pattern, a dynamic merchant sector can have some autonomy, while the central state also exerts control and supervision. This pattern was revealed by the late-Qing reformers' attempts to stimulate industrialization supervised by the state, while, at the same time, to energize and regulate merchants by creating chambers of commerce. The same can be said of the Nationalist regime's efforts to co-opt the most powerful of the formerly autonomous merchant associations to focus their energies on modernization. This particular pattern was somewhat successful and had strong overtones of state corporatism.[59]

Second, differences between the dualism of the Qing and of the Nationalist historical periods are clear. In the Qing era, the relationships between merchants and the state were relatively benevolent. The state compromised their desire for state supervision with the need for a vibrant merchant life and made efforts to accommodate merchant activity. In contrast, the state in the Nationalist era was more coercive. The government in this period wanted to use new state-dominated associations to enforce strong controls and to cause rapid industrialization, although this method did not work in practice. So, for both eras, state control was the goal, but they each tried to achieve this goal in different ways and therefore produced different results. This tactical difference between the ways that the states used to reconcile both autonomy and control is instructive when we consider the post-Mao period. The question is raised here of whether the post-Mao state will follow the Nationalist coercive model or the Qing model of social accommodation and legitimatization to meet this same goal.[60]

Continuity:

Although the Maoist period stood for more than two decades in which the typical pattern was interrupted, yet, one can still identify three specific aspects of historical continuity in the periods before and after Mao. The first, and most important, aspect is that the late-Qing, Nationalist and the post-Mao reformers all have acknowledged that a functional necessity exists to harness the skills and resources of the merchant or business elite.[61] The second is that some continuity exists between pre- and post-1949 institutions. Many federations, for example, such as the ACFIC (a business federation) that were established in the early 1950s, were actually old associations adapted to the new socialist context. The ACFIC was once again updated in socialist clothing in the 1980s. These organizations have not, however, stayed the same, as they have undergone qualitative changes in terms of their goals, methods and links to the state, particularly in the 1956 "transition" and during the Cultural Revolution (1966-1976).[62] The third aspect is an enduring cultural and intellectual context that supports a dual role and can conceivably result in the adoption of similar solutions. In other words, the issue of state control of the business elite and related associations has always been in the same cultural and intellectual context, even though interruptions occurred during the golden age and during Maoism. In this sense, the question involves the extent to which the state should control business, and not whether control should exist in the first place.[63]

Merchant-State Dualism in the Post-Mao 1980s

Merchant-State dualism in the era of post-Mao reform in the 1980s with reference to foreign investment is reflected in two aspects. One is that the post-Mao leadership is able to use its strengths to reap the benefits that the Chinese government identified with foreign direct investment, while guarding against its perceived problems. Second, progress in liberalization was sustained, but marked by a "two steps forward, one step back" pattern,[64] i.e., liberalization was uneven, and often careful and hesitant, but nevertheless undeniable. Despite the government's maintenance of strong controls in some areas, an overall liberalization took place in the policy toward foreign investment during the course of the 1980s.[65]

China's Dual-edged Foreign Investment Strategy:

The reform era's open policy did not discard the point of view that direct foreign investment could have potentially negative effects. The post-Mao leadership instead thought that China would be able to selectively sustain the positive aspects of foreign investments and to remove any negative factors. The leadership believed that the existence of a consolidated socialist state was their primary strength and that this would enable China to control the effects of foreign investment. The core of the Chinese attempt was to use foreign investment to boost economic development while retaining control of capital investment through the form of joint equity ventures.[66] The government was, in a number of ways, effective at maintaining strict controls over many issues. However, at all levels it was under pressure to make significant liberalization in the investment regime.[67]

Power Structure and Decision Making

The Chinese government is a classic example of a Leninist party-state, since the party directly controls the workings of the state. At the same time, the Chinese system has been one of personal authoritarianism, in that one person has held the reigns of power over the party, state, and military for most of the PRC's history. China's potentially democratic institutions, such as the NPC and the CPPCC, have had no power until recently.[68]

The Politburo Standing Committee (PBSC) makes all critical decisions concerning the economy, social policy, foreign affairs, defense, science and technology, education, and culture. The PBSC does not have to answer to any other organ of the Party or government, with the exception of a group of highly esteemed Party Elders, headed by Deng Xiaoping from 1987 to 1997. This group wielded clandestine veto power over the decisions of the PBSC.[69] Support from these Elders as well as wide-reaching political authority were granted to Deng by a secret 1987 Politburo resolution. This resolution granted three retiring Party Elders the power to override Politburo decisions. However, the retired Elders have not used this power to intervene since the death of Deng Xiaoping in 1997. The current Party Elders led by Jiang Zemin do not possess the same authority that Deng Xiaoping once commanded.[70]

While the power to make decisions is given to the Party, the role of the state is to implement these decisions. The Party and the state have organizational structures that are separate, highly developed, yet partly overlapping. That is, the top government posts are occupied by Party members, while those who hold Party posts are generally more powerful than officials of the state in the same area of governmental activity.[71]

The Politburo has not made its decisions by outright voting but rather by consensus. Since the time of Deng Xiaoping, collective leadership has been emphasized. This type of leadership is in stark contrast to the dictatorial domination over the top leaders wielded by Mao Zedong.[72] Jiang Zemin also emphasized collective decision making in his report to the 1997 15th Party Congress, in which he stated that: "In according with the principles of collective leadership, democratic centralism, individual consultations, and decisions by meetings, we should improve the mechanisms of debate and decision making within party committees so as to give fuller play to the role of full sessions of the party committees."[73]

The Politburo's new transparency and image of accountability under Hu's leadership clearly show Hu Jintao's personal goals in striving for institutional reform in the Politburo and in improving inner-party democracy. Publicity has recently been given to meetings of the Politburo under Hu's leadership. Efforts have also been made to underscore the Politburo's accountability to the Central Committee, efforts embodied in Hu's report to the Third Plenum.[74] In spite of publicity given to the full Politburo and its increase in accountability, the Politburo Standing Committee, nevertheless, remains the key decision-making group among the top leadership.

The sensitivity of the Standing Committee's role is borne out by the continuing degree of secrecy surrounding it. In this respect, the image of party transparency and accountability is only enhanced by the media attention to the activities of the full Politburo, attention which has little impact on the inner workings of the top leadership of the Politburo Standing Committee.[75]

The Chinese government is thus centralized enough to implement the above mentioned two-fold foreign investment strategy. The Chinese leadership is able to define the role for foreign investment in the country's economy, politics and culture. Decentralization may have weakened the plan, as well as the role of the national government in joint venture approval, but the government is still able to assert its authority despite these factors. Measures such as controls of exports, of domestic content, of foreign exchange, and of profits and technology transfer,[76] have allowed China to capture what it believes is a legitimate share of investment benefits.

Liberalization in the 1980s: Uneven and Hesitant, but Progressive

Another aspect of merchant-state dualism in the 1980s is that liberalization was uneven, and often careful and hesitant. It was, nevertheless, undeniable. Despite the situation that the Chinese economy became fairly independent, merchants did not achieve autonomy in a linear way, as the liberalization process was marked by a pattern of "two steps forward, one step backward." Nor, on the other hand, were merchants under the complete control of the state. Their position stood somewhere in between.

Rather than remaining static, the Chinese communist reform process after Mao has shifted recurrently between the extremes of restriction and liberalization. The first phase of reform (1979-mid 1983) set out a stringent policy of controls, a policy of controls which was to a certain extent repeated at the start of the second phase of reform (late 1983-mid 1986). Much of the second phase saw liberalization turn into a significant trend, which was carried on with particular emphasis during the third phase (late 1986-1988).[77]

Even though the overall trend was the progression towards liberalization, attempts were still made to protect against potentially negative effects of this liberalization. Four periods of restriction took place during this general trend. These were: the 1981-82 Backlash against Unhealthy Ideological Effects; the 1983-84 Anti-Spiritual Pollution Campaign; the 1987 Campaign against Bourgeois Liberalization; and the 1989 Tiananmen Square Massacre and the following witch-hunt.[78] Each period will be discussed further below.

The first period of restriction began in early 1981 and saw a backlash against the effects of the first wave of economic reform in 1979-80, which was perceived as ideologically unhealthy. In 1981, Deng Xiaoping was engaging in his characteristic-balancing act between various factions and tendencies in the leadership. This carried on into 1982 but gradually wound down as the new reformist party chairman—Hu Yaobang—consolidated his power. The second period of restriction took place in late 1983, and saw a similar type of backlash against what was known as "spiritual pollution" (*jingshen wuran* 精神污染), which was perceived to have come about as a result of increased interaction with the outside world following the Open Policy. The targets for this campaign were diverse, including prominent Party members (including Zhou Yang) and the corrupt and degenerate influences that were alleged to have been imported from the West, such as rock music, fashion and pornography. As economic reforms were proving effective, especially in agriculture, and as reformist leaders were grasping the opportunity to push the reform process forward, this backlash was extinguished relatively quickly. The third period of restriction saw a backlash in early 1987 in response to the moves towards political liberalization in late 1986 that had been encouraged by reform leaders such as Hu Yaobang and Zhao Ziyang. The demonstrations by students for "democracy and freedom" at the end of 1986 and beginning of 1987 also played a part here. In January 1987, a widespread movement was launched by the government against "bourgeois liberalization," accompanied by Hu Yaobang's dramatic resignation as Party General Secretary on the 16th of January. Other high profile targets were selected, including Fang Lizhi, the astrophysicist. Deng was the one, who concerned about the balance of power, threw his weight behind Zhao Ziyang, which effectively brought the backlash to an end. The fourth period of restriction saw the biggest backlash which followed the students' demonstrations of May and June and the Beijing Massacre of June 4th, 1989. Key opposition figures, including Chen Yizi, Yan Jiaqi, Wan Runnan, Su Shaozhi and their overall political sponsor Zhao Ziyang, were attacked. The process of economic reform also generally slowed. This backlash distinguished itself from the others by being far more violent than its predecessors. This reform process shows the great influence that Deng and the Elders had over post-Mao politics. Deng had so great an influence because he had been given the right to intervene in the policymaking process of the party and the state by a secret 1987 Politburo resolution. His control was further solidified by his position as chair of the Central Military Commission.

The Rise of Significant Autonomy of Merchants in the 1990s

If the 1980s' attempts at reform were uneven and hesitant, the 1990s witnessed the substantial autonomy of the merchants in China's political economy.

The scope and role of planning in the Reform era saw significant changes. The *guidance* plan replaced the *mandatory* plans of the Mao era in the 1980s. In this *guidance* plan, the government gave inducements to state-owned enterprises to comply with the plan via a range of particular sanctions and benefits. At this stage, businesses were able to view the plan as being just a part of their responsibilities rather than—as before—being their sole responsibility. As a result, businesses were permitted to sell products on the market outside of the plan.[79] The *guidance* plan was replaced in the 1990s by *indicative* plans. These plans laid out general goals and suggestions rather than enterprise specific requirements.[80]

The movement from planning to regulation has inevitably been accompanied by a shift in government and business relationships. These relationships have been shaped by economic factors in China, because the primary requirement for China's continued development and stability is fast, if not breakneck, economic growth.[81] Despite a pervasive authoritarianism, however, the economic circumstances of firms and industries come to determining the interaction between government and business. Therefore, national economic policies in China cannot be seen as being merely the result of clear intentions of an autocratic leader or leadership circle but rather as the result of bureaucratic and technocratic bargaining and general concerns for the economy. In addition, the policy process is influenced by trade associations and other intermediaries on behalf of their members. More commonly, firms will lobby their regulators directly.[82]

The increased importance of merchants was also symbolized by representation of private interests in the Party's ideology. Jiang Zemin has left two legacies: one is a campaign for internal reform and discipline of the Party; the other is a fundamental revision of Party ideology, which was announced in 2000 and written into the Party's constitution in 2002. This ideology, known as "The Three Represents," called upon the Party no longer to think of itself as representing only its traditional Marxist constituencies, the workers and peasants, but also to represent "the developmental demands of China's advanced social productive forces, the forward trend of China's advancing culture, and the basic interests of the broadest number of China's people." These were code words for making the Party a more urban and bourgeois regime. The ideological shift was further consolidated in Jiang Zemin's invitation to private entrepreneurs to join the Party, which he did in a speech on the Party's eightieth anniversary on July 1, 2001.[83] This positive attitude towards merchants was further endorsed by current Party chief, Hu Jintao, in his two and a half hour speech presented at the 17th Party Congress on October 15, 2007. Hu stated in this speech: "We will promote equitable market access, improve the financing environment and remove institutional barriers in order to promote development of individually-owned businesses and private companies as well as small and medium-sized enterprises."[84] The Chinese Communist Party's 11th Five Year Plan covering the years 2006 through 2010 and passed in October 2005 is seen as the Hu Jintao-Wen Jiabao administration's economic program. This Five Year Plan extends merchant autonomy by opening new sectors to Chinese private capital. It explicitly says that state monopolies over certain sectors—meaning natural resources, utilities and telecommunication—will be opened to investment and ownership diversification. This Plan also grants permission to establish small and medium-sized financial institutions of different ownership types. In particular, this means that some private banks will be allowed, on an experimental basis, in Zhejiang and Jiangsu provinces.[85]

Merchants Gain the Upper Hand:

The Chinese state, as a developmental regime, has an ideological orientation towards business. The central place of merchants in achieving government objectives and the merchants' authoritative knowledge give industry a privileged position at the policy table.[86] Historically, ownership either privately or by the state has been seen as the dividing line of the economic and political activities of a business. This has been joined by other factors now, including size, industry concentration and technological sophistication. Direct and more comprehensive access to the state is given to large firms regardless of their ownership status—rather than to their smaller counterparts. This may seem unsurprising in some ways, but it runs counter to the conventional notion that state-owned businesses in China have more political power than privately or foreign owned ones. Increasingly, in China, size rather than ownership or nationality is the determining factor that sets a company's ability to influence public policy.[87]

Since the 1990s, businesses have interacted with the government through various direct and indirect channels. Associations along with other intermediaries bridge the gap between the Chinese state and businesses.[88] This in turn produces corporate political action. Corporate political action scholars focus intensively on the firms' participation in the governmental process, their attempts to influence government decision-making and to construct a favorable business environment for themselves.[89]

Direct interaction between the government and companies represents the most important form of contact. This direct interaction makes use of a legacy from the Mao era emphasizing direct interaction between the government and businesses. This originally only applied to state owned businesses but has now been extended to both domestic and foreign privately owned firms.[90]

Since the 1990s, both sides have had regular contact before new policies are adopted. The government also commonly asks for industry opinion with regard to economic regulation.[91] These exchanges of opinions are initiated by both sides and occur during the process of considering specific laws and regulations, as well as during the ordinary process of regulatory oversight, which can sometimes lead to a new policy initiative.[92]

At one end of the spectrum, national and regional ministries hold formal hearings as a way of finding out industry opinions. This practice is rapidly expanding and is officially encouraged by the people's congresses.[93] At the other end of the spectrum, businesses and associations will regularly invite officials to press conferences and product releases, and use these events to mention policy issues or at least to heighten the importance of the industry in the officials' minds. The business executives can also go to the capital to actually meet government officials in person. In addition, many larger domestic and foreign businesses maintain branch offices in Beijing with the prime objective of keeping in close contact with their regulators.[94]

More specifically, firms often try to influence the making of government policy in the following ways: a) the direct participation in politics by the National People's Congress on behalf of business. The CEOs and presidents of several enterprises have been engaging in politics directly as representatives of the National People's Congress. In name, their participation is on behalf of the people. In fact, these industrial leaders are pursuing their own interests as well. In particular, they are aiming for a more favorable political environment for their companies. This includes lobbying for such things as the construction of roads, a reduction in the social burdens that businesses now carry, and change in businesses' administrative authority.[95] b) Connection (*guanxi*)-based lobbying. Enterprise leaders use their own or their friends and relatives connections with government officials to get their goals accomplished. For example, when pricing regulations for pharmaceutical products were set in 2001 by the National Development and Planning Commission, leaders of Ha Pharmaceutical Group in Helongjiang province immediately went to Beijing immediately to lobby against such regulations (*gongguan*).[96] c) Charitable contributions. Just as many Western corporations make charitable contributions, so do many Chinese enterprises. In particular, many companies in China contribute to the Hope Project, a project that helps children who cannot afford to go to school. Other charitable contributions include some to the Red Cross, and to educational institutions. Corporate charitable contributions are also made to relief funds. Since China suffers from almost yearly natural disasters, including the seasonal flood of the Yangzi River and the summer and autumnal drought in the north, the Chinese government regularly asks individuals and various enterprises to contribute to the relief funds. Through these charitable contributions, Chinese corporations not only enhance their public image, but increase the strength of their ties to the government as well. The companies' charitable contributions display a sense of social responsibility, which builds favor and trust with the government.[97] d) The giving of money or the quasi giving of money. China seems to lack laws or rules to distinguish explicit bribery from informal gift-giving. Therefore many Chinese enterprises use money or quasi-money giving as a means of privately influencing government policy decision-making. Such gifts include, for example, paying for the children's education of government officials, redecorating houses of government officials for little or no charge, and giving officials and their families tickets to purchase items for free. Their opaqueness to outsiders is what makes these activities popular, not their normality. However, these activities will be looked upon as bribes if an official is under inquiry.[98] e) To be a "proud enterprise of local government." Firms use this approach to influence government policy decision-making. This approach is not well known among foreigners. A series of indexes has been developed by China to measure the political performance of local government officials. This index can help to determine their political future. The condition of the local economy is one such index. A "proud enterprise of the local government" is a large-scale, manageable enterprise that is known throughout China. Such an enterprise can alleviate local unemployment, help to develop the local economy and bring in revenue. Local government policies are favorably geared towards the development of this type of enterprise in order to attract them or to prevent them from relocating to other areas once established.[99]

Just as significant as the existence of multiple paths of interaction and the growth in communication on matters of policy in China is that official norms which stress co-operation between the two sides on the basis of shared interests have weakened. The norm that stresses secrecy in the policy making process has also weakened, due to the increased ability of the business community and other members of society to defend their own interests.[100]

The increased impact of business on policy-making, the increased ability of the business community to defend its own interests and the changing official norms are exemplified in the following two episodes that happened in the 1990s: a "tax revolt" in March 1998 and collective lobbying for price cartels in July of that same year.

In January of 1998, out of a concern that the television industry was overheating, Zhu Rongji suggested to the Ministry of Finance (MOF) that it prepare a special consumption tax on televisions sets. Since Zhu thought that the industry needed to be cooled down, he suggested and approved such a tax.[101]

In March 1998, a meeting was organized by companies between the television makers and officials from the State Economic and Trade Commission (SETC), the State Taxation Administration (STA), and Ministry of Information Industry (MII). These companies also invited representatives and reporters from the major media, including the Xinhua News Agency, Economics Daily and China Electronics news. At this meeting, the companies insisted that despite the popular opinion that the television industry was sizzling, companies were making only a limited amount of profit due to all-out price wars in this sector. In addition, they argued, such a tax on the television industry would have a negative effect on overall employment, which was weak in other sectors of the economy. Aside from this meeting, television manufacturers presented their case to officials in several ministries. MII was in complete agreement with the views of the manufacturers. In addition, some larger companies were able to persuade deputies to the National People's Congress (NPC) to voice concerns about the proposed consumption tax. The intense lobbying by the television manufacturers yielded results. A journalist from the Economics Daily who was in attendance at the meeting wrote a report about it for the State Council. This report fell into the hands of Zhu Rongji himself. Because of this report (and perhaps because of statements by NPC deputies), Zhu changed his mind concerning the consumption tax and ordered the Ministry of Finance to shelve all plans for it.[102]

In July of 1998, Erdos and 12 other Chinese firms paid a visit to the State Economic and Trade Commission (SETC), an agency charged with overseeing Chinese industrial policy. The firms who made the visit included: the state owned electronics producer Changhong from Sichuan (which was at the time the dominant player in the Chinese color television market); the video machine manufacturer Idall from Guangdong (which was almost single handedly responsible for bringing digital video into average Chinese households); the Qingdao Beer Group, based in Shandong, the country's most famous and dominant brewer; and even Beijing's famous Wangfujing Department Store. These companies were all quite different in temperament, products, location, and form of ownership. Nevertheless, they all had two common characteristics: they were all very sizeable enterprises, and they had been negatively affected by a fall in prices that had been sweeping across China. Thus they were all in dire straits. An overcapacity in production had left many industries producing far beyond what could be consumed by current demand. The natural consequence was deflation, a deflation which was draining these firms of profits.[103]

A letter delivered by the companies requested that the government encourage minimum price floors. The firms argued that only through coordination could "vicious competition" (*exing jingzheng* 恶性竞争) in their industries be brought to a stop and orderly market behavior restored. The SETC was receptive to their plea and encouraged associations in various industries to help their companies establish "self-discipline prices" (*zilujia* 自留价). These were the price floors that were requested to halt the tumble in prices. It was an important political victory with major ramifications for the entire economy of China.[104]

Based on former perceptions of Chinese politics, the above two scenarios would seem to be rare instances of business intrusion into a state-dominated policy process. By the mid-1990s such scenarios accurately reflected the increase in the autonomy that business gained from the state.

From a larger perspective, this modernizing of business activities reflects Jiang's political philosophy. From 1997 onward, Jiang made several attempts to remold the CCP. The vision he espoused was a neo-authoritarian one, in which the CCP would be a party of modernizing, educated elites who could discern the national interest without recourse to the tangled processes of democracy.[105] This vision explains Jiang's coastal development strategy. At any rate, current President Hu Jintao portrays himself as a left leaning populist leader whose government places a premium on increasing social fairness and equality. Hu has called for creating a "harmonious society," a society which places great emphasis on decreasing economic disparities, building a social safety net, and providing basic public health care. Quite understandably, the less privileged social groups, particularly those in the interior and northeastern areas of China, view Hu and *tuanpai* （团派） leaders as their chief advocates among the top leadership of the Party.[106]

The State Gains the Upper Hand:

Government and businesses exist in a mixed state of potential co-operation and tension. At times the government bureaucracy may take a position on policy that meets industry interests. At other times the two parties may disagree or the government may not recognize an issue that is important to industry.

The decline in planning and micro-management did not mean that the government would sit by passively on the sidelines as the market operated. To the contrary, the Chinese economy has been heavily regulated. The National People's Congress laid down over 420 laws and regulations in the period between 1980 to early 2002; the State Council laid down 920; and the local people's congresses laid down 7,000—most of which were related to the economy.[107] These figures are just the tip of the iceberg since they do not incorporate the thousands of other—more narrowly targeted—regulations, measures, rules, notices, decisions, and orders that have been laid down by national and local ministries, bureaus and offices. These regulations cover all aspects of business, including entry to and exit from the market, property rights, accounting, labor, credit provision, production, investment, distribution, taxation and commerce.[108]

In fact, the CCP was still very much in control of the merchants during the 1990s. Two events make this fact clear: the first is the way Li Changchun dealt with several high profile bankruptcies of financial groups in the province of Guangdong; the other is the way Zhu Rongji dealt with a US $6.4 billion smuggling scandal involving Lai Changxing, during the time of Jia Qinlin's administration in the city of Xiamen.

In 1997, Jiang sent Li Changchun to the province of Guangdong to take over as provincial Party secretary. Li's appointment resulted in a shakeup of the leaderships of the province's cities, and took away the reigns of power over the province from an independent and entrenched local leadership. As a provincial Party secretary, Li undertook reform of the financial institutions. The Guangdong International Trust and Investment Corporation (GITIC) and the Guangdong Enterprises (Holdings) Group (GDE) were two large financial firms controlled by the local Party leadership and their families. In 1997-1998, during the height of the Asian financial crisis, GITIC owed creditors about US $4.5 billion, while GDE owed US $6 billion. A vast portion of this debt was not only unsecured, but had not even been reported to the central government's foreign exchange administration as required.[109]

Li took charge of the situation by setting up a group of industry specialists led by former central bank deputy governor Wang Qishan to assess the situation. In late 1998, backed by Zhu Rongji in Beijing, Li forced GITIC to declare bankruptcy and GDE to restructure. When foreign creditors complained that a bankrupt GITIC would hurt China's sovereign credit, Li responded to those foreign creditors that if they believed that the Chinese government would come to the aid of a private financial institution solely because of its executives' personal connections, then the Chinese government could rightly be accused of failing to exercise due diligence. However, the provincial government did cover GDE's debts since it was a provincial government agency.[110]

A $6.4 billion smuggling scandal was uncovered in the port city of Xiamen in 1999. Zhu Rongji said that this was the biggest smuggling case in the history of the PRC and vowed to investigate it. The smuggling operation was allegedly run by Lai Changxing and his company, the Yuanhua Group. His company had allegedly bribed members of the local customs administration and military command so that they could import black-market automobiles, gasoline, cigarettes, and a wide range of other controlled commodities without government permits. Lai was a close friend of Jia Qinlin and of Jia's wife Lin Youfang. Lin Youfang, as general manager of the provincial government's foreign trade corporation was involved in controlling import and export. Although Jia's involvement has been widely suspected, it has not yet been proven.[111]

These two events indicate another aspect of Jiang Zemin's philosophy. He believes that the Party should be more disciplined, with a spirit that recalls its origins in the 1930s and 1940s. He articulated this approach in "The Three Stresses". "The Three Stresses" campaign was an attempt by Jiang to save the CCP from internal collapse. This was at a time when the Party was threatened by widespread corruption and regional disobedience to central and provincial orders. Jiang first put forward this philosophy in 1995, comparing it to the Party rectification campaigns launched by Mao in Yan'an in the 1940s.[112]

This bringing of discipline to the Party is also consistent with the views of Hu Jintao's administration. Hu mentioned the problem of the Party cadres many times in his opening address at the 17th Party Congress on October 17, 2007. He even devoted all of sub-section VI consisting of two paragraphs in section XII to the topic of corruption. Hu stated in sub-section VI that: "The CPC never tolerates corruption or any other negative phenomena. This is determined by its nature and purpose. Resolutely punishing and effectively preventing corruption bears on the popular support for the Party and on its very survival, and is therefore a major political task the Party must attend to at all times. ... We must see to it that all cases involving violation of law and discipline are thoroughly investigated and dealt with, and that all those involved in corruption are severely punished according to law without fail."[113]

Hu not only said these words, but put them into action as well. In August 2006, the central leadership dispatched a team to Shanghai to investigate diversion of Shanghai pension funds into various speculative schemes, especially real estate deals. By the end of September 2006, this investigation had ensnared Chen Liangyu, first party secretary of Shanghai and a prominent member of Jiang Zemin's "Shanghai faction."[114] This scandal eventually led to Chen's fall from power. This Shanghai Pension Fund scandal will be explored in more detail shortly.

This would indicate that studies based only on economic factors overstate their case. Additionally, a party/state is not a passive actor. Instead, it always tries to shape society.[115] After all, the political institutions of China conditioned their bureaucrats and businesses alike to behave in a common manner amongst themselves and in relation to each other, no matter what their position in the government or the economy. This shows that no single independent variable is all-powerful, and both economic and political circumstances are the factors that shape relationships between government and business.[116]

The Composition and Dualistic Nature of Merchants

The limited autonomy of merchants is shown through trade associations, trade unions and the actual role of the merchants themselves. Each of these factors is explored in more depth below.

Trade Associations in History:

One can gain an initial insight into the role of these organizations by looking at the historical record of merchant associations in China. In Qing China, these merchant organizations were neither completely autonomous nor wholly dominated by the state. These guilds were actually positioned mid-way between state and society and often performed public (*gong*) acts on behalf of the state that exceeded their own commercial activities. Guilds and other associations were, on the one hand, self-regulating bodies that had a lot of freedom to supervise their own business activities. On the other hand, they did not have the authority to challenge the state to promote their own private interests. In the twentieth century, traditional associations adapted to the modernizing nation-state, with the creation of chambers of commerce, which were designed to both unleash commercial power for China and to put controls on this growing and dynamic group.[117]

Today's System of Trade Associations:

This historical dualistic role of associations has been reshaped in the post-Mao context. Even though some individual associations were started by enterprises, the driving force behind China's post-Mao system of associations was the government itself, which created the system not as a consequence of a market economy but in anticipation of it.[118]

The independence of associations can usually be compromised, if they are: 1) started by the state; 2) required to register/affiliate with a government agency; 3) staffed by government officials; and 4) reliant on financing from the government.[119]

If one examines these four dimensions of autonomy in the case of China, then it becomes obvious that an affiliation with a "responsible business department" is the most consistent bond between government and associations. This is followed by associations created by the state and associations that are staffed and influenced by government officials.

Increasingly, associations are financed by members and their own business activities. To summarize, associations may have varying degrees of autonomy but, in general, close government involvement is still widespread.[120]

Trade Unions:

According to the Leninist model of classic dualism, trade unions must set their priorities in the order of increased productivity and labor protection. The dual role of trade unions includes the mobilization of labor production and the protection of member rights and interests. Production tasks are defined as including those which involve the union management of labor, such as maintaining discipline, motivating members to higher productivity, and educating them in production, management and ideological issues. Two functions make up the "protective" role of unions here. These functions are the guardianship of the legal rights of members against arbitrary management and the protection of labor interests. Yet, precedence will effectively be given to production tasks rather than tasks that fall within the scope of guardianship.[121]

The role of trade unions also involves the resolution of discord to ensure the harmonious relationships between the labor force, management, party and government. This means that unions should seek to blend any discordant individual or group interests with the overall national interest embodied in party and state policies. In effect, this means that unions have to place party and government policy over and above protecting the interests of their membership.[122]

A Brief History of Trade Unions in China:

Unlike trade unions in Eastern Europe and the Soviet Union, Chinese trade unions are characterized by institutional weakness. This is based on various connected historical, social, political, and economic factors.[123]

Contrary to the classic dictates of Marxism, the Chinese Communist Party (CCP) rose to power via a peasant-based strategy of revolution in a peasant society. The proletariat here was virtually excluded from taking part in the revolutionary struggle after 1927, which in turn removed trade unions from the Chinese communist movement's mainstream. Trade unions in China came to represent a working class that was weak and small in number in a peasant society, a society which was rooted in the Maoist appreciation of the virtues of the peasant rather than the proletarian. Therefore, the Chinese trade union movement began in the post 1949 period from an especially disadvantaged position, and was ill prepared to establish itself in the industrial hierarchy. Lacking any tradition of autonomous action, Chinese trade unions were quickly subordinated to the CCP as an auxiliary structure. As the Chinese had decided to follow the Soviet model, the new structure of Chinese trade unions therefore took on the Soviet style, which included the ideological rationale of the dual functions of production and protection. During much of the post 1949 period, party policy dictated that production was virtually the sole focus of trade union activity. Any trade union concern over the welfare of workers was condemned as "economist," i.e. that it reflected an unhealthy focus on material benefit.[124]

Nevertheless, the post-Mao leadership did have a general re-orientation of China's economic, political and social policy, which included reassessing the role of trade unions. Present policy—in contrast to previous priorities—specifies the representation of workers' interests as the primary focus of trade union work. (This change in policy, however, has only slightly changed the reality of the situation.) This does not violate the dual functioning role of the unions, but it does show a significant shift in Chinese policy. The current trade union line is the most unequivocal expression of party support for its welfare role in the post-1949 period. Moreover, the trade union may still be subordinated to the party, but current policy acknowledges a limited autonomy for trade unions.[125]

The Dualistic Role of Merchants Themselves:

- The Composition and Social Status of China's New Business Elite

The new business elite in China is now considered to be part of a global bourgeoisie, however, its structure was formed by the country's unique history and context which makes it rather complex.

First of all, one has to consider the "old-line" managers. These managers tend to be in their late forties or fifties and usually have several years of on the job experience which has led to their senior position. Most of these managers do not have university degrees or any schooling on Western managerial techniques apart from perhaps overseas visits to a foreign parent company for short periods of technical training.[126] These managers' political "reliability" and their lack of formal management training can hold them back from making bold initiatives or taking those responsibilities that would go against standard practice in state-owned enterprises. Gradually, these "old-line" managers are increasingly being eased aside or have learned to transform themselves into more effective managers.

China is unique in the strange fact that the Cultural Revolution disrupted education, which prevented a proportion of the population who would have studied at universities from 1967-1969 from doing so. Many members of this cohort—known as *laosanjie* ("three old ranks 老三届")—are now in their mid-fifties. They were unable to return to school after they had finished compulsory work in either villages or factories, work which they had performed in responses to Mao's call. Despite this fact, many of them have risen to senior roles based on their intelligence and determination. This generation forms a special layer of the business elite in China.[127]

Other important groups are in these new business elite as well. These include former government officials—who are said to have resigned their official positions to jump into the business world. These are known as *xiahai* （下海).[128] Another group in these new business elite is the children of high-level Party or government cadres, known as "princelings" or *taizidang* （太子党）. For instance, Deng Zhifang, the son of Deng Xiaoping, controlled one of Capital Iron and Steel's Hong Kong-listed affiliates—Shougang Concord Grand Group, a property development company. Afterwards, Deng Zhifang resigned as chief executive officer and vice-chairman of Shougang Concord Grand Group to protect himself from Jiang's purge of Chen Xitong (with whom Deng was involved), the then Politburo member and Party secretary of Beijing.[129] Another example of "princelings" is the case of Li Peng's son, Li Xiaopeng and Li Xiaolin. These two took charge of two of the biggest power companies in China, Huaneng Power International and China Power Investment. They used their personal connections to the government to help the companies gain lucrative contracts. Another one of Li Peng's sons, Li Xiaoyong, became involved in a futures brokerage house, Xinguoda, that collapsed in 1998. This collapse has been the subject of many protests by investors in the company.[130] Another example of a princeling is Ye Minghua. Ye is the president of the Shenzhen-based Xianke and is the fourth son of Ye Ting. Ye Ting was a general in the civil war who fought with Deng Xiaoping. He was eventually killed by the Nationalist Party. Ye Minghua was then adopted and raised by Zhou Enlai. Zhou had done this for other orphans as well, most notably former premier, Li Peng.[131] Both these groups can use their contacts in official channels to give them an advantage when making business deals. The personal connections of these former officials and *taizidang* are impressive and can, in many cases, help them gain entry into leadership circles.[132]

In addition, many of the first entrepreneurs in the post-Mao period were not from respected groups in society. Many were the unemployed and former convicts, and operated on the edges of "socialist legality." All of this tended to hurt the image of business as a whole. Recent corruption scandals involving members of the business elite, particularly former government officials, have also had a negative effect on the image of business. Still, the financial success of the business elite nowadays has resulted in a considerable increase in their status and prestige in post-Mao China, especially with young people.[133]

Merger of the State and Merchants:

The post-Mao Chinese state has had significant impacts on both government and on merchants—they have become dependent on each other and could even be termed mutually inter-penetrated. Thus, one can not readily say that real "autonomy" exists for social forces coming from the Chinese state. The interdependence here does bring about collaboration in some cases where merchants and bureaucrats work together to expand the single pot of state resources, channels and sales outlets.[134]

On one hand, no real autonomy of economic power exists at this point for a private sector and no real division of labor in the cities between economic and political power. Any urban Chinese entrepreneur who wants to run a business of some size will have to rely on the state and state institutions as the principal sources of capital for a start-up. Additionally, the payback for business activity is great if given entrée to state production and guidance via its regulatory and informational structures. These benefits keep the new merchant sector dependent on the state. In most cases, the new business elite do not have independent means of production, and it does not have access to independent capital, material supplies and methods of operation. These factors strengthen merchant ties to—and sometimes dependency on—the state and its representatives.[135]

On the other hand, state officials including party cadres, bureaucrats and enterprise managers have engaged in exchanges with the new merchant elite with a view to collusion, incorporation or simply the extraction of profits, skills, connections and time. By doing this, the officials are not only dependent simply on the state, but also sometimes dependent on the new private sector as well. This has resulted in an amalgamation of the business and official classes. One could, in fact, claim that these exchanges are made with a single blended class. This blended class can be compared to the bureaucratic-capitalists of late dynastic times or the gentry-merchants of the ancient period.[136] From this perspective, the liberation of society is actually more of an incorporation of society at both times—past and present, even though the terms have altered dramatically.[137]

The urban Chinese entrepreneur is therefore neither wholly a private operator nor simply a member of the state. Any entrepreneur that wants financial success in the cities has to be involved in both of these groups. The state is not only happy to benefit from private profits but also from the dependency of the merchants. In addition, the advantages of these central merchant-state ties are also shown in the joint ventures, which bring together merchant skills and needs with the connection and supplies of the bureaucracy. Alternatively, they may benefit smaller scale collective businesses that seek to be tied to the neighborhood committees of the state.[138] The merger of state and merchant is more directly revealed by the fact that the leaders of most large Chinese state-owned enterprises are wearing two hats—the president of the enterprise, as well as the official of a government ministry. Their dual status determines their dual roles and functions.

For example, the infamous leader of Capital Iron and Steel from 1979-1995, Zhou Guanwu, initially joined the steelmaking company in 1950. In the 1980s, he was appointed Vice Minister of Metallurgy—this was an honorary position that did not affect his allegiance to his company. He created the prosperity of the company in the 1980s, including promoting a preferential profit-retention plan. However, he was also largely responsible for a range of questionable investments into a bank, an iron mine and a new factory. These investments brought the company to the brink of insolvency. The only way to stop his actions was to remove him from his position, which was done in 1995.[139] His replacement, Bi Qun, was Vice Minister of the Metallurgy Industry (MMI), and the supposition was that his loyalties would therefore lie with the government, rather than with Capital Iron and Steel. Nevertheless, he is not all-powerful in the company, and has to share authority with other senior leaders of Capital Iron and Steel who have been with the company for long periods.[140]

The steel factory, Baosteel, displayed a similar streak of independence. Several years after it began production, the company proved that it was far more efficient that any other steel factory in China. The Ministry of the Metallurgy Industry (MMI) and senior Chinese leaders, especially Wu Bangguo, from the early 1990s preferred that Baosteel be encouraged to merge with other steel companies. In this way the company would be "the strong supporting the weak." The long-standing Chairman of Baosteel, Li Ming, who had played a key role in the success of the company, strongly opposed mergers that would burden the company with the problems of weaker ones. He went so far as to voice his opposition publicly in an interview in 1997 with a foreign journalist.[141] In late 1998 when the merger did finally happen, Li Ming had no option but to resign. His replacement was Xu Daquan, who—like Bi Qun—was a senior metallurgy bureaucrat from Beijing. Despite Li's resignation, the remaining board of directors at Baosteel remained dominated by those who had long tenure at the company.[142]

In cases when a major personnel overlap occurs between a state-owned company and the local government that holds its registration, then the situation can become more complex. For example, the Yonggang Group was established in 1984 by Wu Dongcai who was, at the time, the party secretary for Yonglian Village. With funds from the village and surrounding townships, Wu built Yonggang, which was successfully turned into a company employing 2400 people producing over one million tons of steel for construction every year.[143] In this case, the economic entity—the company—and the political entity—the village—became identical.

While working as Yonggang's party secretary and chairman, Wu has retained his position of party secretary and committee leader for the village. Other village cadres also held senior positions at the company. One of Yonggang's vice presidents was the daughter of Zhangjiagang city's party secretary.[144] Similarly, Ni Runfeng, became president of China's largest TV manufacturer, Changhong, in 1985. He is also an alternate member of the Central Committee of the Chinese Communist Party.[145]

The Dark Side of the State-Merchant Relationship:

The relationships between officials and merchants often have a darker side as evidenced by a recent probe into corruption. The government has been investigating an investment of US $400 million, which equals about a third of the assets of the pension fund, by the Shanghai pension fund into Fuxi. This investment essentially allowed the company, Fuxi, to purchase the Shanghai-Hangzhou motorway. Two senior city government officials and the head of the motorway company (one of the richest people in the country) were detained by the government as a consequence of the biggest scandal that Shanghai had seen for decades.

Qin Yu, the governor of one of the districts in Shanghai, is currently under investigation in the scandal. Qin was previously a personal aide to Chen Liangyu. Chen was a member of the Communist party politburo and the party secretary for Shanghai, as well as a leader of the "Shanghai Gang" which was well-known in the time of General Secretary Jiang. His apparent involvement in the

Fuxi scandal illustrates the complicated web of ties between the government and business that characterize today's China.

According to many analysts, the Chinese President, Hu Jintao, is happy to let the allegations of taking bribes weaken the allies of his predecessor Jiang Zemin. Aside from the matter of Beijing politics, the scandal has come to symbolize those often-questionable ties between government officials and the new generation of millionaire entrepreneurs. Their rapid accrual of wealth is often based on a network of connections.

The rise of Zhang was incredibly rapid—he made some money in trading textiles and then—in February 2002—he established Fuxi. Just one month later, he won the concession for the Hangzhou motorway with the help of the investment from the Shanghai pension fund. This helped place him 16th on the latest Forbes list of China's richest people, with an estimated wealth of US $605 million—all at the age of 32.

Public pension funds are technically limited by the government to investing in government bonds; however, loopholes in the system are being used by many funds to invest in secretive real estate and transport deals. Critics claim that these undisclosed investments can only breed corruption; however, the fund managers are also under strong pressure to generate high returns.

Beijing could use the Shanghai scandal to push for reform. The National Council for Social Security Funds, for example, which is the current manager of the central government's pension fund, has already disclosed information on how and where it invests.[146]

Notes

1. Carl J. Friedrich and Zbigniew K. Brzezinski, *Totalitarian Dictatorship and Autocracy,* New York: Praeger, 1961.

2. David S. G. Goodman, *Groups and Politics in the People's Republic of China,* Armonk, NY: M. E. Sharp, 1984.

Victor C. Falkenheim, *Citizens and Groups in Contemporary China,* Ann Arbor: Center for Chinese Studies, University of Michigan, 1987.

3. Andrew G. Walder, *Communist Neo-Traditionalism: Work and Authority in Chinese Industry,* Berkeley: University of California Press, 1986.

4. Andrew G. Walder, "Workers, Managers, and the State: The Reform Era and the Political Crisis of 1989," *China Quarterly,* No. 127, September 1991, p. 467-492.

Andrew G. Walder, "A Reply to Womack," *China Quarterly,* No. 126, June 1991, p. 333-339.

5. Margaret M. Pearson, *China's New Business Elite,* Berkeley and Los Angeles, California: University of California Press, 1997, p. 23.

6. Robert Dahl, *Who Governs?* New Haven, Conn.: Yale University Press, 1961; and C. Wright Mills, *The Power Elite,* New York: Oxford University Press, 1959.

7. Scott Kennedy, *The Business of Lobbying in China,* Cambridge, Massachusetts: Harvard University Press, 2005, p. 45, 53.

8. Ibid., p. 26-27, 53.

9. Wlodzimierz Brus, "Political Pluralism and Markets in Communist Systems," *Pluralism in the Soviet Union: Essays in Honor of H. Gordon Skilling,* edited by Susan Gross Solomon, New York: St. Martin's Press, 1983, p. 108-130.

10. Pearson, 1997, p. 32.

11. Philippe C. Schmitter, "Still the Century of Corporatism?" *The New Corporatism: Social-Political Structures in the Iberian World,* edited by Fredrick B. Pike and Thomas Stritch, Notre Dame, IN: University of Notre Dame Press, 1974, p. 93-94.

12. David Ost, "Towards a Corporatist Solution in Eastern Europe: The Case of Poland," *East European Politics and Society,* Vol. 3, No. 1, winter 1989, p. 152-174.

Andrew Arato, "Civil Society against the State: Poland 1980-1981," *Telos,* Vol. 47, 1981, p. 23-47.

13. Daniel Chirot, "The Corporatist Model and Socialism: Notes on Romanian Development," *Theory and Society,* Vol. 9, No. 2, 1980, p. 363-381.

14. Valerie Bunce and John M. Echols III, "Soviet Politics in the Brezhnev Era: 'Pluralism' or 'Corporatism'," *Soviet Politics in the Brezhnev Era,* edited b Donald R. Kelley, New York: Praeger, 1980, p. 1-26.

15. Zhao Ziyang, "Advance along the Road of Socialism with Chinese Characteristics," Report delivered at the Thirteenth National Congress of the Communist Party of China, *Beijing Review,* Dec. 20, 1987, p. 18. Zhao Ziyang, "On Separating Party from Government," *Beijing Review,* December 14-20, 1987, p. 18-20.

16. Andrew J. Nathan, *Chinese Democracy,* New York: Alfred Knopf, 1985.

17. Pearson, 1997, p. 35-38.

18. Zhang Jing, *Fatuanzhuyi* (Corporatism), Beijing: China Social Sciences Press, 1998.

19. This part is referred to Kennedy, 2005, p. 40-44.

20. Pearson, 1997, p. 39; and Gordon White, *Riding the Tiger: The Politics of Economic Reform in Post-Mao China,* Stanford: Stanford University Press, 1993.

21. This part is summarized from Pearson, 1997, p. 39-43, 117, 144.

22. Schmitter, 1974, p. 106.

23. Pearson, 1997, p. 39.

24. Schmitter, 1974, p. 120.

25. Pearson, 1997, p. 39.

26. This part summarized Pearson, 1997, p. 34-35, 143-144.

27. Kennedy, 2005, p. 53.

28. David L. Wank, *Commodifying Communism: Business, Trust, and Politics in a Chinese City,* Cambridge: Cambridge University Press, 1999.

29. Andrew J. Nathan and Bruce Gilley, *China's New Rulers: The Secret Files,* New York: The New York Review of Boks, Inc., 2003, p. 28.

30. Catherine Gelb, "First Hand," *China Business Review,* Vol. 30, No. 2. March/April 2003, p. 65-69.

Ming-Cheng M. Lo and Eileen M. Otis, "*Guanxi* Civility: Processes, Potentials, and Contingencies," *Politics and Society,* Vol. 31, No. 1, March 2003, p. 131-162; and Hongying Wang *Weak State, Strong Networks,* Oxford: Oxford University Press, 2002.

31. This part is referred to Pearson, 1997, p. 41, 145-159. Frederic C. Deyo, "Coalitions, Institutions, and Linkage Sequencing—Toward a Strategic Capacity Model of East Asian Development," *The Political Economy of New Asian Industrialism,* edited by Frederic Deyo, Ithaca, NY: Cornell University Press, 1987, p. 232-233.

Frederic C. Deyo, "Economic Policy and the Popular Sector," *Manufacturing Miracles: Paths of Industrialization in Latin America and East Asia,* edited by Gary Gereffi and Donald L. Wyman, Princeton: Princeton University Press, 1990, p. 179-204.

Robert Wade, *Governing the Market: Economic Theory and the Role of Government in East Asian Industrialization,* Princeton: Princeton University Press, 1990.

Hung-mao Tian, *The Great Transition: Political and Social Change in the Republic of China,* Stanford: Hoover Institution Press, 1989, p. 46.

32. This definition is given by author herself, a definition which, however, is based upon the central theme of Pearson, 1997, as well as upon Gordon White, "Prospect for Civil Society in China: A Case Study of Xiaoshan City," *The Australian Journal of Chinese Affairs,* No. 29, January 1993, p. 63-87.

33. Pearson, 1997, p. 44.

34. Susan Mann, *Local Merchants and the Chinese Bureaucracy, 1750-1950,* Stanford: Stanford University Press, 1987, p. 18-21; and Wellington Chan, *Merchants, Mandarins and Modern Enterprise in Late Ching China,* Cambridge, MA: Harvard University Press, 1977, p. 15-18.

35. Mann, 1987, p. 20; and Yen-ping Hao, *The Commercial Revolution in Nineteenth-Century China: The Rise of Sino-Western Mercantile Capitalism,* Berkeley: University of California Press, 1986.

36. Chan, 1977, p. 214-216; Mark Elvin, *The Pattern of the Chinese Past: A Social and Economic Interpretation,* Stanford: Stanford University Press, 1973, p. 172, 268; Joseph Fewsmith, *Party, State, and Local Elites in Republican China: Merchant Organizations and Politics in Shanghai, 1890 -1930,* Honolulu: University of Hawaii Press, 1985, chapter I; Jacques Gernet, *Daily Life in China on the Eve of the Mongol Invasion, 1250 -1276,* Stanford: Stanford University Press, p. 86-88; and William Rowe, *Hankow, Commerce and Society in a Chinese City, 1796-1889,* Stanford: Stanford University Press, 1984, chapters 8 and 9.

37. Pearson, 1997, p. 45-46.

38. Ibid., p. 48.

39. Marie-Claire Bergere, *The Golden Age of the Chinese Bourgeoisie, 1911-1937,* translated by Janet Lloyd, Cambridge: Cambridge University Press, 1989, p. 38-40.

40. Ibid., p. 46-51; 39-40.

41. Chan, 1977, p. 215; Elvin, 1973, p. 292, 293; Fewsmith, 1985; Mann, 1987, p. 12-21; and Rowe, 1984, p. 282-286.

42. Chan, 1977, p. 25-57, 239.

43. Pearson, 1997, p. 50-52.

44. Ibid., p. 52.

45. Bergere, 1989, p. 240, 140; David Strand, "Protest in Beijing: Civil Society and Public Sphere in China," *Problems of Communism,* Vol. 39, May-June 1990, p. 4; and Keith Schoppa, *Chinese Elites and Political Change: Zhejiang Province in the Early Twentieth Century,* Cambridge, MA: Harvard University Press, 1982, p. 7.

46. Hao, 1986, p. 59-63.

47. Fewsmith, 1985, p. 51-60; Bergere, 1989, p. 207-217; Sherman Cochran, *Big Business in China: Sino-Foreign Rivalry in the Cigarette Industry, 1890-1930,* Cambridge, MA: Harvard University Press, 1980, chapter 5; and Kuang-sheng Liao, *Antiforeignism and Modernization in China, 1860-1980,* Hong Kong: Chinese University of Hong Kong Press, 1984, p. 73-79.

48. Bergere, 1989, p. 219-225.

49. Fewsmith, 1985; and Christian Henriot, *Shanghai, 1927-1937: Municipal Power, Locality, and Modernization,* translated by Noel Castelino, Berkeley: University of California Press, 1993.

50. Henriot, 1993, p. 52-54.

51. Pearson, 1997, p. 56-57.

52. Ibid., p. 58.

53. Ibid.

54. Willy Kraus, *Private Business in China: Revival between Ideology and Pragmatism,* translated by Eric Holz, Honolulu: University of Hawaii Press, 1991, p. 52-54; and John Gardner, "The Wu-fan Campaign in Shanghai: A Study in the Consolidation of Urban Control," *Chinese Communist Politics in Action,* edited by A. Doak Barnett, Seattle: University of Washington Press, p. 477-539.

55. Kraus, 1991, p. 50-58; Thomas N. Thompson, *China's Nationalization of Foreign Firms: The Politics of Hostage Capitalism, 1949-1957,* Baltimore: School of Law, University of Baltimore, 1979, and Ping Sun, "Individual Economy under Socialism," *Peking Review,* Vol. 27, No. 33, August 13, 1984, p. 26.

56. Pearson, 1997, p. 36-40.

57. Nathan and Gilley, 2003, p. 193.

58. Ibid., p. 194.

59. Ibid., p. 60-61.

60. Ibid., p. 61-62.

61. Ibid., p. 63.

62. Richard Suttmeier, "Riding the Tiger: The Political Life of China's Scientists," *Citizens and Groups in Contemporary China,* edited by Victor C. Falkenheim, Ann Arbor: Center for Chinese Studies, University of Michigan, 1987, p. 123-158.

63. Joseph Fewsmith, "The Dengist Reforms in Historical Perspective," *Contemporary Chinese Politics in Historical Perspective,* edited by Brantly Womack, New York: Cambridge University Press, 1991, p. 23-52; and Harmon Zeigler, *Pluralism, Corporatism, and Confucianism: Political Association and Conflict Regulation in the United States, Europe, and Taiwan,* Philadelphia: Temple University Press, 1988.

64. Barry Naughton, "Hunkering Down: The Wen Jiabao Administration and Macroeconomic Recontrol," *China Leadership Monitor* No. 11, Summer 2004.

65. This is author's own ideas, which is, however, enlightened by the themes in Margaret Pearson's another book, *Joint Ventures in the People's Republic of China: the Control of Foreign Direct Investment under Socialism,* Princeton, New Jersey: Princeton University Press, 1991.

66. Pearson, 1991, p. 1-7.

67. Ibid., p. 202-206.

68. Nathan and Gilley, 2003, p. 10.

69. Nathan and Gilley, 2003, p. 8.

70. Ibid., p. 75.

71. Ibid., p. 9.

72. H. Lyman Miller, "Hu Jintao and the Party Politburo," *China Leadership Monitor,* No. 9, Winter, 2004, p. 6.

73. Ibid.

74. H. Lyman Miller, "Party Politburo Processes under Hu Jintao," *China Leadership Monitor,* No. 11, Summer, 2004.

75. Miller, Winter, 2004, p. 7.

76. Nathan and Gilley, 2003, p. 100-126.

77. White, 1993, p. 52; and Pearson, 1991, p. 208.

78. Thomas B. Gold, "Party-State versus Society in China," *Building a Nation-State: China After Forty Years,* edited by Joyce K. Kallgren, Berkeley, California: University of California Press, 1990, p. 129-131.

79. Barry Naughton, "China's Experience with Guidance Planning," *Journal of Comparative Economics,* Vol. 14, No. 4, December 1990, p. 743-767.

80. Kennedy, 2005, p. 47.

81. Nathan and Gilley, 2003, p. 200.

82. Kennedy, 2005, p. 3 and 164.

83. Nathan and Gilley, 2003, p. 91-92.

84. Hu Jintao, "Hold High the Great Banner of Socialism with Chinese Characteristics and Strive for New Victories in Building a Moderately Prosperous Society in all Respects," Report to the Seventeenth National Congress of the Communist Party of China on October 15, 2007, *Beijing Review,* No. 45, November 8, 2007, at http://www.bjreview.com.cn/document/txt/2007-11/20/content_86325.htm.

85. Barry Naughton, "The New Common Economic Program: China's Eleventh Five Year Plan and What It Means," *China Leadership Monitor,* No. 16, Fall, 2005.

86. Charles E. Lindblom, *Politics and Markets: The World's Political Economic Systems,* New York: Basic Books, 1977, p. 170-188.

87. Kennedy, 2005, p. 3 and 171.

88. Ibid., p. 46.

89. Boddewyn JJ and TL Brewer, "International Business Political Behavior: New Theoretical Directions," *Academy of Management Review*, Vol. 19, 1994, p. 119-143.

90. Barry Naughton, *Growing Out of the Plan: Chinese Economic Reform, 1978-1993,* Cambridge: Cambridge University Press, 1995, p. 26-55.

91. Liu Guangcai, "Zuohao defang renda gongzuo qiantan" (Superficial Exploration of Doing Good Local People's Congress Work), *Fazhi Ribao* (Legal Daily), March 11, 1999, p. 7.

92. Kennedy, 2005, p. 48.

93. Shen Xiaojie, "Dianxin Zifei Sheji Xin Biaozhun" (Telecom Fees Establish New Standard), *Zhonghua Gongshang Shibao* (China Business Times), February 8, 1999, p. 2; and Frank Ching, "Seeds of Change," *Far Eastern Economic Review,* September 30, 1999, p. 22.

94. Kennedy, 2005, p. 49.

95. Institute of Marketing and Strategy Management, "An Investigation to the Peoples Representative Conference of Hongshan District of Wuhan City and Wuhan City, Hubei Province of China," conducted by IMSM, School of Management, Huazhong University of Science and Technology, 2002.

96. "Sino-America Smith Kline Ltd, Bristol-Myers Squibb Ltd and Shanghai John-son-Johnson Ltd bargain with State Development Planning Commission," *China Business*, January 28, 2002.

97. Gao Yongqiang, "How Firms Influence the Government Policy Decision-making in China," *Singapore Management Review,* January 1, 2006.

98. Ibid.

99. Ibid.

100. Ibid., p. 51-52.

101. Kennedy, 2005, p. 117.

102. Ibid., p. 117-119.

103. Ibid., p. 1.

104. Ibid., p. 2-4.

105. Nathan and Gilley, 2003, p. 190.

106. Li Cheng, "China: Riding Two Horses at Once," Foreign Policy Web, John L. Thornton China Center, The Brookings Institution, October 30, 2007.

107. "Huge Market for Legal Workers," *China Daily,* March 21, 2003.

108. Kennedy, 2005, p. 28.

109. Nathan and Gilley, 2003, p. 118-119.

110. Ibid.

111. Ibid., p. 123-124.

112. Ibid., p. 90-91.

113. Hu Jintao, *Report,* 2007.

114. Li Cheng , "Was the Shanghai Gang Shanghaied? The Fall of Chen Liangyu and the Survival of Jiang Zemin's Faction," *China Leadership Monitor,* No. 20, Winter, 2007.

115. Bruce J. Dickson, *Red Capitalist in China: The Party, Private Entrepreneurs, and Prospects for Political Change*, Cambridge: Cambridge University Press, 2003, p. 22.

116. Kennedy, 2005, p. 17.

117. Pearson, 1997, p. 116-117.

118. Gordon White, Jude Howell, and Shang Xiaoyuan, *In Search of Civil Society, Market Reform and Social Change in Contemporary China,* Oxford: Clarendon Press, 1996, p. 99, 102.

119. Kennedy, 2005, p. 37-39.

120. Ibid., p. 40.

121. Alex Pravda and Blair A. Ruble, "Communist Trade Unions: Varieties of Dualism," *Trade Unions in Communist States,* edited by Alex Pravda and Blair A. Ruble, Boston, MA: Allen & Unwin Inc., 1986, p. 1-6.

122. Ibid., p. 3-4.

123. Jeanne L. Wilson, "The People's Republic of China," *Trade Unions in Communist States,* edited by Alex Pravda and Blair A. Ruble, Boston, MA: Allen & Unwin Inc., 1986, p. 219.

124. This part summarized Wilson, 1986, p. 219-224.

125. Ibid., p. 243-245.

126. Franz Schurmann, *Ideology and Organization in Communist China,* Berkeley: University of California Press, 1968; Eduard B. Vermeer, "Chinese Management Training Programs: A Review," *China Information,* Vol. 3, No. 2, August 1988, p. 51-62; and David Brown and Michael R. Jackson, "Meeting the Challenge to Provide Effective Managers in the Changing Chinese Environment: A Systemically Structured Analysis of the Requirements for Management Education," *Advances in Chinese Industrial Studies,* Vol. 2, *The Changing Nature of Management in China,* edited by Nigel Campbell, Sylvain R. F. Plasschaert and David H. Brown, Greenwich, CT: JAI Press, 1991, p. 117-135.

127. Pearson, 1997, p. 7.

128. Lora Sabin, "The Growth of Non-State Sector Employment," *China Quarterly,* No. 140, December 1994, p. 963; and Tan Hongkai, "Officials Turned Entrepreneurs Center of Dispute," *China Daily,* January 27, 1993, p. 4.

129. Nathan and Gilley, 2003, p. 179-180.

130. Ibid., p. 159.

131. Kennedy, 2005, p. 110.

132. Pearson, 1997, p. 9, 145.

133. Lora Sabin, "The Growth of Non-State Sector Employment," *China Quarterly,* No. 140, December 1994, p. 961; and Nicholas D. Kristof, "China Applauds as Its Officials Plunge into Profit," *New York Times,* April 6, 1993, p: A6.

134. Dorothy J. Solinger, "Urban Entrepreneurs and the State: The Merger of State and Society," *State and Society in China: The Consequences of Reform,* edited by Arthur Lewis Rosenbaum, Boulder: Colorado: Westview Press, 1992, p. 121-122.

135. Ibid., p. 123.

136. Mann, 1987, p. 21-23; Wang Jingyu, "The Birth of the Chinese Bourgeoisie," *Social Sciences in China,* Vol. 3, No. 1, March 1982, p. 220-240; and Editorial Board for Modern and Contemporary Chinese History, *Historical Research,* "Chinese Historical

Studies of Early Modern China's Bourgeoisie," *Social Sciences in China,* Vol. 5, No. 1, March 1984, p. 9-31.

137. Dorothy J. Solinger, "Urban Entrepreneurs and the State: The Merger of State and Society," *State and Society in China: The Consequences of Reform,* edited by Arthur Lewis Rosenbaum, Boulder: Colorado: Westview Press, 1992, p. 124.

138. Ibid., p. 126-132.

139. Edward Steinfeld, *Forging Reform in China: The Fate of State-Owned Industry,* Cambridge: Cambridge University Press, 1998, p. 165-224; Susan L. Shirk, *The Political Logic of Economic Reform in China,* Berkeley: University of California Press, 1993, p. 242-243; and Holman A. Jenkins, Jr., "Hong Kong's Market Stops Believing in 'Miracles,'" *Asian Wall Street Journal,* November 6, 1997, p. 10.

140. Kennedy, 2005, p. 72.

141. Matt Miller, "The Hottest Thing in Cold-Rolled Steel," *Business Week,* September 8, 1997.

142. Eight of the board's fourteen members were carry-overs from the original Baogang, including its general manager, Xie Qihua, who is also an alternate member of the Central Committee. And four are from the two companies that Baogang absorbed, Shanghai Metallurgy Group and Meishan Iron and Steel.

143. Kennedy, 2005, p. 73.

144. David Zweig, *Freeing China's Farmers: Rural Restructuring in the Reform Era,* Armonk: NY: M. E. Sharpe, 1997, p. 307-318.

145. Kennedy, 2005, p. 107.

146. The information of this section is provided by Geoff Dyer, "Shanghai 'Scandal' Exposes Darker Side of Economy," *Financial Times,* September 14, 2006.

CHAPTER III CURRENT ILLUSTRATIONS OF DUALISM IN CHINA'S FDI

Merchant-State Dualism Today

Since the Fourth Generation leadership came into power, the Chinese state has continued to give merchants a significant degree of autonomy, which has been reflected by a flood of overseas investments by cash-rich Chinese banks, insurers, and pension funds. As an example, the mandate to manage the initial overseas investments of the $50 billion state pension fund was awarded to ten international financial groups. Additionally, in January 2007, the U.S. Fund manager, Franklin Templeton, created an unprecedented joint venture agreement with China's largest insurer, China Life. This arrangement—for the first time—allows China Life to invest a significant proportion of its fast growing assets abroad.[1] This arrangement is in keeping with the overall reformist philosophy and personal preferences of Premier Wen Jiabao.

The administration of Wen Jiabao had a relatively successful first year of reformist economic policymaking, after he became Premier in March 2003. This was a time of strong economic growth, fueled by an increase in both exports and new domestic markets. The continued opening up of China's markets, along with increasing privatization, helped to increase both domestic and foreign investment, as well as economic growth in many sectors of the economy.[2]

In 2006, Chinese banks, insurers and fund managers received approval for overseas investment for the first time. This was given via a quota system known as the Qualified Domestic Institutional Investor scheme (QDII). Under this scheme, over $100 billion of investment could be funneled through the QDII in the ensuing two years.[3] This change in policy shows how committed China is to liberalizing the inflow and outflow of its money.

Following the Asian financial crisis of 1997-1998, leaders of emerging economies like China accepted as a matter of course that unrestricted flows of capital might cause speculative attack, capital flight and currency devaluation similar to the events that took place in Thailand and Indonesia. Therefore, they believe that countries should maintain strict controls on capital, so long as they do not yet have a solid and sound banking system, flexible interest rates and a flexible exchange rate—as is the case with China at present.[4] This reveals the impact on the policy formulation process by technocrats and the new left economists in China.

Some of the QDII program restrictions probably will be lifted by Beijing. This relaxation of controls may well hinge upon Beijing's assessment of how the first wave of experimental equity-type products work, including an equity-type product that is co-managed by the U.S. firm, Lehman Brothers.[5] This indicates that the final decision will be made cautiously by leading policy-makers after having been vetted for minimal impact and risk.

The National Social Security Fund (NSSF):

An example of increasing autonomy given by the Chinese government to merchants is the case of the National Social Security Fund (NSSF). In 2000, the central government established the NSSF, which was to be used as a last resort pension fund. Much of the NSSF's assets have been raised through a government policy, which directs state-owned enterprises listing overseas to set aside 10% of their proceeds to go into the fund's coffers. Around US $27 billion worth of assets are in the fund according to the official records of the NSSF. When considering the recent sharp rise in the shares of these companies, the total assets of the fund are probably closer to $40 billion.[6]

The NSSF has given investment mandates to 10 international groups—including UBS, Primo, INVESCO, State Street, Alliance Bernstein and Black Rock. These mandates include global equity, US equity, Hong Kong equity and global fixed income and are widely viewed as "trophies" for fund managers, which could help them win more business in China and across Asia from cash rich institutions. These new mandates offer a unique opportunity for the U.S. companies, such as Alliance Bernstein, State Street, Janus and T. Rowe Price, to access the capital market in China, since they have so far avoided accessing China's domestic fund market, a move which is viewed as expensive as foreigners have to buy minority stakes in fund joint ventures to do so.[7]

On the other hand, for the first time, the NSSF would allow Chinese institutions and individuals to invest holdings and savings in overseas markets. Beijing is currently studying such a detailed plan. The management of the fund's money has been debated in Beijing for many years, and most of its assets have been left in low interest yielding bank accounts in China. The concerns about supervising investment overseas and the pressure that come from local stock exchanges to alternatively invest the money in local equities is balanced against the probability that investing this money overseas would bring in higher returns. In the typical Chinese way of managing new reforms, the fund has, in recent years, been allowed by the government to leave hundreds of millions of dollars in offshore Chinese listings overseas rather than bringing the money back to China.[8] This shows conclusively that the Chinese government continues to increase the autonomy it is granting to merchants.

China's Reform and Liberalization of Banking:

Another example of increasing autonomy of Chinese merchants is the greater freedom that has recently been given to Chinese banks. Although the general trend of financial reform has been one of gradual liberalization, the sale of significant stakes in state-owned banks to foreign institutions has moved very quickly. Prime Minister Wen Jiabao has often chaired meetings of the Finance Work Committee. These meetings have resulted in major changes in policy. The committee meeting of February 2002 laid the foundations for major reforms in the large state banks. The government has poured an enormous amount of money into the banks, allowing them to write off most of their bad loans. For example, in 2003, the Chinese government had injected US $45 billion into the State-owned banking sector by strategically drawing from the foreign currency reserves.[9] At the same time, the government was restructuring the banks in an attempt to improve their operations. This includes the re-capitalization of the three largest institutions, followed by their listing overseas.[10]

According to the China Banking Regulatory Commission, 154 foreign banks had been allowed to do business in local currency in 25 Chinese cities by the end of 2005.[11] In 2005, the three largest banks in China—the Industrial & Commercial Bank of China (ICBC), the Bank of China and the China Construction Bank—have raised over $40 billion. Although China's banks have a history of bad loans, fraud and poor disclosure, yet global investors view them as the best way to access the fastest growing major economy in the world. "Right now, investors see Chinese banks as high margin and high growth."[12]

Opinion has changed significantly about the banks over the last two years. For a long time, Chinese banks were considered to be inefficient arms of the state that were expected to give out money when the government told them to rather than when they had commercial reasons to do so. Beijing is now trying to promote a more commercial practice by changing this long-term image.[13]

The government in China has injected more than $60 billion into the three largest banks since 2003. During this period, strategic foreign investors have also spent over $20 billion buying minority stakes in them.[14] For example, $3.1 billion was invested in the Bank of China by a consortium led by the Royal Bank of Scotland Group PLC. This deal—announced in August 2006—bought them around a 10% stake in the bank. Other investors, known as cornerstone investors, agreed to invest $180 million. These 12 investors include the Bank of Tokyo-Mitsubishi UFJ Ltd., Ping An Insurance Co., Li Ka-Shing's Cheung Kong Holdings Ltd., and Hutchison Whampoa Ltd. They will not be allowed to sell the shares they buy for a year. Additionally, Temasek Holdings Pte Ltd., the Singapore government investment company, has committed to add to its 5% stake and to purchase an additional $500 million of shares.[15]

Other strategic investments include the UK-based RBS rival HSBC with a 19.9% stake in the Bank of Communications. The Bank of America has an 8.5% stake in the China Construction Bank. Goldman Sachs and UBS also have significant stakes in the Industrial and Commercial Bank of China and the Bank of China respectively.[16] Although the introduction of foreign investors into the Chinese banking system exemplifies the new merchant autonomy, it had led to domestic criticism of the government's practice of selling shares in state-owned banks to foreign financial institutions. Although the debate has been vigorous, thus far it has had limited impact on economic decision-making, which is still dominated by finance-oriented technocrats.[17]

Strategic Stakes in Chinese Banks

Purchaser	*Target*	*Date*	**Current Stake** (%)
Allianz	Industrial & Commercial Bank	Jan. 2006	2.3
American Express	Industrial & Commercial Bank	Jan. 2006	0.5
Bank of America	China Construction Bank	Jun 2005	8.5
Goldman Sachs	Industrial & Commercial Bank	Jan 2006	5.8
HSBC	Bank of Communications	Aug. 2004	19.9
Li Ka-shing	Bank of China	Aug. 2005	2.0
Merrill Lynch	Bank of China	Aug. 2005	0.7
RBS (directly)	Bank of China	Aug. 2005	4.3
Temasek	China Construction Bank	Jul 2005	6.0
Temasek	Bank of China	Aug. 2005	4.7
UBS	Bank of China	Sept. 2005	1.3

Source: *Financial Times* Research November 10, 2006.

Led by the Bank of China, the Big Four Chinese banks are well on their way to "Going Global." This outward move will initially be directed at the international banking center of Hong Kong. Also, these first steps on the path towards "Going Global" have already borne fruit as can be seen recently from the first foreign investment by a Chinese bank. China's biggest bank, the Industrial and Commercial Bank of China, purchased a 90% stake in a small Indonesian bank—this is the first foreign acquisition made by a Chinese bank.[18] The Indonesian bank, Bank Halim Indonesia, is a small bank based in Surabaya, East Java and is controlled by the Halim family, which also runs Indonesia's largest cigarette maker, Gudang Garam.[19]

Industry experts state that this purchase allows ICBC to obtain a banking license for Indonesia in a situation where local banks are coming under regulatory pressure to consolidate. From its perspective, ICBC stated that the Bank Halim acquisition would give it the valuable experience needed to expand into international financial markets. Indonesia is the biggest market in Southeast Asia. It has a young population and a growing middle class. In addition, its local banks are under-capitalized.[20]

Most recently, the Industrial and Commercial Bank of China announced plans on October 17, 2007 to open a subsidiary bank in the United States, as a part of its "Going Global" strategy. This strategy also involves Russia, Australia and the Middle East. Jiang Jianqing, Board Chairman of the ICBC, said recently in the Beijing news briefing: "Preparations have been going on smoothly. We hoped to receive the approval from American authorities as early as possible."[21] (Jiang is also a delegate to the 17th National Congress of the Communist Party of China.) More importantly, this intention or plan is another indication of the regional and international ambitions of ICBC. The Bank Halim deal is the first acquisition by a Chinese bank outside China,[22] although various joint ventures took place between foreign banks and China's big banks. According to the UNCTAD's *World Investment Report 2007,* the total foreign assets of China's State-owned banks had reached US $28.4 billion by the end of 2006.[23] These investments are also expected to increase at a rapid pace in the next few years. Thus, merchant autonomy as far as outward investment is also on the rise in China.

In order to implement an overseas development strategy, the China Construction Bank announced its intentions to buy the 17 Hong Kong and Macau branches of the Bank of America Corp., for $1.2 billion. The China Construction Bank is China's third largest bank with assets of over $645 billion, so this purchase represents a modest expansion for them outside of mainland China. The Bank of America itself additionally owns 8.5% of the China Construction Bank, purchased before the Chinese bank made an initial public stock offering of $9.2 billion in October 2005.[24]

Guo Shuqing, the Chairman of the China Construction Bank, may opt to buy a 20% stake in Bear Stearns, which could cost up to US$4 billion. This could be a controversial move in the U.S., as it would be the first time that a Chinese state-owned company has been accepted as a shareholder by Wall Street.[25] In any event, it is evidence of the new autonomy of Chinese merchants.

Some have voiced their concerns that another round of defaults may occur given the new spurt of lending by Chinese banks in recent years. "The vast majority of credits are not being correctly priced so we will maybe have another cycle of mis-allocation of credit." According to a recent report by the International Monetary Fund on lending by Chinese banks during the period of 1999-2004, banks still did not operate on a commercial basis. Guo stated that the report by the IMF did make some "sensible points" but that it was "too pessimistic about the true picture."[26]

Another example of increasing merchant autonomy is that banks are now beginning to diversify their investments outside traditional corporate banking services. For instance, the Bank of China became the first Chinese bank to move into full international competition outside the country's protection of domestic markets by purchasing a global aircraft leasing company—Singapore Aircraft Leasing Enterprise—for $965 million, beating three other bidders.[27] This deal highlights the increasingly international ambitions and the financial resources of the largest lenders in China, following government bailouts and international initial public offerings.

Although the Bank of China is considered to be the most "international" of the Big Four Chinese banks, it has historically confined its direct offshore activities to more traditional corporate banking services. Via their ownership of Singapore Aircraft Leasing, however, the bank could gain valuable experience in developing alternative sources of business.[28] This in turn could lead to further diversification and further autonomy.

Another example of increasing merchant autonomy is the appearance of new banking practices and financial services accompanying the enlarging middle class in China. Estimates are that 350,000 millionaires have been created by the economic miracle in China. This fact, along with China's lack of laws on wealth management, has made the country an attractive prospect for wealth management groups on a global basis. In addition Chinese banks still lack credit assessment expertise despite their heady stock market valuations. The co-operation between the two parties in the RBS transaction in terms of corporate markets are claimed to combine the local corporate relationships of the Bank of China with RBS's global skills in selling and structuring deals.[29]

Overseas investors in Chinese banks tend to offer them Western expertise and technical knowledge. The deal made by the Royal Bank of Scotland (RBS), however, involves exclusive deals that span three areas of joint ventures—credit cards, wealth management and corporate markets. In addition, RBS made the commitment to keep their stake until at least August 2008, on the basis that Beijing would give unspecified protection against loss on their investments.[30]

The prospect that China will continue to be in growth mode and the faith that the Bank of China will be able to stop its previous bad lending practices have fostered mutual trust among both Chinese and overseas executives. Although the Chinese government still owns about 80 percent of the capital of banks. Sir Fred, the RBS Chairman, states: "The political system is stable and we assume that the reform mindset will remain."[31] Thus, the rise of the new wealthy class has spurred on the development of new banking practices, such as the investment of foreign capital in Chinese banks.

Another sign of the increased autonomy of merchants is the emergence of a new urban middle class and the new services necessary to meet their emerging needs. Demand is strong for innovative domestic banking services from the urban middle class in China. This can be seen in the resources that domestic lenders such as the Everbright Bank are deploying to the retail sector. The Everbright Bank was founded in 1992 and currently ranks in the Top 10 of China's lenders. In February 2007, the bank announced through local media that its total assets had risen to US $77 billion last year—this represents a 16.4% increase over the previous year. The focus of the bank will be personal loans, home mortgages, credit cards and automobile loans. This retail business of the bank hardly existed four years ago, as most of the Beijing-based bank's portfolio was dedicated to corporate loans. China's Qualified Domestic Institutional Investor scheme has given the bank a US $500 million quota for offshore investments.[32]

Thus far, we have seen that policy making continues to be dominated by a group of finance-oriented technocrats, informally led by central bank head Zhou Xiaochuan. These technocrats have continued to craft policies that apparently have been successful.[33]

Although China has given significant autonomy to merchants by opening its banking industry based on its pledge for the WTO, at the same time, a crucial fact also highlights the state's continued control in these sectors. That is, all foreign investors who have paid large amounts of money can only take minority stakes in China's big financial institutions. This means they have an inability to exercise any effective control over the banks in which they have invested, despite token representation on their boards and in senior executive ranks.[34] In addition, as with all Chinese state-owned companies, a Communist Party committee has a role in operating the banks. The role of these committees can be seen in the following two events.

The first reminder of who is in control of China's banking system is the case of Zhang Jianguo, who held the position of President at the Bank of Communication and who had guided the bank through its Hong Kong IPO. In July 2006, he was transferred abruptly to a rival bank—the China Construction Bank— in the role of Vice Chairman. This move was made on the orders of the Communist Party.[35] This episode indicates that foreign investors like HSBC might own large stakes and seats on the board in Chinese banks, but there is no doubt where the real power is in these supposedly publicly-listed companies. This indicates that although corporate interests are increasing in importance, they are still dominated in some cases by the Chinese Communist Party.

Yet another reminder of the Communist Party's power is its ability to designate certain Chinese banks as financiers of overseas resource exploitation projects. A senior executive at the China Development Bank has announced that the bank—the largest development institution measured by assets in the world—will be putting more resources into the overseas expansion of Chinese enterprises, particularly in natural resource projects. The China Development Bank had previously sought international financing opportunities in the energy and minerals areas, and their lending for foreign projects had undergone rapid growth with anticipation of further increases. The bank is likely to play an integral part in financing the overseas push by China's state-owned enterprises,[36] as was decided by the CCP.

All of the big five banks of China have been experiencing an increase in autonomy. Rural finance is also being reformed by the Chinese government, particularly in the case of the Agricultural Bank of China, which is the last one of the big five state banks to undergo restructuring. The government envisions the same makeover for the Agricultural Bank of China that it applied to other state lenders. This will involve recapitalization which will probably be funded by foreign reserves, followed by listing overseas and then investment from strategic foreign partners. However, the bank poses a challenge to foreign investors, since the rural economy in China is weak.[37]

An Increase in Chinese Banking Violations:

Generally, the dualistic functions of banking officials have been best revealed by banking violations. They wear two hats as the leaders of "private," yet state owned enterprises. The government of China is trying to overhaul the banking sector, which is weighed down by bad debt. Their efforts have been slowed by various scandals that highlight poor corporate governance and vulnerable internal controls.

The China Banking Regulatory Commission provided information that the misuse of funds increased 31% in 2005 over 2004. The commission's audits had revealed 1,272 criminal actions, and it had been able to recover around 1.47 billion Yuan. China's banking watchdog had found irregularities in 2005 that involved around 767.1 billion Yuan—around $95.1 billion—in mainland banks. This shows just how far China has to go to clean up its financial sector.[38] This also shows the current merging of state officials and merchants, which is not without its problems.

As mainland banks are in the global spotlight, and as foreign banks take stakes in them, the banking regulator had disciplined 6,826 staff at the institutions in question, including 325 senior managers.[39] In order to improve sector co-ordination, China is contemplating setting up a "super regulator" to manage the finance and banking sectors.[40]

Chinese government is currently focused on reform of the capital markets, where development has badly lagged behind in growth in the real economy, it is more specifically addressing the issue that the capital markets and brokerages are governed by numerous elements, making them difficult to sell off. These elements include separate regulators for banking, insurance and securities, as well as the central bank—the People's Bank of China. Local governments are also significant shareholders in brokerages.[41] On a larger scale, these regulations and reforms in the Chinese banking system indicate that the merchant is subordinate in his power to the government. At the same time, these specific economic policy measures are testament to a much more regularized policymaking process in China than has previously been observed. Wen Jiabao's government systematically aggregates advice from agencies within the government bureaucracy. It then slowly and deliberately evaluates that advice and formulates its policy decisions. This means that not only is the policymaking process time consuming, but also that bureaucratic interests are represented disproportionately, and that the policymaking process is more a function of government agencies. While this type of decision making process produces steady and gradual change, it may very well have long-turn costs in decisiveness and creativity.[42]

China Aims to Develop Ten Accountancy Firms:

Banking is not the only financial industry which is experiencing increased growth and autonomy. In order to cut back on its reliance on foreign accounting groups, China will develop at least 10 accountancy firms in this decade which are capable of offering comprehensive international services. A draft policy paper released in October 2006 by the Chinese Institute of Chartered Accountants (CICPA) outlines this goal. The Ministry of Finance is backing the move to create robust local accounting firms, according to Chen Yugui, CICPA secretary general. According to Chen, policymakers are troubled about the weakness of China's accounting infrastructure as well as the situation that the big four international accountancy firms KPMG, PwC, Deloitte and Ernst & Young presently monopolize the auditing of Chinese companies listed overseas.[43]

According to the draft of the policy, China will develop 10 accountancy firms by the year 2010 with the capabilities to support the international needs of domestic companies that "Going Global." In addition, another 100 firms large enough to serve big domestic enterprises are planned. This policy highlights the shortage of experienced accountancy professionals in China. Some have called for the development of 1,000 "senior professionals able to handle globalized services." A deal has already been signed by the CICPA to train several accountants with the Institute of Chartered Accountants in England and Wales.[44] Thus, accountancy will soon experience growth but a growth subject to government's regulation and control.

Chinese Outward Cooperation in the Financial Markets:

Another indicator of increased merchant autonomy is the recent move of Chinese FDI into the financial markets. Xinhua Finance, a Tokyo listed Chinese company, acquired Glass Lewis on December 14, 2006. Glass Lewis is one of the two biggest U.S. shareholder advisory groups, and the deal cost Xinhua Finance $45 million. Xinhua Finance is China's biggest provider of financial information. This deal shows how rapidly the market for corporate governance and shareholder proxy advisory services is growing as the institutional investors are now making more and more investments outside of their home markets. According to the two firms, this deal will combine Xinhua's expertise on geopolitical and macroeconomic research with Glass Lewis's knowledge of corporate governance and accounting. Glass Lewis has stated its intention to expand coverage of Chinese and emerging market businesses and to give China access to objective investment research and proxy advisory and voting services.[45] This will also help improve China's skills in credit assessment.[46]

Opening of the Booming Chinese Aviation Industry:

The government's opening of overseas investments in the booming Chinese aviation industry is another example of increased merchant autonomy. Chinese regional airports are struggling to meet demand, and are keen to absorb external capital and management expertise. The Taiwan-based China National Aviation Corporation (CNAC), for example, has launched a mainland China-focused aviation infrastructure fund. The CNAC will use their knowledge to capitalize on the fast growth of China's aviation market over the next few years. The funds would be invested in some of mainland China's 140 airports, as well as into aviation-related businesses, including aircraft leasing.[47]

In another example, the Hong Kong airport authority paid $244 million in April 2005 to buy a 35% stake in Hangzhou Xiaoshan International Airport. This airport covers the capital of the Zhejiang province and the Yangtze River Delta region around Shanghai.[48]

Another deal (finalized in August 2005) saw the Hong Kong airport authority commit to setting up a $46 million management venture with an under-used airport in Zhuhai, which is a special economic zone near Hong Kong. In this agreement, Hong Kong's airport authority will take on management control at the facility for 20 years in order to develop it as a low cost carrier center.[49] These examples show that the Chinese government is willing to absorb the inward FDI in the booming Chinese aviation industry, which is a positive step towards reform and liberalization. In turn, the industrial business interests are more weighted.

Corporate Restructuring and Incremental Decision Making

Since Hu-Wen assumed power in 2003, significant policy innovations regarding corporate restructuring have been continuous. This indicates the reformist, corporate and commercial mindset of the top leadership. This mindset will perhaps result in an increase in the autonomy of the merchant. In most other cases, however, the mindset of the current leadership fosters a larger and growing role for bureaucracy. Examples of such increasingly important bureaucracies are the State Asset Supervision and Administration Commission (SASAC), and the National Development and Reform Commission (NDRC).

As for the corporate sector, a positive step towards greater corporate autonomy has been the development of the conversion of state shares from non-circulating to circulating, as well as the management buyout (MBO), as will be explained in the next paragraph. All of these corporate restructurings demonstrate a pattern of cautious, incremental, and bureaucratic-dominated policymaking on the part of the current administration.

Since Wen became premier, management buyouts have become an important issue in China. MBOs take place when managers of an existing state-owned enterprise take control of its operations. Since 2000, management buyouts have increased in frequency. They have fast become the preferred means for privatizing state-run and collectively run firms. Although the government never uses the word "privatization", the state-run firms are often restructured, with steep cost cutting measures followed by listing on the stock markets. At the end of 2003, the SASAC began to systematically promulgate laws and regulations at the end of 2003 for MBOs. These regulations set general principles for MBOs and ban so-called "camouflaged MBOs." SASAC's overall policy has been to provide a degree of transparency and oversight to privatization, but without making the privatization process completely transparent. Although privatization has been increasing, with a corresponding increase in merchant autonomy, the SASAC has not committed itself completely to an ultimate objective of complete privatization.[50]

The SASAC is even more ambivalent about the transformation of non-circulating state shares into circulating shares than it is about the process of privatization. Although this conversion of shares allows the state to have more flexibility in its ability to enhance the value of its assets, the SASAC's mission is still to represent the government in its role as owner of state-owned enterprises. The SASAC is, in essence, the ownership interest behind the non-tradable state shares. Thus, concerning the conversion of shares, the SASAC plays a role in both ownership and management of the central government's enterprises.[51] Nevertheless, the SASAC by allowing this conversion of shares is taking one more step towards corporate and commercial interests on the part the government.

In sum, the recent increase in merchant autonomy and in the autonomy of corporate governance indicates the top leadership's overall commitment to opening up China and integrating it with the world economy. The current generation of leaders all believes that the first requirement for China's continued development and stability is fast, indeed breakneck, economic growth. Economic growth is considered the key to political stability because it provides jobs and a rising standard of living for a sufficient amount of people to give the regime a broad base of support.[52] This striving for economic growth has made the Central Financial and Economic Affairs LSG an increasingly important locus for the making of China's foreign economic decisions and for their coordination and implementation. During the process of implementing this growth, technocratic and bureaucratic personnel are needed to help with the problems of poverty in the Chinese interior, the failure of some SOEs transformations and macroeconomic management in general. Thus, the opinions of the technocrats and bureaucrats will carry more weight than they did before.

Despite the Recent Increase in Merchant ***Autonomy, the State Still Maintains Control***

Despite the significant autonomy merchants have received, the Chinese government continues to maintain a certain degree of control over them. This control is reflected in that the Chinese government has the ability to select, rethink, and limit the merchant-related inward FDI, so that it is concentrated on the high-tech sector, financial management, market services, as well as other specific industries that are important to China. More and more, the Chinese Government is focusing on the policy objective of increasing the quality rather than the quantity of FDI. This policy objective has been indicated by both the Ministry of Commerce and the National Development and Reform Commission. For example, in 2006 the Chinese Government implemented new rules and the screening on foreign takeovers. The Chinese government has also come up with a list of industries over which will remain under State control based on antitrust and "national economic security" concerns. In July 2006, the Government began to introduce regulatory restrictions in FDI in real estate in order to keep China's real estate market from overheating. Seven industries were deemed to be of strategic importance and are thus to remain under State control: telecommunications, petroleum, defense, electricity, coal mining, civil aviation and ocean shipping.[53]

China is Encouraging the Emergence of Accounting "National Champions"

The strength of the Chinese government is also reflected in its attempt to develop through a regulatory process a new type of accountant. The Director General of the Ministry of Finance's accounting regulatory department, Liu Yuting, has indicated that he would like the development of China's accounting firms to catch up with the country's spectacular economic growth. He said: "As Chinese companies list abroad, we also hope that Chinese auditing firms can go global too. After all, the entry of foreign companies into China happened along with the introduction of foreign auditing firms here." His comments highlight official unease over the reality that China's biggest companies depend on the services of foreign accountants to raise capital.[54]

The Big Four accounting firms—KPMG, PwC, Deloitte and Ernst & Young—have moved ahead with ambitious plans to expand in China. Today's China is unlikely to create a credible rival to the Big Four, given that the country lacks experience in international disclosure requirements, accounting rules and audit procedures. In order to get official approval, the Big Four have sought to curry favor with officials by providing training and consulting services, and seconding personnel to various bodies, including the Finance Ministry and the China Securities Regulatory Commission.[55] This shows the continued importance of government approval for foreign merchants—in this case, accounting firms—to gain entrance into China.

The Chinese Government's Selectivity in Accepting Inward FDI:

An example of the Chinese government's aforementioned selectivity in accepting inward FDI is its dealings with Airbus. Airbus has chosen the Tianjin plant for its assembly line. Tianjin won the tender against competition from its rivals Shanghai, Xi'an and Zhuhai. The assembly line probably will be set up as a joint venture between Airbus and Chinese groups. In the long run, this factory could help China set up a commercial airliner industry of its own, which is a national objective of the Chinese government.[56]

Airbus already uses some state-owned Chinese companies to supply it with wing components, doors and landing gear. Technological and trade problems are unlikely with this new assembly plant, as the work in China involves less technological intensity than other areas of the plane making process. Airbus has also opened a new engineering centre in Beijing, with the aim of training 200 local engineers.[57]

Inward FDI Constrained in High-Tech:

The Chinese government has been tapping the brakes on inward FDI in manufacturing, but not on those sectors engaged in advanced technologies. Some examples of inward FDI in the manufacturing and high tech sectors include foreign TNCs' US $1 billion investment in China's integrated circuit industry in 2005.[58]

The US chip manufacturer Intel has proposed setting up a new plant in the north-eastern city of Dalian—a proposal under consideration by the Chinese government. Intel already has bases for chip assembly and testing in Shanghai and the Western city of Chengdu, but—as yet—does not have a manufacturing facility in the country. The new factory is not likely to make micro-processors, as the US government would not give an export license for such a sensitive technology.[59]

Construction of such a fabrication plant by the world's largest chipmaker would have a significant impact on China's emerging semi-conductor industry. It would also allow Intel to expand into the fast growing IT market in China.[60]

However, this move to transfer market-leading technology to China could also spark concerns in the U.S., since some Washington officials see China as an economic and military rival.[61] This constraint of inward FDI in the high-tech sector by the Chinese government shows that it still maintains a degree of control over merchant autonomy.

China Digests Japan's Bullet Train Technology

China has introduced a range of Japanese style "bullet trains." These trains have been assembled locally and demonstrate that China has completed the transfer of foreign world-class high-speed rail technology. According to the Beijing Ministry of Railways, the country's success in assimilating foreign technology can be seen in these modified versions of the Japanese E2-1000 Shinkansen.[62]

Beijing is determined to ensure that local companies will enjoy the benefits of planned 5,400 km high-speed lines in the four years following 2006. Berlin had earlier proposed extending a magnetic levitation train line in Shanghai, but was turned down, since they refused to pass on the "core aspects" of maglev expertise that Beijing asked for. Nowadays, China Railways obviously already grasps the core technologies for trains operating over 200 km/h, given the various types of high speed rail travel available.[63] This is an example of governmental control of inward FDI in the high-tech sector, as well as of merchants, since China accepted Japan's offer of technology but not Berlin's. China clearly preferred Japan, since it was forthcoming about the nature of its technology, whereas Berlin was not.

In addition, China's constraints on inward FDI in the high-tech sector can be viewed as part of the Chinese government's efforts to be conscientious in implementing the Outline of the National Program for Long- and Medium-Term Scientific and Technological Development (2006 – 2020).[64] This outline was set out in the 17th Party Congress Report.

Inward FDI Tied to 2008 Beijing Olympics:

The newly liberalized aviation industry in China and the growing middle class has led many carriers to take the opportunity to launch their own flights to Chinese cities. For example, Mesa Air, in conjunction with its Chinese partner, Shenzhen Airlines, anticipates that it will have 20 aircraft flying by the time of the 2008 Beijing Olympics. However, Cathay Pacific, the international carrier of Hong Kong, has not been successful in its attempts to get a larger slice of the mainland market, as a result of political opposition against its efforts.[65] This is an example of governmental control of inward FDI in the airline business. In addition, this is an example that the Chinese government is linking inward FDI to the 2008 Beijing Olympics.

FDI Constrained in the Chinese Specially Needed Industry:

Chinese governmental control over merchants is illustrated in constraint of FDI in industries in which China is facing difficulties. By using inward FDI, China is hoping to be able to improve the situations of its problematic industries. Prices for oil are so high that investment is being encouraged into projects that can convert coal to gas and liquids to be used as fuel or as chemicals for industrial use. All these products are in high demand in China. Royal Dutch Shell, for example, stated in June 2006 that it would consider a coal-to-liquids joint venture plant in the western Ningxia region.[66]

The UK listed mining company, Anglo American, and Shaanxi set up a joint venture initially in 2004. Anglo American is currently undertaking a feasibility study to assess the viability of a coal mining and processing complex, which could be potentially worth $4 billion in the northern province of Shaanxi. This proposed joint venture illustrates strong interest among international businesses in helping to develop the rich reserves of coal in China. Coal is, after all, the main fuel for China's booming economy.[67]

Investment in high-budget coal conversion plants in China is likely to increase sharply in the next few years. Currently, around 30 coal-to-oil projects are at the detailed planning stage or under feasibility study in China.[68] This investment in the coal-to-oil project reflects the current leadership's overall economic thinking as stated in the report of the 17th Party Congress: "We must keep to the new path of industrialization with Chinese characteristics ... the transition from relying heavily on increased consumption of material resources to relying mainly on advances in science and technology ..."[69]

FDI in the Recycling Industry:

The Chinese government is also allowing inward FDI in the recycling business. Recycling is another newly booming business in China. China's internal sector for waste treatment and recycling is growing quickly, because of economic growth and pressure on the government to make improvements to the environment.

The following case concerning FDI in the waste paper treatment and recycling is a significant part of the 11th Five Year Plan (2006-2010). The relevant part of the Five Year Plan states that China must build an economy that economizes on resources, a "cycling economy" and an "environment-friendly society." The government is instructing local officials on the merits of the five R's: rethink, reduce, re-use, recycle, and repair.[70] Recycling is also mentioned in the report of the 17th Party Congress: "Promoting a conservation culture by ... pattern of growth and mode of consumption. We will have a large-scale circular economy and considerably increase the proportion of renewable sources in total material consumption ... Awareness of conservation will be firmly established in the whole of society."[71]

The French company Veolia Environmental Services is a global leader in waste treatment and recycling. They are expanding their paper recycling and scrap metal recycling operations in China to tap into this huge demand and the relatively favorable prices given to waste products in China. The Chinese market is still "immature" and is largely dominated by small players at a local level. Veolia wants to help organize the recycling sector in a professional way and also to acquire Chinese companies in the sector to utilize their highly localized networks.[72]

The profile of recycling business in China was given a boost through the success of Zhang Yin. She runs a wastepaper business and is estimated to be the richest person in the country according to one survey, with net worth of $4.7 billion. Now listed in Hong Kong, her Nine Dragons business started in the early 1990s, when she set up wastepaper collections in the U.S. The wastepaper collected was sent to China to be recycled into cardboard boxes.[73] These are yet more examples of the Chinese government allowing inward FDI in sectors that the government believes have a great necessity for it.

In sum, with government control and policy regulation, FDI may continue to rise in China's high-tech and industrial sectors, but overall, is likely to stagnate in the manufacturing sector. Nevertheless, the quality of FDI in manufacturing is improving. The economic impact of the 2008 Olympic Games in Beijing and the 2010 World Expo in Shanghai, together with rising FDI in services and high-tech manufacturing, might bring about a new round of growth of FDI in China. However, policy changes related to foreign M&As and to FDI in real estate, along with rising labor costs, in particularly in the coastal provinces, could have an unfavorable impact on the growth of such FDI.[74]

China's "Rethinking" of Its Inward FDI and Economic Nationalism

That the state still retains control over merchants is illustrated by various backlashes concerning foreign investment in the Chinese economy. These include restrictions on foreign investment in China's construction machinery sector, overseas investment in the communications industry, and foreign investment in the media sector, out of concern for its cultural security.

The Carlyle Case in the Construction Machinery Industry:

An example of the backlash against inward FDI in the construction machinery industry is the case of Carlyle. Carlyle, a U.S. private equity firm, announced in October 2005 that it had committed to buy an 85% stake in Xugong for $375 million. Xugong is a listed company whose parent group is controlled by the local government of Xuzhou city in the Jiangsu province.[75] Now over a year later, Beijing still has not given its approval to the deal, and the deal seems to have been caught up in a backlash over foreign investment in China's economy. At the same time, the rival construction group, Sany Heavy Industry, fiercely campaigned against the proposed takeover, and took measures, including posting a strongly nationalistic web log that was written by the company's Chief Executive.[76] In October 2006, Carlyle and Xugong altered the terms of the deal to turn it into a joint venture in an attempt to defuse political resistance. Under this deal, Carlyle would buy a 50% stake in Xugong and hoped that this would get them official ministry approval in a matter of weeks. The government body that controls state-owned companies, the Assets Supervision and Administration Commission (SASAC), agreed to the new deal. However, the revised deal has not been approved by other bureaucratic agencies in Beijing. Carlyle is still waiting.[77] This shows increasing reluctance on the part of the government to allow inward FDI in the machinery construction sector.

The Carlyle case illustrates the three dimensions of the overall decision-making and political thinking of the top leaders.

First, Zhu's plan of SOEs reform was to create a trimmed-down state sector of efficient, profitable, high-tech enterprises, along the lines of the state sector in contemporary Germany or France. However, he only wanted to sell off to private investors (foreign or Chinese) SOEs that did not occupy leading positions in their sectors. Wen is committed to Zhu's overall strategy of privatizing failing state-owned enterprises, with the exception of those in strategic sectors such as arms production and energy.[78] Wen also considers manufacturers of construction machinery as being of national strategic importance and thus that they should be maintained under public ownership. He will not allow private investors to purchase them under any circumstances. This attitude towards public ownership was further confirmed in the most recent 17th Party Congress, at which Hu Jiantao stated that: "We need to uphold and improve the basic economic system in which public ownership is dominant and unwaveringly consolidate and develop the public sector of the economy."[79]

Second, the Carlyle case also reveals the conservative philosophy of the top Chinese leadership, in particular, Zeng Peiyan, who is the vice-premier in charge of state investments in industry and infrastructure, a Politburo member, and chairman of the State Development Planning Commission (as well as being a crony of Jiang Zemin) is considered to be on the more cautious side of the policy spectrum with regard to large state enterprises, state banks, and industrial ministries. Zeng is also an extremely capable policymaker. His believes that he can steer the market economy, and he seems to have adequate faith that this can in fact be done. Many of the Chinese leadership seem to side with Zeng. These leaders include Vice Executive Premier, Huang Ju, NPC chairman, Wu Bangguo, and CPPCC chairman, Jia Qinglin. Huang's and Wu's Shanghai-based careers have given them familiarity with the state-owned sector, and they believe that many SOEs must and can be saved. On this basis, Zeng and his followers call for further state investment in SOEs to upgrade their technology as well as to improve their management.[80]

However, the Chinese Communist Party's 17th Congress, which convened from October 15-21, 2007, resulted in a changing landscape of the delicate personnel and policy balances struck among the old leadership. The most notable changes were the retirement of Zeng Qinghong, the death of Huang Ju, and the purge of Chen Liangyu. In addition, Shanghai Party Secretary Xi Jinping was elevated to the No. 6 position in the hierarchy of the Politburo Standing Committee. Li Keqiang, Liaoning Province CCP Secretary, was also promoted to the PBSC, just one rank below Xi Jinping.[81] These changes will assuredly produce a new balance among this collective leadership.

Despite the personnel changes in the 17th Party Congress, this optimistic attitude towards SOE reform still exists. In fact, it dominates the current leadership's industrial philosophy. For example, in the 17th Party Congress report, Hu Jintao states that: "We will improve the modern corporate structure and optimize the distribution and structure of the state sector of the economy to enhance its dynamism, dominance and influence."[82] This thinking is manifested in the program of the current administration—"Revitalizing the Northeast Region and Old Industrial Bases." This confidence in SOEs is also demonstrated in the decision finally made in May 2007 to have 159 central government State-owned enterprises begin paying dividends to the government.[83]

Third, the Carlyle case also seems to be an example of the model of "fragmented authoritarianism." This model posits that a complex matrix of relevant bureaucracies and interests produce decisions through extensive bargaining and coordination; efforts to gain consensus dominate the whole process.[84] This fragmentation of interests inherent in the model might help to explain why the

Assets Supervision and Administration Commission (SASAC) agreed to the new deal, while other relevant bureaucracies did not.

The PCCW Case in the Communications Industry:

Another example of government backlash against inward FDI is in the communications industry. In 2005, the state-owned telecom company, China Network Communications, acquired a 20% stake in PCCW (Hong Kong's primary carrier), a stake second only to that of the PCCW Chairman Richard Li. In 2006, the Macquarie Bank of Australia and TPG/Newbridge of the USA each proposed offers up to $7 billion to acquire Li's holdings in PCCW. Richard Li would have preferred to sell his 23% PCCW holding for this sum to foreign private equity groups, but China Network Communications objected to this on nationalist grounds. Their stance was that PCCW ought to be "owned and managed by the people of Hong Kong."[85]

Richard Li was upset at this governmental interference, and, as a result, he opted to sell his shares to the investment banker Francis Leung for a mere US $1.3 billion. In turn, Leung divided up these shares—12% went to the private charitable foundation led by Li Ka-shing, Richard Li's father; 8% went to the Spanish company, Telefonica; and Leung kept 2.65% for himself. China Network Communications is now bigger than any other PCCW shareholder, sitting on the top of the shareholder pile. It now has control of the major provider of fixed-line and broadband internet services in Hong Kong.[86] Beijing's successful blocking of Richard Li's sale of his shares to foreign investors is yet more evidence of Beijing's control of merchant activities.

This process has also raised concerns and created political waves in Hong Kong. Legislators there are concerned with having a Beijing-controlled company responsible for controlling its core telecom network.[87] Aware of the sensitive political nature of the transaction, China Network Communications announced that it did not intend to control the board of PCCW, and that it would not do so in the future.[88]

This further testifies to Zhu's and Wen's reformist philosophy concerning SOEs. Although they are both committed to privatizing and reforming failing state-owned enterprises, they maintain that strategic sectors, such as banking, telecommunications, transportation, arms production and energy are to be kept firmly within government control.

Inflows in Media—National Cultural Security:

The continued control of merchants by the Chinese state can also be seen in setbacks in the liberalization of the press. Specifically, the Chinese government has halted new foreign investments in China's TV groups, and has also banned the issuing of stock in its newspapers.

The government finds some investments too controversial to approve. In December 2006, for example, the State Administration of Radio, Film and Television (SARFT) announced that Beijing had put a halt to landmark rules that had been originally laid down in 2004. These rules had allowed foreign investors to buy minority stakes in television programming, distribution and movie production. In addition, China would no longer approve the creation of program production companies. The decision to restrict foreign companies' activities to one-off co-operation projects highlights Beijing's reluctance to give away influence over the media sector.[89]

International media groups, such as the News Corp., Time Warner and Viacom, have worked for years to gain more access to China, one of the world's most strategic media markets. In 2005, however, it became clear that the government had changed their heart on equity involvement, when SARFT limited most foreign companies to just one such venture, and banned any businesses that were considered "unfriendly" to China. The government feared that if it opened up the TV and film production sectors, it ran the risk of allowing international conglomerates to establish a dominant position in local media markets. Therefore, the Communist Party set out tighter restrictions on media involvement by foreign companies, so that it could protect "national cultural security". At the same time, Beijing hopes that local companies will get the opportunity to assimilate the management and technology skills necessary to gain global competitiveness while keeping control firmly in Chinese hands. For instance, China Central Television (CCTV), the state broadcaster, was encouraged to increase efficiency and raise creativity by spinning off production and other non-broadcasting units.[90]

A similar trend happened in the setback of press liberalization. Beijing did a U-turn on its 2005 plans to allow foreign newspapers to print in China. These companies had been transporting newspapers to the mainland prior to this. This newspaper liberalization was suspended by Beijing because of the role that the international media played in the so-called "color revolutions" in Georgia, the Ukraine and Kyrgyzstan.[91]

In addition, China has also banned local newspapers from publicly issuing shares following a 2005 corruption scandal at the IPO pioneer—*Beijing Youth Daily*. A number of Beijing's media advertising managers and staff were arrested for economic problems. This move angered investors and harmed the company's share price. Another reason for the ban is that the Chinese government has begun to realize that if its communications media are to list, they must have very well established management structures. However, traditionally, the industry lacks this experience.[92]

The setback to the liberalization of FDI into the Chinese media, including the press, was brought about for the above mentioned corporate and managerial reasons. In addition, this setback to inward media-related FDI is in keeping with the Propaganda Department's overall critique of neoliberalism, which is in consonance with widespread feelings about neoliberalism in the Chinese population in general. The Propaganda department's critique of neoliberalism began as a scholarly research project carried out within the Chinese Academy of Social Sciences (CASS). According to a widely accepted anecdote, Li Changchun, the Politburo Standing Committee member responsible for propaganda, initiated this research program upon his return from a visit to Cuba in 2003.[93]

What is more, the Propaganda department apparently caused this media FDI setback because Hu Jintao opened the door to critiques made by the left in general, and the critique of neoliberalism in particular, with his speech to the Fourth Plenum of the CCP in October 2004. This speech has never been published.

However, many people believed that in it, Hu advocated tight control of the press, and emphasized the need for continuing vigilance against foreign cultural intrusions.[94] These comments undoubtedly legitimized some of the criticisms made against neo-liberalism, and indirectly of the setback in the liberalization of inward FDI directed towards media.

At a higher level, this reflects another aspect of Hu's philosophy on addressing the problems of the Party. Hu Jintao and his followers, including Wen Jiabao and Luo Gan, wish to strengthen internal Party mechanisms to improve the behavior and quality of cadres. Wen has also said that that the Party should strengthen its ideological and political training and be more attentive to recruiting and promoting cadres who are committed ideologically and ethically, as well as being technically proficient.[95]

The setback to media-directed inward FDI is also in keeping with Hu's overall personal style. Hu's idea of leadership is not to impose a new vision. He is a rule-keeper rather than a rule-bender, a balancer rather than a visionary.[96]

Interestingly enough, although the government has, over the last two years, slowed down its cautious liberalization of the media industry to protect "national cultural security," it has also simultaneously encouraged local media groups to make higher contributions to economic growth, and has tried to find an expanded role for private capital in publishing and distribution. The government has encouraged book publishers to list their shares on mainland China and Hong Kong stock markets. For example, in March 2006, Liaoning Publishing Group was given permission to become the first publisher in China to list in Hong Kong. Another example is the recent back-door listing of the distribution company, Shanghai Xinhua Media. The Sichuan Xinhua chain store, a distributor based in western China, also has plans for an IPO.[97] The decision to ban newspaper listings, but to allow them for publishing and distribution companies, reflects officials' attempts to balance the commercial development and benefits of the media industry without losing political control over it.[98]

These setbacks in liberalization of the media indicate that the Chinese government is still very much in control over merchant activities. At the same time, however, the government is trying to strike a balance between political control and its own commercial benefit by liberalizing its policies for publishing company merchants. It must be kept in mind, however, that the media are not merchants in the traditional sense, since most media in China are owned by government entities.

PRC Champions Locals via Regulating Inflows of FDI:

The Chinese government's control over its merchants also extends to the Internet industry. Given their importance, it's no wonder that online businesses have become active in the Chinese economy. Nevertheless, Chinese companies such as Tom Online and Alibaba.com posed strong challenges to eBay. Jack Ma, the founder of Alibaba, argued that only locally controlled Internet businesses should have a chance of succeeding in China. He has deployed clever promotional techniques and a fee-free business model to build his market share and consolidate his dominant position in consumer online auctions. The auction site of Alibaba's Taobao had shown faster growth than eBay in terms of both users and completed deals—it was responsible for approximately 60% of consumer-to-consumer online transactions for the third quarter of 2006. Based on this circumstance, estimates are that eBay will pay $40 million for a 49% stake in a joint venture with Tom Online, which will result in the launch of a new online auction site in 2008.[99]

eBay's decision to work through a locally controlled joint venture is similar to the route that Yahoo, the US portal, took when it switched its struggling China site to Alibaba last year. Google and Amazon have also struggled to compete with Chinese rival, Baidu.com, the NASDAQ-listed online search provider. A "cut and paste" business model where a service provider tries to use the same business model that worked in their domestic market is unlikely to work in China.[100]

In 2007, Baidu has plans to enter Japan, which is a rare and ambitious move for a Chinese Internet company. The plan is to take on Yahoo and Google who are already firmly entrenched in Japan. Baidu is doing this, because they have specific strengths in non-English searches and because Japan has high Internet use. However, Japanese online habits are also different from those that Baidu has experienced in its domestic market. Plus, in Japan, Baidu will lack the indirect support of the Chinese Internet censors. These censors have helped Baidu tremendously, since they have often disrupted and blocked Google's services.[101]

China operates the most extensive, technologically sophisticated, and broad-reaching system of Internet filtering in the world. China temporarily blocked access to Google in September 2002; requests for Google's site were redirected to Chinese search engines. According to the company, Google negotiated with Chinese officials, and eventually access was restored. However, the Google cache and certain keyword searches are now blocked. For example, Chinese users can not access Web sites with sensitive keywords, such as "falun."[102]

The Baidu and Yisou search engines filter by keyword and remove certain search results from their lists, such as "free Tibet" and "falun." Interestingly, when a user requests a banned keyword, the filtering system terminates that user's connection to the destination server by sending a TCP reset packet to the user. Compared to similar efforts in other states, China's filtering regime is pervasive, sophisticated, and effective.[103]

Stark difficulties face foreign internet companies in China, difficulties which eventually led to eBay's decision to close its main online auction website in China, and replace it with a minority-invested joint venture. These same difficulties also highlight China's influence over its merchants, since—at least in the case of the Internet—the government championed what were essentially local issues via the regulation of the inflows of FDI.

Macroeconomic Re-control through Administrative Measures in 2004 and 2006

The decision of Chinese policymakers to use administrative measures and not standard macroeconomic policy to cool down the economy in 2004 is the most obvious and direct example of the state's control over merchants. The difficulties of an overheated economy became clear in the first quarter of 2004, although they had been recognized since spring 2003, The Politburo of the Chinese Communist Party decided to strengthen macroeconomic policies dramatically in a meeting held on April 26, 2004. This was followed by numerous meetings and activities, which led to the imposition of significant administrative controls over land use and investments. The instruments chosen to impose the macroeconomic recontrol were similar to those of the era of planned economies. However, these old methods do not work well with the market operations that now dominate the Chinese economy.[104]

Within four days of the April 26th meeting, an urgent directive ordering the suspension and re-inspection of thousands of investment projects was issued by the State Development and Reform Commission (SDRC)—the former State Planning Commission. These moves represented a major reorientation of Chinese macroeconomic policy. The political impact of these moves is significant—new leaders have been brought into the center of the economic decision-making process, and overall economic policy has shifted towards a somewhat more conservative direction. The economic impact of these measures is also significant. The administrative measures made in 2004 to cool the economy were not very successful. It turns out that the macroeconomic policy set by the PBC was more responsible for the slight cooling the economy in 2005 than the administrative measures made by the NDRC. Although perhaps not a step backward, these administrative measures are at least an indication that the reformist approaches to economic policy, in place through the first year of the Wen administration, have not achieved their goals.[105]

Chinese leaders turned their economic policy to face the danger of another overheating in the summer of 2006. The policy so developed involved a powerful combination of monetary and administrative measures. Only administrative measures were taken during the previous economic contraction of 2004. The policy instruments this time—unlike those in 2004—have been well coordinated across financial, macroeconomic, and administrative measures. The policy instruments have even included a slight acceleration in the rate of appreciation of the RMB exchange rate.[106]

Chinese policymakers became increasingly aware of the need to step up measures to cool the overheated economy throughout 2006. The People's Bank of China (PBC, the central bank) and the NDRC—main centers of Chinese economic policy—took measures from April through August to reduce investment demand. The first of these measures came from the PBC on April 28, 2006, when it raised interest rates on loans by 0.27 percentage points. The PBC again raised loan interest rates by another 0.27 percentage points on August 18, 2006. Meanwhile, the NDRC was also participating in this macroeconomic policy shift by enacting a whole host of measures to reign in investment. In particular, on June 13, 2006, the NDRC, together with the Ministry of Land and Resources and the China Bank Regulatory Commission, issued the directive, "Opinion on Strengthening the Adjustment of Fixed Investment and Rigorously Controlling the Start of New Investment Projects." On August 1st, the NDRC Investment Bureau along with the Ministry of Land and Resources, the State Environment Protection Bureau, the State Safety Administration, and the Bank Regulatory Commission set out the "Guiding Opinions on Rectifying New Investment

Projects." This regulation has a very precise set of criteria for the approval of new projects. While the NDRC in general agrees with PBC monetary policy, it also sees a necessity for NDRC's administrative measures in order to ensure stability and moderation in monetary policy.[107]

In mid-August of the same year, the State Council also joined this movement for macroeconomic contraction. At its August 16th meeting, the State Council rebuked the government of Inner Mongolia for failing to implement macroeconomic policies. As a result the Autonomous Region chairman was instructed to write a self-criticism.[108]

What is more, the government, in order to help cool the economy, appreciated the RMB currency, or gains in value. In general, Chinese policymakers are extremely reluctant to let the RMB appreciate rapidly for a variety of reasons. However, the rapidly growing overall trade surplus, along with the macroeconomic factors i.e. economic overheating, led administration to appreciate the exchange rate, though by relatively modest amount. On September 22, 2006, the value of the RMB was 4.4 percent greater than its pre-July 2005 value.[109]

China's attempt to control investment in 2006 appears quite similar to the attempts it made in 2004. However, many lessons had been learned in the interim. For example, PBC policy and NDRC policy was more coordinated in 2006 than in 2004. Also fiscal and exchange rate policy were more in keeping with the overall direction of macroeconomic policy than in 2004. However, in both instances, the Chinese government had to resort to intervention by the administration to do what monetary policy alone could not. The costs of these interventions by the administration were the creation of new distortions in the economy.[110]

The separate measures prescribed by PBC and NDRC demonstrate the existence of two important power centers, power centers that perceive the economy quite differently. One power center, the PBC, advocates a greater reliance on financial and monetary policies. Although the PBC is willing to go along with some administrative measures that are suitable for China's less developed financial markets, it is reluctant to rely excessively on administrative means to control investment. The other power center, the NDRC, looks favorably upon the use of administrative measures. The reason for this is that the use of such measures is in accord with the NDRC's broader agenda of implementing industrial policy that is specific to each sector. Bureaus and bureaucrats within NDRC gain power and influence anytime a shift occurs towards administrative measures by the government.[111]

In view of the existence of the two power centers, the full package appears to be somewhat of a political compromise, which carefully balances bureaucratic divisions and the interests they represent. The process of economic decision making, therefore, seems to be caught up in the balance of forces between the financial bureaucrats and the industrial bureaucrats, between the PBC and the NDRC. However, these specialists have learned to cooperate with each other, and to act within the boundaries set by the Communist Party Politburo.

Up until now, the Politburo has not permitted the PBC to break away from the policy of gradualism and stability. Therefore, no matter what the thinking of the PBC, including that of some PBC officials who would like to see more dramatic policies, the role of the PBC is limited to giving advice and making policy within the boundaries set by the top political leadership.[112] This Politburo guideline is expressly stated in its 17th Party Congress report: "We will improve the state planning system. We will give play to the guiding role of national development plans, programs and industrial policies in macroeconomic regulation and combine the use of fiscal and monetary policies to improve macroeconomic regulation."[113]

The Interplay between State Control and Merchant Autonomy

The Case of China Mobile:

Recent lessons indicate that most of the time, both the state's control and the merchants' autonomy are not static but rather mutually change and influence each other. The conflicting interests between corporate executives and the government, as well as the interaction between the two can be revealed in the activism of China Mobile on the global stage. Although the Chinese government owns China Mobile, the company seems to be driven more by corporate interests than government interests. The company has been linked with many mergers in the last two years that would have seen it expand into Pakistan, Yemen, Uzbekistan, Ghana, Paraguay and many other countries. The reality is that the company has a small presence in Hong Kong and, other than that, its activities are in the domestic Chinese market. The reported expansions were either speculative or the deals did not work out.[114] What is clear is that the company does have the ambition to extend its reach beyond mainland China. But even this ambition is not without checks, it is the control and observation of government officials.

In 2005, the company failed in a bid to buy a stake in Pakistan Telecommunications. Later, however, it was successful in its acquisition of China Resource People, a Hong Kong-based mobile operator. The company still wants to beef up operations by acquiring overseas companies.[115] In the last two years, for example, it has been linked to CSL (a Hong Kong based mobile operator), Reliance Telecom of India, and Millicom. All of these companies are in emerging markets and, as such, are attractive prospects for telecom companies.[116] China Mobile has also tried to access the developed world. It recently investigated the third-generation mobile assets of Hutchison Whampoa in Italy and the UK.[117] Its desire to buy the Luxembourg-based company cooled after recent overseas site visits by senior executives to assess the assets.[118]

Considering plenty of growth opportunities still exist at home, and the domestic market is still relatively young, governmental officials are afraid that China Mobile may be taking on more overseas risk than it is prepared for. Wang Xueqing, a Chinese official and a telecom industry expert under Beijing's powerful National Development and Reform Commission, calls for restriction for China Mobile's activism. Wang believes that the operator is flush with cash all too easily earned from its dominant position in the Chinese market and is keen to find something to spend it on, instead of returning it to the state. As a result, the public assets may be put in danger. "This is a matter of 'taking another person's child to go wolf-hunting'," he says. "A state-owned enterprise like China Mobile should not be making this kind of tremendously risky overseas investment." [119]

However, the Chairman of China Mobile, Wang Jianzhou, reflecting more the corporate rather than the governmental interests of his company, has stated that: "Our 'Go Global' policy has not changed. We are still searching for opportunities abroad to grow our earnings." When asked if he viewed the failure of the bid for Pakistan Telecommunication as a set-back, he commented that: "There is no such a thing as failure in acquisition. If you go to a mall and decide not to buy something because you don't want to pay a high price, that's not a failure." [120]

This episode highlights the reality that when government sees corporate autonomy going too far and taking what it sees as unnecessary risks, it exercises stringent control, since the government feels business would be well served to do so—regardless of the ambitions of the businesses themselves.

An interplay happened between state and corporate interests in the Chinese telecommunications industry. This interplay is shown in the existence of four major competitors in the Chinese telecommunications market. This creation of four competitors in the Chinese telecommunication markets implements the philosophy of the top leaders as stated in the 17th Party Congress: "We will deepen the reform of monopoly industries by introducing competition, and strengthen government regulation and public oversight of them."[121]

Three of these four companies, China Netcom, China Mobile, and China Telecom, came into existence in 1999-2000, when the Chinese government decided to split up the monopoly of China Telecom (which is the fourth company). In spite of the break up, **China Telecom** is still the largest provider of telecommunications services in the China. Its area of service includes 21 provinces in southern China.[122]

The second largest provider of telecommunications services in China is **China Netcom**, whose service areas in the northern 10 provinces of China. In August 1999 when Chinese Telecom was broken up with the backing of Jiang's son, Jiang Jinheng, the Chinese government gave Netcom (whose headquarters are in Shanghai) a third of China Telecom's assets.[123]

The largest state-owned mobile phone company in China is **China Mobile**. It has over 349.66 million customers, thus making it the world's largest mobile phone by number of subscribers. It was split off from former China Telecom in 2000. It now maintains a 65% share of the Chinese mobile market. [124]

On July 19, 1994, the Ministries of Electronic Industry and the State Council founded **China Unicom** as a state-owned corporation. Ninety percent of China's wireless market is controlled by Unicom and China Mobile.[125]

The reality that four state-owned telecommunication companies compete and cooperate in Chinese telecommunication markets shows that state on one hand recognizes the necessity of corporate competition and breaking up the monopoly; on the other hand, these are all state owned companies and so are within state control.

The Case of Chinese Steelmakers:

Another example of the interplay between state control and merchant autonomy is revealed in the recent negotiations for the price of iron ore. Chinese Association of the Iron and Steel Industry have dictated that all Chinese steelmakers are banned from having individual iron ore price negotiations for contracts with international miners for 2006, apart from the Shanghai Baosteel Group Co.[126]

The government has backed the association in this move, which is designed to set discipline for the industry. Baosteel has been set as the representative of all Chinese steelmakers in negotiations for the price of iron ore. Baosteel has held talks with BHP Billiton, Rio Tinto and Vale do Rio Doce of Brazil. These three companies together account for approximately 70% of global iron ore production.[127]

In 2005, Chinese companies agreed to a steep 72% increase over the previous year in the price of iron ore. Mining companies are seeking another increase of 20% for 2007 in consideration of the huge steel production and need for ore in China. Global steelmakers are almost certain to see price increases for iron ore in 2007 at the upper end of market expectations after China's Shanghai Baosteel Group Corp. reached a deal with Brazilian mining giant Cia. Vale do Rio Doce for a 9.5% rise, following on a 20% increase in 2006 and a 72% gain in 2005.[128]

Facing surging high process, the State Reserve Bureau, which is affiliated with China's primary economic planning body, the National Development and Reform Commission, pledged to manage these commodities better by indicating that it will take a more active stance towards trading futures on domestic markets in order to minimize the effects of global commodity price surges.[129] At the same time, the National Development and Reform Commission states that it will continue revamping pricing systems for natural resources, including prices for electricity, natural gas and coal, so that they can reflect global price changes more quickly.[130]

Baosteel Group will increase prices on its core steel products in the second quarter of 2007 by about 10% from the previous quarter, according to information from the *Shanghai Securities News*.[131] At the same time, Beijing has also begun to close down the private sector, which accounts for one-third of output from the iron and steel industry, in order to avoid economic "overheating".

This episode demonstrates that government—at least in certain special circumstances—has the ability to regulate industry and control its direction to what is sees as being in the best interests of business.

While the government's efforts to control overseas price negotiation in the iron and steel industry have been successful; its attempts to close the domestic private steel makers in order to avoid economic overheating have been less so.

Despite a government edict, semi-legal steel plants in China are on the increase, which is giving rise to worries about an investment bubble. For instance, one small plant based to the east of Beijing in Tangshan is a primitive operation that produces H-bars, which are long thin rods made from cheap slabs of steel for use in construction. The factory is the kind of place that Beijing claims it wants to close—it belches out smoke and spills out untreated waste water—but local officials are turning a blind eye to its existence, so business carries on as usual once the sun has set.[132] These steel merchants are clearly operating on the periphery of governmental control.

Interestingly, in the 1950s, during Mao's Great Leap Forward, this kind of operation was a common sight, as millions of people set up basic furnaces to forge steel in their backyards. Nowadays, similar facilities are being set up by thousands of small entrepreneurs, with an eye on profits rather than politics. The Tangshan plant, for example, is run by a husband-and-wife team. Estimates show that one third of the industry's output has come from the private sector in this way.[133]

Realizing a danger of "overheating," an army of bureaucrats in Beijing shaped economic behavior via "administrative measures." These measures include new rules, approvals and warnings. However, to get these planning tools to work is becoming more difficult, as the private sector is growing fast and the economy is getting more diverse.

The authorities in the Tangshan area have closed down some small plants, but many still operate. In fact, the provincial government ordered the closure of the night-shift plant, but it remains open because the district government has not enforced the directive.[134]

The truth is that local officials cannot easily close down these small steel operations. They often spring up in poorer areas and make big contributions to local government. As local officials in China are virtually completely judged on the economic growth they create, it's not difficult to understand why they consider creating jobs more important than cleaning air.[135] China is governed by a form of authoritarianism but it is a decentralized one. Beijing's writ has its limits.

Natural resources, whether overseas or domestic, are always a subject of some controversy in rapidly-growing nations like China. On the one hand, China's hunger for natural resources has led to the significant autonomy of Chinese merchants from the state, an autonomy that was given to them so that they could produce the raw materials necessary to sustain China's fast economic growth. This autonomy has given Chinese merchants worldwide exposure to various industries from the iron ore mines in Australia to the oil fields of the Sudan, and has been a big factor in forcing up global prices to generational highs. On the other hand, China has constantly maintained that the military, electric power, oil, coal, telecommunications, aviation and the shipping industries would remain under absolute state control. China wants to keep key state industries in sectors considered to have important national security implications in its own hands.

The desire to keep certain industries under complete governmental control is in keeping with Zhu and Wen's agenda of reform. From a larger perspective, it is also in keeping with the philosophy of the leadership under both Jiang and Hu. When China carries out bold economic reform and modernization, it must do so on the basis of national unification, ethnic cohesiveness and social stability.

The Case of Aluminum:

The most explosive growth in production has been seen in alumina—the bauxite powder that makes aluminum. When local smelters began to complain that alumina shortages were causing price hikes and leaving them short on materials, the state opened up the industry. Private companies—supported by their local governments—saw the potentially enormous profits that could be made if they got alumina quickly to market and invested a lot of capital into building new production plants. Production rose so rapidly that China will go from importing 7 million tons of alumina in 2005 to having no net import of alumina in 2008.[136]

Chinese production of alumina will increase is anticipated to increase from around 4.3 million tons a year in 2000 to in excess of 27 million tons a year by the end of the decade. This swing is projected on the mix of high prices on a global basis and on the state decision to allow private companies to enter what has long been a state monopolized sector. This production explosion in alumina has had effects all over the world which are now impacting China itself. Global prices stood at $650 a ton in 2006, but have now dropped to approximately $250. Consequently, many of the plants set up in the last two years—if the economics show that they cannot function at costs below $300 a ton—will now have to close down.[137]

Since it realized a danger of "overheating," the NDRC changed economic behavior through administrative measures which ended the tax-free aluminum policy. These measures by the NDRC mean that China is putting a stop to its preferential tax policy on aluminum imports and aluminum exports from July 2005. This is one of the more recent attempts to try to slow the growth of some energy-intensive industries.

This move is also an attempt to restrict the alumina processing trade and eventually decrease exports of aluminum products, which are highly energy dependent. The former preferential tax policy was known as tolling. This former policy permitted aluminum smelters in China to import and process alumina tax-free if the finished aluminum was re-exported. Industry sources as well as traders have indicated that the move by the NDRC would reduce the supply of Chinese aluminum on the international markets, while increasing the domestic supply at home. China is a major exporter of aluminum to Asia, aside from being the world's largest spot buyer of alumina.[138]

The Case of Iron Ore:

Iron ore provides a consistent source of material. However, the environmental impact of mining ore causes problems. Plants in China were constructed quickly and cheaply with none of the requirements that multi-nationals have to go through, such as feasibility studies to test out business and environmental issues. The 70% increase in global iron ore prices in 2005 is another factor that promoted the rapid construction of iron ore mines. This rapid construction, however, has caused problems. The new mines are mainly based in Northern China—a drought-stricken region. The mining operations in this region may have pushed production in the country up by around 40% in 2006, but they are using up scarce and valuable water. Besides, the focus of these Chinese private mines is on quick profit. However, the quality of Chinese ore is poor—it takes around 10 tons of dirt to yield a ton of ore.[139] All this is severely damaging the environment around the mines. But, in the short term, these private mines have turned a significant profit. Facing these challenges, the Chinese government is attempting to take various measures to balance and control these private mining operations. Although the above environmental concerns are rational reaction by the government, the power wielded in this case by top governmental officials was not only meant to show the strength of the state, but also to show the state's commitment to the Hu-Wen administration's environmental-friendly philosophy. This environmentalist worldview is also seen in Hu Jintao and Wen Jiabao's economic program—11th Five Year Plan from 2006 through 2010. The Plan emphatically advocates environmental protection. It marks the first occasion that the Chinese government has been so strongly committed to the protecting the environment. The Plan calls for greater enforcement of pollution laws, better mechanisms to eliminate the worst polluters, great investments in controlling pollution and increasing water quality, and more investment in natural areas.[140]

Many references to environmental issues are also contained in Hu Jintao's 17th CCP Congress report. In fact, all of paragraph 4 under section IV is dedicated to this topic. This report states: "Our economic growth is realized at an excessively high cost of resources and the environment."[141] It goes on to state: "We must adopt an enlightened approach to development that results in expanded production, a better life and sound ecological and environmental conditions, and build a resource-conserving and environment-friendly society that coordinates growth rate with the economic structure, quality and efficiency, and harmonizes economic growth with the population, resources and the environment, so that our people will live and work under sound ecological and environmental conditions and our economy and society will develop in a sustainable way."[142]

The Case of Copper Taxes:

In order to regain control and to maximize the benefits available from its huge resource-intensive industries, China is going to impose new export taxes on copper. Chinese firms import raw copper and refine it to manufacturer wire and copper sheets, and then export it overseas to meet the needs of higher value niche market products. The Chinese government plans to raise taxes on certain types of refined-copper and copper-alloy ingots from current rate of 5% to 10%. Other copper and part-copper products that are currently untaxed will also be taxed at a rate of 10%. The government is also increasing taxes on copper because copper plants use energy intensively, as well as poisonous and carcinogenic chemicals, and are, therefore, often situated by rivers to harness hydropower.[143] The government anticipates that in the long term these higher taxes on input will push manufacturers away from industries that are energy-intensive and high-polluting, in favor of manufacturing higher-valued goods to cover the tax costs. The above copper tax reflects the administration's overall policy in the 11th Five Year Plan. This Plan advocates the collection of fuel taxes, improvements in the design and collection of natural resource taxes, and imposing further taxes on sectors that consume raw materials.[144]

These cases, i.e., aluminum, iron ore, and copper, show that the Chinese government alternately tightens and loosens its control over merchant autonomy in these industrial sectors. This robust process of governmental control and adjustment of the industrial sectors is clearly part of a sustainable process of industrial development in China. This sustainable process has often been referred to as the "Scientific Outlook on Development" (*kexue fazhan guan* 科学发展观). According to the 17th Party Congress, the Scientific Outlook on Development "takes development as its essence, putting people first as its core, comprehensive, balanced and sustainable development as its basic requirement, and overall consideration as its fundamental approach."[145] Premier Wen Jiabao has stated that development is the key to resolving all of China's problems. Development, however, is not measured merely by growth in the GDP. Development requires emphasis on human resources, that is, on putting people first (*yiren weiben* 以人为本), as well as emphasis on the diversification of capabilities. Development must be sustainable, and sensitive to the capacity of the natural environment and human society. As a matter of fact, everything that the Chinese government must do to "soften" the current rush to economic growth is precisely that which will make long-term development sustainable.[146] This "Scientific Outlook on Development" was added to the Party Constitution along with "Marxism-Leninism-Mao Zedong Thought, Deng Xiaoping Theory, and the Important Thought of the Three Represents."[147] According to the 17th Party Congress report: "It is an important guiding principle for China's economic and social development and a major strategic thought that we must uphold and apply in developing socialism with Chinese characteristics."[148]

China's Trillion-Dollar Reserves—State and Merchan Become One

State control and merchant autonomy can even embody themselves in one thing at the same time. This can be illustrated by some of the consequences of China's foreign exchange reserves shooting past the trillion-dollar mark. On the one hand, the government is setting up an institution responsible for managing China's towering stack of foreign currency holdings. This illustrates state control. On the other hand, a portion of China's foreign reserves may be invested in overseas securities to make more profit. This illustrates the commercial and business oriented mentality of the administration. This also reveals the two tilts of the economic policy makers.

By the end of 2006, China had the world's largest foreign reserves estimated at US $1,066 billion.[149] This was a result of huge trade surpluses and large inflows of capital. These reserves have also become a magnet for the world's global fund management giants.[150] Intense discussion is now taking place in China about how these reserves should be managed and spent. The management and spending of these reserves reveal the consensus and balance reached between the two factions within the top leadership.

At the top level, the economic decision makers have two somewhat different orientations. One group of economic policymakers tilts towards a more conservative direction. This group has backgrounds in the bureaucracy, is somewhat more attuned to political considerations, and is close to Jiang Zemin. An example is Vice Premier Zeng Peiyan, who is in charge of state investments in industry and infrastructure, and Executive Vice Premier Huang Ju, who is in charge of fiscal and financial matters. By contrast, a slightly less conservative role is being played by those technocrats who were most involved in making the blueprints of reform, working under Wen Jiabao, and who are most closely attuned to economic considerations. Zhou Xiaochuan, the head of the Central Bank, is an example of this group.[151] However, this landscape is currently changing after the 17th Party Congress, with the retirement of Zeng Qinghong and Wu Yi, the death of Huang Ju, as well as the addition of Xi Jinping and Li Keqiang to the Politburo Standing Committee.

On the one hand, those technocrats who tilt towards economic considerations have paid special attention to South Korea's recent move in which some of its reserves are allowed to be managed like a mutual fund, under the guidance of foreign banks. Those decision makers have also been scrutinizing the model of Singapore, which established the Government Investment Corporation and Temasek Holdings to manage its foreign reserves and direct investments respectively.[152]

On the other hand, the more cautious bureaucratic decision makers are treating its huge foreign reserves carefully, since any capital losses that result from a change in currency values could bring harsh criticism to the central bank. Wen Jiabao has decided to give equal importance to both commercial profits and to the maintenance of stability by giving its control to two agencies simultaneously.[153]

In doing so, Beijing has delegated to the State Administration of Foreign Exchange (SAFE), an agency under the central bank, the task of continuing to manage the major part of the reserves.[154] This money has been kept in its reserves as a kind of hedge against financial volatility. This traditional use of foreign reserves is illustrative of state control, as well as of the intentions of the conservative decision makers.

At the same time, China just commissioned a special state investment agency to invest a portion of its huge foreign reserves in October 2007, following a decision made by the State Council at the Central Financial Work Meeting in January 2007. This agency is China Investment Corp (CIC), the country's long-awaited gigantic state investment arm. This proactive approach to the management of reserves follows the examples of the Republic of Korea and Singapore. Its aim is to prudently manage the reserves, and to do so more profitably and efficiently. It is headed by Lou Zhiwei, the company's newly-appointed board chairman, who is also deputy secretary general of the State Council. Lou Jiwei has stated that "We will maintain transparency of company operations on the premise of safeguarding our commercial interests,"[155] These guidelines that pursue commercial interests are exemplified by the actuality that in May 2007, the company, though not yet formally established, invested US $3 billion for a 9.9% stake in the private equity firm Blackstone (United States).[156] This arrangement in turn reveals the commercial orientation of the top policy makers. China's management of its trillion dollar foreign reserves illustrates that state control, in the form of SAFE, and merchant autonomy, in the form of CIC, can exist in the same thing at the same time.

The Chinese government has already conducted research into dividing a portion of this reserve for investment, separate from the normal foreign exchange reserves. This portion for investment is expected to be possibly US $200 billion.[157] The attempt to reach an agreement on such an amount indicates that policymaking under the Wen Jiabao State Council has tended to emphasize bureaucratic consensus-building rather than prompt decisiveness. As a result, policymaking has often been slow and incremental.

Notes

1. Florian Gimbel, "Overseas Markets Prepare for an Inflow as China Turns on the Tap," *Financial Times,* February 13, 2007.

2. Barry Naughton, "Hunkering Down: The Wen Jiabao Administration and Macroeconomic Recontrol," *China Leadership Monitor* No. 11, Summer 2004.

3. Ibid.

4. Ibid.

5. Ibid.

6. Florian Gimbel, "China Widens Pension Fund Mandates to Foreign Groups," *Financial Times,* November 30, 2006.

7. Ibid.

8. Richard McGregor, "Beijing Looks Overseas to Invest Holdings," *Financial Times,* May 2, 2006.

9. UNCTAD, *World Investment Report 2006,* p. 55.

10. Richard McGregor, "China Considers Establishing Powerful Financial Watchdog," *Chinese New Agency,* September 11, 2006, p. 4.

11. UNCTAD, *World Investment Report 2006,* p. 57.

12. Kate Linebaugh, "ICBC Completes World's Biggest IPO," *The Wall Street Journal,* October 20, 2006, p. C4.

13. Kate Linebaugh, "Bank of China Sets Big Offering—Its June IPO May Fetch $9.8 Billion, The Nation's Largest Ever," *The Wall Street Journal,* May 10, 2006.

14. Ibid.

15. Ibid.

16. Sundeep Tucker, "RBS Shows Skeptics it has Learned the Rules of the Game in China," *Financial Times,* November 10, 2006.

17. Barry Naughton, "Waves on Criticism: Debates over Bank Sales to Foreigners and Neo-Liberal Economic Policy, *China Leadership Monitor* No. 17, Winter, 2006.

18. Andrew Yeh and John Aglionby, "ICBC to Pursue Buying Most of Bank Halim," *Financial Times,* January 2, 2007.

19. Shawn Donnan and Geoff Dyer, "ICBC Poised for First Foreign Acquisition by Chinese Bank," *Financial Times,* September 28, 2006.

20. Andrew Yeh and John Aglionby, "ICBC to Pursue Buying Most of Bank Halim," *Financial Times,* January 2, 2007.

21. Xinhua News Agency, "China's Largest Lender to Open Subsidiary Bank in U.S.," *People's Daily,* October 17, 2007.

22. Shawn Donnan and Geoff Dyer, "ICBC Poised for First Foreign Acquisition by Chinese Bank," *Financial Times,* September 28, 2006.

23. UNCTAD, *World Investment Report 2007,* p.47.

24. James T. Areddy, "Bank of America Sells Asia Branches to Chinese Lender," *The Wall Street Journal,* August 25, 2006.

25. Geoff Dyer, "CCB Chief Repeats Denial," *Financial Times,* April 24, 2006.

26. Ibid.

27. Mure Dickie, Sundeep Tucker and Assif Shameen, "BoC Buys Singapore Aircraft Leasing for $965 Million," *Financial Times,* December 12, 2006.

28. Ibid.

29. Ibid.

30. Sundeep Tucker, "RBS Shows Skeptics it has Learned the Rules of the Game in China," *Financial Times,* November 10, 2006.

31. Ibid.

32. Andrew Yeh, "Switch to Booming Retail Sector for Bank," *Financial Times,* March 19, 2007.

33. Barry Naughton, "Waves on Criticism: Debates over Bank Sales to Foreigners and Neo-Liberal Economic Policy, *China Leadership Monitor* No. 17, Winter, 2006.

34. Tom Mitchell and Sundeep Tucker, "HSBC Faces $800 Million Cash Call to Maintain BoCom Holding," *Financial Times,* November 21, 2006.

35. Ibid.

36. Andrew Yeh, "CDB to Boost Loans for Projects Outside China," *Financial Times,* December 7, 2006.

37. Richard McGregor, "China's Policy Shift Signals Boost to Overseas Investment," *Financial Times,* January 22, 2007.

38. Reuters News Agency, "China Crackdown Racks Up Banking Violations," *The Wall Street Journal,* February 7, 2006.

39. Ibid.

40. Richard McGregor, "China Considers Establishing Powerful Financial Watchdog," *Chinese New Agency,* September 11, 2006.

41. Ibid.

42. Barry Naughton, "Incremental Decision Making and Corporate Restructuring," *China Leadership Monitor* No. 15, Summer, 2005.

43. "China to create 10 big accounting firms, cut reliance on foreign groups," *AFX News*, October 4, 2006, at
http://www.forbes.com/business/feeds/afx/2006/10/03/afx3064785.html.

44. Mure Dickie and Barney Jopson, "China Aims to Develop 'Big Ten' Accountants," *Financial Times,* October 3, 2006.

45. Jeremy Grant, "Xinhua to Buy Glass Lewis in $45 Million Deal," *Financial Times,* December 15, 2006.

46. John Plender, "Credit Binge? Too Bad," *Financial Times,* December 18, 2006, p. 22.

47. Sundeep Tucker and Tom Mitchell, "Executives at CNAC Plan $1 Billion Fund," *Financial Times,* November 21, 2006.

48. Ibid.

49. Ibid.

50. Barry Naughton, "SASAC Rising," *China Leadership Monitor* No. 14, Spring, 2005.

51. Barry Naughton, "Incremental Decision Making and Corporate Restructuring," *China Leadership Monitor* No.15, Summer, 2005.

52. Nathan and Gilley, 2003, p. 200.

53. UNCTAD, *World Investment Report 2007,* p. 47.

54. Barney Jopson, "China to Promote Rivals to 'Big Four'," *Financial Times,* June 8, 2006.

55. Ibid.

56. Daniel Michaels and Bruce Stanley, "Airbus Move to Build in China May Pose a Longer-Term Risk," *The Wall Street Journal,* October 27, 2006.

57. Andrew Yeh and Doug Cameron, "Airbus Studies Plans for Assembly in China," *Financial Times,* June 9, 2006.

58. UNCTAD, *World Investment Report 2006,* p. 57.

59. Mure Dickie and Chris Nuttall, "Intel Keen to Build Chinese Plant," *Financial Times,* January 28, 2007.

60. Ibid.

61. Ibid.

62. Mure Dickie, "China 'Digests' Japan's Bullet Train Technology," *Financial Times,* February 1, 2007.

63. Ibid.

64. Hu Jintao, *Report,* 2007.

65. Andrew Yeh and Doug Cameron, "Mesa Teams Up with Shenzhen Airlines," *Financial Times,* December 23, 2006.

66. Andrew Yeh and Mure Dickie, "Anglo American Shows China Interest," *Financial Times,* November 16, 2006.

67. Ibid.

68. Ibid.

69. Hu Jintao, *Report,* 2007.

70. Barry Naughton, "The New Common Economic Program: China's Eleventh Five Year Plan and What It Means," *China Leadership Monitor,* No. 16, Fall, 2005.

71. Hu Jintao, *Report,* 2007.

72. Richard McGregor, "Veolia Taps into China's Appetite for Recycling," *Financial Times,* January 29, 2007.

73. Ibid.

74. UNCTAD, *World Investment Report 2006,* p. 59.

75. Tao Jingzhou, "Why China Must Turn Away from Economic Nationalism," *Financial Times,* November 15, 2006.

76. Mure Dickie, "H&Q Buys China Engineering Stake," *Financial Times,* November 9, 2006.

77. Geoff Dyer and Sundeep Tucker, "Carlyle Clears China Deal Hurdle," *Financial Times,* November 14, 2006.

78. Nathan and Gilley, 2003, p. 205-207.

79. Hu Jintao, *Report,* 2007.

80. Ibid., p. 207-208.

81. David Shambaugh, "China's 17th Party Congress: Maintaining Delicate Balances," Brookings Northeast Asia Commentary, October 30, 2007.

82. Hu Jintao, *Report,* 2007.

83. Barry Naughton, "Strengthening the Center, and Premier Wen Jiabao," *China Leadership Monitor,* No. 21, Summer, 2007.

84. Margaret M. Person, "The Case of China's Accession to GATT/WTO," David Lampton ed. *Making of Chinese Foreign and Security Policy in the ERA of Reform, 1978-2000,* CA: Stanford University Press, 2001, p. 346.

85. Sundeep Tucker and Tom Mitchell, "Telefonica in Talks over PCCW Stake," *Financial Times,* November 8, 2006; and Tom Mitchell and Sundeep Tucker, "Netcom Move on PCCW Rings Alarm Bells," *Financial Times,* November 14, 2006.

86. Ibid.

87. Sundeep Tucker, Tom Mitchell and Justine Lau, "CNC Takes Largest PCCW Stake," *Financial Times,* November 13, 2006.

88. Tom Mitchell and Sundeep Tucker, "Netcom Move on PCCW Rings Alarm Bells," *Financial Times,* November 14, 2006.

89. Mure Dickie, "Beijing Halts New Foreign Investment in TV Groups," *Financial Times,* December 8, 2006.

90. Ibid.

91. Mure Dickie, "Share Ban is a Blow to Press Liberalization," *Financial Times,* December 4, 2006.

92. Ibid.

93. Barry Naughton, "Waves on Criticism: Debates over Bank Sales to Foreigners and Neo-Liberal Economic Policy, *China Leadership Monitor* No. 17, Winter, 2006.

94. Ibid.

95. Nathan and Gilley, 2003, p. 220-222.

96. Ibid., p.85.

97. Mure Dickie, "Share Ban is a Blow to Press Liberalization," *Financial Times,* December 4, 2006.

98. Ibid.

99. Chris Nuttall and Mure Dickie, "Ebay Tries to Fix its Strategy in China," *Financial Times,* December 20, 2006.

100. Ibid.

101. Mure Dickie, "Baidu Plans Japanese Foray," *Financial Times,* December 5, 2006.

102. "Internet Filtering in China in 2004-2005: A Country Study," at http://www.opennetinitiative.net/studies/china/#toc2

103. Ibid.

104. Barry Naughton, "Hunkering Down: The Wen Jiabao Administration and Macroeconomic Recontrol," *China Leadership Monitor* No.11, Summer, 2004.

105. Barry Naughton, "Economic Policy in 2004: Slipping behind the Curve?" *China Leadership Monitor* No. 13, Winter, 2005.

106. Barry Naughton, "Another Cycle of Macroeconomic Crackdown," *China Leadership Monitor,* No. 19, Fall, 2006, p. 1.

107. Ibid., p. 2-4.

108. Zheng Weiqiang, "PRC Macroeconomic Reconrtol Enters Its Third Phase (Guonei hongguan tiaokong jinru disan jieduan," August 23, 2006.

109. Naughton, Fall, 2006, p. 6-7.

110. Ibid., p. 10-11.

111. Ibid., p. 5.

112. Xia Bin, "There is No US-Style Pattern of Progressive Rate Increases in China (Zhongguo bucunzai meiguoshi de jiaxi zhouqi," August 25, 2006. Xia Bin is the head of Finance Research Institute of the Development Research Center.

113. Hu Jintao, *Report,* 2007.

114. Justine Lau, "China Mobile Wants to be a Big Face in the Global Market," *Financial Times,* January 3, 2007.

115. Sundeep Tucker and Justine Lau, "China Mobile to Renew Search for Acquisitions," *Financial Times,* July 5, 2006.

116. Justine Lau, "China Mobile Wants to be a Big Face in the Global Market," *Financial Times,* January 3, 2007.

117. Ibid.

118. Sundeep Tucker and Justine Lau, "China Mobile to Renew Search for Acquisitions," *Financial Times,* July 5, 2006.

119. Mure Dickie and Justine Lau, "China Mobile Set to Extend Its Reach," *Financial Times,* May 29, 2006.

120. Justine Lau and Mure Dickie, "China Mobile still Looking to Buy Abroad," *Financial Times,* August 21, 2006.

121. Hu Jintao, *Report,* 2007.

122. Yang Lan, *China Telecom Group Corporation—International Development Strategy Analysis* (zhongguo dianxin jituangongsi—guojihua fazhan zhanlue tantao), Master Thesis, Jinan University, May 2003, p. 14-15.

123. Zhou Lina, *A Study on Internationalization of Telecommunication Industry—Internationalization Strategy of Telecommunication Industry in China* (dianxin chanye guojihua fazhanyanju—jianlun zhongguo dianxin Chanye guojihua zhanlue), Mater Thesis, Harbin Engineering University, February 2002, p. 37.

124. Jason Singer and Jason Dean, "China Mobile Nears $5.3 Billion Deal for Millicom," *The Wall Street Journal,* May 25, 2006.

125. Yang Lan, *China Telecom Group Corporation—International Development Strategy Analysis* (zhongguo dianxin jituangongsi—guojihua fazhan zhanlue tantao), Master Thesis, Jinan University, May 2003, p. 14-15.

126. Glenys Sim, "Beijing Warns Its Steelmakers," *The Wall Street Journal,* February 23, 2006.

127. Ibid.

128. Paul Lupinacci, "China's Steelmakers Set Pace in Iron-Ore Pricing," *The Wall Street Journal,* December 22, 2006.

129. Ibid.

130. Terence Poon and Victoria Ruan, "Chinese Inflation Accelerated a Bit During January," *The Wall Street Journal,* February 23, 2006.

131. Glenys Sim, "Beijing Warns Its Steelmakers," *The Wall Street Journal,* February 23, 2006.

132. Geoff Dyer, "Furnaces Burn on as Beijing Tries to Cool the Economy," *Financial Times,* August 3, 2006.

133. Ibid.

134. Ibid.

135. Ibid.

136. Richard McGregor, "China Digs for the Raw Materials It Needs to Sustain Breakneck Growth," *Financial Times,* December 5, 2006.

137. Ibid.

138. CCTV.com, July 21, 2005 at
http://www1.cei.gov.cn/ce/doc/ceni/200507211366.htm

139. Peter Marsh, "Steel Giants Hope Red-hot China will Cool Down," *Financial Times,* November 6, 2006, and Richard McGregor, "China Digs for the Raw Materials It Needs to Sustain Breakneck Growth," *Financial Times,* December 5, 2006.

140. Naughton, Fall 2005, p. 4-6.

141. Hu Jintao, *Report,* 2007.

142. Ibid.

143. Andrea Hotter, "China Sets Copper Taxes to Better Manage Sector," *The Wall Street Journal,* March 20, 2006.

144. Naughton, Fall 2005, p. 5.

145. Hu Jintao, *Report,* 2007.

146. Naughton, Fall 2005, p. 2.

147. Shambaugh, October 30, 2007.

148. Hu Jintao, *Report,* 2007.

149. Richard McGregor, "China Plans a Policy Switch on Massive Foreign Reserves," *Financial Times,* January 22, 2007.

150. Richard McGregor, "The Trillion Dollar Question: China is Grappling with How to Deploy Its Foreign Exchange Riches," *Financial Times,* September 25, 2006.

151. Barry Naughton, "Hunkering Down: The Wen Jiabao Administration and Macroeconomic Recontrol," *China Leadership Monitor* No.11, Summer, 2004.

152. Ibid.

153. Richard McGregor, "Beijing Closer to Managing Foreign Reserves More Actively," *Financial Times,* February 14, 2007; and Richard McGregor, "The Trillion Dollar Question: China is Grappling with How to Deploy Its Foreign Exchange Riches," *Financial Times,* September 25, 2006.

154. Richard McGregor, "Beijing Closer to Managing Foreign Reserves More Actively," *Financial Times,* February 14, 2007.

155. Xinhua News Agency, "China's trillion-dollar kitty is ready," *China Business,* October 2, 2007.

156. UNCTAD, *World Investment Report 2007,* p. 44.

157. Ibid.

CHAPTER IV DECISION-MAKING AND POLITICAL GIVE-AND-TAKE IN FDI

The Decision-Making Structure Related to Outward FDI

The Central Leadership has centralized control over the entire political economic system and its processes of policy making. The Central Leadership includes a) the paramount leader, i.e., the Party General Secretary; b) the Politburo Standing Committee in charge of Finance and Commerce and c) the Central Financial and Economic Affairs LSG (*zhongyang caijing lingdao xiaozu* 中央财经领导小组). These three constitute the top leadership taken as a whole with regard to the economic decision-making. The Party Secretary General and his inner leadership circle have the ultimate foreign economic policy decision-making power for China.[1]

Since the 16th Party Congress in November 2002, General Secretary Hu Jintao and Premier Wen Jiabao have made most of the important foreign and economic policy decisions together with the members of the Politburo Standing Committee, and their top aides in the party, government, and military. When Wen became Premier, he followed a pattern set down by Zhu Rongji in 1998. At that time, Zhu decreased the number of ministerial-level agencies from 50 to 29. Wen hopes to reduce the number of ministerial organizations even further to 21.[2] Under Wen's leadership, eight new or radically restructured commissions were set up. Of the eight new commissions, four represent radical departures from currently existing agencies. These four are the National Development and Reform Commission (NDRC); the State Banking Regulatory Commission; the State Assets Supervision and Administration Commission (SASAC); and the State Telecommunications Regulatory Commission.[3] The 17th Party Congress has selected a great number of leading economic personnel, though the scale of leadership change is less dramatic than that of the 2002 16th Party Congress, which had seen a sweeping turnover of leadership.[4]

The Financial and Economic Affairs LSG has a key role in the process of making decisions. It provides an opportunity for the central Party leadership in charge of financial and economic affairs to meet in person with the leading officials of various governmental institutions: the top bureaucrats and technocrats. Cross-ministerial jurisdiction or interest is often involved in decisions at this level. Therefore, the policy preferences and recommendations of the LSG have a great impact on the final outcomes, despite that the LSG is not in itself a decision-making body.[5]

For much of the 1980s then-Premier Zhao Ziyang headed the Central Financial and Economic Affairs LSG. In the early 1990s, its official head was Jiang Zemin, with Zhu Rongji as his deputy. In reality, however, Zhu was in overall charge of the financial and economic sector.[6] Starting from 2002 16th Party Congress, Hu Jintao has been the official head of the fourth generation leadership, with Wen Jiabao as his deputy in overall charge of the financial and economic sector. Zeng Peiyan and former vice premier Wu Yi have been identified as a member of the LSG.[7] Since the 2007 17th Party Congress, although Wen Jiabao still chairs the LSG, Li Keqiang, who is a new Politburo Standing Committee member as well as a new executive vice-premier, will become vice-head of the Finance and Economic LSG with overall responsibility for economic affairs. Zhang Dejiang is expected to take over control of foreign economic relations and responsibilities for commerce held by State Councilor Wu Yi during the previous administration. Wang Qishan will take over from Zeng Peiyan and be given supervisory authority over industry and industrial policy, including high technology and energy.[8]

The primary bureaucratic institution responsible for designing, studying and implementing the foreign investment, trade and economic policies under the guidelines established by the central leadership is the *MOFTEC or Ministry of Commerce*. The Ministry of Commerce's policies and measures are in line with the instructions given by the Party's General Secretary, Hu Jintao and the chief of State Council, Wen Jiabao. One of the most important changes in economic positions after the 17th Party Congress is the designation of Chen Deming as the new Minister of Commerce. Chen was executive vice-head of the NDRC since June 2006, and has replaced the former Minister of Commerce, Bo Xilai, who was sent to Chongqing to be Party secretary.[9]

Overall, the 17th Party Congress was careful to follow institutional rules, including those regarding retirement age and redistribution of seats. It also witnessed efforts by political forces to carefully balance differing interests in the Party and institutions.[10] Although the political process of the 17th Party Congress has shaped the economic leadership to some degree, some key posts are still unfilled, especially with large financial institutions. We will not know the full extent of the change in government until the upcoming 11th National People's Congress meets in March 2008, because of the inevitable adjusting to new positions and the running of new bureaucracies.

Aside from the appointing of successors in the central Party leadership made at the 17th Party Congress mentioned earlier, Luo Gan retired and was replaced by Zhou Yongkang, Minister of Public Security. In addition, Wu Guanzheng also retired and was succeeded by He Guoqiang, head of the Central Discipline Inspection Department. Both Zhou Yongkang and He Guoqiang, who are in charge of internal investigative mechanisms, are associates of Zeng Qinghong.[11] Also, Li Yuanchao, an ally of Hu Jintao, will become Director of the CCP Organization Department and will manage the process of nominating changes in personnel.[12] The new leadership seems generally balanced. No deep policy disputes or factional splits seem to be evident. What is more, several of the new reformers have been promoted. The institutional portfolios of the leadership seem appropriate as well. The Politburo Standing Committee seems to be constituted these days more by statutory position than personalities or political favoritism. This is clearly an indication of the increasing institutionalization of the party-state.[13]

The Decision-Making Process Concerning FDI

By all accounts, in the period before the 16th Party Congress, top level decision making was carried out according to the standard procedures of a communist-style system. The Standing Committee of the Politburo had the last word on every key issue, including decisions regarding overseas FDI. Although the State Council and the Premier had nominal control of most economic policymaking, the Standing Committee had strict powers of oversight and held the final power of decision-making. Then party secretary, Jiang Zemin, was, as is well known, expert at retaining power over the final say. Thus the Standing Committee was in tune with Jiang's desires. Jiang maintained his control in the party by giving way on issues that were of lesser political concern to him. Hence the Standing Committee did in fact have some power of its own, and did decide the outcome of some key policy decisions regarding the economy. Jiang, however, remained at the center of power.[14]

Under the present leadership, the process of making policy in China is more regularized than it has been for a long time. The government of Wen Jiabao systematically seeks and gathers advice from bureaucratic agencies within the government. Step by slow step, it considers and evaluates this advice and produces policy decisions. Without doubt the policymaking process is now filled with deliberation, and proceeds only by slow, small steps. All of this, of course, indicates a greater representation of bureaucratic interests, and that the government agencies themselves contain, as it were, the policy making process. The slow and steady nature of this process, however, might have the long term cost of stifling decisiveness and creativity.[15]

The representation of technocrats in the new State Council after the 17th Party Congress has declined, with a concomitant increase in the representation of politicians.[16] Several powerful groups of economic technocrats played important roles during the first administration of Wen Jiabao (2003-2008). The important roles played by technocrats occurred at the level of the State Council itself, and at the level of the economics ministries and commissions immediately below the State Council. As for the level of State Council, two of the vice-premiers, Zeng Peiyan and Wu Yi, were primarily economics bureaucrats. The influence of the technocrats in the State Council was reinforced by the fact that the executive vice-premier, Huang Ju, played a small role. Huang had been diagnosed with liver cancer shortly into his term, and suffered a reduction in influence. An equally experienced group of technocrats was at work at the ministerial level in the next tier down. This group was represented by the governor of the People's Bank of China, Zhou Xiaochuan, and by the industrial head of the NDRC, Ma Kai.[17]

On the other hand, the second term of the Hu-Wen administration is now packed with politicians. The current vice-premiers have all served as provincial Party secretaries in at least two provinces. Consequently, little room is left for technocrats. Li Keqiang has the sharpest profile of all the politicians in the new State Council. Zhang Dejiang is another politician with a poor record of performance in Guangdong (Zhang is also a patron of Jiang Zemin).[18] In short, China's top economic team is in the process of being formed. Although the process is incomplete, some clear patterns are emerging. Internal Communist Party politics not only pave the way for selecting economic bureaucrats, but also condition the process of job selections. The State Council is now oversupplied with politicians and undersupplied with technocrats.[19] Once again, politics drives economic personnel choices in China.[20]

China's "Going Global" Policy

While China's "Going Global" strategy was first brought about in the mid-1990s, Jiang Zemin promulgated the formal policy decision of "Going Global" at the turn of the last century. He then stated: "At this time of energetically expanding export, we shall, with proper steps and leadership, organize and support a group of enterprises with advantages and strengths to go abroad to make investments and set up factories there, particularly in Africa, Central Asia, the Middle East, Eastern Europe and South America."[21] The current leadership of Hu Jintao and Wen Jiabao have endorsed and promoted this policy. They have promulgated a series of policies and measures encouraging enterprises to go abroad so as to promote the overseas Chinese investments.

In particular, the responsibility for implementing and coordinating the policy rests with the Ministry of Commerce (MOFCOM). In this light, China's appearance on the global stage can be viewed as a result of MOFCOM's active execution of the policy of the central leadership. MOFCOM itself does not have the final authority to make major decisions on issues related to foreign investment. As MOFCOM states in its Statistic Yearbook, it acts in the spirit of the 16th Party's Congress and in the spirit of the Economic Affairs Conference of the Central Government in its efforts to speed up the pace of implementing the strategy of "Going Global."

The National Development and Reform Commission (NDRC) is another central Government Agency involved in the implementation of the policy. That is, China's outward FDI projects for any foreign investment of US $30 million or more must obtain approval from the NDRC. In addition, any foreign investment of US $200 million or more must obtain approval from the State Council.[22] One purpose of this approval system is to stop China's overseas companies from competing against each other. A series of regulations has increasingly formalized China's policy on outward FDI. Examples of such are:[23]

- 2004 *Interim Administrative Measures on the Approval of Overseas Investment Projects* (NDRC)

- 2004 *Circular on the Supportive Credit Policy on Key Overseas Investment Projects Encouraged by the State* (NDRC and the Export-Import Bank of China)
- 2005 *Provisions on Issues Concerning the Approval of Overseas Investment and Establishment of Enterprises* (MOFCOM)
- 2006 *Opinions on Encouraging and Regulating Chinese Enterprises to Carry Out Overseas Investments Cooperation* (MOFCOM and relevant departments). The "opinions" are the first guiding outline document which regulates and encourages the strategy of "Going Global" in an all-around way.[24]
- Various other regulations and circulars on foreign currency management, statistics, performance assessment and State-owned asset management.

The expansion of China's outward FDI appears to have been increased by the policy of "Going Global." This policy is the second most important force driving Chinese outward FDI today according to a recent survey conducted by the Asia Pacific Foundation of Canada and the China Council for the Promotion of International Trade.[25] At the same time, certain government regulations may have hampered the effectiveness of this policy. For example, a 2005 survey of Chinese companies found that most thought that the approval process was more complicated than necessary, and that the restrictions on the use of foreign exchange were too strict.[26] An important step in addressing these concerns is the July 1, 2006 decision by the State Administration of Foreign Exchange to put an end to quotas on the purchase of foreign exchange for overseas investment.[27]

Political Give-and-Take between Merchants and the State in FDI

Merchant-State dualism is also reflected in the aspect of political give and take. State gives up its political control in exchange for its economic gains, gains which in the long term still serve the state's political ends. One illustration of the dualistic role of merchants in China is the political give-and-take occurring in the global hunt for oil by large-scale state-owned enterprises. Domestically, the Chinese government gives these merchants an enormous role in the global economy in exchange for serving the state's larger political economic goals. Internationally, China gives up its political interests and prestige with some nations, in exchange for economic benefits from other nations.

China's Role in Africa:

China stands out as an attractive partner for Africa in four ways. First, China's growing demand increases prices for African products which are generally raw materials like oil, copper and zinc. Second, China demands no standards of political transparency or economic reforms when deals are done. Third, China pays no attention to their internal abuse of human rights when making deals. Fourth, it is a one-stop shop that offers investment, trade, skilled labor and military weapons, as well as diplomatic protection, which is given by its United Nations Security Council veto.[28]

- **Sudan.** In a move that helps China greatly, it has invested $4 billion in the Sudan, the country believed to hold the largest untapped reserves of oil in

Africa. The China National Petroleum Corp., for example, holds a 40% stake in Greater Nile Petroleum, which owns oil fields, a pipeline, a large refinery and a port. In 2005, China was responsible for buying more than half of the Sudan's oil exports. On the other hand, the Sudan was responsible for 6% of China's oil imports, which is equivalent to about 200,000 barrels a day.[29] Due to China's large oil interests in the Sudan, China has had to contend with claims that the Sudan has not made enough of an effort to halt the violence in Darfur. China contends that the issues with Darfur and the economic and energy cooperation and trade deals between China and the Sudan are two different issues. In fact, one Chinese official even criticized U.S. policy by asking: "The United States has unilateral sanctions against the Sudan—has it been useful?"[30]

- **Angola.** Angola's offshore wells have made it the second-largest oil producer in Africa. Through February 2006, it was responsible for 13% of all oil imports to China, which made it China's primary supplier. In order to get additional oil rights, China has pledged at least $3 billion in loans to Angola and has sent over engineers and trained workers to help to develop oilfields. China is now also the largest aid donor to Angola.[31]
- **Nigeria.** Nigeria is Africa's largest oil producer, but the country has only recently become a major supplier to China. In March 2006, the largest publicly held oil company in China, CNOOC, purchased a 45% share of the equity in the "OML130" marine petroleum exploitation license of Nigeria for US $2.268 billion. It has also purchased 35% of a Niger Delta exploration license for $60 million.[32]
- **South African** president, Thabo Mbeki, gave a pointed warning in 2006 that Africa should watch out not to fall into a "colonial relationship" with China. His comments matched Western concerns that China is not only taking over its position in Africa but also undermining the efforts to link trade and aid with good governance. Nonetheless, China and South Africa signed agreements in 2007 that covered the export of South African fruit to China, co-operation deals on energy and minerals, and economic pacts.[33]
- **Zambia.** China has invested $170 million in Zambian mines.[34] The relationship between the two countries, however, has been difficult since Michael Sata, a presidential candidate in Zambia's 2006 elections, accused China of the exploitation and maltreatment of local workers.[35]
- **Elsewhere in Africa.** CNOOC has shown activism in Equatorial Guinea, Chad and Gabon. It has also become a major weapons supplier and trading partner of Zimbabwe, a country run with unfettered corruption by the global outcast Robert Mugabe.[36]

As China reinforced overseas expansion with increasingly aggressive lending tactics, it has created a series of hidden debts in Africa. China has stated that it will not impose detailed conditions on its loans for governments in Africa and other developing areas.[37] The development ministries and international aid agencies in developed countries are becoming increasingly worried that China's push into Africa could undo the work they have done over the past decade in writing off official debts in Africa and in ensuring that aid money was well spent.[38]

China has made a lot of deals with countries such as the Sudan, where it won valuable oil concessions. This provides an illustration of China's achievement of its economic benefits at the expense of its prestige on the world stage. In the case of the Sudan, the Chinese government is turning a deaf ear to world protests arising from the Sudanese government's handling of the troubles in the Darfur region. The World Bank's human rights and environmental safeguards regulations will not allow Western countries to operate in the Sudan. According to the European Investment Bank, an EU-backed financial institution, they and other multilateral banks lose projects in Asia and Africa to Chinese banks simply because the Chinese "don't bother about social or human rights conditions."[39]

Chinese officials have argued that their country cannot immediately follow the same lending rules as rich donor countries. They claim that China is also helping African countries by building roads, railways, hospitals and schools in return for natural resources.[40] China's relinquishing its international image in return for its economic benefits indicates the state's attempt to balance its political and commercial interests in the international arena.

At the same time, China's global hunt for resources by the large-scale state-owned enterprises is also a case illustrating the above mentioned process of central decision making and the subsequent implementation of such a policy. The overall decision-making structure regarding policy involves three groups of actors: the central leadership, the major economic bureaucracies and institutions, and working-level officials in the economic affairs establishment.[41]

China's Role in Latin America:

The story is very similar in Latin America. Repressive, paranoid and regionally ambitious regimes that want to use their oil and ore reserves to buy weapons and tanks are increasingly seeking to partner with China. The Bush administration has even held discussions with China to try to halt the role China plays in training and advising military forces in the southern neighbors of the U.S. That China and South America have mutually beneficial needs and resources is causing problems for the United States, as the region has fabulous metal, energy and agricultural assets and is being run more and more by ideologues willing to find buyers who will not impose restrictions on them as the U.S. does. China is now the second largest trade partner in Latin America, ahead of Europe.[42]

- **Brazil.** This—the largest South American country—exports iron ore, soybeans, cotton, oil and sugar to China and has set up joint arrangements to develop satellites and aerospace equipment. In the short term, China has committed $10 billion in additional investments.[43]
- **Argentina.** China has committed to agreements worth $20 billion in investments over a period of 10 years. CNOOC is also developing an offshore oil field.[44]
- **Venezuela.** This country is the third most important foreign source of oil to the US, but the political and social disputes between the two countries have resulted in Hugo Chavez looking for alternative partners. His plans include doubling oil exports to China to 300,000 barrels a day—this represents about a fifth of the 1.5 million barrels that are sent to the U.S. a day. The Chinese are in

the process of buying stakes in several oil fields, which would make their output unavailable to the U.S.[45]

- **Ecuador.** This country is one of the top three oil producers for the West Coast of the United States. The Chinese have already bought one oil field and are in negotiations to buy more.[46]

China is clearly willing to risk a soured relationship with U.S. and other international governments by engaging with repressive Latin American regimes in return for their natural resources and economic benefits. This willingness of China to risk its reputation in Latin America is similar to its willingness to do so in Africa. Evidently, the current Chinese strategy is to place profits and economic investments above its reputation. Again, China's role in Latin America illustrates the government's give-and-take between its political and commercial interests at the international level.

China's Role in Middle East:

In the Middle East, China has found another repressive state, Saudi Arabia that wants to decrease its dependency on the U.S. As for Iran, the discussions of weapon sales and technology transfer with that country have made it the fastest rising Chinese partner in the region. For example, a Chinese company is expanding the subways in Tehran, another is establishing fiber-optic networks for the city, and still others are taking on auto and electronics factories. It will not be long for Iran to become the largest source of imported oil for China. This would mean that the economic and political interests of China and Iran would be in direct opposition to those of the U.S.[47]

- **Iran**. The Iranian Oil Minister's rare acknowledgement of its difficulty in financing oil projects highlighted the effects of financial sanctions on Iran, which is the second largest producer of oil in the Organization of the Petroleum Exporting Countries.[48] Western officials hope that the financial constraints against Iran will squeeze its oil industry, the backbone of the Iranian economy, and will result in domestic pressure for a change of policy. They also hope that the current regime will listen to international calls for its uranium enrichment program to be suspended. Despite these facts, China's CNOOC still signed a memorandum of understanding with the National Iranian Oil Company for the development of the North Pars gas field. It would bring $16 billion of Chinese investment into the country for the first part of the deal, according to reports from the Fars news agency.[49]

The case of Iran indicates that China's petroleum interests in the Middle East are making China willing to sacrifice its international reputation in return for commercial benefits in the region. However, in the case of Iran, China has been less willing to generate friction with the United States compared with its involvement in the Sudan. In the case of the Sudan, Beijing ignored the language of at least one UNSC resolution that called for an automatic trigger for sanctions if Khartoum failed to stop the atrocities in Darfur.[50] However, China had to balance several competing interests in the case of Iran. These issues include regional stability, energy and other economic ties, and China's relationship with the United States. For the United States, Iran's nuclear ambitions are a sensitive national security issue. Mostly because of pressure from Washington, in February 2006 Beijing voted as a member of the Board of Governors of the International Atomic Energy Agency to report the Iran nuclear issue to the UNSC. China also supported the July 31st UNSC resolution demanding an end to Iran's uranium enrichment program and threatening sanctions if it did not do so.[51] China's slightly different actions in Iran and Sudan show that China's demand for oil affects its international behavior. Although oil is undoubtedly playing an increasingly important role in Chinese foreign policy, Beijing's calculus of foreign policy objectives and economic benefits seems to vary from country to country.

Both Chinese roles in Africa, Latin America and Middle East illustrate the two dimensions of modern leadership's thinking:

First, China's willingness to give up political prestige for its own economic benefit in the global hunt for oil mentioned above indicates that the current generation of leaders is more pragmatic and economic in their thinking. This is more true considering the alternatives open to China. China can gain economic benefits without damaging its international reputation, such as it is doing in the case of Canada and of Central Asian Countries. China's leaders' pragmatic and economic thinking is further highlighted by the observation that in other, non-economic sectors, especially foreign affairs, Chinese leaders are more aware of international opinion.

Second, that China is relinquishing its world political standing for its economic benefit also shows that as continuous economic growth becomes its leaders' primary agenda, the centrality of economic development is dictating that China's foreign political and security policies serve its economic interests.

Government Support

Chinese FDI in Africa, Latin America and the Middle East all share similar features. That is, the Chinese government has facilitated PRC Companies' acquisitions for its offshore FDI. This view is widely held. Underlying reasons are obvious: because of China's economic boom, the state feels under an imperative to secure natural resources abroad; the acquisition of foreign assets is encouraged by China's surplus foreign exchange reserve; and there is a strong political desire to see Chinas biggest companies grow into full-fledged international firms through overseas expansion.

A perception exists that this will lead China to benefit from the advanced technology, management expertise and distribution networks of businesses that are acquired. However, observers have pointed out that Beijing does not have a single agency powerful enough to be an effective coordinator of overseas investment, an agency such as Japan's renowned Ministry of International Trade and Industry, which flourished in the 1960s and 1970s. Moreover, China's central government has not enacted any centralized plan along these lines, although at a strategic and policy level, it coordinates state-owned enterprises' (SOE's) overseas investment activities with regard to certain industries.[52]

As of now, government backing has mainly take the form of financial and political support:

Financial Support

The government of China provides Chinese companies with direct and indirect financial support. This support takes the form of loans made at below market rates, providing investment for infrastructure, and aid to the governments of states that produce natural resources. Such support by the Chinese government entails the use of the so-called "policy banks" to help the government secure foreign oil assets. These "policy banks" include the Export-Import Bank of China and the China Development Bank—both of which control lending directed by the state.[53] The NDRC and China Eximbank made an announcement in 2004 that the bank would give preferential terms on credit given to Chinese companies for "state-encouraged key overseas investment projects." These projects were to include those geared towards the development of natural resources.[54]

One of the chief beneficiaries of these preferential credit terms appears to be CNOOC. When the company made its US $18 billion offer for Unocal, CNOOC is said to have received US $7 billion by way of its wholly state-owned parent company, and from its ultimate owner, the government of China. The terms of this US $7 billion dollar loan are said to have been quite favorable to CNOOC: it would reportedly pay no interest on US $2.5 billion of the total amount and only 3.5% interest on the remaining amount. The total life of the loan is said to have been 30 years.[55] A second source of funds for Chinese companies is bridging loans provided by Chinese banks. For example, when CNOOC made its bid for UNOCAL, it was backed by a US $6 billion loan facility from a state-owned bank.[56]

As for indirect financial support, the Chinese government has provided a panoply of financial incentives to the governments of states which produce natural resources, in hopes that these states will provide China's oil companies with investment opportunities. Such financial incentives have taken the form of foreign aid, as well as the construction of basic infrastructure by Chinese firms. Such aid and infrastructure development projects further Beijing's larger foreign policy objectives of developing China's political and economic influence on the world stage and of creating Chinese companies that are competitive on a worldwide basis. In fact, many investments and acquisitions made by the national oil companies of China are directly connected to investments by other Chinese firms in non-oil infrastructure. This is the case in Africa in particular, since this continent, is in general, in dire need of basic infrastructure.[57]

A good example of this strategy is that a financing package given by China's Eximbank to Luanda convinced Angola to reject Royal Dutch-Shell's plan to sell its stake in Block 18 to the Indian firm ONGC Videsh. The stake was instead awarded to the Chinese firm Sinopec.[58] The financing package in question was a $2 billion line of credit extended to the Angolan government in 2004 by China's Eximbank. The line of credit had an extremely low interest rate of 1.5% over 14 years, and was to be used to finance infrastructure development projects by Chinese companies.[59] In fact, China Eximbank's Vice President Li Jun described this financial arrangement between the bank and the Angolan government as an exchange of "loans for oil."[60] Eximbank provided Angola with US $3 billion more in credit in 2006.[61]

What is more, grants and low- and no-interest loans for pharmaceuticals and health programs have been offered to oil producing states by the Chinese government. Such offers include one made by Wu Bangguo to Nigeria in November, 2004[62] and one by Hu Jintao to Kenya in April 2006.[63]

Political Support

Part of the reason for the surge in overseas Chinese FDI has been political support by the Chinese government. In March of 2006, Chinese Primer Wen Jiabao stated: "We will support qualified enterprises in going global, making overseas investments, conducting international business in conformity with general international practices, and establishing processing centers, marketing and service networks, and R&D centers in other countries."[64]

This is particularly true regarding oil investments. The Chinese government supports Chinese oil companies in several ways: 1) through summit meetings between Chinese leaders and their counterparts in oil producing states, 2) through the involvement of China's leaders' negotiations for some projects and 3) through leveraging China's membership in international organizations, such as the WTO and UNSC.[65] China conveys to oil exporting countries the importance Beijing places on their relationship by means of trips abroad by Chinese leaders and invitations to their foreign counterparts to visit Beijing. Energy cooperation agreements are often entered into during such meetings and provide both governments with a "deliverable" impression. Certain Chinese leaders sometimes directly participate in negotiations for specific mergers and acquisitions. This usually happens when the countries involved have large oil reserves that are felt by the Chinese to be of strategic significance. Examples of such countries are Kazakhstan, Russia, and Iran.[66]

The success of CNPC's bid for PetroKazakhstan is attributed by the Chinese media to the personal involvement of Hu Jintao in the negotiations, as well as to the generally good relations between Beijing and Astana.[67]

In 2003, the Chairman of the Chinese Standing Committee of the National People's Congress, Wu Bangguo, attended the Asian Forum for Peace Conference in the Philippines. He proposed at that forum multilateral exploration of the oil and gas fields in the South China Sea. This agreement broke the deadlock concerning an energy exploration in the South China Sea, since ownership of this area had been under dispute. CNOOC and the Philippine National Petroleum Exploration Company signed a memorandum of intent to explore jointly potential oil and gas resources in the South China Sea, a mere three months after Wu Bangguo's proposal. This memorandum was signed on the Island of Bali by the Chinese Premier Wen Jiabao and the leaders of the ten countries of the Association of Southeast Asian Nations.[68]

Notes

1. Nathan and Gilley, 2003, p. 40, 41, 47,

2. Barry Naughton, "The Emergence of Wen Jiabao," *China Leadership Monitor,* No. 6, Spring, 2006, p. 42.

3. Ibid., p. 42-45.

4. Alice Miller, "China's New Party Leadership," *China Leadership Monitor,* No. 23, Winter, 2008, p. 1.

5. Lu Ning, 2001, p. 47.

6. Ibid.

7. H. Lyman Miller, "Party Politburo Processes under Hu Jintao," *China Leadership Monitor,* No. 11, Summer, 2004, p. 12.

8. Barry Naughton, "China's Economic Leadership after the 17th Party Congress," *China Leadership Monitor,* No. 23, Winter, 2008, p. 3.

9. Ibid., p. 7-10.

10. Joseph Fewsmith, "The 17th Party Congress: Informal Politics and Formal Institutions," *China Leadership Monitor,* No. 23, Winter, 2008, p. 10.

11. Ibid., p. 6.

12. Shanbaugh, October 30, 2007.

13. Ibid.

14. Barry Naughton, "Economic Policy after the 16th Party Congress," *China Leadership Monitor,* No. 5, Winter, 2003, p. 40.

15. Naughton, No. 15, Summer, 2005, p. 8.

16. Naughton, No. 23, Winter, 2008, p. 3.

17. This section summarized Naughton, No. 23, Winter, 2008, p. 3-5.

18. Naughton, No. 23, Winter, 2008, p. 6.

19. Ibid., p. 10.

20. Ibid., p. 5.

21. Wang Hui, "Implementing Vigorously the Opening Strategy of 'Going Global'," *Almanac of China's Foreign Economic Relations and Trade 2001,* China's Ministry of Foreign Trade and Economic Cooperation (MOFTEC), p. 94. Wang Hui was Director General of Department of Foreign Trade, MOFTEC.

22. Erica Downs, "The Brookings Foreign Policy Studies Energy Security Series: China," The Brookings Institution, December 2006, p. 40.

23. The following regulations are referred to UNCTAD, *World Investment Report 2006,* p. 210.

24. Wu Xilin, "Implementation of the Strategy of 'Going Global' in China in 2006," *China Commerce Yearbook 2007,* Chinese Ministry of Commerce, p. 419. Wu Xilin is Director General of the Department of Foreign Economic Cooperation, Ministry of Commerce in China.

25. Asia Pacific Foundation of Canada, 2005.

26. Yao Yang and Yin He, "Chinese Outward Investing Firms: A Study for FIAS/IFC/MIGA," Beijing: China Center for Economic Research, Peking University, 2005.

27. See MOFCOM website: www.mofcom.gov.cn/aarticle/b/bf/200605/20060502256191.html.

28. Jon D. Markman, "How China is Winning the Oil Race," MSN Money at http://moneycentral.msn.com, April 26, 2006.

29. Ibid.

30. Shai Oster, "Beijing Hosts Big Africa Summit as West Watches," *The Wall Street Journal,* October 25, 2006.

31. Jon D. Markman, "How China is Winning the Oil Race," MSN Money at http://moneycentral.msn.com, April 26, 2006; and Andrew Yeh, "China Ventures on Rocky Roads to Trade with Africa," *Financial Times,* June 20, 2006.

32. Markman, April 26, 2006.

33. Alec Russell, "Hu and Mbeki Forge Ahead with Closer Ties," *Financial Times,* February 7, 2007.

34. Michael Peel and Rebecca Bream, "Bars to a Copper Bonanza," *Financial Times,* December 22, 2006.

35. Russell, February 7, 2007.

36. Yeh, June 20, 2006; and Markman, April 26, 2006.

37. Alan Beattie and Eoin Callan, "Chinese Lending Creating New Wave of Hidden Debt in Africa, IMF Says," *Financial Times,* December 8, 2006.

38. Shai Oster, "China is Seeking a Broader Role in Africa," *The Wall Street Journal,* October 24, 2006.

39. Alan Beattie and Eoin Callan, "Chinese Lending Creating New Wave of Hidden Debt in Africa, IMF Says," *Financial Times,* December 8, 2006; and Oster, October 24, 2006.

40. Ibid.

41. Lu Ning, 2001, p. 40.

42. Markman, April 26, 2006.

43. Ibid.

44. Ibid.

45. Andy Webb-Vidal, "Chavez on Oil Export Mission in China," *Financial Times,* August 24, 2006.

46. Markman, April 26, 2006.

47. Ibid.

48. Najmeh Bozorgmehr and Roula Khalaf, "Iran Admits Sanctions Hurting Oil Investment," *Financial Times,* December 21, 2006.

49. Ibid.

50. Downs, December 2006, p. 50.

51. Ibid., p. 50-51.

52. "The Challenges Facing Outbound Chinese M&A: PRO Companies' Acquisition Campaigns Share Some Generic Features—Some of These Features have Facilitated, While Others have Militate Against, Offshore Acquisitions," *International Financial Law Review,* Vol. 24, Issue 12, December 2005.

53. Downs, December 2006, p. 41.

54. National Development and Reform Commission and China Export Import Bank, "Notice on the Policy of Giving Credit Support to the State Encouraged Key Overseas Investment Projects (Guanyu dui guojia gulide jingwai touzi zhongdian xiangmu jiyu xinguo zhichi zhengce tongzhi," October 27, 2004 at www. Ndrc.goc.cn.wzly/jwtz/jwtzzn/t20050714_35633.htm; and Wang Xiaobing, Cao Haili, He Yuxin, Zhang Fan and Huang Shan, "The Path to 'going global' (zouchuqu zhi dao)," *Caijing,* No. 142, September 19, 2005.

55. Kate Linebaugh, "How Favorable is Oil Bid's Financing?" *Wall Street Journal,* June 30, 2005; and "State Rivals Stretch Majors in Bidding Wars," *Petroleum Intelligence Weekly,* July 4, 2005.

56. *International Financial Law Review,* December 2005.

57. Downs, December 2006, p. 41-42.

58. "China Edges Out India for Angolan Prize After Political Move by State Sonangol," *International Oil Daily,* October 22, 2004; "Chinese Victory Parade for PetroKazakhstan Win," *Indian Express,* August 24, 2005; and "China and Angola Sign a US $2 Billion Oil Repayment Agreement (ZhongAn qian 20 yi Mei yuan shiyou huanhuo," *Wen Hui Bao,* October 19, 2004.

59. "China in Africa Digest 8-24 January," *BBC Monitoring Africa—Political,* January 31, 2005; "China Supplies Funds with Fewer Conditions," *Financial Times,* November 14, 2005.

60. Li Jun, "China Export Import Bank: Strengthen Policy-oriented Financial Work, Support the Development of Overseas Contracted Projects (Zhongguo jinchukou yinhang: jiachang zhengcexing jinrong fuwu, zhichi chengbao gongcheng fazhang," China International Contractor's Association (Zhongguo duiwai chengbao gongcheng shanghui), October 9, 2005.

61. Thomas Pearlman, "China Agrees to Extend Extra US $2 billion in Oil-Backed Loan for Angola," *Global Insight Daily Analysis,* June 23, 2006; and "Chronology-Chinese-African Deals," *Reuters,* May 23, 2006.

62. "Nigeria and China to Develop Lake Chad Basin Blocks," *World Markets Analysis,* November 12, 2004.

63. Vahid Oloro, "China to Prospect for Oil," *All Africa,* May 1, 2006.

64. Stand & Poor's Ratings Direct, "Behind the Chinese M&A Surge," *Business Week,* July 26, 2006.

65. Downs, December 2006, p. 42.

66. Ibid.

67. He Qing and Yang Juan, "Background to the 'Supplementary Agreement': CNOOC tries to Strengthen State Tactics (Buchong xieyi de beihou:Zhonghaiyou qianghua guojia celue," *21st Century Economic Herald (21 shiji daobao),* December 26, 2005.

68. Tang Weibin, "China's Petroleum Security and Energy Diplomacy (Zhongguo shiyou anquan he nengyuan waijiao)," *Journal of China Foreign Affairs University (Zhongguo waijiao xueyuan xuebao),* No. 76, June 2004, p. 77.

CASE STUDY ONE
THE IRON AND STEEL INDUSTRY

Introduction:

There has been a tendency in Europe for iron and steel enterprises to merge. A similar tendency is also occurring in America and Northeast Asia. Because of these mergers and acquisitions, the iron and steel enterprises are more productive, and can react in a coordinated fashion to market changes resulting from supply and demand. Between 2003 and 2004, there were many successful mergers in European iron and steel enterprises. For example, the world's number one iron and steel giant, Mittal steel, purchased Arcelor, the world's second largest iron and steel enterprise.

The world's large iron and steel companies usually grow and develop through domestic and overseas transnational annexation. The Japanese Nippon Steel Corporation is the result of the merger of two iron and steel companies, Yawata and Fuji, and has become one of world's most dominant iron and steel corporations. British Steel Corporation was formed by the conglomeration of 14 iron and steel plants by the English government in 1967. This corporation, because of its continuous worldwide growth, increased its production and market share. Examples such as these prove that domestic industrial reorganization and structural adjustment, along with foreign mergers and acquisitions, is an effective, economical, and fast way to develop a country's iron and steel enterprises.

In light of the above experiences and tendencies of the world's large iron and steel companies, the Chinese government under Wen Jiabao has formulated its industrial policies for developing the iron and steel industry. Specifically, on July 20, 2005 the National Development and Reform Commission (NDRC) posted their Steel Industry Development Policy.[1] The import of this document is to severely limit the creation of new steel mills; to concentrate production in a smaller number of more efficient and larger plants; to benchmark industry progress by the use of technical standards; and to reach targets concerning energy and water conservation. This document also has a regional aspect to it with new construction concentrated in southern coastal areas with deepwater ports and access to global ore and energy resources, where there is also strong demand.[2] Most of these intentions are in line with the current leadership's overall political and economical thinking and have been effectively enforced since 2005. These correlations between central decision-making and industrial enforcement will be explored in detail in the following sections concerning the Chinese iron and steel industrial enterprises.

NDRC's Development Policy for the Steel Industry

These new guidelines recognize the role of the iron and steel industry as a pillar and fundamental industry in the national economy. They also intend to develop this segment to satisfy domestic demand, as well as to make China a global iron and steel producer. The first chapter of the NDRC's guidelines elaborates the above objective of the policy in six articles. By an increase in the quality of products, most of the requirements of crucial sectors of the national economy would be fulfilled. These sectors include construction, machinery, petrochemical, automobile, household appliances, shipbuilding, transportation, railroad, and the military industry. According to the guidelines, mergers and acquisitions would pave the way for forming big conglomerates by 2010. The top 10 domestic iron and steel enterprises would account for over 50 percent of production and over 70 percent by 2020.[3] Some of the relevant clauses of these guidelines regarding consolidation, restructuring, quality improvement and investment will be further illustrated in the specific cases which follow.

Internal Structural Adjustment in Chinese Iron and Steel Enterprises:

Chinese iron and steel enterprises recently faced an internal structural adjustment, i.e. the formation of major industrial groups through domestic combination and reorganization, which in turn can build a solid foundation for transnational acquisition. The outcome of this structural adjustment was the Chinese government's decision to create the Baoshan Steel Corporation, the Anshan Iron and Steel Company, the Capital Steel Corporation, and the Wuhan Steel Corporation, which now form the four (4) largest iron and steel enterprise groups. These four were formed by the reorganization of mid- and small-scale enterprises on the basis of geographical or product proximity. These four companies lead Chinese foreign investment in the iron and steel sector.

This internal combination and reorganization to form large iron and steel conglomerates is in keeping with the objective of the NDRC Steel Industry Policy. According to Article 20, chapter V, there are to be two 30-million-ton steel enterprises and several 10-million-ton steel enterprises which would be internationally competitive enterprises by 2010.[4] This NDRC industrial objective is in keeping with Wen-Zhu's agenda to invigorate key state enterprises in sectors considered to have important national security implications, such as the iron and steel industry.

The reorganization of the Chinese iron and steel enterprises follows the principle to assimilate horizontally allied iron and steel companies and to incorporate vertically the production of raw materials and the processing of steel and iron products. The principle also includes limiting the diversification of operations and management, unless it is in an appropriate context and condition.

The Chinese iron and steel industry's export distribution shows the following pattern. a) With regard to America and Western Europe, China mainly exports thick steel plate, since China has a competitive advantage in the relevant technology. In addition, the quality of such thick steel plate is high as is local demand for the product. In particular, between 1995 and 1999, Anshan Iron and Steel Company sold 260,000 tons per year of thick steel plate to the U.S., Canada, and Belgium.[5] b) With regard to Japan, China mainly exports ordinary steel products. Japan produces mostly high quality steel products, but consumes mostly ordinary steel products. This demand for ordinary steel is filled from Chinese exports. c) As for Southeast Asia and the Middle East, they remain the last untapped major markets for China's iron and steel industries. Southeast Asia requires a great deal of iron and steel for its economy, but its local industry cannot meet this demand. Thus, Southeast Asia offers an ideal investment opportunity for Chinese iron and steel companies. In particular, the potential market for Chinese steel related investment in Malaysia and Indonesia is huge. In fact, some experts predict that these two countries will eventually become large centers of steel production for that region.

The Three Stages of the Construction of the Baoshan Steel Corporation:

The construction of the Shanghai Baoshan Steel Group Corporation (referred to below as Baosteel) moved China's large-scale iron and steel enterprise from the area of the mines to the area of the markets, thus bringing it closer to both domestic and foreign resources, including ore and coal. Before Baosteel, China's large-scale iron and steel enterprises were all built near mines, with the intention of "developing the mining industry," in accordance with the Chinese proverb "One does not make a meal without the rice". The location of Baosteel in Shanghai brings the iron and steel enterprise to the market, and makes full use of Shanghai, an industrial city rich in human and technological resources. This changed the tradition of locating large-scale iron and steel enterprises inland away from the coast.

The three-stage construction of Baosteel cost upwards of US $10 billion. The cost of the first two stages entailed about 1/9 of the total national investment in the metal industries. On December 20, 2000, the three stages of Baosteel's construction were completed. From December 23, 1978 up to 2000, Baosteel had produced 11 million tons of steel, and 7.536 million tons of steel products per year. The first stage of the construction of Baosteel was started on December 23, 1978 and completed on September 15, 1985 with an investment of US $1.6 billion. For the next 15 years, Baosteel replaced nearly 30% of the imported steel used for automobiles, the petroleum industry, electrical appliances, and ships. Baosteel now sells in 27 countries and produces income of US $3.615 billion. Baosteel also pays off nearly US $1.25 billion on its government loans including principal and interest. The second stage of the construction of Baosteel started in January 1986 and was completed in April 1992 with an investment of US $2.15 billion. During this stage, Baosteel introduced the hot rolling line and technology to hot roll coils, sheets and plates. The third stage of the construction of Baosteel began on December 23, 1993. This stage introduced the competitive system, and the notion of a corporation as a legal entity. The construction time for this stage was 1/3 of that of the first and second stages.[6]

The main products of this project are used for urgently needed high-quality galvanized sheets for passenger vehicles, household electrical appliances, silicon steel plates for the manufacture of electrical machinery, and tinplate for food and drink containers and cans. This new production by Baosteel eliminated the need for importing these products. The completion of the project coincided with a change in Baosteel's product structure from the construction of steel plate for manufacturing purposes to the construction of steel for passenger vehicles and electrical appliances. Baosteel's quality up-grade for its steel products reflects the Chinese government's overall strategic objective. That is, by up-grading quality, most of the requirements of the crucial sectors of the national economy would be fulfilled. This technology up-grade also reflects Article 34, chapter VIII of the guidelines, which reads "(there should be a) promotion of steel in various new application areas including the use of high strength, corrosion proof steel. High strength plate and sheet, H-section and reinforcement steel with high strength etc. should be given active encouragement."[7] As a result of Baosteel's product up-grades, other industries related to Baosteel production, like the rubber and coal industries, also strengthened their own competitive advantage by their association with Baosteel. They did so by introducing and independently developing new technology. In spite of these advances, Baosteel's core competitive advantage is still less than that of the Japanese Nippon Steel Corporation and the Korean POSCO, which are first-class multinational corporations.

Diversification v. Specialization:

Several years ago, the Baoshan Steel Corporation's strategic target was "to develop into a major industrial group, primarily focusing on the steel and iron industry, while simultaneously engaging in trade, investment and finance." But in June 2003, Baosteel determined a new overall strategic target, which was to "become principally a steel corporation, first-class and multinational, with only tangential interests in those other industries."[8] According to Baosteel insiders, minor branches of the corporation and those that do not rank among the top in the nation, are to be eliminated. This reflects the current leadership's reformist philosophy to restructure large corporations under state's control, to split off or discard non-core businesses, and to build strong, competitive corporations around a few core businesses.[9]

After a business develops past a certain stage, the enterprise must continue to maintain profits. This inevitably makes the enterprise choose between two roads, specialization or diversification. There are quite a few successful large enterprises that engage in diversification to maintain their development, like G.E. Diversification itself is not wrong; rather the question is how to diversify effectively. Before diversification can occur, the chief product of the enterprise must have achieved absolute superiority. This is especially true when an enterprise is to diversify into non-related industries. After a Chinese enterprise reaches a certain stage in its development, its motivation for diversification results from its insufficient knowledge of the cycle of industrial development and its eager desire to seek a richer profit domain. Nevertheless, Baosteel is not enticed to diversify into non-related industries. It is quite content concentrating on the development of steel for vehicles and electrical appliances; what diversification it has engaged in is confined to closely related industries, such as the mining of iron ore. Baosteel has decided to concentrate its efforts in the production of high-end iron and steel, as an alternative way to diversify.

The Layout of the Industrial Strategy of Baosteel:

Baosteel, the sixth largest steel producer in the world, recently invested in the stock of Handan steel in order to become its biggest shareholder. This is part of Baosteel's strategic plan, as well as a fulfillment of the government's industrial policy. According to Hebei Province's plan, the province will form Tangshan and Handan steel in the northern and southern parts of the province respectively. These two enterprises are expected to produce 10 thousand tons of steel per year. In 2006, the Handan steel group established a strategic alliance with two of Hebei's large privately owned iron and steel enterprises—the Hebei Wenfeng and Delong iron and steel companies. Therefore, since Baosteel already controls Handan steel, it can now easily control the iron and steel production of Hebei province. This is in keeping with the provisions of Article 20, chapter V of the NDRC's guidelines that state "large companies should be publicly listed."[10] These provisions also require all large firms to convert to joint stock companies; to seek listing on the stock exchanges; and to accept ownership stakes from diverse parties, specifically including private Chinese firms (*baokuo minying ziben zainei).*[11] These NDRC requirements are also consistent with Wen Jiabao and Zhu Rongji's overall philosophy of privatizing state-owned enterprises by ordering them to issue stock.

Before Baosteel acquired Handan steel, Baosteel and Maanshan steel, two major industries in the eastern part of China, officially signed a strategic alliance. This alliance is regarded as a major restructuring of the iron and steel industry in the East China area, and a significant realization of China's policy for the development of the iron and steel industry. This is consistent with the NDRC guideline that "smaller inefficient producers in East China should merge with large enterprises."[12] The dispersed nature of the Chinese steel industry and its uneven distribution throughout the country are the main reasons for excessive investments in the iron and steel industry, as well as the cause for disorderly competition in the industry. Therefore, China's industrial policy clearly requires a large-scale concentration and amalgamation of domestic iron and steel and a restructuring of the industry. Against this backdrop, Baosteel and Maanshan steel made a decision to form an alliance. Thus, there is also a high likelihood that Baosteel will purchase Maanshan steel in the near future.

Four months after forming its strategic alliance with Baosteel, Maanshan steel spent US $44 million to purchase Hefei steel and iron, the largest state-owned enterprise in Anhui province. The resulting Maanshan-Hefei steel and iron limited liability company has capital of US $63 million, 71% of which is held by Maanshan.[13] Shanghai's Baosteel is clearly a beneficiary of this transaction through its valuable alliance with Maanshan. Baosteel will completely control the market in Anhui province, further consolidating its leading position in Eastern China. The acquisition of Hefei steel by Maanshan steel is persistent with specific clauses in the NDRC guidelines that promote consolidation within the industry and the elimination of the smaller enterprises by enhancing the investment criteria. These clauses state that "the enterprises must own 40 percent or more of the total equity, leaving not more than 60 percent of borrowed capital for new investment (Article 23, chapter VI)."[14] They also state that "for inter-regional investment, the enterprise must reach a production level of either 5 million tons of ordinary steel or 0.5 million tons of special steel in the previous year."[15] At the same time, the guidelines also strictly limit the creation of new steel mills: "no new integrated steel, iron and rolling mills should be constructed (chapter III)."[16] A strong message here is that China does not need capacity expansion of iron and steel production, therefore it can limit investment in that industry.

In March 2006, when Mittal Steel had close contact with Xinjiang Bayi iron and steel, Baosteel, in spite of the great geographical distance, quickly acquired the Bayi iron and steel group, the largest such enterprise in the Xinjiang Autonomous Region. Since it is Xinjiang's largest iron and steel enterprise, Bayi steel is rich in coal. Baosteel, by fully utilizing its technology, personnel, management and marketing, may use Bayi steel's geographic position to expand to markets in Xinjiang, and even to other markets in northwest China.

With its strategic alliances with Maanshan, Bayi, and Handan steel, Baosteel's strategic layout becomes clearer by the day. First, Baosteel's consolidation reflects a clear-cut vision in the new policy in favor of the formation of large units by means of consolidation, merger and restructuring. This vision is consistent with Wen Jiabao and Zhu Rongji's overall philosophy of reforming state-owned enterprises. This is a philosophy of "grasping the large and letting go of the small"—i.e., of selling off small SOEs that do not occupy leading positions in their sectors, while pouring new money into the sector front runners.[17] Second, from a longer term perspective, Baosteel's industrial layout and alliances are consistent with China's overall plan for the direction of the iron and steel industry. That is, mergers and acquisitions will pave the way for the formation of large conglomerates. As noted earlier (see page 3), two 30-million-ton steel enterprises and several 10-million-ton internationally competitive enterprises are to be set up by 2010 (Article 20, chapter V).[18] This, in turn, is in line with the leadership's vision of economic growth based on large state-owned conglomerates.

Foreign Steel Enterprises Enter the Chinese Iron and Steel Industry:

New guidelines restrict foreigners to less than a majority stake in domestic iron and steel enterprises. Article 23, chapter VI of the NDRC guidelines states that "overseas investors must possess independent technology and steel production of 10 million tons or more of ordinary steel or 1 million tons of special steel production in the previous year. No controlling share status would be granted to foreign investors."[19] Once again, the implication is that China does not need large investments in its iron and steel industry for the expansion of capacity, but rather for the up-grade of technology.

What is more, this provision of the NDRC guidelines immediately derailed pending acquisitions by multinational firms in China's steel industry. The multinationals Arcelor and Mittal were each seeking controlling stakes in Shanghai-listed steel firms, as well as in the steel firms Hualin and Laiwu in the provinces of Hunan and Shandong, respectively.[20] These plans came to naught because of the new regulations. Mittal steel did not obtain the consent of the Chinese government to become a majority shareholder in Hualin, and thus was compelled to become the second largest stockholder. As a result, as of September 2005, the Hualin iron and steel group held 37. 673% of its own shares as a state-owned shareholder; while the world's biggest iron and steel group, Mittal steel, held 36. 673% of Hualin's foreign capital shares.[21] Similarly, in February 2006, the world's second largest iron and steel Arcelor purchased a minority 38. 41% share of Laiwu steel's stock, the eleventh largest steel producer in China, and thereby entered Shandong province's steel and iron industry.[22] Nevertheless, foreign companies have continued to invest in the Chinese iron and steel industry. For example, the Russian company, SeverStal, has expressed its intention to invest in Tong steel in Jilin province, and Mittal has engaged in negotiations to purchase the Baotou and Kunming steel factories.[23] Since Chinese policy does not allow foreign companies to hold a majority stake in domestic iron and steel enterprises, further inflows of foreign investment into the Chinese iron and steel industry for the purpose of up-grading technology remains uncertain.

Chronology of Baosteel's Overseas FDI:

On April 23, 2004, Baosteel and the Australian Rio Tinto Group formed a joint venture, the Baoruiji mining company. Baoruiji was immediately ready to go into production. Baosteel holds 46 % of the stock in the joint venture, while the Rio Tinto Group holds 54 %. In the coming 20 years of this joint operation, Baoruiji is expected to supply 200 million tons of high quality iron ore to the Baoshan Steel Corporation. The Rio Tinto Group is one of the three largest global ore suppliers. Its subsidiary, the Hamersley Iron company, is one of Baosteel's long-term suppliers. Baosteel is currently aiming to produce high-quality steel, so 95 % of its iron ore is imported.[24] This is because the general quality of domestic iron ore is not suitable for the production of high-quality steel. The guarantee of a long-term, stable, high quality supply of imported iron ore has thus become Baosteel's lifeline.

On May 25, 2004, Baosteel also pooled capital with the Brazilian CVRD Corporation to set up the Baohuarui mining industry company. The CVRD Corporation is Brazil's largest producer and exporter of iron ore, and also one of the world's most diversified mining companies. In addition, it is one of the world's Top 500 corporations. China's resource strategy in South America takes into consideration its favorable geopolitical conditions as well as its abundance of resources. South America is a key to China's strategy of the development of mineral resources. South America is a large area rich in resources with a small population. South America's economy is also complementary to China's economy. For example, Venezuela and Brazil are among the world's greatest producers of oil, iron ore, and agricultural products, all of which are desperately needed by China. On the other hand, China's mechanical and electrical products, its light industrial products, and its textile products, have a strong competitive advantage over those same products produced in Venezuela and Brazil. China's fast economic development requires not only South America's minerals, petroleum, iron ore, and non-ferrous metal, but also its grain, meat, and milk products. At present, South American countries like Brazil, Venezuela, Argentina, Chile, and Peru all consider China a good market for their exports because of China's rapid economic growth. These exports to China also help the domestic economic growth of the South American countries.[25]

Baosteel's overseas investments in the iron ore industry precisely reflect the government's efforts as prescribed in the NDRC guidelines, Article 28, chapter VII: "the state should encourage large-scale enterprises to develop iron ore resources." It is also in keeping with the dictates of Article 30, chapter VII: "support should be given to large enterprises to set up overseas production bases of iron ore, chrome ore, manganese ore, nickel ore, scrap and coking coal."[26]

Most of Japan's steel products leave the country because of its export of containers, the production of which is one of Japan's strongest industries. Most of Germany's steel products leave the country through the export of automobiles, production of which is one of Germany's largest industries. The export of Chinese steel has experienced something similar, in that at one time it was mostly due to the export of one specific steel product, in this case, a pipeline. In 1998, China exported a significant amount of steel to the Sudan. The reason for this was that the China Petroleum and Natural Gas Corporation had invested in a Sudanese petroleum project, which made use of steel from the Baoshan and Wuhan steel corporations for a pipeline.

Baosteel's Distribution of Steel Products in South China:

There is a large presence of international enterprises in China's iron and steel markets because of these enterprises' investments in related products. For example, on July 26, 2001, China announced a project for the "transportation of natural gas from the west to the east". This resulted in bids from seven enterprises for the pipeline steel, including bids from Baosteel and several Korean and Japanese corporations. Baosteel was the only domestic company participating in the bidding process. Japanese enterprises led by Nippon Steel Corporation bid US $429 per ton, Baosteel bid US $395 per ton, while the South Korean company, POSCO, bid the low price US $228 per ton, thereby becoming the successful bidder.[27] Moreover, the Japanese company, Nippon Steel Corporation, as well as others successfully bid on the Three Gorges Dam Project. Learning from these examples, Baosteel also started to prepare its strategic investment in steel related products.

On December 3, 2004, Baosteel made its first investment in a steel related industry, namely Foshan Baosteel Stainless Steel Processing & Delivering Company, a large project in the city of Foshan Shunde in Guangdong province. The resulting company has become a center for the production of cutting instruments. At present, this company is the largest center of production of stainless steel in China.[28] This project's completion symbolizes the three principal parts of Baosteel's South China strategy, i.e., the production of carbon steel, special purpose steel, and stainless steel.

On the one hand, Baosteel's strategy in high-end steel products reflects the government's attempts to provide a clear road map for the industry in the coming years by benchmarking industry standards with technological parameters. On the other hand, Baosteel's South China strategy is in line with the NDRC provision that "South Central and South Western China, since they are abundant in water resources, should encourage large integrated steel mills to put up facilities near their ports."[29] This provision also reflects the current leadership's economic and environmental consciousness.

Aside from reasons of governmental policy, Baosteel's rapid appearance in South China was at least in part due to the city of Guangzhou's desire to become the "Oriental Detroit." As far as Baosteel is concerned, Guangzhou represents a foothold in the South China automobile manufacturing industry. At the present time, nearly all of Guangdong's automobile manufacturing enterprises use steel produced by Baoshan. The presence of the Foshan Baosteel Stainless Steel Processing & Delivering Company helps solidify Baosteel's status in this Eastern "Detroit", thereby consolidating its leading position in the domestic steel market.

In addition, Baosteel also considered the city of Zhanjiang in the province of Guangdong for the formation of the Zhanjiang-Baoshan Steel Corporation, whose scale was planned to be larger than that of the Shanghai Baosteel corporation. Moreover, Zhanjiang-Baoshan steel was intended for the manufacture of fine steel, especially steel used for the manufacture of automobiles, as well as for other specialized products.[30] With the arrival of five Japanese Toyota automobile parts manufacturing businesses in Shunde, a Guangzhou-centered eastern automobile production complex is emerging in the Zhujiang Delta. Other cities in this industrial zone include Nansha, Huadu, Foshan Shunde, Nanhai, as well as Huizhou, Zhongshan, and Zhanjiang. Baoshan-Zhanjiang Steel Corporation is planned to be the largest enterprise in this Zhujiang Delta, as well as one of Guangdong's 50 strongest enterprises. This move is in line with the government's intention to develop this segment of the Chinese steel industry so that it is internationally competitive and satisfies domestic demand. It is also in keeping with the government's desire to encourage industrial growth in quantity, quality and variety.

The Beijing Capital Iron and Steel Group:

Since the recent reforms and changes in policy in China, the Beijing Capital Iron and Steel Group (also known as the Shougang Group) has developed into a transnational conglomerate with operations in steel and iron, machinery, electricity, the mining industry, the ship building industry, construction, finance and so on, 18 industries in all. It consists of more than 100 large and middle scale enterprises, spreading over 11 provinces, cities, and autonomous regions. It is involved in more than 70 joint ventures, and more than 70 scientific and technological research institutes. It has invested in a total of 28 overseas enterprises in 13 countries in an area covering the Americas, Europe, Southeast Asia, the Middle East and the Commonwealth of Independent States (CIS), as well as others.[31] See Table 5.1 for details.

Table 5.1 - Capital Iron and Steel's FDI in Geographical Distribution

	Hong Kong	Southeast Asia	The U.S.	Latin America	Western Europe	Eastern Europe	Total
Number	10	5	3	8	1	1	28
Share (%)	36	18	11	29	3	3	100

Source: *The Capital Iron and Steel Statistical Yearbook 2000.*

The Capital Iron and Steel Group introduced into China advanced steel rolling and casting technology by purchasing 70% of the stock of the American engineering company, Mesta, in 1987.[32] In order to guarantee a supply of iron ore, the Capital Iron and Steel Group on November 5, 1992 spent US $120 million to purchase a Peruvian iron ore company.[33] The Capital Iron and Steel Group also established its own bank, the Huaxia Bank.

The Agenda and Relocation of the Company:

The Capital Iron and Steel Group recently decided to move some of its operations out of Beijing. This move will reduce the production of iron and steel in Beijing's Shijingshan factory district, while retaining 3.5 million tons of productivity. The relocation of the Capital and Iron Steel Group reveals the government's environmental concerns, as well as other strategic purposes. This relocation also follows the overall spirit of the NDRC guideline that there should be "restrictions on capacity in areas short of water and large cities like those in North China" (Article 10, chapter III).[34] This relocation is also in keeping with Article 11, chapter III of the same guidelines: since "northeastern China is short of water and iron ore, it should focus on meeting local demand without seeking an expansion of production capacity."[35]

Capital Iron and Steel's relocation will shift the center of production of high quality iron and steel from Beijing to Caofeidian in Hebei province. Caofeidian has a deepwater port, which is convenient for the importation of iron ore. This is in keeping with the NDRC provision that "regions abundant in water resources should encourage large integrated steel mills to put up facilities near their ports."[36] In Shunyi, a satellite city of Beijing, the construction of the model Shouqin project will focus on cold rolling, environmental protection, and energy circulation, as well as on economically efficient production of wide thick plate.[37] This is consistent with the NDRC guidelines, Article 12, chapter IV: "the industry should improve the level of environmental protection, encourage the comprehensive usage of resources, save energy and cut costs."[38] Although the relocation and restructuring of the Capital Iron and Steel Group has been primarily driven by the environmental concerns of the Chinese government, it also gives an indication of the personal philosophy of the top leadership. Wen, for example, seems to be more sensitive to environmental concerns than other Chinese economic policymakers past or present.[39]

In 2005, the Capital Iron and Steel Group exported 635,000 tons of iron and steel, and expanded its market to 26 countries and five continents.[40] During the period of the eleventh Five-year Plan, from 2006 – 2010, the Capital Iron and Steel Group plans to implement a three-stage developmental strategy, including structural adjustment, transformation, and economic growth. The first step, which should be completed by the end of 2007, is to complete the structural adjustments and capitalist oriented reforms in the headquarters and to continue with technical research and development, as well as personnel adjustment. Other parts of the first step include the aforementioned relocation of the plant, the completion of the Beijing Shunyi cold rolling project and the employment of plate production technology.[41] The preservation of Capital Iron and Steel's headquarters in Beijing at a center of R&D and high-tech Shunyi project is consistent with Articles 14-15, chapter IV of the NDRC guidelines, which state that "support should be given to enterprises to set up R&D facilities with a view to upgrading technologies."[42] This first step will also lay a solid foundation for the construction of the Caofeidian project.

The second step of the developmental strategy will be completed by the end of the year 2010. It will include the completion of Caofeidian project, which is expected to produce 9 million tons of high quality steel plate. The completion of the second stage will also bring about a significant improvement in the product structure and the industrial layout, as well as strengthening direct investment in overseas capital markets.[43] These first two steps are in accordance with the NDRC guidelines that state "although no new integrated steel, iron and rolling mills should be constructed (chapter III), enlargement and improvement of existing facilities will be permitted (chapter II)."[44] This is also in keeping with Zhu Rongji and Wen Jiabao's overall philosophy of reforming state-owned enterprises. That is, they wish to create a trimmed-down state sector of efficient and profitable high-tech enterprises, along the lines of those in contemporary Germany or France.

The third step, to be completed after the year 2010, will make the Capital Iron and Steel Group one of the world's largest enterprises, as well as a dominant company in the Chinese domestic iron and steel industry. By that time, the Capital Iron and Steel Group is expected to be producing 15 million tons of iron and steel per year.[45] This is yet another example of the NDRC's agenda as set for in Article 20, chapter V, i.e., that "two 30-million-ton steel enterprises and several 10-million-ton internationally competitive enterprises should be set up by 2010."[46]

The Overseas FDI of the Capital Iron and Steel Group:

In the early 1990's, the Capital Iron and Steel Group purchased a Peruvian iron ore plant for US $120 million, and acquired 98.4% of its stock. The Capital Iron and Steel Group thereby obtained unlimited rights to develop and use the mineral resources in the Marcona Mine, a mining area of 670.7 square kilometers. This area has a known iron ore reserve of approximately 1.4 billion tons. Moreover, the grade of ore is good, with an iron content of over 50%. The majority of the minerals there are visible from the surface, and suitable for open-air mining.[47] This promised to be a huge source of iron ore resources for the Capital Iron and Steel Group. However, the Peru iron ore project has been operating at a loss for the past several years as a result of poor management. Recently, the Capital Iron and Steel Group sold off a portion of its stock in the Peruvian iron ore project, but still maintains a controlling share. At present, the production of ore is far less than what was hoped for.

In 2003, the Capital Iron and Steel Group and the Brazilian Hamersley Iron corporation entered into an agreement whereby Hamersley would supply the Capital Iron and Steel Group with 6 - 7.5 million tons of iron ore annually. The Capital Iron and Steel Group also signed a long-term agreement with Brazil-based Companhia Vale do Rio Doce (CVRD) for the acquisition of 1.175 - 3.105 million tons of iron ore per year. The Capital Iron and Steel Group also has agreements with BHP and Robe River for 1 million and 1.6 million tons of iron ore annually.[48]

The Capital Iron and Steel Group and the Australian Mount Gibson Iron ore company (Mount Gibson Iron) reached an agreement on June 23, 2005 to develop jointly the Australian Extension Hill hematite project. On this occasion, the Capital Iron and Steel Group invested US $105.4 million. The Mount Gibson Iron Ore Company is one of Australia's most famous, with its headquarters located at Perth.[49] One of the incentives to mine hematite is that it is used in the production of hematite balls, which are very profitable. This joint venture between the Capital Iron and Steel Group and Mount Gibson Iron is the second largest foreign investment in a minerals corporation after the Capital Iron and Steel Group's Peru project. This joint venture is also the Capital Iron and Steel Group's first investment in an Australian minerals corporation.

On June 14, 2006, the Mount Gibson Iron Ore Company sold 73% of its stock to the Capital Iron and Steel Group for US $46.1 million. After trying for the past two years, the Capital Iron and Steel Group finally obtained the controlling rights to the Western Australia Extension Hill area's magnetite project. Mount Gibson has been exporting hematite stone to China since February 2004. The Capital Iron and Steel Group has indicated that the reason it purchased the Australian Extension Hill area's magnetite project is to guarantee a supply of resources. In 2006, the Capital Iron and Steel Group required more than 17 million tons of iron ore. In 2007, it is estimated that this requirement will surpass 20 million tons. China depends on the world's three largest iron ore companies, Australian BHP-Billiton Company, Australia's Rio Tinto company and Brazil's CVRD. These three companies provide China with over 60% of its required ore.[50]

In 2004, India replaced Brazil as China's second largest supplier of iron ore behind Australia. Iron ore is at present India's largest export to China, constituting approximately a quarter of China's total amount of imported iron ore.[51]

India has many kinds of iron ore, such as hematite and magnetite, whose quality satisfies the requirements of China's large-scale iron and steel enterprises. India currently anticipates a broader cooperation with China's iron and steel enterprises. Thus, India has become one of China's staple suppliers of raw materials. India has also reduced the red tape required for China to mine in India in the hope of attracting more Chinese investors.

Some of China's steel enterprises are currently setting up mines in Mongolia. By the end of 2004, more than 50 Chinese companies were investing in Mongolian mining enterprises, making Mongolia the fourth largest supplier of minerals for China, after Australia, India, and Brazil. The Capital Iron and Steel Group and Baosteel are both currently investing in Mongolia. One of the Capital Iron and Steel Group's investments went into production in 2006 at a cost of US $11.6 billion with an anticipated annual production of 1.5 million tons of iron ore. Baosteel has also signed an agreement for the mining of iron ore with a Mongolian company. This agreement will take effect in 2007.[52]

On September 30, 2005, the Capital Iron and Steel Group devised a plan to construct a steel mill in Thailand. The Capital Iron and Steel Group planned to invest US $2.42 billion to construct an iron and steel plant to supply the steel markets of Thailand and the rest of Southeast Asia. It was also planned that this steel mill would be constructed in Rayong province, about 180 kilometers from Bangkok.[53] There are high expectations for this steel mill since there is no other supplier of iron and steel for Southeast Asia and South Asia except for India. The steel produced by the Capital Iron and Steel Group's Thai factory is expected to help with the reconstruction of several Southeast Asian countries following the tsunami of 2004.

In June 2006, the African country, Gabon, decided to hand over the COMIBEL iron ore project to a Chinese enterprise for development with an expected production of 500 million tons of iron ore annually. However, the difficulties in mining are expected to be huge, and could drive up investment past US $732 million.[54] China's resource investment in African countries reveals its strategy concerning geopolitics and resource distribution. Many African nations have maintained good political relations with China for many years. China is using these hard-won political relations with African nations to foster economic and trade relations in the hope that Chinese can play a significant role in the development of the rich mineral resources in the African continent.

The Capital Iron and Steel Group's overseas activities regarding iron ore are in line with the Chinese government's policy of "Going Global," which was first promulgated by the Chinese Communist Party at the turn of the century. This policy is specifically reflected in Article 28, chapter VII of the NDRC guidelines: "the state should encourage large-scale enterprises to develop iron ore resources," as well as Article 30, chapter VII: "support should be given to large enterprises to set up overseas production bases of iron ore, chrome ore, manganese ore, nickel ore, scrap and coking coal."[55]

The Capital Iron and Steel Group-Peru Project:

The Capital Iron and Steel Group's purchase of the Peruvian state-owned company, Hierro de Peru, was perhaps the most bitter of all China's foreign investments. It also caused great harm to China's image in South America. In 1993, the Capital Iron and Steel Group purchased this Peruvian corporation at a cost of US $120 million, a bid 4 times higher than that of the closest competitor. The Capital Iron and Steel Group also promised at that time that it would invest another US $130 million in this iron ore project.[56]

In June of 2002, in this small town with a population of only 13,000, many workers blocked the entrance to the mine, and demanded an increase in daily wages of 85 cents, as well as a daily distribution by the employer of canned milk. The workers' demands were refused. The Capital Iron and Steel Group was caught off guard when it decided to freeze the wages of the Peruvian workers, since strikes rarely occur in China. Faced with this situation, the Capital Iron and Steel Group's ultimate solution was to bring in 270 workers from China, who had been given intense training in Spanish before their arrival in Peru.[57] After the Capital Iron and Steel Group decided to let these Chinese workers return home, they were replaced with inexpensive local temporary workers. At first, these temporary workers were not provided with any medical or housing benefits. According to Peruvian law, however, once workers join trade unions, they are authorized to obtain these benefits. The temporary workers then promptly set up their own trade unions, and, accordingly, asked for higher wages and better living conditions from their Chinese employer. The slogans and writings everywhere in San Juan Marcona bear witness to ten years of continuous protests and strikes.

The Capital Iron and Steel Group's actions in San Juan Marcona alienated the company from the local workers and the community. The Capital Iron and Steel Group has not fulfilled its promise to the Peruvian government to improve the production of iron ore. Rather, it paid US $2.5 million to the Peruvian government as fines for the breach of this promise. One consequence of the Capital Iron and Steel Group's failure to keep its promise was a reduction in the rate of overall safety in the production of iron ore. According to the Peruvian Labor Department, in 2003 there were 170 accidents, resulting from the production of iron ore, two of which resulted in death. The situation in 2004 was somewhat better.[58]

The eruption of the financial crisis in Asia in 1997 caused a dramatic drop in the market demand for iron and steel. This drop severely hurt the Capital Iron and Steel Group's commercial prospects. For eight years the Capital Iron and Steel Group could only break even in the Peruvian iron ore project, although the price of iron and steel has undergone a remarkable rise recently. What is more, the Capital Iron and Steel Group has refused to comment on the labor problems it encountered in Peru.

However, as the experience of the Capital Iron and Steel Group in Peru shows, trade unionism could prove to be one of the thornier issues that Chinese enterprises may face in their overseas investments.

Consequence of the Upsurge in Demand for Iron Ore:

China's rapidly growing economy, particularly in the areas of automobile manufacturing, the real estate industry and light industry, is driving its demand for iron ore to new heights. This skyrocketing demand, in turn, is causing a global rise in the price of iron ore. Today, China is the world's largest consumer of iron ore. The amount of iron ore imported by China is astonishingly huge, so much so that China is occasionally referred to as "The Global Magnet," because it attracts so much iron ore.

In 2005, the increasing demand for iron ore on the part of the world's major economies caused the price of ore to rise 71.5% compared to the price of a year earlier. The world's ten largest producers of iron ore are China, Brazil, Australia, India, Russia, the Ukraine, the U.S., Canada, South Africa and Sweden. Part of the rise in price of iron ore was caused by a worldwide economic recovery.

However, the major reason was an increase in China's demand for steel, iron, and other raw materials. Australia, Brazil, India and South Africa control the global iron ore markets since they are the greatest exporters. Among these giants, Australia ranks first, followed by Brazil and then India. Australia accounts for 36% of exports, Brazil for 35%, India for 9%, South Africa for 5%, and Canada for 4% with other countries accounting for the remaining 11%. Thus, Australia and Brazil account for more than 70% of the world's iron ore exports. It is a recognized fact that Australian ore is the highest quality.[59]

The world's chief iron ore importers are the Asian and European countries. Japan, South Korea, Britain, France, Germany, and Italy are all net importers of iron ore. Italy in fact relies completely on imports for its iron ore.

China is not only the world's largest producer of iron ore, but also the world's largest importer of iron ore. While China's iron ore resources are abundant, they are dispersed geographically and are of relatively poor quality. Most of China's iron ore mining enterprises are generally small scale, and lack advanced mining technology. Because of this, the resulting gap between the demand for iron ore and the production of iron ore in China is bound to increase. For the amount of iron ore imported by China between 2000 and 2004, see the following charts concerning the total amount of iron ore imported by China, according to the *Chinese Statistics Yearbook.*

Chart 5.1 – Imported Iron Ore in China 2000-2004

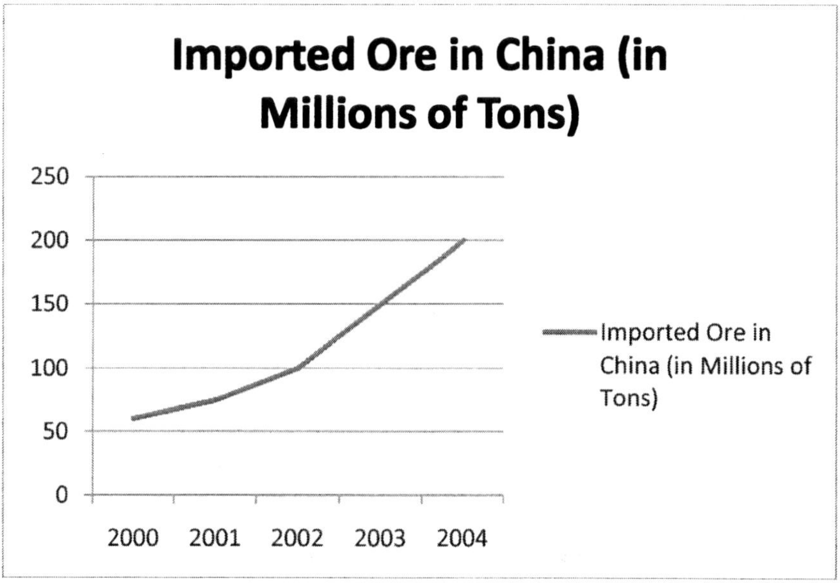

Source: *Chinese Statistics Yearbook,* 2000-2004

Chart 5.2 – Amount of Money for Importing Iron Ore in China 2000-2004

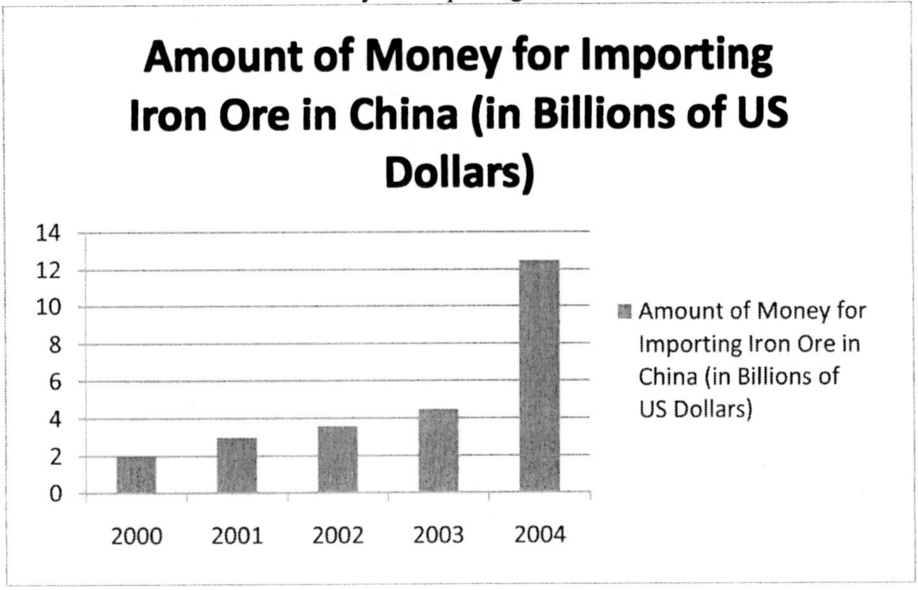

Source: *Chinese Statistics Yearbook,* 2000-2004

On January 31, 2004, Baosteel and the Brazilian CVRD company entered into an agreement to pool capital in Brazil, and to construct a steel mill there. Before this, Baosteel and the Australian Hamersley iron ore limited company entered into the Baoruiji joint venture, and developed the western Australian Paraburdoo iron ore together. On March 1, 2004, the Wuhan Steel Corporation, Tang steel, Maanshan steel and Sa steel announced a joint venture with the Australian BHP Billiton company to establish and manage the Australian Jimblebar iron mine.[60] Therefore, China's overall strategy regarding mineral resources is through trade and foreign direct investment to establish a stable supply of mineral resources for its national economic development. The guiding principle of this strategy is to serve the national economic growth and development.

In addition to the above mentioned reasons for China's demand for iron ore, namely, the increasing production of China's iron and steel industry, as well as the poor quality of China's domestic supply of iron, another factor driving China to explore resources on a global level is government policy. In particular, the NDRC guidelines Article 28, chapter VII state that "the state should encourage large-scale enterprises to develop iron ore resources." [61] Article 30, chapter VII of the same guidelines states "support should be given to large enterprises to set up overseas production bases of iron ore, chrome ore, manganese ore, nickel ore, scrap and coking coal."[62] This industrial policy of the NDRC is in line with the central leadership's overall strategy of "Going Global."

In 2003, at the symposium concerning the population, resources, and the environment, General Secretary Hu Jintao stressed that domestic Chinese resources are insufficient, with the situation becoming worse by the day. Some important domestic supplies of mineral resources are close to being exhausted. Therefore, Hu continued, China must increase its efforts for "Going Global" in order to obtain the use of overseas resources.[63] In the meeting concerning the central economy in November 2003, General Secretary Hu Jintao pointed out that the impact of the lack of resources on economic growth is increasing, particularly the lack of sufficient quantities of crude oil, iron ore, energy, and non-ferrous metals. Although imports are increasing greatly, Hu went on to stress that China was still having difficulty meeting its domestic needs. Thus, he concluded, China must persist in implementing its "Going Global" strategy.[64] On October 12, 2004, Premier Wen Jiabao pointed out that China must simultaneously engage in both domestic and overseas resource development. First, he stated, China must increase its exploration for domestic supplies of resources. Second, China should use its policy of "Going Global" to increase its foreign supplies of resources.[65]

In spite of the positive aspects of the policy of "Going Global," an excessive dependence upon foreign mineral resources can impair China's economic security and development. An excessive dependence on overseas resources is causing disarray in the competition between domestic companies. The result is often shortsighted behavior on the part of the steel companies. First of all, the excessive dependence upon overseas resources tends to make the domestic mining industry chaotic, in that enterprises tend to concentrate on rich reserves and abandon poor ones. This will eventually drive up the cost of mining domestic minerals. Then, these increased production costs will naturally be passed on to the consumer. Finally, China's national resources as a whole also suffer a risk of loss due to China's excessive dependence on foreign resources, in that once work is finished at a mine, and the mine pit is filled, the ore which was deemed unprofitable to extract will be forever lost.

Therefore, China would be benefited by being diligent in the attention it pays to the consumption of resources. Since there is only a limited amount of domestic resources in China, the recycling of raw materials will become more and more important. For example, one third of the world's gold output comes from recycling. The Chinese government would be well served to take protection and care in the development and use of mineral resources, according to the principle that one must develop with protection, and protect the development. That is to say, one is obliged to employ reasonable use, protection and management of valuable mineral resources. China would be better off if it made more efficient use of its mineral resources. This could be accomplished by strengthening the regulation of policy, by letting market forces optimize the disposition of the resources, and by creating a new pathway for the conservation of resources and economic development.

Suggestions for Chinese Steelmakers' Future Overseas FDI:

In the future, if the market is the goal, China might choose the area of Southeast Asia for investment. It is an area of high economic growth, its iron and steel industry is still in its preliminary stages, and demand for the steel and iron in this geographic area is very substantial. Thus, Southeast Asia is a market which the Chinese steel and iron industry might favor. China might think of first establishing a base of production of iron and steel in either Indonesia or Malaysia, and then use its existing trade relations with some members of the Association of Southeast Asian Nations (AESAN) in order to gain a foothold in the markets of other members in the association.

If natural resources are the goal, China might select Africa, Oceania and South America for investment, since they are home to resource rich mining companies. In addition, the Chinese iron and steel industry requires a stable flow of resources such as iron ore. In particular, China's large-scale iron and steel enterprises might choose the following countries as their primary area for foreign investment in the development of resources: Brazil, Australia, Canada, Chile, Peru, and South Africa. In addition, China might also investigate ways of reducing the cost of marine transportation of these minerals, which would thus reduce the overall cost of ore.

If technology is the aim, China might choose the European and North American steel enterprises for investment. Although the steel and iron industry has already passed its prime in the European and North American nations, their technology is still more advanced than China's. Therefore, China might look towards Europe and America for advanced technological expertise in the iron and steel industry. This would help reduce the gap between China and the West in technological development. China might initially adopt a strategy of purchase and acquisition, and then gradually transfer its efforts into the building and construction of iron and steel plants in these areas.

The Chinese iron and steel enterprises might also learn how to exploit the foreign capital markets. There is a great amount of funds available in the international monetary markets, enough to solve any financial problems that Chinese iron and steel companies are facing. Some of China's largest enterprises have had great success in obtaining international funding. For example, the Chinese metallurgy import-export company obtained an international bank loan of US $81.2 million, and contributed another US $34.8 million of its own money to obtain 40% of the rights to the China-Australian Channar Iron Ore project, a company whose total worth is US $280 million. The China International Trust Investment Company (CITIC) was able to obtain an international loan in order to acquire 10% of the stock of the Australian Portland aluminum factory. Also CITIC, using an international bank consortium loan, financed the purchase of 50% of the stock of the Canadian Celgar Pulp mill at a cost of US $62 million. This mill produces 180,000 tons of paper pulp yearly. In addition, the Capital Iron and Steel Group through a Hong Kong-listed shell company bought the Hong Kong Dongrong company. Because of the Capital Iron and Steel Group's successful management of the Dongrong company, its investment rose in value. The Capital Iron and Steel Group, through the International Jiayi financing company, also issued US $183 million worth of bonds.[66]

Conclusion:

In short, the overall restructuring of the Chinese iron and steel industry, represented in particular by Baosteel and the Capital Iron and Steel Group, closely follows the NDRC's Iron and Steel Industrial Development Policy of

China released on July 20, 2005. These guidelines not only undoubtedly follow the central leadership's political and economic thinking, but also clearly demonstrate the power and influence of the NDRC. The NDRC's new Industrial Policy for the steel industry, among many others areas, illustrates an effort by economic bureaucrats to step up the pace of corporate restructuring. These efforts in turn reflect Wen Jiabao's working style, i.e., letting policy be made by powerful supra-ministerial agencies, such as SASAC and NDRC. This type of policymaking will result in greater representation of bureaucratic interests, and a policymaking process that is more contained within government agencies.[67]

The Chinese iron and steel industry is a clear-cut example of the governmental policy favoring the creation of large industrial units by means of consolidation, merger and re-structuring. It is also clear that China requires investment in its iron and steel industry not for any expansion of production capacity, but only to up-grade its existing technology. This is obvious from the fact that the target production capacity for Chinese steel of 340 million tons by 2010 [68] just matches the projected level of consumption and is quite achievable by current indications. Hence, there is no need for China to increase production capacity.

However, if the Chinese iron and steel industry follows the benchmarks set by the best in the industry with regard to technological parameters, such as energy consumption, coke rate, BF productivity and cost of production, it will provide a clear road map for the Chinese steel industry in the coming years. Regarding the national steel policy, these industrial benchmarks are excellent tool for evaluating the performance of the industry in its journey towards global competitiveness.

With regards to steel making, China has approximately 290 companies, with a total productivity of 134 million tons.[69] In general, China exports mostly unfinished metallurgical products, such as coke, pig iron, ferroalloy, and billet, which are mostly low value products. China's imports, on the other hand, are mostly high-tech metallurgical products, which are usually of high value. In order to reduce the export of these low value products, chapter VII of the NDRC guidelines provides that "export of coke, ferroalloy, pig iron, steel scrap and semi-finished products which consume much energy and generate pollution should be restrained by reducing or withdrawing export tax rebates."[70]

China also has a low level of craftsmanship and equipment. These disadvantages cannot be offset by the low cost of manpower in China. There is currently an oversupply of low valued ordinary steel products in China, especially steel used for construction, whereas the national economy urgently needs high scale and high valued products, which are currently undersupplied, and thus have to be imported. These include steel used for passenger vehicles, electrical appliances, bearings, and gears. In response to this, the government, on the one hand, is trying to reduce the continued use of out-dated equipment by providing in Article 17, chapter IV of the NDRC guidelines that "construction and use of outdated processes and facilities like steel making by the cupola process, primitive sintering and coke, BF below 300 cubic meters, converters below 20 tons, EAF below 20 tons etc should not be permitted."[71] The guidelines go on to state that "enterprises should also be discouraged from using the outdated second-hand iron and steel production facilities that have been abandoned at home and abroad" (Article 18, chapter IV).[72] On the other hand, the government is encouraging the adoption of new technology by providing in Articles 14-15, chapter IV of these same guidelines that "support should be given to enterprises to set up R&D facilities with a view to internalizing and upgrading technologies, like high quality furnace charges, oxygen-enriched coal injection, large-scale BF and Converters, ultra-high power electric arc furnaces, secondary refining, continuous casting, controlled cooling, and so on."[73]

The marketing strategies of China's iron and steel industry are still relatively in their infancy. There is currently no marketing theory, which takes into account China's historical and regional characteristics. For example, the only marketing practice used in the competitive process is the lowering of prices, rather than more sophisticated techniques that might, for example, include advertising, and increasing the quality of products.

Nevertheless, led by the Capital Iron and Steel Group, China's iron and steel enterprises have been participating on a large scale in joint multinational ventures. The Capital Iron and Steel Group has conducted a bold, multi-level exploration in foreign investment and operations. There are several aspects to the Capital Iron and Steel Group's foreign investment, such as seeking technological and managerial experience, obtaining a supply of natural resources, obtaining global financing, expanding its market, promoting the export of labor and equipment, and engaging in international projects. Apart from the Capital Iron and Steel Group, since November of 1987, many other Chinese iron and steel companies have also been engaging in joint multinational ventures. One example is the joint venture in Western Australia between the China metallurgical import-export company and the Australian Hamersley Iron Ore company. Chinese companies, one after the other, such as the Anshan Iron and Steel Company, the Shanghai Baoshan Steel Group Corporation, the Capital Iron and Steel Group, and the Wuhan Steel Corporation, have established trading companies of various sizes in Hong Kong, the U.S., Japan, Germany, Singapore, and Thailand as a first step in establishing overseas FDI. In addition, the Chinese metallurgical industry is also engaging in contracts for overseas projects.

As a direct result of the increase in production in China's iron and steel industry, since 2003, China has surpassed Japan and the European Union to become the world's largest importer of iron ore. Today, with over 50% of its ore coming from imports, China is by far and away the world's largest importer of iron ore.[74] One reason for this is that the Chinese domestic supply of iron ore is not ideal. As a consequence of China's increasing demand, the world's three largest exporters of ore, Australian BHP-Billiton Company, Australia's Rio Tinto company and Brazil's CVRD, have significantly increased their price for ore at the same rate. In response to this simultaneous increase in price, the Chinese Association of the Iron and Steel Industry has dictated that all Chinese steelmakers are banned from having individual iron ore price negotiations for contracts with international miners for 2006, (with the exception of the Shanghai Baosteel Group Co.),[75] since such individual price negotiations tend to drive the price of ore even higher. The Chinese government has backed the association of the iron and steel industry in this move. Baosteel has been designated as the representative of all Chinese steelmakers in negotiations for the price of iron ore.

China has learned that it is not to its advantage to be excessively dependent upon overseas resources; these foreign resources at best should only supplement the domestic supply. Taking this into account, China would be benefited by developing a suitable strategy for the simultaneous use of foreign and domestic resources.

Notes

1. "Gangtie chanye fazhan zhengce (Steel Industry Development Policy)," at http://www.ndrc.gov.cn/zcfb/zcfbl/zcfbl2005/t20050719_52618.htm

2. Barry Naughton, "Incremental Decision Making and Corporate Restructuring," *China Leadership Monitor,* No. 15, Summer 2005, p. 6.

3. Sushim Banerjee, "New Policy of China—a Lesson for Others," *Steel RX,* September 19, 2005.

4. "Gangtie chanye fazhan zhengce (Steel Industry Development Policy)," at http://www.ndrc.gov.cn/zcfb/zcfbl/zcfbl2005/t20050719_52618.htm

5. Liu Dexue, Jia Xiaoxia, and Zhang Feng, "Large Scale Iron and Steel Enterprise's Internationalization Analysis and its Strategic Choice (daxing gangtie qiye guojihua jingying zhuangkuang fenxi yu fazhan zhanlue xuanzhe," *Metallurgy Economy and Management (yejin jingji yu guanli),* No. 1, 2001, p. 36.

6. Ruan Haier, "The Modern Baosteel was Fully Completed (xiandaihua baogang quanmian jiancheng)", *China Metallurgy Newspaper (zhongguo yejinbao)*, Dec. 22, 2000.

7. "Gangtie chanye fazhan zhengce (Steel Industry Development Policy)," at http://www.ndrc.gov.cn/zcfb/zcfbl/zcfbl2005/t20050719_52618.htm

8. Ding Bo, "Implication of the Investment Principles of Baosteel (baogang touzi fazhe qishi)", *Jiefang Daily*, March 1, 2005.

9. Andew Nathan and Bruce Gilley, *China's New Rulers: The Secret Files,* New York: New York Review Books, Inc., 2003, p. 205-206.

10. "Gangtie chanye fazhan zhengce (Steel Industry Development Policy)," at http://www.ndrc.gov.cn/zcfb/zcfbl/zcfbl2005/t20050719_52618.htm

11. Naughton, 2005, p. 7.

12. "Gangtie chanye fazhan zhengce (Steel Industry Development Policy)," at http://www.ndrc.gov.cn/zcfb/zcfbl/zcfbl2005/t20050719_52618.htm

13. Ma Fengtao, "Baosteel's Strategic Investment and Layout for an Iron and Steel Kingdom (baogang zhanlue touzi buju gangtiediguo)", *Investment Report (touzi baodao),* No. 6, 2006, p. 52-53.

14. "Gangtie chanye fazhan zhengce (Steel Industry Development Policy)," at http://www.ndrc.gov.cn/zcfb/zcfbl/zcfbl2005/t20050719_52618.htm

15. Ibid.

16. Ibid.

17. Nathan and Gilley, 2003, p. 206.

18. "Gangtie chanye fazhan zhengce (Steel Industry Development Policy)," at http://www.ndrc.gov.cn/zcfb/zcfbl/zcfbl2005/t20050719_52618.htm

19. Ibid.

20. Naughton, 2005, p. 6.

21. Ma, 2006, p. 52-53.

22. Ibid.

23. Ibid.

24. Ding Bo, "Baosteel Invests in Australian Iron Mine (baogang touzi aozhou tie-kuang)", *Jiefang Daily,* April 23, 2004.

25. Luo Yuanhua, "Situaiton on China's Mineral Resources and its Development Agenda (woguo kuangchan ziyuan xingshi ji fazhan guihua silu," *Land and Resource Scientific Management (guotu ziyuan guanli),* No. 5, May 2001, p. 7-9.

26. "Gangtie chanye fazhan zhengce (Steel Industry Development Policy)," at http://www.ndrc.gov.cn/zcfb/zcfbl/zcfbl2005/t20050719_52618.htm

27. Xie Xiangqian, Zhang xianping, "Analysis on the Internationalization of China's Iron & Steel Enterprises (zhongguo gangtie qiye guojihua yingxiao fenxi)," *Journal of Wuhan Metallurgical Manager's Institute (wuhan yejin guanli ganbu xueyuan xuebao),* Vol. 13, No. 3, Sept. 2003, p. 18.

28. Chen Yongru, "Baosteel Invests Billions of Dollars to Build Huge Steel Factory in Zhanjiang (baogang touzi baiyi meiyuan zhanjiang jian juxing gangchang)," *South Daily (nanfang ribao),* Dec. 3, 2004.

29. "Gangtie chanye fazhan zhengce (Steel Industry Development Policy)," at http://www.ndrc.gov.cn/zcfb/zcfbl/zcfbl2005/t20050719_52618.htm

30. Ibid.

31. Liu Zhiyong, "Shougang's Personnel Strategy in its Overseas Management (shougang kuaguo jingying zhongde rencai xiyin zhanlue)," *Enterprise Management (qiye guanli),* 1994, p. 13.

32. Dong Zhuomin, Guan Zhian, "International Management and Chinese Iron and Steel Enterprise's Overseas Acquisition (guojihua jingying yu zhongguo gangtie gongye kuaguo jianbing)," *Metallurgy Management (yejin guanli),* Aug. 1998, p. 41.

33. Liu, 1994, p. 13.

34. "Gangtie chanye fazhan zhengce (Steel Industry Development Policy)," at http://www.ndrc.gov.cn/zcfb/zcfbl/zcfbl2005/t20050719_52618.htm

35. Ibid.

36. Ibid.

37. Zhang Wenji, "Open a New Page (xiankai xinde yiye)," *Front (qianxian),* July 2006, p. 50.

38. "Gangtie chanye fazhan zhengce (Steel Industry Development Policy)," at http://www.ndrc.gov.cn/zcfb/zcfbl/zcfbl2005/t20050719_52618.htm

39. Nathan and Gilley, 2003, p. 208-210.

40. Zhang, July 2006, p.50.

41. Ibid.

42. "Gangtie chanye fazhan zhengce (Steel Industry Development Policy)," at http://www.ndrc.gov.cn/zcfb/zcfbl/zcfbl2005/t20050719_52618.htm

43. Ibid.

44. "Gangtie chanye fazhan zhengce (Steel Industry Development Policy)," at http://www.ndrc.gov.cn/zcfb/zcfbl/zcfbl2005/t20050719_52618.htm

45. Ibid.

46. Ibid.

47. Wang Fengjun, "Shougang Again Purchase Iron Ore in Australia (shougang aozhou zai maikuang)," *21st Century Economic Report (21shiji jingji baodao),* July 4, 2005.

48. Ibid.

49. Ibid.

50. Zhang Yan, "Shougang Spent 311 Million to Purchase an Australian Mine (shougang 3.11 yiyuan maixia aozhou kuangshan)," *Modern Commodity Flows Newspaper (xiandai wuliu bao),* June 14, 2006.

51. Liu Anlin, "Influence and Enlightenment of Iron Ore's Rising Price on China's Economy (dangqian tiekuangshi jiage shangzhang duizhongguo de yinxiang he qishi)," *China Metallurgy (zhongguo yejin)*, Vol. 15, No. 10, Oct. 2005, p. 10.

52. Wang, July 4, 2005.

53. Chen Shanshan, "Shougang Plans to Invest 2.4 Billion Dollars to Build a Plant in Thailand (shougang jihua touzi 24 yi meiyuan taiguo jianchang)," *First Financial Daily (diyi caijing ribao)*, Sept. 30, 2005.

54. Xu Yuli, "Shougang Spent 300 Million RMB to Control Australian Hematite Project (shougang 3 yi konggu aozhou citiekuang xiangmu)," *Shanghai Security Newspaper (shanghai zhengquanbao)*, June 9, 2006.

55. "Gangtie chanye fazhan zhengce (Steel Industry Development Policy)," at http://www.ndrc.gov.cn/zcfb/zcfbl/zcfbl2005/t20050719_52618.htm

56. Li Lintao, "South America—Shougang's Waterloo (nanmei: shougang de "huatielu"?)," *Business Culture (shangye wenhua)*, Mar. 2005.

57. Ibid.

58. Ibid.

59. Data is from The International Iron and Steel Institute (IISI), http://www.worldsteel.org/

60. Wang Jun, Yang bo, and Yu Zipeng, "China Iron Ore Supply & Demand Strategic Analysis (zhongguo tiekuangshi gongxu zhanlue fenyi)," *Economist (jingji xuejia)*, April 2005, p. 40.

61. "Gangtie chanye fazhan zhengce (Steel Industry Development Policy)," at http://www.ndrc.gov.cn/zcfb/zcfbl/zcfbl2005/t20050719_52618.htm

62. Ibid.

63. Lian Changyun, Liu Dawen, Qiu Ruizhao, and Yuan Chunhua, "Thoughts on the Global Mineral Resources Strategy Adopted by China (guanyu zhongguo quanqiu kuangchan ziyuanzhanlue de sikao)," *Geological Bulletin of China (dizhi tongbao)*, Vol. 24, No. 9, Sep. 2005, p. 795-799.

64. Ibid.

65. Ibid.

66. Dong and Guan, Aug. 1998, p. 41.

67. Naughton, 2005, p. 1-8.

68. Banerjee, September 19, 2005.

69. Xie and Zhang, Sept. 2003, p. 16.

70. "Gangtie chanye fazhan zhengce (Steel Industry Development Policy)," at http://www.ndrc.gov.cn/zcfb/zcfbl/zcfbl2005/t20050719_52618.htm

71. Ibid.

72. Ibid.

73. Ibid.

74. Liu, Oct. 2005, p. 7-8.

75. Glenys Sim, "Beijing Warns Its Steelmakers," *The Wall Street Journal*, February 23, 2006.

CASE STUDY TWO
THE OIL AND GAS INDUSTRY

Introduction: Changes in the Geopolitics of Petroleum

The Drop in Status of OPEC – The U.S-Iraq war has changed to a great extent the international pattern of petroleum supply, a pattern which had been in place for more than 30 years. Although the strength of the Organization of Petroleum Exporting Countries (OPEC) had been weakening even before the Iraqi war, it was, nevertheless, in a dominant position in the global supply of petroleum. The oil output of Iraq, a member of OPEC, has been greatly reduced as a result of a series of hostilities with the United States. The political situations in Venezuela and Nigeria are also turbulent. This has caused a drop in their output of petroleum. When OPEC reduces surplus production, there is a corresponding reduction in its ability to influence the global pattern of petroleum distribution. In addition, in the last few years Russia has used its petroleum industry to fuel the development of its economy. At the present time, Russia is the world's largest exporter of natural gas. It plans to be the world's largest exporter of petroleum as well. All these factors have reduced OPEC's influence on the international crude oil supply. In the past, OPEC could unilaterally adopt policy measures, such as raising the price of oil, or decreasing the amount of oil production in order to adjust the global pattern of petroleum distribution. Now, however, the strength of OPEC compared to that of non-OPEC oil-producing countries has changed. OPEC's ability to impact the international crude oil supply and to control the international price of oil has clearly been weakened. As a result of new reserves discovered in non-OPEC nations, OPEC's total proportion of global crude oil production has dropped from 80%-90% to about 50%-60%. Its proportion of global exported crude oil has dropped from above 50% to below 35%.[1]

The Rise in Status of the Non-OPEC Oil-producing Countries – At one point, the Russian petroleum output surpassed that of Saudi Arabia, and reached 2.3 million barrels per day. In recent years, Africa's proven reserves of oil, as well as its production of oil have increased dramatically. Every year the U.S. imports more than 300 million barrels of crude oil from Nigeria, and more than

100 million barrels from Angola.[2] At present, the U.S. imports an approximately equal amount of crude oil from Africa and from Saudi Arabia. Soon, about a quarter of the United States' imported crude oil is expected to come from Africa. The appearance of this new pattern of global petroleum supplies will have a profound influence on world economic development.

Russia, Central Asia, Africa and other oil-producing areas which are not yet controlled by the U.S. will become the world's new focal point for petroleum demand. In the past, China's energy diplomacy tended to deal solely with a few areas. China paid great attention to the Persian Gulf, as well as to South America and Africa. At that time, China did not pay much attention to neighboring regions, such as Russia and Central Asia. Therefore, this lack of attention caused China to fall behind the large western petroleum companies. While these companies were spending large amounts of capital for access to the abundant oil and gas reserves of Russia and Central Asia, China was searching for oil in more far-flung regions. Also, when Russia proposed constructing an oil pipeline to China, China shortsightedly rejected the proposal on the grounds of cost. At that time, China was placing all of its eggs in the Middle Eastern basket, and, therefore, lost its best opportunity to enter the Russian oil market.[3]

China's rejection of the proposed pipeline as well as the energy crisis of 2003-04—when the demand for oil increased by 850,000 barrels per day and when the country was plagued by widespread electrical shortages[4]—highlighted the deficiencies in China's energy policy. This policy is dominated by weak institutions and strong vested interests. Tensions between the government and the state-owned energy companies, as well as a lack of coordination between the conflicting objectives of different portions of the bureaucracy have hindered China from developing a comprehensive national energy strategy. There have been recent attempts to make the Chinese bureaucracy more effective. These attempts are part of an effort to balance administrative and market mechanisms, as well as the interests of the companies and the government in controlling the challenges that face China's energy policy.[5]

Since oil is a source of both economic and military power, it is at the foundation of China's status as a great power. The vice president of the CCP's Central Party School, Li Junru, has stated that the most significant question facing China's peaceful rise to international power is not Taiwan, but rather competition for global energy resources.[6] Oil is at present the only fuel that China imports in significant quantities. Consequently, China is most concerned about securing its supply of this fuel. Oil is also having a greater impact on China's behavior on the international stage.

The Making of China's Energy Policy: Weak Institutions & Strong Firms

Two important aspects of the energy policymaking system have shaped China's energy policies: the weakness of the central government institutions involved in energy and the power of the state-owned energy enterprises.[7] This imbalanced situation has hampered coordination among opposing interests in the energy sector,[8] stunted the growth of a comprehensive Chinese energy strategy,[9] and permitted China's state-owned energy enterprises to have a significant influence on China's energy policy. Because of this, it is the corporate interests of the Chinese energy firms rather than the national interests of the Chinese state that drive China's energy agenda.[10]

Authority, in the case of China's oil sector, is divided between several government agencies. The agency with the most power is the National Development and Reform Commission (NDRC). This agency controls the planning of long-term energy development, the setting of energy prices, and the approval of investments in domestic and international energy projects. The NDRC has at least seven offices that oversee the oil sector, among them the Energy Bureau.[11] There are other government agencies that deal with oil policymaking. These include the Ministry of Land and Resources, which is in charge of surveying natural resources, including oil and natural gas, and which grants licenses for exploration and production. Another such agency is the Ministry of Commerce, which is in charge of issuing licenses for the import and export of oil, as well as for promulgating regulations for foreign firms which make investments in China's energy markets and for Chinese firms which invest in foreign energy markets. There is also the Ministry of Finance, which makes tax and fiscal policies that promote the energy objectives of the central government. The Ministry of Foreign Affairs (MFA) supports the national oil companies (NOCs) in their attempts to acquire opportunities in trade and investment abroad. This is part of the MFA's larger mission to promote commercial relations with other countries. The MFA also tries to make sure that the deals pursued by the NOCs do not run afoul of other foreign policy objectives. The Chinese government created two new institutions in 2005 for energy policymaking. These are the Energy Leading Group (ELG) and its administrative body, the State Energy Office (SEO). These two agencies were created to help China improve its energy policy making system. The creation of these two agencies was supported by experts who favored the establishment of a supra-ministerial body to consolidate authority over the energy sector and to work in concert with other government agencies involved in energy, such as the MFA.[12]

Figure 6.1 Selected Components of China's Energy Bureaucracy

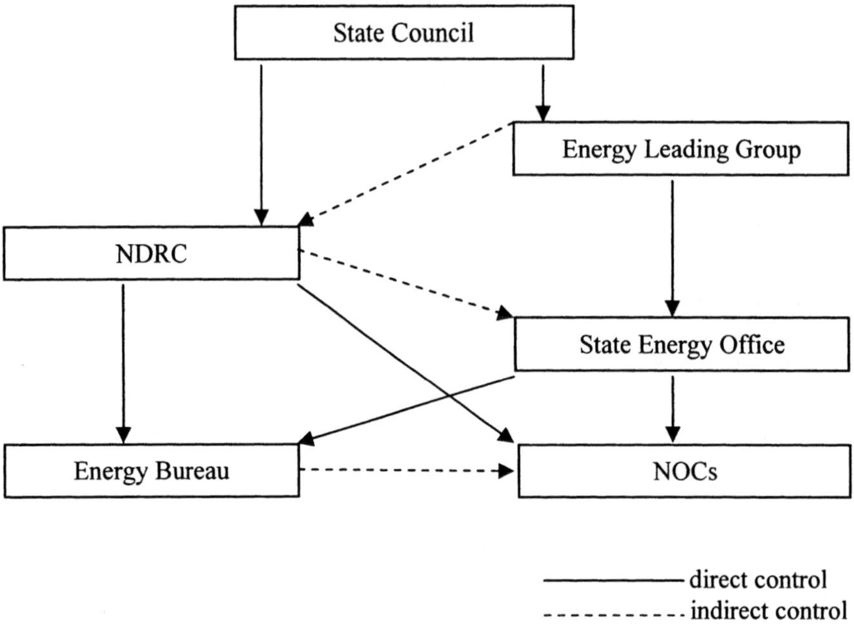

The creation of a high-level government body to oversee and coordinate the energy sector is a reversal of Zhu Rongji's 1993 abolishment of the Ministry of Energy. Zhu did this because he was a strong advocate for market forces in the energy sector. Since the leadership recognized both the need for more effective institutional structural authority, as well as the resistance of influential stakeholders to any changes that would diminish their power, the Energy Bureau was established in 2003 under the NDRC and the ELG and SEO were created in 2005. The balancing of the interests of the various stakeholders is indeed the most challenging aspect of changing the institutional structure of energy policymaking.[13]

The Energy Bureau – The establishment of the Energy Bureau of the NDRC in March of 2003 during the National People's Congress (NPC) was a compromise between several important players in China's energy bureaucracy,[14] including the energy companies and the NDRC. The ability of the Energy Bureau to manage effectively China's energy sector has been limited by a lack of manpower, financial resources and political influence. What is more, since it is an agency *within* the NDRC, the Energy Bureau lacks the power to coordinate among other politically influential players, such as the state-owned energy companies and other ministries.[15]

The Energy Leading Group and the State Energy Office – In 2005 the Energy Leading Group (ELG) was created under the State Council led by Premier Wen Jiabao, as well as the State Energy Office (SEO), which reported directly to the premier himself. The creation of these agencies showed that the leadership, in agreement with many energy experts and officials, was dissatisfied with the then current energy policymaking structure. Although it was the most powerful agency in China's energy policymaking structure, the NDRC did not have the ability to coordinate with other interests such as the MFA. There has in fact been a degree of enmity between the MFA and the NDRC, and the MFA and the NOCs. Chinese diplomats from the MFA have often complained that they do not find out about investments made by China's NOCs until after the fact.[16] These complaints are grounded in the diplomats' concern about the impact of NOC investments on larger foreign policy objectives. In response to the concerns of the MFA, Hu Jintao held a Politburo meeting to discuss the county's energy situation in November 2004. At this meeting, the Politburo members decided to form a leading group and a leading group office for energy.[17] In May 2005 the formal announcement of the establishment of the SEO and the ELG was made, with the publication of Document 2005 (14) by the State Council.[18] The Chinese leadership established the ELG and the SEO in order to determine how to restructure the bureaucracy and reduce the influence of the energy firms. Since China's top leaders realized that a ministry would in all probability become another layer of bureaucracy controlled by vested interests, they decided to form a leading group rather than a ministry.[19]

The importance and power of the ELG is substantial. The ELG has among its ranks some of China's most powerful officials. It is able to intervene in the energy sector to solve problems as they arise. The ELG is not, however, involved in the day-to-day running of the energy sector. The responsibilities of the primary government and Party positions of the ELG members prevent them from routinely getting involved in conflicts of interests that hamper energy policy formulation, whether such conflicts arise within the government or between the government and the state-owned energy companies.[20]

Leading groups do not promulgate concrete policies (*zhengce*). Rather, they issue guiding principles about the overall direction in which bureaucratic activity should proceed (*fangzhen*). A *fangzhen* provides an outline for the promulgation of *zhengce*.[21] Leading group's recommendations have considerable influence on the policymaking process because they usually represent the formation of a consensus by the leading members of the government, party, and military agencies.[22] The establishment of the ELG was made in response to the Chinese leadership's dissatisfaction with the country's ineffective energy bureaucracy and powerful firms. However, the ELG alone cannot alter this situation.

The SEO is not particularly powerful politically. The SEO has the bureaucratic rank of a vice-ministry. This bureaucratic rank is below that of the NDRC and some of the state-owned energy firms.[23] The SEO has a vague mandate, since it overlaps with that of the NDRC Energy Bureau. Some critics have described the SEO as a paper-tiger policy consulting body that merely encourages the writing of reports.[24] Zhu Zhixin, vice director of the NDRC, has called the SEO a "corporate-driven think tank," designed to "serve the Chinese companies as much as possible yet at the same time ensure policies practiced by the commercial sector are not harmful to other areas."[25] Thus the SEO can act as an instrument both for the state-owned energy companies to increase their influence on energy policymaking and for the government to attempt to limit the influence of these same companies.[26]

China's Petrochemical Industry and Sinopec:

Due to a 20-year long process of reform and policy of opening, China's petrochemical industry has grown from virtually nothing to become a global influence. The petrochemical industry has undergone a process of gradual development along with continual adjustments and self-improvement. One factor contributing to the growth of China's petrochemical industry has been the introduction of funding, technology, and management techniques from overseas. In spite of the fact that China's petrochemical industry has benefited greatly from the introduction of foreign funding, China's own foreign direct investment is still in its beginning stages and is only growing slowly. Only the large state-owned petrochemical enterprises, such as China National Petroleum Corporation (CNPC) and China Petroleum & Chemical Corporation (hereafter referred to as Sinopec) have been engaged in direct investment overseas. Middle and small-scale petrochemical companies have yet to take that step.

In August 2004, it was announced that Sinopec ranked number one among China's top 500 enterprises, with sales of US $79.28 billion. Sinopec is a petroleum enterprise which integrates the up, middle, and downstream parts of the petrochemical supply chain. Its upstream crude oil explorations, however, are small in comparison with its downstream oil refinery business. Sinopec's own oil and gas mining only supplies it with 10% of the resources it requires. Over 70% of the total crude oil needed by Sinopec comes from outside the company's own chain of production. This percentage is progressively increasing.[27]

China Petroleum Corporation and the Chinese Petrochemical Company, ranked sixth and eleventh on 2003's list of market capital of the world's oil and chemical companies, with capital market amounts of 94.5 billion US dollars and 35.6 billion US dollars, respectively.[28]

Sinopec has several dozen branch and subsidiary companies. Among the subsidiary companies, there are 12 outside of China that are licensed in local markets. Various subsidiaries of Sinopec can be categorized by labor type and by product type. The types of labor that Sinopec employs include machine manufacturing, petroleum mining, petroleum refinement, production of chemical fiber, retail sales of oil, and construction engineering. The types of products that Sinopec produces include lubricating oil, paraffin wax, polypropylene, polyethylene, and chemical fiber.

The petrochemical industry has a natural tendency to produce multinational corporations because it is by nature a large-scale enterprise. This has in fact been proven to be the case. At present, the international petrochemical market is dominated by a relative handful of multinational corporations. This small group of companies relies on their huge scale, their abundant financial resources, and their advanced technology to occupy the major share of the world's petrochemical trade markets. China is a big consumer of petrochemical products. These major international petrochemical corporations have already established several joint capital enterprises with China. For example, the U.S. DuPont Company has invested in and established 8 joint capital enterprises. The German Bayer has established more than 10 joint capital enterprises. The British B.P. Corporation has established a large-scale project for the production of acetic acid. In addition, BASF, Shell Oil, and Dow Chemical Company have shown enormous interest in developing a large scale ethylene project in China.[29] In fact, these world's oil giants actually make friendly concessions in their joint capital projects with Sinopec. For example, in large projects like the Shanghai Saike, the Nanjing Yang-Ba, the Fujian Chemical Refinery, and the Nanjing acetic acid project, the ratio of Chinese to foreign investment is about 1 to 1. In the joint capital projects involving gas stations, however, most are under Sinopec's control. For instance, in the province of Zhejiang, Sinopec owns 60% of the gas stations, while B.P. only owns 40%. In the province of Jiangsu, Sinopec owns 60% of the gas stations, while the Shell Oil Company owns 40%.[30]

The fact that most of these companies are minority stake share holders reflects the state's overall philosophy of reforming SOEs. Zhu's plan of SOEs reform was to create a trimmed-down state sector of efficient, profitable, high-tech enterprises, along the lines of the state sector in contemporary Germany or France. However, he only wants to sell off to private investors (foreign or Chinese) SOEs that do not occupy leading positions in their sectors. Wen is committed to his overall strategy of privatizing failing state-owned enterprises, with the exception of those in strategic sectors such as arms production and energy.[31] In this case, Wen views China's national oil companies as being of national strategic importance, and, will consequently not allow foreign oil companies to have a majority share.

Sinopec's Inward and Outward FDI:

Sinopec's upstream production of oil is deficient. It only supplies Sinopec with about 20%-30% of the crude oil Sinopec requires. The remainder is virtually all imported.[32] Thus, Sinopec must make up its upstream shortage of resources through trade, purchases, and other acquisitions.

In January 2001, the establishment of the China International Petroleum Chemical Company (SIPC) symbolized the implementation of Sinopec's strategy of globalization. That same year, Sinopec's strategy of foreign investment focused on the Middle East. The Middle East is China's main supplier of crude oil, accounting for approximately 50% of all the oil imported, most of which comes from Saudi Arabia and Iran. 80% of this imported Middle Eastern crude oil goes to Sinopec.[33]

In 2001, Sinopec found its first overseas investment partner, the National Iranian Oil Company. Two years later, Sinopec's first began to drill for oil and gas in the Iranian Zavareh-Kashan mountainous area. This initial drilling turned out to be quite fruitful with a daily production of 1,000 cubic meters of gas. In 2004, Sinopec made overtures towards the Saudi Arabian petroleum company, Saudi Aramco, and started to enter Saudi Arabia's natural gas industry. In March of the same year, Sinopec successfully bid for the rights to develop the natural gas field in the Rub al-Khali Basin Area "B", and was allowed to invest venture capital for this project.[34]

In addition to the Middle East, Sinopec gained the rights to oilfields in Kazakhstan, Azerbaijan, and Kyrgyzstan, in an amount totaling 310,000 tons. At present, China has already succeeded in gaining access to the world's largest area of concentration of oil and gas, namely, Saudi Arabia. It has also participated in local petroleum and natural gas projects in Canada, Iran, Saudi Arabia, Gabon, Kazakhstan, Yemen and Ecuador.[35]

Although many stories in the international media concerning the overseas expansion of China's NOCs have focused on the Chinese government's energy insecurity as the main motivation for such expansion, it is in fact the companies' desire for reserves and profits that are the forces driving the expansion. Some Chinese officials are most assuredly uncomfortable with China's increasing dependence on imported oil. However, China's NOCs, like all other oil companies, continuously need to acquire new reserves to replace what they produce. These have limited opportunities to do so within China. What is more, exploration and production have always been the most profitable aspect of the oil industry. This fact is particularly true for China's NOCs. These NOCs have recently incurred heavy losses in their refining and marketing operations because of an increase in the price of crude oil coupled with state-controlled prices for diesel and gasoline. As a result, China's NOCs are seeking income from exploration and production abroad.[36]

In view of its shortage of upstream oil, Sinopec has chosen a course of outward FDI. In its middle and downstream segments of production, it has employed inward FDI.

This is exemplified by three great joint capital ethylene projects. Sinopec's first joint capital enterprise took place in September 2001 between the Sinopec subsidized Yangzi Petrochemical Company and the German BASF company. The total capital invested in this project amounts to US $2.9 billion, and the ethylene production currently reaches 600,000 tons annually. This joint venture, called the Yang-Ba Petrochemical Company, went into production on June 28, 2005 in Nanjing, China.[37]

The second ethylene project was formed by Sinopec, Shanghai Petrochemical, and BP as the Shanghai Saike Ethylene Project. It has a current annual ethylene production of 900,000 tons, making it the largest in China so far. The total amount invested in this project was US $2.75 billion. This project went into production on June 29, 2005.[38]

The third project involved Sinopec, Exxon-Mobile and the Saudi Aramco Company. On October 21, 2002, it was agreed that this project was to open new markets in the two coastal provinces of Fujian and Guangdong. The total amount invested in this project was US $3 billion, making it Sinopec's most expensive project to date. This project combined the drilling and exploration for oil with its refinement and chemical processing. This project was in its preparation stages as early as 2000 when the two parties established a strategic alliance.[39]

This project began with several goals. The first was to increase the amount of oil refined per year from 4 million tons to 12 million tons. Another goal was to establish a production capacity of 800,000 tons of ethylene per year. The third goal was more focused on downstream production, and involved the management of 600 gas stations in Fujian Province. On July 8, 2005, this tripartite joint capital project went into production.[40]

With respect to other inward FDI projects, Sinopec and the Shell Oil Company cooperated to jointly established approximately 500 gas stations in Zhejiang province. In addition, Sinopec and B.P. jointly formed the Sinopec-BP Petroleum Limited Company to establish and operate 500 gas stations in Hangzhou, Ningbo, and Shaoxing, three cities in Zhejiang province. Besides the above, on September 28, 2005, CNOOC, Shell Oil and Sinopec South China Sea started a joint project in Huizhou, Guangdong province, with the goal of producing 800,000 tons of ethylene yearly. This project employs the world's most advanced petrochemical technology.[41]

In addition, Sinopec and B.P. also signed a joint capital agreement to construct an acetic acid factory in Nanjing with a predicted annual production of 500,000 tons. It has been stated that this project's implementation will satisfy the Chinese domestic demand for acetic acid. It will also consolidate both sides' leading status in the Chinese's acetic acid market.[42]

NOCs' commercial interests have driven Sinopec's inward and outward FDI. China's NOCs overseas oil investments represent a confluence of corporate and national interests. The oil companies have the goal of increasing reserves and profits. The government's objective is to increasing Chinese control over the country's oil supply. The securing of overseas oil assets abroad is important to both the companies and the government. In spite of this importance, the Chinese government and companies have not jointly developed a comprehensive national plan for acquiring overseas oil assets. The NOCs' foreign investments are primarily driven by the companies themselves. Each of these companies has its own corporate objectives in making these investments.[43] As a result, it is often said by China's policymakers that, as far as the NOCs are concerned, "each soldier is fighting his own war"— that is to say, each company is placing its own corporate interests above national ones.[44] However, since 2005, there seems to have been greater cooperation between the government and the NOCs.

China National Petroleum Corporation's (CNPC) Development:

In recent years, through a series of large-scale annexations and reorganizations, the world has acquired a handful of giant petroleum companies, for example, Exxon-Mobile, BP-Amoco, Royal Dutch Shell, TotalFinaElf, and Chevron-Texaco. In 1992, China's petroleum enterprises represented by the CNPC began to enter the international market. The internationalization of Chinese petroleum groups began during the period of the Eighth Five-Year Plan (1989-1994). 1992 to 1995 was the initial stage of the internationalization. During that time, the CNPC signed onto several small projects with overseas investors. By doing so, it accumulated experience, fostered its own talent, and became familiar with the international environment. 1997 until the present has been a stage of steady development. The essential targets of this stage are low risk, high benefit, large and middle scale development projects. Between 1996 and 1997, the CNPC has successively signed onto several large-scale oil and gas development projects in the Sudan, Kazakhstan, and Venezuela. The CNPC is currently involved in 44 overseas petroleum investment projects. Its big three oil and gas projects in the Sudan, Kazakhstan and Venezuela are operating fairly successfully.[45] The CNPC will eventually develop global oil and gas resources in areas, such as central Asia, South America, the Middle East and Africa. Thus, the CNPC will form multiple centers of overseas oil production, and will thereby realize diversification of the developments of all overseas exploration for petroleum products.

The CNPC's Integration of its Downstream Oil-refining:

In the next five years, the CNPC plans to construct five oil-refining bases with a capacity of thousands of tons, two large aromatic hydrocarbon production bases, four chemical fertilizer production bases, and six large-scale ethylene production bases. All of them are planned to be of world-class scale, and to make their owners more competitive. With regard to oil refining, the CNPC continues to complete the construction of five oil refining bases, namely, Dalian petrochemical, Fushun petrochemical, Lanzhou petrochemical, Dushanzi petrochemical, and the Western Pacific petrochemical companies, all of which have huge production capacities. With regard to petrochemicals, the CNPC will construct six large-scale ethylene bases, namely, Jilin petrochemical, Lanzhou petrochemical, Sichuan petrochemical, and several others. With regard to sales, the volume of refined oil sold by the CNPC is projected to surpass 100 million tons, while the sales of major petrochemical products are expected to surpass 25 million tons.[46] The CNPC is still in the preliminary stages of becoming an integrated petroleum company. Its downstream business is relatively small compared with its upstream business. The current investment in infrastructure improvement is part of the CNPC's determination to make its downstream services larger.

In addition, the CNPC and Sinopec jointly established the Maoming petrochemical, Zhenhai petrochemical, and Tianjin petrochemical plants, all ultra large-scale ethylene projects. Ethylene is the upstream raw material for plastic, automobile spare parts, shoes, and textiles. The construction of the Zhenhai ethylene project will alleviate the shortage of such material in light industry in the city of Shanghai and Zhejiang province. In addition, the CNPC subsidized the Fushun petrochemical ethylene project in Liaoning province. This project will resolve the ethylene shortage in the northeastern part of China.[47]

This reflects the government's agenda to create national industrial leaders by consolidation and integration of enterprises in the industrial sectors. The Chinese government has spoken of its ambitions for its oil companies to join the ranks of the world's top oil companies, like ExxonMobil, Royal Dutch-Shell, and BP.[48] The creation of such world-class oil companies is a matter of national prestige. According to Peter Nolan, most senior policymakers "regarded it as a national humiliation that China should have no powerful firms to match those of the advanced economies in general and the United States in particular."[49]

The CNPC and Sinopec's North-South Layout:

The CNPC plans to construct a refinery in the southern city of Qinzhou with a projected output of 10 million tons annually. This is the CNPC's first oil refinery in the south. In the past, the southern market was dominated by Sinopec. Once the project is completed, it will mainly be used for processing crude oil from the Sudan. At present, China's largest overseas holding in oil is from the Sudan. When the oil flows in from the Sudan, it will enter China through the port of Qinzhou, and will be refined and processed locally. These products will supply Guangxi province in particular, as well as the entire Zhujiang River Delta area. Prior to this, the CNPC's market focused on the northern part of China. Its imported crude oil was mainly processed at the Dalian refinery plant, and then shipped to the South through marine transportation. The CNPC's cost of transporting oil from the north to the south amounted to two hundred million dollars each year.[50] The CNPC officials believe that if a refinery plant would be situated in Guangdong province, it would save the company a great amount of transportation costs. Therefore, the strategic importance of the Guangxi province project is substantial. This project has been submitted to the China Development and Reform Commission for final approval. As we can see, this project is mainly driven by commercial interests of the CNPC.

In addition, Sinopec has also considered expanding a small refinery plant in Beihai with current capacity of 500 thousand tons per year into a large scale factory with an annual capacity of 8 million tons. The plan for this project has also been submitted to the China Development and Reform Commission for approval. However, the Chinese government will not allow internal competitive investment between state-owned companies. That is to say, only one of these projects will be approved.[51] This situation reflects the state's role in controlling the competing interests of the companies. In these cases, the companies' objectives conflict with those of the government. China's NOCs have bid directly against each other for oil assets, much to the dismay of the Chinese leadership and analysts, who would rather see things done with central planning, and who would prefer to see the firms operate as a team rather than as competitors. From the Chinese leadership's perspective, perhaps its most important role in this regard has been to encourage the NOCs not to compete against one another for investment projects.[52]

Guangxi province does not consume an inordinate amount of refined oil. However, it has suddenly become an area of interest for two large oil companies. This is because of Guangxi's connection to the anticipated construction of a crude oil pipeline from Burma to China. This pipeline project will enable crude oil from the Middle East to enter China's Guangxi province via a land route through Burma. Although this project has been temporarily put on hold by the China Development and Reform Commission, and an internal staff member once explicitly told a reporter that the project would start sooner or later. Once Guangxi province does become the terminus of the proposed Sino-Burmese oil pipeline, the company that has a refinery plant there will capture the market of the Zhujiang River Delta. Moreover, southwestern China adjoins Vietnam, which also does not have a large refinery plant. Thus, the company that controls the Chinese terminus of this pipeline will have another market in Vietnam.

The CNPC's Oil and Gas Cooperation with Russia and Central Asia:

Energy experts believe that despite the fact that the Middle East is the largest oil resource in the world, it carries with it a fairly large risk because of the instability of its economy and politics, which bear with them corresponding deleterious effects on the oil transportation routes. Moreover, most Middle East oil-producing countries do not open their resources to foreign investment. Therefore, the chief way to obtain oil from this area is through trade rather than foreign direct investment.

However, central Asia and Russia are ideal candidates for Chinese foreign direct investment, not only because these two countries are located outside of the Persian Gulf region, but also because Russia and the five countries in central Asia possess vast oil resources, and their exports travel to China overland. In addition, China has a huge and quite stable market for the consumption of petroleum. This geopolitical closeness and economic reciprocity of the supply of and demand for oil make Russia and central Asia an ideal area for Chinese foreign direct investment and joint ventures in the oil and gas industry. This proposed mutually beneficial cooperation would also promote economic development for China, Russia, and central Asia.

Moreover, Russia and Kazakhstan—which played a negligible role in China's oil import mix ten years ago—accounted for 11 percent of China's crude oil imports in 2005.[53] China has already undertaken the development of oil and gas cooperation projects with Russia and the five countries in central Asia. As of now, these projects include the Chinese "West to East Gas Transmission" pipeline, the Russian Irkutsk-based Kovykta gas field, which provides natural gas to China and South Korea, the Russian Sakha Republic to China natural gas project, as well as the Kazakhstan based Aktobe, and the Turkmenistan Gunorta Eloten gas field projects.[54] The Kazakhstan Aktobe project has been fairly successful. Both its production and its financial condition turned around within five years of the CNPC takeover. It has not only paid off its debt, but its financial status is well into the black. In addition, this project has also vastly contributed to the local economy. Moreover, the Chinese government wants to increase the amount of oil from these areas through two pipeline projects: 400,000 barrels per day pipeline from western Kazakhstan to western China, which is being built in stages and a proposed 600,000 barrels per day pipeline from eastern Siberia to northeastern China. The Siberia project depends on Moscow making a firm commitment. If both pipelines are built and operated at the designed capacity, the combined throughput of 1 million barrels per day would constitute 10 to 20 percent of the 6 million to 11 million barrels per day China is projected to import in 2020.[55]

The CNPC in Africa:

By February 4, 2004, when Chinese president, Hu Jintao, returned to Beijing from his visit to France and three African countries, China had become significantly prominent in its petroleum cooperation with the three African countries he had visited. Hu's companions on this trip included the leaders of the CNPC and Sinopec. On January 31, Total in Gabon, a French-owned petroleum group, signed an agreement with a Sinopec subsidiary, the Lianbang petrochemical company. This agreement guaranteed that the Gabon Khartoum company would supply crude oil to China on an annual basis. On January 29, Zhou Jiping, the CNPC vice president, and the first vice-minister of the Egyptian Petroleum Ministry signed a memorandum in Cairo, agreeing to cooperate for the exploration of oil in 3 areas in southern Egypt.[56] Egypt hoped that China would use the same successful mode of operation as it did in the Sudan. That is to say, that the bilateral collaboration would include exploration, development, the upgrading of old oil fields, the construction of pipelines and refinery plants, as well as project engineering services, the manufacture of equipment and personnel training.

The CNPC has been investing in the African petroleum industry for several years now. It has recently been increasing the amount of its investment. Among all the Chinese projects in Africa, the most noteworthy is the CNPC's investment in the Sudanese petroleum industry. In 1997, the CNPC and the Sudanese government entered into a joint venture with each side holding 50% of the shares. The CNPC has invested in the Sudan more than in any other country. In 1997, the CNPC and the Sudanese Energy Ministry jointly constructed the Khartoum Oil Refinery Company, which was designed to have the appearance of a verdant park. Another successful project between the CNPC and the Sudanese government was the construction of three oil fields and a pipeline project in 1997. This second project, aside from being the CNPC's largest overseas investment in scale, has also proven to be its most profitable.[57] North Africa's Sudan, South America's Venezuela, and the Middle East's Iran and Iraq have become the CNPC's three main strategic regions for its overseas investment.

Starting with the Sudanese project, the CNPC has developed other North African markets one after another, such as those in Libya, Algeria, Amman, and Syria. On July 14, 2003, the CNPC and the Algerian National Oil and Gas Company signed a contract for the development of the Adrar oil field. This contract included terms for the construction of the refinery, the project operation, and its management. On December 22, 2003, both sides also signed a contract concerning the exploration for oil and gas in two other areas.[58]

In recent years, Sinopec has continuously increased the amount of crude oil it imports from Africa. Sinopec is the chief importer of oil for the Chinese. In 1998, 8% of all Chinese imports of crude oil came from Africa. From 1999 to 2002, that proportion was 19 %, 24 %, 22 %, and 23 %, respectively. In 2003, the amount of oil that China imported from Africa's Angola for the first time surpassed the amount of oil it imported from the Middle East's Saudi Arabia. Angola thus became China's biggest supplier of petroleum. Another African country, Nigeria, also exports a considerable amount of petroleum to China.[59]

Venturing into Africa is a superficially attractive option for Chinese enterprises with limited global experience, as they can avoid the kind of competition and rules they face in markets such as the US or the European Union. But Chinese companies are also under great pressure to invest in Africa to fulfill political commitments made by China's leaders, who provide financial incentives, including cheap loans, for the Chinese companies to go overseas. For instance, Chinese enterprises have built highways and bridges in Tanzania, Zambia and

Guinea. They have also constructed a "friendship" sports stadium for Senegal, which switched recognition from Taiwan to the mainland in late 2005. China is likely to finance a US $600 million hydroelectric dam in northern Ghana, which could boost the country's gold and iron ore industries.[60]

Chinese overseas investment in Africa is often seen as part of a larger Chinese state driven energy policy, when it comes to dealing with oil-exporting states whose policies run counter to American interests. For example, the main reason for Beijing's willingness to soften the language of UNSC resolutions, which included automatic sanctions if Khartoum did not stop the killing and dislocation of civilians in Darfur, was China's oil ties to the Sudan. The CNPC is the largest foreign investor in the Sudanese oil field. The operations in 1999 of the CNPC changed the Sudan from a net oil importer to a net oil exporter. This change let the CNPC and the Sudan reap windfall profits from the rise in world oil prices at that time. It is therefore clear that the CNPC's lucrative investments in the Sudan (the company's second largest source of oil after Kazakhstan) have played a significant role in China's recent recalcitrant behavior in the United Nations Security Council.[61]

The rise of the importance of Africa and Central Asia as sources of Chinese oil and the corresponding decline of Southeast Asia is reflected in China's overall strategy of the diversification of its oil supplies. There are two factors which explain the diminishing role of the Asia Pacific region and the increasing importance of Central Asia and Africa in meeting China's demand for oil. First, the demand for oil exceeds supply in the Asia Pacific region. This trend has only increased over the past ten years.[62] For example, Indonesia is now a net importer of oil, though it was the region's second largest oil producer (behind China) and was at one time China's largest supplier. As a result, countries in this region are looking elsewhere for supplies of oil. Second, Central Asia and Africa's oil surplus has grown over the past decade, in contrast to the growing oil deficit in the Asia Pacific region. Moreover, the light, sweet crude oil of West Africa and Kazakhstan are well suited for China's oil refineries.[63]

China's Oil and Gas Investments in Russia:

When Rosneft, one of Russia's oil companies, recently sold shares of its stock for the first time, the CNPC invested US $500 million, thus realizing its goal of being involved in a large scale Russian oil company. However, the CNPC holds less than 1% of the stock in this Russian petroleum company.[64] As a small shareholder, the CNPC cannot control this enterprise. If this is true, then why did the CNPC invest in this Russian petroleum company?

Russia is a huge producer of oil, and it is also China's neighbor. For a long time, Chinese petroleum enterprises have hoped to gain a foothold in the Russian petroleum market for exploration and development. However, China's path to develop Russian petroleum has not been smooth. With the exception of several projects in Sakhalin island, most Chinese attempts to gain a foothold in the Russian market over the past several years have failed. Chinese petroleum enterprises have made little progress in the Russian inland.

Russia has been quite discriminating when it comes to allowing foreign capital to be involved in its oil and gas exploration and development. Russia refuses to allow foreign enterprises to control its strategic oil fields. Every foreign cooperation project of any significance must be decided by President Putin himself. These manifold extra-market factors present obstacles to foreign enterprises which wish to gain entry into Russia's oil fields. China is faced with the additional obstacle of having an insufficient understanding of the Russian energy industry.

In recent years, Russia has increasingly treated China as a foreign business partner. It has clearly felt that energy cooperation with China would reap huge economic benefits. Moreover, as Russia sees increasing conflict in its energy relations with the Western nations, it is turning to China to offset this potential instability in its petroleum markets.

As for the Chinese, their petroleum enterprises—by gaining an increasing amount of experience with the Russian energy industry—have finally come to grasp its complexities. These Chinese companies have also become keenly aware of the complex web of relationships between the various domestic interest groups in the Russian oil industry. This knowledge has greatly enhanced the possibility of successful Chinese investment in the Russian oil industry. In spite of this progress in the opening of Russia's oil industry to China, Russia still places limits on the amount of Chinese investment and still looks chiefly towards its own benefit in each project.

Some experts believe that the current Chinese investments in petroleum enterprises in Russia will not yield large economic benefits, and that some individual projects may even lose money. However, those Chinese enterprises with investments in Russian petroleum are not looking towards an immediate gain but are rather focused on long-term strategic interests. For example, Sinopec bought TNK-BP's subsidiary company, Udmurtneft, but transferred its controlling stockholder's rights to a Russian petroleum company which was not one of the bidders.[65] Sinopec did so because without the support of this Russian petroleum company, Sinopec would not have been able to win the bid for the subsidiary company. Although Sinopec lost some benefit in the transaction by giving up the controlling share, it, nevertheless, succeeded in entering Russia's petroleum exploration market.

The CNPC invested US $500 million to purchase a trivial share of the stock of a Russian petroleum company. The amount of stock purchased by the CNPC did not grant it policy-making power over the Russian petroleum company. However, by entering the Russian petroleum market, the CNPC obtained an opportunity to learn the inner workings of the Russian petroleum industry. The CNPC can also use this investment as a springboard for deeper involvement in the Russian energy industry.

The behavior of the Russian petroleum industry with regard to its cooperation with its Chinese counterpart reflects Russia's concern regarding its economic independence, as well as its national security interests. Specifically, Russia worries that if China gains a majority share of the stock of a Russian energy company, it would result in Russia's loss of control of its oil production and price. This concern of Russia's is heightened by the increasing number of Chinese living in Russia illegally. What is more, the rapid rate of Chinese economic growth is also putting pressure on Russia. China's successful bid for the 2008 Olympic Games, its membership in the World Trade Organization, and Shanghai's sponsoring of the recent World Symposium all make Russia feel ill at ease, especially since Russia is not yet even a member of the WTO.

The CNPC in Thailand:

The CNPC may possibly invest up to US $1 billion in Thailand for oil and natural gas projects.[66] Thailand is not far away from China, and is currently seeking investors from China, South Korea and Japan. China is currently interested in investing in natural gas projects. The Thai government hopes to compete with Singapore to become Southeast Asia's main center for of the petroleum trade. China is also considering constructing an oil pipeline in Thailand to avoid potential problems in transporting oil through the Strait of Malacca. At present, the majority of Middle Eastern petroleum comes to Asia through the Strait of Malacca. This new Thai pipeline will reduce both the risks of pirate attacks in the Strait of Malacca, as well as the distance that the oil has to be transported.

This reflects the Chinese government's efforts to diversify suppliers and transportation routes. This is the key to enhancing oil security. In terms of oil suppliers, China has sought not only to expand the number of countries from which it imports oil, such as Thailand, but to decrease China's dependence on the Persian Gulf, which provided almost half of China's crude oil imports in 2005. In terms of oil routes, both the government and the NOCs want to reduce China's reliance on the routes of oil transportation by sea, through which almost 90 percent of the country's crude oil imports travel, because of their vulnerability to disruption on the high seas by various modern navies.[67] This new Thai pipeline will definitely provide a much needed alternative.

The Origins of "Going Global"

Representatives from China's NOCs assert that the decision to invest in oil exploration and production abroad originated with the companies themselves.[68] The CNPC, the first Chinese oil company to venture overseas, began to set its sights beyond China's borders in the late 1980s in search of reserves and profits. In 1991, the CNPC announced that one of its three main strategies was the internationalization of its operations. The CNPC's first overseas investment was the purchase of a stake in an oil sands development project in Alberta, Canada, which was sponsored by the United Nations.[69] Only after China's oil companies had begun to invest overseas, did the idea arise that acquiring equity in oil abroad enhances China's energy security. Once the link was made between equity in foreign oil and national energy security, China's NOCs were quick to use "energy security" as a reason for paying a premium for certain assets, often in bidding wars between the NOCs themselves.[70]

The CNPC's decision to invest abroad was initially not supported by the Chinese leadership. The top leadership was of the opinion that China's increasing oil imports were a stopgap solution to a situation that could best be solved by increasing domestic oil exploration and production. Additionally, the leadership feared that when Chinese companies investing abroad, it provides opportunities for the companies and their executives to gain riches at the state's expense.[71] However, increasing oil imports and the increasing profitability of the CNPC abroad gradually changed the government's position. By 1997, the Chinese oil companies' strategy of "Go Global" had the support of mainstream industrial, academic, and government circles. This support has continued, especially in light of the energy crisis of 2003-2004.[72]

Therefore, contrary to accepted opinion, the overseas expansion of China's NOCs has been driven from the "bottom-up" rather than from the "top-down." A shift of power and resources away from the central government toward the state-owned energy companies has resulted from the liberalization and decentralization of China's energy sector over the past two decades. The power shift has also resulted in a substantial reduction in the ability of the government to monitor these firms. The NOCs are in the driver's seat and the Chinese government is often just along for the ride, when it comes to deciding which overseas assets should be acquired. In addition, the Chinese government is not the only one along for the ride. The NOCs also "take along for the ride" a variety of other actors, including the companies' minority shareholders. The NOCs also have other forces trying to influence them, including international banks and the governments of oil-producing states.[73]

The Profile of CNOOC & its Outward FDI:

Acquisition may become an important strategy for overseas development for the China National Offshore Oil Company (CNOOC). Through transnational acquisition and purchase, CNOOC can achieve two transformations: one transformation is from being involved in domestic competition to being involved in international competition, the other transformation is from being engaged solely in production to being engaged both in production and capital management.

CNOOC started its global exposure relatively late, but its movements in that direction have all been substantial. In January 2002, CNOOC invested US $580 million to purchase partial interests in Indonesia's five largest oil fields. The Spanish Repsol-YPE Company is currently chief owner of these oil fields. CNOOC at the same time reached an agreement of cooperation concerning petroleum with Australia in the amount of US $12 billion, an agreement projected to last 25 years. In September 2002, in Jakarta, CNOOC and the Indonesian national oil and gas company signed a purchase agreement for liquefied natural gas (LNG) in Indonesian Tangguh project, an agreement projected to last 25 years. In October 2003, CNOOC spent US $25.8 billion to purchase a 5.56% interest in the Australian North West Shelf gas project (NWS—natural gas project).[74]

In addition, Canada has massive reserves of crude oil locked up in the form of "tar sands," a tar-like substance mixed in with sand. The potential oil reserves are huge, second only to Saudi Arabia's, and are projected to last for at least 50 years. Canadian tar sands are extremely attractive to the Chinese. CNOOC invested US $147 million dollars to purchase nearly 17% of the stock of the Canadian MGE energy company, a company engaged in the oil sand mining industry. The MEG energy company is located in Calgary, Canada.[75] This project has provided China with a good opportunity to learn oil sand mining technology and to gain experience in that industry. Thanks to this experience and technology, China recently discovered within its own borders rich reserves of rich sand oil and shale oil. The technologies and experiences acquired from Canada will also help in the mining and extraction of these recently discovered Chinese resources.

According to former chief financial officer of CNOOC, Mr. Qiu, CNOOC needs to establish larger and geographically more diverse reserves to ensure its long-term survival, as do all international oil companies.[76] In addition to making foreign investments solely for profit, CNOOC's investments are also part of a competition among the companies to obtain economic and political benefits from the party-state. Whenever CNOOC obtains foreign oil assets, the company gain influence with key energy officials along with access to capital from state-owned banks. A company is more likely it is to obtain support for subsequent acquisitions, the more assets it acquires initially. This is the case for CNOOC, which does not have the amount of political clout that CNPC and Sinopec do.[77] A Chinese consulting firm has stated that, "here in China, CNOOC's real enemies are CNPC and Sinopec. The little brother among the three has to have more assets to have a louder voice."[78]

Perhaps the most important guidance given by the Chinese leadership has been its advice to the NOCs not to compete against each another for overseas projects. Zeng Qinghong, in the *Study Times* in 2005 (a Communist Party publication), stated that Chinese companies should coordinate their foreign investments.[79] Although the Chinese government—according to some reports—has attempted to direct CNPC, Sinopec, and CNOOC to invest in different geographical area, the companies have not heeded the government's advice. In this same article, Zeng also advised Chinese companies which invest abroad to consider China's political and diplomatic strategies when doing so, not just their own economic benefit. Zeng's warning was probably a response to unsuccessful bid by CNOOC for the Unocal (a U.S. oil company) and the resentment against China it caused in Washington.[80]

Zeng also advised Chinese companies to take each other into account when making foreign investments so as to avoid direct competition with each other. He also urged these companies not to keep a high profile when bidding for projects. The Ministry of Commerce sounded this same warning, trying to stop Chinese companies from paying a "China premium" for overseas investments because of political opposition incited by rivals.[81] What is more, Jiang Zemin, China's former president, has encouraged China's NOCs to make more investments in developing countries that are on good terms with China, including countries in Central Asia and Africa.[82]

Compare and Contrast Sinopec, CNPC and CNOOC:

First, Sinopec, CNPC and CNOOC are influential state-owned Chinese oil companies that have considerable impact on energy sector development. Their influence is due to the fact that they possess the political, financial and human resources the energy policymaking bodies lack. These firms experienced a marked increase in power during the time when Zhu Rongji was in charge of China's economy (1993-2003). After about 1995, Zhu Rongji made great efforts to increase the financial and administrative autonomy of Chinese NOCs. He made this effort out of a desire to make them more financially efficient in light of the coming listing of their subsidiaries on international stock exchanges. In part because of a leadership vacuum in the Chinese energy sector, these three powerful companies have successfully joined their own financial interests in specific projects to a professed interest in Chinese national "energy security." Because of this joining, some of the projects of these three companies drive policy.[83]

Second, each of these three oil companies is constantly looking for new reserves through exploration or acquisition in order to replace what they produce, keep reserves high, and to create a diversification of supply in order to reduce risk. Most oil companies in general, and China's in particular, according to Qiu, need to create bigger and more geographically diversified reserves to help guarantee their growth and survival in the long term. Since there are few opportunities to increase oil reserves for these companies within China, most of these companies are looking abroad.[84]

China's oil companies are at the same time engaging in differing investment strategies. Their respective histories, capabilities, and corporate objectives are driving the foreign investments of Sinopec, CNPC and CNOOC. Although they all wish to diversify their investments, these companies all have different desires and outlooks for risk, profit targets, assessments of future world oil prices, and, to a more limited extent, geographical regions.[85] CNPC is trying to expand in Kazakhstan and the Sudan—areas where its larger operations are located. Sinopec used to be solely a refining and marketing company until the late 1990's. It thus lacks the experience in exploration and production that CNPC and CNOOC have. It is therefore considering any and all geographical areas in its quest to find places for future development. CNOOC has focused on Asia and Africa.[86]

Both Sinopec and the CNPC have sought to increase the attractiveness of their bids for upstream assets by building and investing in pipelines and refineries—projects which the international oil companies view as being of questionable economic value. Nigeria's Kaduna refinery is an example of such a project. CNPC invested US $4 billion in this refinery exchange for four Greenfield blocks, and a proposed export refinery in Lobito, Angola. Sinopec has agreed to build this refinery in Lobito out of a desire to acquire more upstream assets.[87] In the meantime, CNOOC has kept its focus on Asia and Africa. Ever since CNOOC lost its bid for Unocal, some have reported that the company has taken a more opportunistic approach towards the acquisition of assets.[88]

The Government versus the NOCs

China's government and its NOCs will apparently have a relationship of friction at home and more close cooperation abroad. Inside China's borders, the NOCs will keep seeking an increasing degree of autonomy from the government. Outside China's borders, there will continue to be cooperation between the Chinese government and the NOCs. The government support for state-owned oil companies has been successful in the past few years in countries such as in Angola, Kazakhstan, and Nigeria.[89]

The Chinese government and the NOCs both believe that the government has a role in helping companies obtain overseas oil assets. The general opinion in China is that government support is not only necessary, but desirable as well.

The reason for this is that most people think that since other national and international oil companies receive the support of their home governments in acquiring oil assets, the Chinese companies should—in all fairness—receive the same type of support from the Chinese government. The Chinese government has been using many tools, both financial and political, to help secure investment opportunities for China's oil companies. The Chinese government uses such tools not only to give oil companies financial assistance, but also to help improve relations with states which produce oil. The Chinese government often plays a key role in the acquisition of oil assets, and lobbies for specific projects on behalf of China's oil companies.[90]

As it is, the Chinese government supports the NOCs through direct and indirect financial support to China's NOCs. China offers such support by mean of loans—often at below-market rates—and by making investments in the infrastructure of oil producing states, as well as in the states themselves. China's use of these financial instruments involves the "policy banks," such as the Export-Import Bank of China (China Eximbank) and the China Development Bank (which manage state directed lending). Such use of these banks helps to further the government's interest in obtaining oil assets abroad.[91]

Indirect financial support by the Chinese government has taken the form of construction of basic infrastructure in the host country by Chinese firms and the giving of foreign aid. Chinese foreign aid and investment helps to assure the local governments that China can help their country's economic development.[92] The Chinese oil companies are often the beneficiaries of the ensuing good will. Infrastructure investments by Chinese firms not involved in oil are often linked to Acquisitions made by China's NOCs. This is quite certainly the case in Africa, where even basic infrastructure is greatly needed. Nigeria and Angola, among other African oil producers, have demonstrated that they will prefer foreign oil companies that can provide them with beneficial economic packages.[93]

In the political realm, the Chinese government supports China's oil companies through the involvement of China's leaders in some project negotiations, summit meetings between Chinese leaders and their counterparts in oil producing states, and making full use of China's membership in international organizations, such as the WTO. In countries with large oil reserves that China believes to be strategically important, such as Kazakhstan, Russia, and Iran, it is not uncommon for Chinese leaders to participate in negotiations for specific mergers and acquisitions.[94] For example, the success of CNPC's bid for PetroKazakhstan has been attributed by the Chinese media to Hu Jintao's personal involvement in the negotiations, as well as to the generally friendly relations between China and Astana.[95]

In May 2003, Hu Jintao visited Russia and central Asia for the first time as the new president of China. During this trip, the CNPC and the Russian company, YUKOS, signed a mutual recognition agreement concerning the Chinese-Russian pipeline and the long-term purchase and sale of crude oil. This was the largest petroleum supply agreement in Chinese-Russian history.

In 2003, Wu Bangguo, Chairman of the Chinese Standing Committee of the National People's Congress, attended the Asian Forum for Peace Conference in the Philippines. There he proposed the multilateral exploration of the oil and gas fields in the South China Sea. Since ownership of this area had been under dispute, this agreement broke the deadlock concerning possible exploration for energy in the South China Sea. Three months later, China Offshore Oil and the Philippine National Petroleum Exploration Company signed a memorandum of intent to explore jointly potential oil and gas resources in the South China Sea. The Chinese Premier, Wen Jiabao, and the leaders of the ten countries of the Association of Southeast Asian Nations signed this memorandum on the Island of Bali.

In October of 2003, Chinese president, Hu Jintao, conducted an official visit to Australia and New Zealand. During this visit, China Offshore Oil signed an agreement with the Australian Gorgon company to purchase 80 to 100 million tons of liquefied natural gas. This contract has a duration of 25 years, and a value of up to $US 21 billion US. In addition, China Offshore Oil will also obtain 1/ 8 of the rights and interests in this project.[96]

In the beginning of 2004, President Hu Jintao visited Africa and continued China's new chapter of cooperation regarding petroleum with three African countries. During President Hu Jintao's visit to Egypt, Gabon, and Algeria, China signed agreements with Egypt and Algeria to further strengthen their cooperation regarding petroleum.[97]

The Chinese government has also employed its membership in several international organizations to help China's oil companies acquire and secure access to foreign oil assets. For example, Beijing has used its seat on the United Nations Security Council (UNSC) to shield Sudan from economic sanctions for the atrocities in Darfur. The Sudan is home to one of the NOCs' two largest overseas oil projects.[98]

The Failures of China's Big Three Petroleum Giants' Overseas Investments:

The Chinese petroleum corporations' overseas development path has been by no means problem-free. In December 2002, the CNPC attempted to spend a large amount of money (estimated to be above $US 2 billion) to participate in the Russian petroleum company Slavneft's auction of 74.95% of its stockholder's rights. The Slavneft petroleum company possessed more than 4,000 oil wells in Siberia.[99] Some experts worried that after its acquisition, the CNPC would use these oil fields as a strategic petroleum reserve, rather than for production. Finally, the Russian Duma denied CNPC's request based on the fact that the CNPC is a state-owned company, and thus cannot participate in Russia's privatization process. This denial cast a shadow on the prospect of Sino-Russian energy cooperation. Moreover, the long planned China-Russia petroleum pipeline project (originally planned to extend from the Russian Angarsk to the Chinese Daqing) also brought with it disappointment. In December 2002, the Russian government changed its preliminary decision, and decided to place the pipeline's end point in Russia's Far East area, Nakhodka or Vladivostok, out of concern that if the pipeline ended in China, it would make Russia lose control of its petroleum output and price. Another factor in Russia's change of plan was influence by Japan.

This change of plan has had an enormous negative influence on the relationship between China and Russia concerning energy cooperation. China's wish to treat Russia as a long-term energy partner failed, while Russia lost a potential oil market. In March 2003, the CNPC and Sinopec announced their intention to purchase the British Natural Gas Company's 8.33% share of the northern Caspian Sea area project for a price of US$ 615 million.[100] This project is located at one of the world's richest oil and gas reserves. Because this project is owned by a consortium of world-class energy companies who have the right of first purchase as shareholders, the Chinese petroleum companies' bid to purchase a share of the Caspian Sea project failed.

These failures bear witness to the sensitivity surrounding oil and its political and economic characteristics, characteristics which can influence a country's international behaviors. China's oil interests, like those of other countries, will continue to shape its broader foreign policy. Beijing is probably more willing to take actions to gain and maintain access to oil when such actions do not conflict with top U.S. foreign policy objectives.[101] The following section will consider several of the major failed oil projects that China has pursued, as well as the economic and political influence on these projects. All of these failed bids seem to lead to the conclusion that money does not necessarily buy "China's oil security."[102]

Chinese oil company bids for the Russian oil producer, Slavneft, in 2002 and the U.S. oil company, Unocal, in 2005 were defeated by economic nationalism. The increasing perception that the United States regards military power as a legitimate instrument for gaining access to oil[103] has raised awareness in China of the following fact: both oil producing and oil consuming states are constantly intervening in the world markets in order to further their own national interests.[104]

Lessons Learned from CNOOC's Attempt to Purchase Unocal:

CNOOC's attempt to purchase Unocal and its subsequent withdrawal from the transaction attracted world attention. From the perspective of market risk, political risk, and CNOOC's own fame, it was a good decision for CNOOC to withdraw from the bid for Unocal. In determining whether to make this bid, CNOOC invited Goldman Sachs and J.P. Morgan to be its advisors, employed a series of senior consultants to evaluate the political and market risks, and also formed its own Washington Operations Office. Moreover, CNOOC also rolled out an aggressive advertising campaign in the Washington media, including *Roll Call* and *The Hill.*[105]

That deal did not go through after US congressmen warned the Bush administration that approving it would amount to handing over America's energy security to the Chinese government (CNOOC is a state-owned enterprise). Another objection to the CNOOC bid was the fear that Chinese ownership of Unocal would threaten the US oil supply. One of the reasons that political and business circles in the United States challenged CNOOC's purchase of Unocal was the belief that CNOOC was not intending to make the purchase for purely commercial reasons. It was also believed that the Chinese government was providing massive financial and political support behind the scenes. This belief was fostered in part by the fact that during the bidding process CNOOC stressed that it had the support of the Chinese National Assets Commission. Although it wasn't intended to do so, this statement had negative consequences for CNOOC, because the United States has always regarded the Chinese National Assets Commission as an arm of the Chinese government. After this, the Chinese government agencies' attempts to clarify the CNOOC-Unocal transaction as a purely commercial endeavor were felt by some to contradict the previous claims by CNOOC that its actions were approved by the National Assets Commission. In comparison to the Chinese government, the U.S. government handled this matter more carefully. The Bush Administration has not made official comment regarding CNOOC *vis a vis* Unocal. These difference in reaction by the two governments points to a difference of values in the two societies. To the United States, the CNOOC matter was initially to be left to the markets to decide; whereas, to the Chinese, the matter was to be left to the authorities.

However, contrary to widespread belief, CNOOC's attempted purchase of Unocal was not motivated by the dictates of the Chinese government (with the backing of all the resources of the Chinese state) to secure oil and natural gas assets for the China. Since it lacked strong political support from Beijing, CNOOC was attempting to acquire Unocal not only for its oil reserves but also to help transform CNOOC into a truly multinational energy company. More than a handful of U.S. policy makers assumed that the country of origin of an oil company matters because firms, especially state-owned ones, place national over corporate interests. These policy makers also cling to the belief that the acquisition of oil assets by state owned or influenced firms is the best way to enhance a country's security of a supply of oil.[106]

In fact, the Chinese government's reaction to the tumult that reverberated throughout the United States in 2005 because of CNOOC Ltd.'s bid for Unocal gives insight into how Beijing balances energy priorities and foreign policy priorities. CNOOC made its bid was after Unocal had already accepted an offer from Chevron. Many commentators portrayed this bid as an example of how Beijing's wish for oil is becoming a source of tension between China and the U.S. Faced with these circumstances, Beijing gave priority to its relations with the United States over the acquisition of foreign oil assets by a Chinese NOC.[107] The Chinese leadership, never enthusiastic about CNOOC's bid in the first place, requested that CNOOC Ltd. withdraw its offer. The Chinese government did so to prevent any further damage to Sino-US relations and to keep Hu Jintao's planned visit to the United States in September of 2005 on schedule.[108]

Some have pointed out that investors did not approve of CNOOC's attempted purchase of Unocal. As evidence for this, they point to the fact that when CNOOC raised its bidding price for Unocal, its own stock price dropped. When CNOOC announced that it was giving up its attempt to purchase Unocal, its stock price rose strongly that same day. William Blair & Co (WB), CNOOC's second largest stockholder, as well as its largest overseas investor, once mentioned that it would completely divest itself of its holdings in CNOOC, should the takeover occur. This points up WB's disaffection with CNOOC's attempted purchase of Unocal.

The defeat of CNOOC demonstrates that the global advancement of the Chinese energy strategy has not been without difficulties. First, it appears as if the international markets are uncomfortable with China's rise. To them, this is yet another version of the "Chinese Threat." Corresponding to the development of the Chinese economy, there has been a shift in concern about China from the political and ideological domain to the economic and energy domain. On the one hand, the international markets have shown a great demand for goods "made in China"; on the other hand, these same international markets are concerned about the impact of the goods "made in China" on the global economy. The international markets are also concerned about the huge Chinese demand for energy and its potential impact on the global market. It is inevitable that China meet with conflict and challenges when it enters the global energy market. China, as a newcomer to the international energy markets, will naturally meet with some resistance. No matter whether it is the direct purchase of energy resources, or the purchase of stocks in energy enterprises, China has met with formidable resistance. An example of the former is CNPC and Sinopec's attempts to participate in the purchase of the Caspian Sea oil resources, which was brusquely pushed aside. An example of the latter is CNOOC's failed attempt to purchase Unocal.

The Caspian Sea Project Defeat:

In March 2003, the British Natural Gas (BG) company announced that it would sell half of its 16.67% rights and interests in the Caspian Sea oil project—half to the CNPC and half to Sinopec—at a price of US$ 6.15 billion each. The attempt to sell was not successful. The northern Caspian Sea oil project is geopolitically quite significant. This project is managed by a consortium of world-class oil companies, which include BG, Exxon-Mobile, Eni-Agip, Shell Oil Company, Total, ConocoPhillips, and the Japanese Inpex. BG and Exxon-Mobile each own a 16.67% share of the project, while the latter five each hold an 8.33% share.[109]

The British BG group gave as an explanation for the attempted sale of its rights to the CNPC and Sinopec that fact that its future core business was natural gas and not oil, which was what the Caspian Sea project was producing. In addition, BG explained that the Caspian Sea project would not be able to achieve its peak output for several years. During this period, BG claimed, it would have to invest more than US $20 billion. It was therefore less than willing to invest such an amount of funds in a non-core business. Consequently, at the beginning of 2003, BG withdrew from the Caspian Sea mining agreement, and intended to sell its share to the CNPC and Sinopec.[110] The other shareholders of this project, with the exception of the Japanese Inpex, used their right of first purchase to acquire the BG shares. This resulted in the collapse of Chinese attempt efforts to acquire BG's rights in the Caspian Sea oil project.

This was yet another setback for overseas investment by Chinese petroleum enterprises, the first being the failed attempt to purchase the Russian Slavneft petroleum company in 2002. This latest setback is another roadblock for the advancement of overseas investment by the Chinese petroleum industry.

The CNPC and Sinopec's attempt to purchase the northern Caspian Sea oil project has important strategic significance. The Caspian Sea area is considered to be the 21st century's third largest energy reserve after the Middle East and Siberia. The Caspian Sea area has attracted investments from many of the world's giant petroleum companies, and in the process, has become an as it were battlefield for these same companies.

It is estimated that the oil and gas reserves in the four main countries of the Caspian Sea area, namely, Kazakhstan, Uzbekistan, Turkmenistan and Azerbaijan, amount to approximately 10.411 billion tons. Kazakhstan's reserves are the richest, accounting for roughly 36% of the total. Therefore, the struggle for the petroleum of the Caspian Sea area is in essence a struggle for the petroleum of Kazakhstan. In 1995, there were only 50 world oil companies involved in Kazakhstan's petroleum industry. This number increased to 200 by the end of 1998. The major projects there include the Tengiz oil-field development project, the Karachaganak oil and gas field project, and the Kashagan oil field project.[111] The CNPC and Sinopec were trying to purchase the stockholder rights to the Kashagan oil field project. The Kashagan oil field is located in one of the world's richest oil and gas reserves. It was one of the world's largest and most significant oil and gas discoveries of the past 30 years. Since this project is located in Kazakhstan, and thus borders with China's Xinjiang Autonomous Region, it enables China to use its newly built western pipelines to transport the crude oil from Kazakhstan to China's markets in the east.

The Defeat of the Russian Slavneft Auction:

On December 18, 2002, bidding for the Russian petroleum company, Slavneft, was held in Moscow. The auction process only lasted four minutes. With nearly no competition, an investment company won the bid for US $ 1.86 billion, which was only US $ 100 million over the starting price. This winning investment company was set up by the Russian petroleum company, Sibneft, and TNK petroleum company. This successful bid was for 74.95% of the stock of the Slavneft petroleum company.[112] Just a day before the auction, the CNPC announced its withdrawal from this auction, although it was considered a strong competitor.

The Slavneft petroleum company was established by the governments of Russia and Belorussia. It is Russia's eighth largest petroleum company. The Russian government originally held the 74. 95% of the stockholder's rights, which were later put up for auction, and the government of Belorussia held 10.83% of the stockholder's rights. In 2003, the Russian government was faced with unprecedented foreign debts, with some estimates as high as US $ 17 billion US. According to the Russian government's initial plan, it would auction off its 74.95% share of the Slavneft petroleum company, with an initial asking price of US $ 1.7 billion. This auction of some of Russia's state assets was the second largest such sale during the period of Russian privatization. The largest auction was conducted in 1997 for the Russian telephone group. For this second largest auction, there were a total of 14 oil companies applying for participation in the bidding, including the CNPC. The expected sale price was hoped to be about US $ 3 billion.[113]

The CNPC planned to enter the Russian crude oil market through participation in the bidding for the Russian Slavneft. The CNPC's participation in the bidding process aroused suspicion and concern in many quarters that China would use this oil field as a strategic reserve, and just ship the crude oil from Russia to China, rather than making full use of the capacity of the Russian refineries. There was also opposition in Russia itself against the Chinese purchase of an oil field which has strategic significance for Russia. The Russian Siberia petroleum company rose to the defense of Russian owned petroleum, thereby opposing China's involvement in the auction. Before the auction took place, the Russian State Duma drafted a resolution concerning the bidding for the stockholder's rights of the Russian Slavneft petroleum company. The resolution stated that if the CNPC—a completely state owned petroleum company—were allowed to participate in the privatization auction, it would violate the principles of Russian privatization. Because of the involvement of the Russian State Duma, what had originally been a purely business dealing became highly politicized. The then Russian Prime Minister stated publicly that:

> The Chinese government sponsored the CNPC out of a desire to obtain the major stockholders' rights of the Russian petroleum company. This action, beyond its superficial economic goal, also has a deeper political objective. This acquisition will enable China to exert political and economic leverage over Russia. The Russian authorities have prepared for this. If the Chinese insist on participating in this auction, the auction will be cancelled.[114]

Shortly after this announcement by the Russian Prime Minister, the representatives of the CNPC announced on December 17th that they would voluntarily withdraw from participation in the next day's auction. The Russian Siberia petroleum company presently is Russia's fifth largest petroleum company. Once China withdrew from the bidding, the remaining 7 companies had business ties of varying degrees to the Russian Sibneft and the TNK petroleum company, the two eventual winners of the auction. These relationships between the remaining bidders are what caused the final price of the deal to be US $ 1.86 US billion, far below the anticipated price. With this auction, Russia tried hard to give the West an image of a fair and transparent privatization transaction of Russian state assets. This included the presence of foreign bankers, professional auctioneers, public bidding, and live reporting. However, the true fairness of this competition was still held suspect. The *New York Times* on December 19th commented that this bidding was intended to be the most public and competitive in Russian history. However, according to the *Times,* it added a new meaning to the word "opaque". The *Times* stated that: "Obviously, this auction was not carried on in a competitive environment. The Siberian company has won, and Russia's budget has lost."[115]

The failure of all three cases highlights one particular aspect of energy security. That is, that China's oil security is not necessarily procured by money. There is a heightened awareness in China that oil producing and oil consuming nations readily intervene in the world markets on behalf of their own national interests. The perception that the United States sees its military might as an instrument for acquiring oil, the defeat of Chinese bids for the Russian oil company Slaveneft in 2002 and the United States company Unocal by economic nationalism in 2005 have led to this heightened awareness in China.[116]

All three failed cases also indicate that there should be more coordination between the NOCs and the Ministry of Foreign Affairs. The MFA desires to be kept abreast of projects engaged in by the NOCs due to the potential effect of these projects on China's foreign policy objectives. That is, China does not want to see a negative impact on its national prestige, as happened with CNOOC's failed bid for Unocal. On the other hand, the NOCs see a clear need for more information about foreign political and economic risks because of the defeat by anti-foreign nationalism of their bids for Slavneft and Unocal.[117]

Chinese Petroleum Security and Its Countermeasures:

Experts have many different estimates regarding the prospective amount of China's petroleum imports, but they universally believe that it is a foregone conclusion that in the long-term China will import massive amounts of petroleum. The Chinese have been on a roller coast of emotions concerning their oil use and production. In the 1960s, they were overjoyed to cast off the label of "the poor oil country." In the 1980s, they were also glad to have the surplus petroleum to sell to earn foreign exchange. At present, they are dismayed at the prospect of having to import large quantities of oil.

Despite China's massive dependence on imported oil, one must also see that there are few countries in the world that are self-sufficient with regard to petroleum. The problem of petroleum security has become an international question. When the price of petroleum is high, it impacts the economies of many countries. The problem of petroleum security is greater for the United States and Japan than for China. This is because these two countries consume more oil than China. As a result, a high price for petroleum has a greater impact on these two countries than on China. Therefore, Chinese should not be unduly anxious with regard to their supply of petroleum.

Efficient use of energy – one component of Chinese petroleum security is the adjustment of its patterns of domestic consumption to improve the efficient use of energy. China's current oil shortage has resulted from three things: rapid economic growth, a rate of consumption of petroleum that far outpaces China's petroleum production, and the inefficient use of energy. Since these factors were not present in the 1980s, China was able to export oil at that time. Since these factors have come into play since the 1990s, China has been an oil-importing nation. China's oil consumption per unit of GDP is about 30% higher than that of the U.S., and twice that of Japan's. Therefore, the current oil shortage in China was inevitable. In the future, two elements will influence the quantity of China's consumption of petroleum. One is the use of energy efficient technology. Once China increases its use of energy efficient technology, the petroleum consumption per unit of GDP will be reduced. If judged by the ratio of economic output to petroleum input of the United States, China should have consumed 145 million tons of petroleum in 2002. However, in 2002, China produced 167 million tons of petroleum.[118] In other words, if China's ratio of economic output to petroleum input was similar to that of U.S., then China would be self-sufficient with regard to oil. Therefore, if China positively adjusts its industrial structure, and adopts energy efficient technology and efficient management, China will enhance its overall energy efficiency, and largely reduce petroleum consumption per unit of GDP. Therefore, the increase of energy efficiency should be one of China's top priorities.

In addition, China might be benefited by optimizing energy efficiency, and reducing its dependence on petroleum. It could go about doing this: (1) by vigorously promoting energy saving activities; (2) by further improving the patterns of China's energy consumption; and (3) by studying and developing renewable sources of energy, including solar, wind, geothermal energy, and nuclear power.

Chinese experts have given similar insightful advice addressing the challenges facing Chinese oil-shortages. For example, Tong Xiaoguang, a senior consultant for the Chinese Petroleum and Gas Development Company, claims that Chinese foreign direct investment with regard to petroleum should have a new strategy: First, Tong maintains that natural gas is a high quality source of energy. At present, the reserve to production ratio of natural gas is higher than that of petroleum in China. However, natural gas has many limitations because of difficulties in transportation. Therefore, there must first be a market for natural gas before money is invested in exploration and development. China should, he says, use the liquefied natural gas of the Asian Pacific and Middle East, and enhance the proportion of the usage of natural gas in the Chinese energy consumption profile. Second, Tong states that the total amount of global heavy oil and oil recoverable from asphalt is 400 billion tons, and is larger than the conventional petroleum reserves. Moreover, the technology to use heavy oil has been significantly enhanced, and its cost has in turn dropped. In addition, heavy oil can now meet commercial production standards. The heavy oil mining business has garnered the attention of the big international oil companies. Therefore, he holds that China's petroleum companies should seize this opportunity by expanding production in Venezuela's heavy oil industry, and by striving for entry into Canada's oil sand and heavy oil mining businesses. Chinese oil companies can mine the sands and put it in hot-water tanks to separate the sand from the oil, which then gets refined. Third, Tong continues that there should be innovation in the conventional petroleum business as well. The Middle Eastern oil reserves comprise approximately two thirds of the world's total resources. This is a fact that cannot be changed. In the long run, China will still have to depend mainly upon the Middle East for oil imports. In other words, if China can successfully win over the Middle East, it will solve the problem of Chinese use of overseas oil resources. However, it would be difficult for China to enter the market for the exploration of Middle Eastern oil. This is so, because the Middle Eastern upstream oil industry is usually not open to foreign investment, the contractual provisions involved are very strict, and the investment environment is very complex. Therefore, Tong suggests that China should adopt more creative ways to enter the Middle Eastern oil market. For example, China can attract these countries to establish refineries in China with the Middle Eastern countries providing the supply of crude oil for use in these refineries. Another alternative would be for China to go to these resource-rich countries, and establish joint capital refineries, thus expanding China's own sources of oil, and helping China establish possible long-term contracts for the supply of oil.[119]

Safe delivery of energy resources – Another component of energy security for China is the safety of the seaborne transportation routes. The three main methods of transporting oil are by ship, by pipeline, and by rail. For China, the most vulnerable method of transporting oil is by ship. That is because some of the larger nations, such as the U.S. and India, have continuously tried to control the Strait of Malacca, while China does not have the naval power to do so. In reference to the fact that about 80% of China's oil imports pass through the Strait of Malacca, Hu Jintao, in the Central Economic Work Conference of November 29, 2003, spoke of the "Malacca Dilemma," expressing his concern about the security of energy imports into China.[120] There is also apprehension in Beijing that the United States might try to interfere with the flow of oil into China through the Strait of Malacca, should there be a conflict between China and Taiwai.[121] What is more, this strait is filled with various risks and uncertainties. Among them are unceasing border disputes, rampant piracy, a huge amount of passenger and cargo traffic, the presence of enormous fishing boats, and an overall general chaos in the strait—all of which gravely affect the security of navigation through the strait.

There are other analysts who have more positive views concerning oil transported to China by sea. They argue that not only is it highly unlikely that China will go to war with another country, but also that it would be next to impossible to blockade China. They also argue that in spite of this vulnerability, i.e., that 80% of Chinese imported crude oil is shipped through the Strait of Malacca, Japan's dependency on oil shipped through the Strait of Malacca is more severe than that of China's. Over 90% of Japan's imported oil is transported through the Strait of Malacca. Northeast Asia's China, Japan, and South Korea are three of the world's five greatest oil-consuming nations.[122] The majority of the petroleum imported by these nations must travel through the Strait of Malacca. In this sense, this navigation route is not only the petroleum lifeline of China, but of these three countries as well.

Despite the fact that China is uncomfortable with its dependence on the United States Navy for the protection of its oil that passes through the Strait of Malacca, many analysts see this as a long-term reality for China. This discomfort and difficulty have caused China to consider other routes to transport its petroleum. For example, some have suggested a transportation channel through the peaceful Kara isthmus at the southern tip of Thailand as a replacement for the Strait of Malacca. This project has won the support of the Thai government. If completed, it would fulfill the wish of many Asian countries to possess a route of oil transportation, which bypasses the Strait of Malacca. However, because of massive construction costs, including the cost of excavating a canal or constructing a pipeline through the narrow Kara isthmus, this project has not got beyond the planning stages.

Moreover, China is also considering developing its transportation of oil over land by pipeline. For example, China is looking into the possibility of building a pipeline from Burma into China for petroleum from the Middle East.

For petroleum that originates in Iran, China is considering constructing a pipeline to China through Afghanistan. China is also urging that the present pipeline extending from Iran to India through Pakistan be extended to China.

Aside from this, China also believes that another way of guaranteeing security of transportation through the Strait of Malacca (and thereby the security of the transportation of petroleum through the South China Sea) is for China to establish long-term, stable, and constructive diplomatic relations with the U.S. and to make every effort to avoid conflict and confrontation with India. For example, on March 29, 2002, Cao Gangchuan, Chinese Secretary of Defense as well as State Council member, visited India. There he pointed out that China and India would take a long-range approach and a broad view of the future. They would embark on a strategy for both countries' long-term benefit, both with regard to bilateral relations and the maintenance of marine transportation security. He also stated that China and India would carry out joint maritime maneuvers, and would jointly attack piracy and other criminal marine activities.

Moreover, China is strengthening its dialogue with the Southeast Asian countries concerning mutual security, and fostering mutual cooperation with these countries for maritime security. To this end, in October, 2003, Premier Wen Jiabao and the ten leaders of the Association of Southeast Asian Nations signed the Southeast Asian Friendship and Cooperation Treaty in the Indonesian island of Bali.[123] This treaty will improve cooperation among these countries regarding energy and the security of the oil navigation routes used by China.

Energy cooperation among the energy consuming countries – cooperation among the energy consuming nations is the third component of China's petroleum security. China and Japan's struggle over the Angarsk-Daqing or Angarsk-Nakhodka pipeline indicates that the relationship between these two countries concerning oil is one of competition rather than one of cooperation. Russia is a net exporter of energy; while China and Japan are net importers of energy, and in competition for the same Russian oil and gas. Although it seems that Russia has the upper hand in its petroleum diplomacy, and can decide exactly how much of its energy China and Japan receive, in actuality, this is not the case. Oil and gas are Russia's two top exports, closely linked with Russia's financial revenue, as well as with the stability of its economy and society. Loss of either China's large stable market for oil or Japan's large demand for oil would cause an inestimable economic loss for Russia. Therefore, Russia cannot recklessly play the card of petroleum diplomacy, and obtain any advantage from the struggle between China and Japan. Instead of being competitive, it would be to the mutual benefit of both China and Japan to carry on joint energy development, technological exchange, and diplomatic cooperation. Such cooperation would also help to build mutual trust and to resolve the dispute concerning the development of oil and gas in the East China Sea.

Similar rules also apply to the energy relationship between China and India. It would be beneficial for both countries if this relationship were more cooperative than competitive concerning energy. Political relations between India and China are currently at their historical peak. Moreover, India, like China, is a huge consumer of energy. What is more, India has a strong presence in the Indian Ocean, through which petroleum bound for China must pass. Therefore, it is essential for China to develop a cooperative energy relationship with India, rather than a competitive one.

The Debate about Whether Equity Oil Enhances Energy Security – Some Chinese officials believe that equity oil enhances energy security. This belief arises from a suspicion of the international market, as well as an expectation that China's NOCs will place national interests over corporate interests in a time of crisis. According to the holders of this belief, if a foreign company enters into an agreement with the Chinese government, both the government and the company own the oil in the ground, such as in a production sharing contract. Under this type of contract, the firm pays a certain amount to extract oil and splits the output with the government. Those who believe that equity oil enhances China's energy security do not assume, as do Western oil industry analysts, that oil will always be available on the world markets—albeit at a fluctuating price. Such people also hold that the NOCs would be able to send their foreign equity production to China should China finds itself in a position where it has money but is unable to buy oil.[124] A fear of such a scenario has already been expressed by NDRC officials.[125] What is more, those who make the case for equity oil argue that the oil produced by Chinese companies abroad is immune to fluctuations in world oil prices. It can thus, they argue, provide China's consumers with cheaper oil than that available international market.[126]

However, it seems to be the case that even if China were to secure overseas sources of oil, it would not be a guarantee to China of a supply of oil more reliable and less expensive than that available on the international market. When oil that is produced abroad by Chinese companies is shipped to China, it is highly probable that it would be exposed to the same transportation risks as oil purchased on the spot market by Chinese companies. Moreover, production of oil overseas is subject to a variety of risks in the host country.[127] It is also unlikely that equity barrels could serve as a buffer against price fluctuations for Chinese consumers. This is because the oil market is a global one and the price of oil is the same in every location.[128] Even if Beijing were successful in an attempt pressure Chinese oil companies to sell oil below the price on the world market, only a minority of Chinese consumers would be benefited with cheaper oil in the short-term. Such a tactic would bring with it the long-term cost of preventing China's oil companies from the opportunity to take advantage of higher prices, and thereby deny them funds for investment in other oil exploration and development projects.[129]

Executives of many Chinese oil companies have asserted both publicly and privately that they are not in agreement with the idea that with the notion that acquisition of oil assets abroad can enhance China's energy security.[130] Employees of China's NOCs, both present and former, have been quick to point out that that the notion that equity oil can improve China's energy security is supported chiefly by people who are not directly involved in the oil industry. The supporters of this policy, they claim, are primarily those in politics and the media, people who do not understand the workings of the oil business.[131]

The Chinese populace has begun to question the connection between the foreign acquisitions of China's NOCs and the country's oil supply, at least according to what can be gleaned from public debates. It used to be the case that there was almost universal approval for the acquisition of equity oil to meet the China's oil needs. Dissenters have begun to come forward in recent years.[132] For example, some critics have pointed to Japan's recent failures to enhance its energy security through overseas oil exploration and production as an example of the potentially high costs and meager returns of investments that are politically influenced.[133] Still others have noted that equity barrels on foreign soil would be of no use to China in the event of a war or other regional conflict. In a similar vein, some experts involved in the "China's Peaceful Rise and Energy Security Forum" came to the conclusion that China should not look with any great hope towards equity oil as a remedy for its oil deficit—it should look towards international trade instead to cure the deficit.[134]

Conclusion:

The idea that energy self-sufficiency is a complete cure for China's energy security seems to have passed its prime. Chinese officials and analysts now reluctantly acknowledge that the country will remain dependent on imported oil. As a result, experts and pundits alike are no longer asking whether or not China should import large quantities of oil, but rather how China can manage the risks associated its dependence on imported. In the 1990s, there was some fear about whether China had enough monetary resources to meet all of its oil needs. The present concern is now whether there will be enough oil available on the world market for China to buy.[135]

As for its domestic oil supplies, China's proven oil reserves are only sufficient for a little more than ten years. The Daqing Oil Field has passed its oil-producing peak. Only the western area of China or the deep seabed might have undiscovered reserves. If China's oil imports come only from one or two areas, if these imports depend on only one avenue of transportation, and if the difficulty of forecasting the price of oil becomes too great, China's energy supply will be exposed to vulnerability and risk. This is a latent threat to Chinese economic development. In order to overcome these risks and to meet the companies' desires for reserves and profits, as well as the companies' needs for continuous acquisition of new reserves to replace what is produced, Chinese petroleum enterprises unceasingly strive to develop investments in overseas oil resources.

Chinese companies have already entered the oil industries of Venezuela, Ecuador, the Sudan, Kazakhstan, Iran, and Canada through stock purchase, property transfer, and oil-field bidding. The Chinese government has signed and officially endorsed 28 petroleum exploration and development projects. These projects are distributed over four continents and 12 countries. These 12 countries are spread over the strategic areas of the Middle East and North Africa (in particular, the Sudan); Central Asia and Russia (in particular, Kazakhstan) and South America (in particular, Venezuela.)[136] As for oil pipelines, one from Kazakhstan to China was completed in 2005. Russia has already decided to construct a branch of an oil pipeline leading to the Chinese city of Daqing, which is expected to be completed by 2008. Moreover, Russia is also preparing to construct natural gas pipelines to China and South Korea. China has also recently reached agreements to engage in several natural gas projects in the Middle East, Indonesia, and Australia.

A pattern does seem to emerge from the data concerning Chinese foreign oil assets. Most production seems to be limited to a handful of countries (and is under the control of the CNPC) although Chinese oil companies have investments in many countries (table 6.1). About 450,000 barrels per day of equity oil were produced by Chinese oil companies abroad in 2005, which accounted for 15 percent of total oil imports.[137] The Sudan, Kazakhstan, and Indonesia accounted for 79 percent of the NOC's production of overseas equity oil in 2004, amounting to 372,370 bpd (table 6.2).[138] The CNPC alone accounted for 89 percent of all of the foreign equity oil production of China's oil companies in 2004 (table 6.3).[139] Angola and Nigeria will apparently become major sources of foreign equity production with recent investments by Sinopec (Block 18) and CNOOC, respectively.[140]

Table 6.1 Selected Countries in Which China's Oil Companies Have Signed Contracts for Equity Participation.

Algeria	Cuba	Iraq	Myanmar	Sudan
Angola	Ecuador	Kazakhstan	Niger	Syria
Azerbaijan	Equatorial Guinea	Kenya	Nigeria	Thailand
Canada	Gabon	Libya	Oman	Tunisia
Colombia	Indonesia	Mauritania	Peru	Venezuela
Cote D'lvoire	Iran	Morocco	Russia	UAE
		Turkmenistan	Yemen	

Table 6.2 Chinese Oil Companies' Foreign Equity Oil Production by Country, 2004

Country	**Barrels per day**	**Share (%)**
Sudan	134,752	36
Kazakhstan	110,452	30
Indonesia	46,941	13
Other	80,225	21
Total	372,370	100

Source: CNPC website; *CNOOC Ltd. Annual Report 2004; Sinochem Annual Report 2004;* and *21st Century Business Herald*

Table 6.3 Chinese Oil Companies' Foreign Equity Oil Production by Company, 2004

Company	**Barrels per day**	**Share (%)**
CNPC	329,810	89
CNOOC	29,941	8
Sinochem	8,603	2
Sinopec	4,016	1
Total	372,370	100

Source: *Platts; 21st Century Business Herald; CNOOC Ltd. Annual Report2004; Petroleum Intelligence Weekly;* and *Sinochem Annual Report2004.*

However, when one surveys the difficulty and complexity that Chinese enterprises encounter when they "go global", it is clear that the path which large-scale state-owned Chinese enterprises must follow in making overseas purchases is not smooth. It may even be said that the path is quite rocky and far from smooth. For example, there was the failed attempt by the CNPC and CNOOC to purchase the Caspian Sea oil project in 2003. There was also the CNPC's abortive attempt to acquire the Russian Slavneft at the end of 2002. All of these have left a deep impact on Chinese petroleum enterprises. The CNOOC's attempt to buy Unocal, and China's Mineral-Metallurgy Group's efforts to buy the Canadian Noranda reveal the typical risks and difficulties involved in such endeavors. Initially, in order to facilitate a petroleum cooperation project with the Sudan, the CNPC made many diplomatic overtures to the Sudanese government. However, fighting between the troops of the Sudanese government and guerrilla forces brought great risks for the CNPC's Sudanese petroleum investment. Moreover, CNPC's stake in Sudan's oil fields may also become vulnerable to attack in the way western oil interests in Nigeria have been, if it fails to deliver clear benefits to locals. There are signs of local resentment in Sudan, though projects in Susan seem to be progressing smoothly. Even in South Africa, a relatively developed economy, textile job losses have been blamed on Chinese imports. Similar complaints are emerging in Nigeria. In addition, Chinese enterprises in Africa also have to manage the risks, such as power and water shortages. Faced with all the above challenges, the CNPC deeply feels that investing in overseas oil is like dealing with the devil. Yet it would seem unwise and economically unfeasible not to face risk and difficulty in order to gain scarce resources.

On a broader scale, the Chinese government will continue to try to equalize the effect of state and market forces in China's energy sector. On the one hand, former Premier Zhu Rongji seems to have had more faith in market forces than the current leadership of China. Some Chinese analysts are quick to point out that Zhu Rongji's confidence in market forces is at least partly responsible for the energy crisis of 2003-2004. These analysts maintain that it was this poorly-placed confidence that led him to shut the doors of China's Ministry of Energy and correspondingly ratchet up the power and autonomy of China's state-owned energy companies. This, in turn, they maintain, brought about ineffective institutions and powerful firms—a phenomenon that many see as the Achilles' heel of China's energy policymaking apparatus. This view of the situation has only served to empower those officials and analysts who would like to see the establishment of a standing ministerial or supra-ministerial body to oversee the energy sector. Most analysts who hold this view see a movement towards recentralization with the establishment of the SEO and the ELG.[141]

On the other hand, the continuing debate about whether China should re-establish a Ministry of Energy, as well as the fact that the Chinese leadership decided to create the SEO and ELG instead of a Ministry of Energy seem to be indications that it is easier to create new institutions than to change the power structure among the existing ones. It is quite difficult to bring about effective institutional change in China's energy sector because any such reorganization will create shifts in power that are fraught with difficulties for the parties involved.[142]

Notes

1. Tang Weibin, "China's Petroleum Security and Energy Diplomacy," *Journal of China Foreign Affairs University,* No. 76, June 2004, p. 74.

2. Ren Dong, "New Pattern of the World's Petroleum Supply," *Economic Guidance,* June 9, 2003.

3. Ibid.

4. International Energy Agency, *Monthly Oil Market Report,* December 13, 2005, p. 48.

5. Erica Downs, "The Brookings Foreign Policy Studies Energy Security Series: China," The Brookings Institution, December 2006, p. 1.

6. "What could prevent China's peaceful rise? Central Party School Deputy Director: China's increasing demand for resources could give rise to international friction" (Shenme hui zudang Zhongguo heping jueqi? Zhongyang dangxiao fuxiaozhang: Zhongguo dui ziyuan xuqiu zengjia keneng yinqi guoji moca), *China Affairs* (Zhongguo shiwu), March 8, 2004 at www.chinaaffairs.org/detail.asp?id=41680.

7. Downs, December 2006, p. 16.

8. Mai Tian, "New Authority to Oversee Energy Sector," *China Daily*, April 30, 2005, *Dow Jones*; and Olivia Chung, "High-level office to tackle China energy shortages," *The Standard*, January 12, 2005.

9. Huang Hui, "The National Energy Leading Group is only the first step," (Guojia nengyuan lingdao xiaozu zhi shi di yi bu), p. 40–42; Wang Yichao, "China's energy sector moves from crisis to new administration," (Zhongguo nengyuan cong weiji dao xinzheng), *Caijing*, No. 23, 2005; and "China to set up energy regulator under SDRC," *Reuters News*, March 28, 2003.

10. See Philip Andrews-Speed, *Energy Policy and Regulation in the People's Republic of China,* Kluwer Law International, 2004, p. 56 and chapters 5 and 12.

11. Chen Ting, "The Energy Bureau's Dilemmas," (Nengyuan ju kunjing), *21st Century Business Herald* (21 Shiji jingji baodao*)*, May 10, 2004, at www.nanfangdaily.com.cn/jj/20040510/chj/200405100076.asp.

12. This section summarized Downs, December 2006, p. 16-18.

13. See "The New Energy Institution: Ministry of Energy or Energy Supervision and Management Commission?" (Xin nengyuan jigou: nengyuanbu haishi nengyuanwei?), *China Entrepreneur* (*Zhongguo qiyejia*), February 6, 2005; and Wang Yichao, "The Case of the Energy Bureau: Will it be a transitional product long in the making?" (Nengyuanju zhi ju: hui shi yige manchang guodupin ma?), *Caijing*, No. 8, April 20, 2003.

14. "Will China reestablish the Ministry of Energy?" (Zhongguo chongjian nengyuanbu?), *Business Watch Magazine* (Shangwu zhoukan), May 5, 2005, p. 51.

15. Olivia Chung, "High-level office to tackle China energy shortages;" and "China delays setting up Ministry of Energy due to complexity of problems," *Agency France Press*, December 3, 2004.

16. Downs, December 2006, p. 19.

17. "The New Energy Institution: Ministry of Energy or Energy Supervision and Management Commission?" and Zheng Min and Chu Fujun, "Is the Ministry of Energy almost here?"

18. "State Council document number 14 specifies the establishment of the Energy Leading Group," (Guofa 14 hao wenjian mingque: Guijia nengyuan lingdao xiaozu chengli), *China Petroleum News* (Zhongguo shiyou wang), May 30, 2005.

19. Interview with industry insider, Beijing, China, April 12, 2006 in Downs, December 2006, p. 20.

20. This paragraph referred to Downs, December 2006, p. 21.

21. Jing Huang, *Factionalism in Chinese Communist Politics,* Cambridge University Press, 2000, p. 414–417; and Kenneth Lieberthal and Michel Oksenberg, *Policy Making in China: Leaders, Structures and Processes*, Princeton University Press, 1988, p. 26–27.

22. Downs, December 2006, p. 20-21.

23. Ibid., p. 20.

24. "Calls for upgrading the NDRC Energy Bureau to a general energy directorate are heard again," (Guojia Fagaiwei jiang shengge wei guojia nengyuan zongju de shengyin youqi), *Economic Observer* (Jingji guancha bao), February 19, 2006.

25. Interview with industry insider, Beijing, China, April 12, 2006 in Downs, December 2006, p. 21.

26. Downs, December 2006, p. 21.

27. Feng Zhiyong, Yu Laiwen, and Chen Ming, "Analysis on Chinese Petrochemical Enterprise's International Management," *Management of Chemical Industry*, Nov. 2005, p. 8.

28. Xiao Xi, "Create Petrochemical Industry's Wal-Mart," *Scientific Technology Daily,* July 30, 2005.

29. Guo Hui, "About Strategy of China's Petrochemical Enterprise's Internationalization," *Petro-Chemical Technology & Economy,* Vol. 15, No. 4, 1999, p. 8.

30. Ibid.

31. Nathan and Gilley, 2003, p. 205-207.

32. Li Xinmin, "Focus on China Petrochemical International Project's Construction," *Economic Reference Newspaper,* Sept. 13, 2005.

33. Ibid.

34. Ibid.

35. Ibid.

36. Erica Downs, "China's Quest for Overseas Oil," *Far Eastern Economic Review,* September 2007, p. 53.

37. Zhang Nianqing, "Among Joint Venture Giants, Sinopec Speed up its Internationalization," *Beijing Youth,* Oct. 24, 2002.

38. Yu Guoming, "Management towards Globalizaiton," *China Petrochemical Newspaper,* June 27, 2001.

39. Zhang Nianqing, "Among Joint Venture Giants, Sinopec Speed up its Internationalization," *Beijing Youth,* Oct. 24, 2002.

40. Yu Guoming, "Management towards Globalizaiton," *China Petrochemical Newspaper,* June 27, 2001.

41. Li Xinmin, "Focus on China Petrochemical International Project's Construction," *Economic Reference Newspaper,* Sept. 13, 2005.

42. Ibid.

43. Downs, December 2006, p. 35.

44. "The two oil giants fight loudly overseas, competition forces prices down and both sides suffer," (Liangda shiyou jutou haiwai da xiang zaoyu zhan jingxiang yajia liangbaijushang), *Economic Reference News* (Jingji cankao bao), June 28, 2004; "The going global strategy faces many difficult problems, should state enterprises or private enterprises have priority?" (Zouchuqu zhanlue mianlin zhuduo nanti, guoqi youxian haishi minqi youxian), *China Business Times* (Zhonghua gongshang shibao), December 9, 2004; and "China will shock South Asia by digging a canal in Thailand to Bypass the Strait of Malacca," (Zhongguo piekai Maliujia kaizao Tai yunhe jiang zhendong NanYa), *Economic Monthly* (Jingji Yuekan), July 3, 2003.

45. Hua You, "CNPC International Management Good News," *China Mining Industry Newspaper,* April 12, 2003.

46. Xu Jinjing, "CNPC Substantially Promote its Oil Refining Industry," *First Financial Daily,* March 24, 2006.

47. Wang You, "Investing 61.8 Billion Yuan, Sinopec and CNPC Preparing Huge Ethylene Projects," *First Financial Daily,* May 30, 2005.

48. For more information on China's quest for national champions, see "The dragon tucks in," *The Economist*, June 30, 2005; "The Struggle of the Champions," *The Economist*, January 8, 2005; "China's companies: a special issue," *China Economic Quarterly*, Vol. 7, No. 3, 2003; and Peter Nolan, *China and the Global Business Revolution,* Houndmills and New York: Palgrave, 2001.

49. Peter Nolan, *China and the Global Business Revolution,* Houndmills and New York: Palgrave, 2001.

50. Li Yanzheng, "Investing 13 Billion Yuan, CNPC Greatly Interfered in Sinopec's Domain," *Shanghai Security Newspaper,* April 22, 2006.

51. Ibid.

52. This point referred to Downs, December 2006, p. 39.

53. Downs, December 2006, p. 32.

54. Hua You, "CNPC International Management Good News," *China Mining Industry Newspaper,* April 12, 2003.

55. Downs, December 2006, p. 32.

56. Guo Dapeng, "Hu Jintao's Trip to Africa full of Petroleum Cooperation," *Financial Times,* February 7, 2004.

57. "CNPC Constructs the Sudan's Largest Refinery," *Shanghai Economic Newspaper,* May 22, 2003.

58. Guo Dapeng, "Hu Jintao's Trip to Africa full of Petroleum Cooperation," *Financial Times,* February 7, 2004.

59. Shai Oster, "China is Seeking a Broader Role in Africa," *The Wall Street Journal,* October 24, 2006.

60. Andrew Yeh, "China ventures on rocky roads to trade with Africa," *Financial Times,* June 20, 2006.

61. Downs, September 2007, p. 54.

62. *BP Statistical Review of World Energy 2006*, p. 8 and 11.

63. Maryelle Demongeot and Judy Hua, "Analysis—No let up seen yet for China sweet crude imports," *Reuters News*, November 12, 2004.

64. Wang Xiaoyu, "Prospects of China's Investment in Russian Energy Industry from the View of CNPC's Shares of Stock in Russia's Rosneft," *China Youth,* July 26, 2006.

65. Ibid.

66. Jiang Jingping, "CNPC Intends to Invest in Thai Oil and Gas Projects," *Natural Gas Industry,* Dec. 2004.

67. Downs, December 2006, p. 30-31.

68. Tong Xiaoguang, "Implement the 'going out' strategy to fully utilize oil and gas resources abroad," (Shishi 'zou chu qu' zhanlue chongfen liyong guowai youqi ziyuan), *Land & Resources* (Guotu ziyuan), No. 2, 2004, p. 6-9.

69. Downs, December 2006, p. 38-39.

70. Ibid., p. 39.

71. Ibid.

72. Tong, 2004, p. 6.

73. Downs, September 2007, p. 53-54.

74. Du Jiang, "CNOOC Seeking the Way to International Markets," *China Academic Journal,* March 2003, p. 50.

75. An Pei, "CNOOC Involved in Overseas Tar Sands Exploration," *China Land and Resources Newspaper,* April 20, 2005.

76. Qiu Zilei, "Why CNOOC purchases overseas assets," (Zhonghaiyou weihe shougou haiwai zichan), in *Talking to Financial Reporters* (Geicaijing jizhe jiangke), Beijing: CITIC Publishing House, 2004, p. 129-144.

77. Downs, December 2006, p. 36.

78. Neil Gough, Eric Ng and Mark O'Neill, "CNOOC gains tactical edge from battle; Higher profile will help No. 3 producer take on 'big brothers,'" *South China Morning Post,* August 4, 2005.

79. Zeng Qinghong, "The current economic situation and party construction work," (Guanyu dangqian jingjji xingshi he dang jian gongzuo), *Study Times* (Xuexi shibao), No. 301, September 2005.

80. "Zeng Qinghong: Chinese companies investing abroad must maintain a low profile and focus on practical results," (Zeng Qinghong: Woguo qiye dao haiwai touzi fazhan yao duo zuo shao shuo zhuyi shixiao), *Xinhua News Agency,* September 9, 2005.

81. Downs, December 2006, p. 39.

82. Chen Huai, "The way to solve China's oil supply and demand;" Zhang Kaiyu, "CNPC Accelerates Implementation," p. 10; and Tong, 2004, p. 6.

83. Downs, December 2006, p. 21-23.

84. Ibid., p. 36.

85. Zhang Yange and Liu Zhaoqiong, "A change of tactics in foreign oil and gas acquisitions, China tries joint bids," (Haiwai youqi shougou huanzhao, Zhongguo changshi lianhe jinggou), *Economic Observer* (Jingji guancha bao), June 16, 2006.

86. Downs, December 2006, p. 40.

87. Ibid.

88. Ibid.

89. Ibid., p. 49.

90. Ibid., p. 41.

91. Yang Zilin, "Thoughts on accelerating the implementation of the 'going abroad' strategy," (Guanyu jiakuai shishi 'zou chu qu' zhanlue de sikao), *Seeking Truth* (Qiushi), No. 7, 2005, p. 47–49; and "Going abroad concerns future generations," (zou chu qu' shiguan zisun houdai), *International Herald Leader* (Guoji xianqu daobao), October 14, 2004.

92. Gao Shuqian, "The current state of the development of the Nigerian oil industry and prospects for Sino-Nigerian oil cooperation," (Niriliya shiyou fazhan xianzhuang ji ZhongNi shiyou hezuo qianjing), March 23, 2005.

93. Downs, December 2006, p. 41-42.

94. Ibid.

95. He Qing and Yang Juan, "Background to the 'supplementary agreement': CNOOC tries to strengthen state tactics," ('buchong xieyi' de beihou: Zhonghaiyou qianghua guajia celue), *21st Century Economic Herald* (21 shiji jingji daobao), December 26, 2005.

96. Du, March 2003, p. 50.

97. Shai Oster, "China is Seeking a Broader Role in Africa," *The Wall Street Journal,* October 24, 2006.

98. Downs, December 2006, p. 42.

99. Kang Yiming, "Thoughts on China's Petroleum Company's 'Go Global' Strategy," *Geological Techno-economic Management,* Vol. 26, No. 2, April 2004, p. 11.

100. Ibid.

101. Downs, December 2006, p. 50.

102. An Fengquan, "Reflections on security triggered by high oil prices," (Gao youjia yinfa anquan sikao), *China PetroChem,* (Zhongguo shiyou shihua), No. 5, 2004.

103. Christian Constantin, "China's Conception of Energy Security: Sources and International Impacts," Institute of International Relations, Working Paper no. 43, University of British Columbia, March 2005, p. 14.

104. Downs, December 2006, p. 15.

105. He Jun, "CNOOC-UnocalIncident: What do We Need to Learn?" *China Management Newspaper,* August 8, 2005.

106. Downs, September 2007, p. 55-56.

107. Downs, December 2006, p. 51.

108. Wang Fang, Francesco Guerrera and Joe Leahy, "Beijing 'never behind' bid for Unocal" *Financial Times,* August 6, 2005.

109. Carola Hoyos, "Eni's Kashagan Oil Field Hit by Delays," *Financial Times,* February 23, 2007.

110. Shi Xi, "China Petroleum Companies' Overseas Acquisition Path," *International Economic Cooperation,* Vol. 6, 2003, p. 21.

111. Carola Hoyos, "Caspian Oil Field to Produce 25% More," *Financial Times,* November 26, 2006.

112. Xu Na, "CNPC Obstructed in its Expansion to Russia," *International Economic Cooperation,* No. 1, 2003, p. 38.

113. Ibid.

114. Ibid. p. 39.

115. Sabrina Tavernise, "Oil Auction In Russia: Some Scowl, Others Giggle," *New York Times,* December 19, 2002.

116. Downs, December 2006, p. 15, 37-38.

117. Ibid., p. 49.

118. Ji Xing, Xi Xiaolin, Xian Jialin, and Li li, "China's Petroleum Security Strategy Discussion," *China Energy,* Vol. 26, No.1, January 2004, p. 17.

119. Liu Qianru, "Under the New Situation, How Chinese Petroleum Companies Go Out More Efficiently—Interviewing Liu Keyu, Zhang Weipin, Tong Xiaoguang, Zhang Hang, and Han Gensheng," *International Operation,* Vol. 13, No. 3, 2005, p. 27-28.

120. Shi Hongtao, "Energy security runs up against the 'Malacca Dilemma;' Will China, Japan and Korea cooperate?" (Nengyuan anquan zaoyu 'Maliuya kunju' ZhongRiHan nengfou xie shou), *China Youth Daily* (Zhongguo qingnian bao), June 15, 2004.

121. Downs, December 2006, p. 14.

122. Tang Weibin, "China's Petroleum Security and Energy Diplomacy," *Journal of China Foreign Affairs University,* No. 76, June 2004, p. 76.

123. Tang Weibin, "China's Petroleum Security and Energy Diplomacy," *Journal of China Foreign Affairs University,* No. 76, June 2004, p. 77.

124. Downs, December 2006, p. 37.

125. Zhang Yuqing, "Implement the 'go abroad' development strategy of the oil industry," (Shishi shiyou gongye 'zou chu qu' de fazhan zhanlüe), *Macroeconomic management* (Hongguan jingji guanli), No. 10, 2000, p. 5–6; and "Xu Dingming, Deputy head of the Transportation and Energy Department of the State Planning Commission discusses China's overseas oil exploration and development," (Guojia jiwei jiaonengsi fusizhang Xu Dingming tan Woguo jingwai shiyou ziyuan de kantan kaifa), *China Economic Herald* (Zhongguo jingji daobao), October 8, 1997.

126. Xu Yu, "The Communist Party Central Committee Deploys a Strategy to Break Out of Energy Encirclement," (Zhongyang bushu nengyuan tuwei zhan), *Wen Wei Bao,* June 5, 2005; and "How can the increasingly tight energy problem be solved? Chinese People's Political Consultative Conference Member places hope in acceleration of the pace of China's oil Companies 'going abroad,'" (Ruhe yingdui riqu jinzhang de nengyuan wenti? Quanguo zhengxie weiyuan jiwang Zhongguo shiyou jiakuai 'zou qu chu' bufa), *China Petroleum News* (Zhongguo Shiyou Bao), March 16, 2005.

127. Downs, December 2006, p. 37-38.

128. Paul Blustein, "Many Oil Experts Unconcerned over China Unocal Bid," *Washington Post,* July 1, 2005.

129. Downs, December 2006, p. 38.

130. Peter S. Goodman, "Big Shift in China's Oil Policy," *Washington Post,* July 13, 2005, p. D1; and Qiu Zilei, "Why CNOOC purchases overseas assets," (Zhonghaiyou weihe shougou haiwai zichan), *Talking to Financial Reporters* (Gei caijing jizhe jiangke), Beijing: CITIC Publishing House, 2004, p. 136–137.

131. Downs, December 2006, p. 38.

132. Ibid.

133. Goodman, July 13, 2005, p. D1; and Qiu, 2004, p. 129–144.

134. "The implementation of China's energy security strategy during peaceful rise," (Zai heping jueqi zhong shixian Woguo de nengyuan anquan zhanlue), *Think Tank Express* (Naoku kuaican), No. 16, July 20, 2005.

135. Downs, December 2006, p. 14-15.

136. Sun Ling, "Briefly Discuss China's Energy Diplomacy," *Science and Technology of West China,* March 2006, p. 91.

137. Zhang Haiyun and Liang Guohua, "CNPC's 2006 News Conference," (Zhongshiyou 2006 nian xinwen zuotanhui xianchang zhiji), *China Oil News Web* (Zhongguo shiyou wang), January 18, 2006.

138. China National Petroleum Corporation, "Overseas Work," January 5, 2006; CNOOC Limited, *Annual Report 2004*, p. 3; Sinochem Corporation, *2004 AnnualReport*, p. 14; Chen Jibao, "16 billion Renminbi: Sinopec continues to focus overseas," (160 yi: Zhongshihua jixu xiazhu haiwai), *21st Century Business Herald* (21 shiji jingji daobao), May 25, 2005; Winnie Lee, "In a bid to grow overseas, PetroChina, CNPC form JV," *Platts Oilgram News*, June 13, 2005; "Western passage: CNPC and CNOOC break into the Caspian," (Xibu tongdao: Zhongshiyou Zhonghaiyou chuangru Lihai), *21st Century Economic Herald* (21 shiji jingji daobao), September 19, 2005; and CNOOC Limited, *Annual Report 2004*, p. 3; and "China's Foreign Drive Faces Long Road Ahead," *Petroleum Intelligence Weekly*, March 14, 2005.

139. China National Petroleum Corporation, "Overseas Work;" CNOOC Limited, *Annual Report 2004*, p. 3; Sinochem Corporation, *2004 Annual Report*, p. 14; and Chen, May 25, 2005.

140. Downs, December 2006, p. 43.
141. Ibid., p. 48.
142. Ibid.

CASE STUDY THREE
THE ELECTRICAL APPLIANCES INDUSTRY

Introduction:

The world's center of the manufacture of electrical appliances is usually located in the country which is home to the current large international brands. In the 1960's, the center of manufacture of electrical appliances was located in the U.S. and Europe, which housed such electrical appliances manufacturers as General Electric, Whirlpool, Maytag, Simons and Electrolux. In the 1970s, the center shifted to Japan, which at the time was home to Panasonic, Sony, Toshiba, Sanyo, Hitachi, and Sharp. The center again shifted in the 1980s, this time to South Korea, home of the world-class brands LG, and Samsung.

The Chinese electrical appliance industry grew rapidly from the 1980's to the mid-1990's. The industry's average rate of profit at that time was 20%-30%. Because of the attraction of these high profits, various Chinese provinces gradually introduced numerous production lines for electrical appliances. During the ten-year period between 1986 and 1995, the total output of the Chinese electrical appliance industry had an annual growth rate of 32.1%.[1] This was accompanied by an increase in the percentage of Chinese households that owned electrical appliances. The color television and the refrigerator, which were once considered upscale consumer products, came to be considered household necessities during this period.

The profits of the Chinese electrical appliance started to diminish in the mid to late 1990's. During this time, the profit margin for most products was 3%-5%, with some products even having a profit margin of zero.[2] This precipitous drop in profits seems to have been sparked by price wars for color television sets, wars which came about because of over-saturation of the market. This was soon followed not only by losses in the markets for color televisions, but also in the market for VCD players. Eventually, in 2001, entire Chinese electrical appliance industry posted its first net loss ever. This was companied by a large-scale decrease in the production rate of electrical appliances.

As for domestic market competition, the Chinese electrical appliance industry has evolved from a pattern of corporate competition, which it followed in the 1980s, to an oligarchic pattern of competition which it is following today. Over its 20 years of development, the Chinese market for domestic electrical appliances has become increasingly concentrated. At present, as for the domestic color television market, the top 4 brands account for approximately 62% of the total market; as for the domestic refrigerator industry, the top 4 brands account for approximately 72% of the total market share; in the case of the domestic air-conditioner market, the top 5 brands account for 54% of the market share; and in the case of the market for domestic washers and dryers, the top 4 brands occupy about 69% of the total market share.[3] This indicates that the domestic electrical appliance market in China is starting to be controlled by a handful of companies. Thus, the competition in electrical appliance industry has already begun to enter an oligarchic era. By means of mergers and acquisitions among domestic companies, an industry can keep a few leading enterprises, enterprises with pricing power and the ability to keep a good profit margin and rate of growth. In addition to the above economic reasons, this domestic consolidation also reflects the government's overall reform agenda, starting with the efforts of Chinese planners in the 1990's. During that decade, these planners tried to merge state firms to create big "national champions," illustrating the vision of growth based on large State-owned conglomerates.[4]

During this period of oligarchic competition, there has been a gradual slowdown of industry production, and corresponding decrease in the industry-wide profit margin. This clearly indicates that the Chinese electrical appliance industry has entered a mature period. It is against this background that china has become one of the world's centers for the manufacture of electrical appliances. Of course, Chinese electrical appliance enterprises have been seeking to increase their presence in the international market. For example, Haier and Huawei have chosen to increase their presence by concentrating on internal growth (as opposed to acquisition of other companies). They established overseas manufacturing bases, as well as a marketing and research network. The Chinese company, Galanz has turned itself into a global manufacturer of microwave ovens by selling its ovens to other companies for resale under the other companies' own brand names. In this way, it has become the world's greatest producer of microwave ovens. Midea and Changhong have engaged in strategic cooperation to increase their worldwide market presence, and have developed the market through their alliance. The Fuyao Glass Company has its factories firmly located in China, but it obtains its raw materials from overseas, and has its markets overseas as well. TCL and Lenovo have engaged in acquisition of other companies as means of increasing their presence on the global stage (acquisition of other companies is fast becoming the first choice of many Chinese enterprises when they decide to go global). The road of acquisition, however, is certainly not smooth.

Electrical Appliance Companies' Interaction with the Government:

The consumer electronics industry' economic characteristics are prominent, and, as a consequence, so is the pattern of the industry's politics. If the iron and steel industry is an illustration of direct governmental control, as manifested in the successful enforcement of the government's industrial policies; then the oil and gas industry is an illustration of strong commercial interests driving national interests. The dearth of human resources in the central government's policy making bodies is contributing to Beijing's reliance on the national oil companies for support and advice. The state-owned energy companies have an abundance of such resources.[5] The electrical appliance industry is, however, more a combination of private ownership and state control, and is driven more by market concerns rather than by political ones. At the same time, the influence of large non-state companies has been growing. In addition, tensions over the old norms of government-business relations, particularly industry deference to the government, has increased.[6]

All consumer electronics firms that seek to influence national government policy consider direct interaction with the government to be of primary importance. Large SOEs are attached to the government on administrative matters, and so have more regular contact with it. The leaders of these SOEs regularly meet with national-level officials. The directors of major television producing companies regularly interact with officials at all levels of the national bureaucracy, including the Ministry of Information Industry (MII), the State Economic and Trade Commission (SETC), the Ministry of Foreign Trade and Economic Cooperation (MOFTEC, now the Ministry of Commerce), the General Administration of Customs, and the Ministry of Finance.[7] The government still quite often appoints the senior executives of these firms. These executives often must get government approval for investments, and have often been compelled to take actions they otherwise would not have. An example of this government interference in corporate matters is the case of Mudan, which used to be one of China's most successful television manufacturers. It is now buried in debt because the government compelled it to take over four other government-owned factories in Beijing.[8]

Despite this strong government involvement, there has been a greater clarity of firms' profits and losses and a clearer perception of the functions of most executives regarding policy-centered relations. All of this has sharpened the distinction between SOEs and the government. In 1985, for example, Changhong's president, Ni Runfeng, took up his post. In spite of his being an alternate member of the Chinese Communist Party Central Committee, he has been extremely loyal to his company. He shares this devotion to his company with the heads of all China's large consumer electronics makers.[9] The old monist framework has been weakened in the electrical appliance industry, because of the importance of economic policy. In the consumer electronics industry, the leaders of large SOEs are astutely aware of and keenly interested in influencing the direction of policy. For example, officials often discuss policy at the firms' initiative.

This practice gives firms a degree of influence on policy debates. One executive said, "When the interests of enterprises and the government are not the same, enterprises will proactively provide opinions."[10]

One result of direct relations in the industry is that companies are increasingly critical of government intervention in the market. More and more, companies are willing to act on that belief by challenging the authority of the government openly. An increasing number of Chinese companies have taken action on their displeasure with government authority.[11] For instance, state-owned, as well as private companies have criticized the government's intervention with regard to certain policy issues. These policy issues include those of pricing and competition, and the setting of technical standards.[12] As will be treated shortly, firms in these cases have openly acted on their viewpoints, although they were quite aware that in doing so they were violating the official standards of deference and cooperation.

As has been stated, interaction between the electronic consumer executives and government officials occurs in an open and direct fashion. What is more, there are three national-level associations which were formed to look after the interests of the electrical appliance industry. At first glance, all of these national associations appear to have the same degree of embedded autonomy from the government. Just as is the case with the other industries, the central government was the driving force for their creation.[13] However, despite their origin in the government and their continued contact with the MII, the associations are autonomous, at least to a certain extent. None of them receive any funds from the government and none of them are run on a day-to-day basis by current or former government officials.[14]

The Number Four Machinery Industry Ministry became the Ministry of Electronics Industry (MEI) in 1982. It later merged with two other ministries in 1998 to become the Ministry of Information Industry. The Number Four Machinery Industry Ministry had established the National TV International Competition Committee in 1979 to help it regulate TV makers. In 1986, MEI transformed the National TV International Competition Committee into the China Electronic Video Industry Association (CVA, *Zhongguo dianzi shixiang hangye xiehui*). In the same way, the China Electronic Audio Industry Association (CAA, *zhongguo dianzi yinxiang gongye xiehui*) was started in 1981 as the National Recorder Inter-Factory Competition Committee (*quanguo luyinji changji jingsai weiyuanhui*). In 1983 it became the China Recorder Industry Association (*zhongguo luyinji gongye xiehui.*) In 1986, it increased its scope to cover all audio products—radios, stereo equipment, compact disc players, etc. Two years later, the China Electronics Chamber of Commerce (CECC, *zhongguo dianzi shanghui*) was created to take the place of MEI's sales bureau. This sales bureau had been shelved as part of a larger restructuring effort by the government.[15]

Domestic Price Competition and Its Effects on Globalization

A good example for illustrating the interesting, delicate and complex interaction between the electrical appliance companies and the national government is price competition. When prices decline across the economy, it places companies into one of two opposing sides. One side thinks a decline in prices is "dumping" (*qingxiao*). This "dumping", they maintain, is a consequence of "vicious competition" (*exing jingzheng*) that must be checked, either by intervention of the government, cartels organized by associations or the companies themselves. Companies which operate more efficiently tend to view such "checking" actions as going against the principles of a free market. As a result, these more efficient companies oppose any efforts to restrain competition. Despite the existence of two opposing sides in the "price decline" question, any one company's policy position depends on its circumstances at any given time.[16]

In early 1998, Gaoluhua, a manufacturer of television sets, initiated the price cuts that led to an attempt at price floors.[17] Soon after this round of price cuts started, the CVA gave assistance to its ten largest members in the creation of a "market working committee," which was formed to help stabilize prices. Yet some members of the cartel soon began to disregard the establishment of price floors, and began selling goods at below the agreed upon price. In July of 1998, one of the largest manufacturers of color TV sets in China, Changhong, signed an appeal to the SETC in hopes of gaining more authority for associations to organize cartels, whose purpose would be to help stabilize prices. In August of 1998, the SETC responded positively to this appeal by issuing the notice "Idea on Instituting Industry Self-Discipline Prices for Some Industrial Products". This notice encouraged associations to set price floors or ceilings for twenty-one products. Despite its previous failure, the CVA and some members responded to the SETC's August 1998 notice with another attempt to form a valid cartel for the purpose of stabilizing prices. CVA was under the impression that support from the SETC and the MII might help the cartel in maintaining price stability. It did not, and prices soon began falling rapidly once again.[18]

Changdong was following any strategy it hoped would lead to a monopoly over the television set manufacturing industry, even though that might mean calling for lowering prices one day, and on the next day, criticizing the very price wars it had started the day before. In November 1998, Changdong boldly announced that it had purchase most of the available color television tubes in China.[19] Changhong's actions gave it a distinct advantage over its competitor, especially since it came right after a well publicized crackdown on smuggling. Changhong was hoping that its market share would grow dramatically during the upcoming Spring Festival, when TV sales were at their peak, because it owned many of the available color tubes. Since they found CVA to be useless in the face Changhong's actions, several large television manufacturers created a "lobbying group" to pressure the MII and customs to agree with their request to set a price floor. They made an appeal to the Politburo member responsible for industrial policy, Wu Bangguo. In a tense New Year's Eve showdown between the government and the major TV manufacturers, hosted by the MII without the presence of the CVA, the wronged TV manufacturers implored the government to increase the quota for tube imports and to force Changhong to part with some of its tubes. Even though the government refused to give in to the manufacturers' requests that night, they eventually did lift the quotas on tube imports and Changhong later "voluntarily" sent some of its tubes to its competitors.[20]

Once the battle for market share was joined, television manufacturing companies acted even more brazenly, and increasingly challenged the authority of the government. In early April 1999, the MII and SDPC began to realize that the battle for control of the color TV market was becoming much too fierce. As a result, they issued compulsory price floors for both color TVs and picture tubes. However, this reassertion of government power in the marketplace proved fruitless. In a matter of days after the issuance of the mandate, companies were beginning to sell TVs at prices well below the mandated floors.[21] Eight of the country's eleven picture tube manufacturers formed a cartel to limit production in May of 1999. All of the eight were members of the China Vacuum Parts Association's Color Picture Tube Sub-Association. They included several joint venture producers, including Japan's Matsushita and South Korea's LG. Since the MII and SDPC officials realized they could not stop the eight, the officials, to everyone's surprise, condoned the action of the tube manufacturers in forming the production cartel. However, some of the cartel members soon broke ranks by selling below the agreed upon price and by producing more than they were allowed. In the following summer of 2000, nine large TV producers (which did not include Changhong) followed suit and announced the formation of a private price cartel, the China Color TV Enterprise Summit. The SDPC called the formation of this cartel illegal. However, it took no action against the cartel. The TV producers' cartel collapsed within a matter of days, as was becoming usual for such associations.[22]

All of the TV companies' cartels ended in failure. However, their formation illustrates the companies' attempts to gain control of the market and to change public policy for their own benefit. The formation of cartels also illustrates the companies' willingness, when they are unsuccessful, to disregard the opinions of the government and to take matters into their own hands The China Video Association was involved in the early efforts. It was later pushed aside by the government and large SOEs, on the grounds that it was merely impeding their own purposes.[23] This extreme price competition in the domestic Chinese electronics market is one of the major factors pushing Chinese electrical appliance companies to "Go Global."

TCL's Developmental History:

TCL was organized in 1981, and its development has undergone three stages: (1) *Specialization Stage.* In 1981, an electronic engineering company in the Huiyang district formed a joint venture with a Hong Kong business, the TTK Family Electrical Appliance Company. This company specialized in the production of audio cassette tapes. It was one of China's first 12 joint venture enterprises. In 1985, TTK and another Hong Kong business jointly established the TCL Communication Equipment Company. In 1986, this company developed China's first hands-free speaker telephone. (2) *Diversification Stage.* In 1992, TCL decided to ally with the Hong Kong Great Wall Electronic Group in order to break into the color television industry. In 1993, TCL's King brand color television went into production, and within three years, it was one of China's top three selling color televisions. In 2001, while most Chinese color television manufacturers were losing money, TCL realized a profit of more than 300 million RMB Yuan. Currently, TCL's King brand color television is still the main source of the company's profit.[24] In 1998, TCL tried to break into the IT industry by manufacturing computers for home use. In 1999, TCL established an air conditioning research center, and began to produce air conditioners for resell by other companies. (3) *Internationalization Stage.* In 1997, TCL decided to establish a global presence by deciding to become a major international producer of electronic communication products. After two years of preparations, TCL's internationalization strategy officially started in 1999. For the first 20 years of its existence, TCL's growth was rapid and steady. For the past 13 years since the mid-1990s, TCL has maintained an annual growth rate of 42.65%. This has made it one of China's fastest growing industrial manufacturing enterprises.[25]

TCL has formulated a clear strategy for internationalization. Li Dongsheng, the CEO of TCL, laid out this strategy as follows: a) TCL will still depend on the Chinese domestic market for the majority of its income; b) TCL will use its leading products, the color television and the cell phone, to break into the international market; c) TCL will promote its own brand of products in the markets of the developing nations; d) in the developed countries, TCL will become an original equipment manufacturer (OEM) whose products will be resold by other companies under other brand names; and e) TCL will acquire well-known local brands on the international market.[26]

The TCL's process of internationalization has gone through two stages: (1) *The Primarily OEM Stage* – For a long time, TCL's internationalization mainly depended upon exportation, carried on chiefly in OEM form. (2) *The Brand Exportation and FDI Stage* – In 1998, orders for TCL's products were drastically reduced as a result of the Asian Financial Crisis. This made the company determine to develop its own international market, to establish its own sales network, and to promote its own brand rather than being chiefly an OEM provider. As TCL's CEO Li Dongsheng said, it was the Southeast Asian Financial Crisis that compelled TCL's internationalization.

In 1998, TCL entered the Vietnamese market by purchasing the Hong Kong owned Vietnamese color television producer, DONACO. After owning the company for four years, TCL became one of the top three producers in the Vietnamese color television market, third only to LG, and Samsung. In August 2000, TCL entered the Indian market, and is currently one of India's top ten producers of electrical appliances. In October 2002, TCL purchased the German Schneider Electronic Company, and used this as a foothold to gain entry into the European Union market. In January 2004, TCL became the world's largest color television producer by acquiring the French company, Thomson.[27]

TCL's internationalization was moved by the stick of the Southeast Asian Financial Crisis and the keen competition between domestic producers of color television, and by the carrot of other markets, such as the U.S., European Union, India and Southeast Asia. Specifically, Usha Haley, business professor at the University of New Haven, believes that China-based companies wish to enter foreign markets is that those markets are perceived to be less competitive than the domestic Chinese markets. Haley points to several reasons why it is difficult for Chinese companies to make profits domestically. One is that there is little, if any, protection for intellectual property rights in China, so that competitors of a given company—who don't have to put much time or money into research and development—can easily and cheaply produce "bootleg" products to compete with those of the original manufacturer. "It's not that Chinese companies are invading the West", Haley says, "it's that they are escaping from China."[28]

Haley notes that another reason why Chinese electrical appliance companies' enter foreign markets is to help the Chinese companies overcome their deficiencies in areas such as service expertise and cutting-edge technology. "Technology is an especially important issue for Chinese companies that view themselves as global competitors. Because customers are so price sensitive, and margins are so razor thin, Chinese companies often lack the resources to make sustained investments" in research and development, states Haley.[29] In addition, says Haley, another reason for Chinese companies to go abroad is the potential upside from merging with Western firms. For example, the Chinese computer firm Lenovo has gained valuable management experience from its deal with IBM.[30]

The Chronology of TCL's Acquisitions:

In 1999, TCL initially established a subsidiary company in Vietnam. During the next five years, TCL gradually improved its brand small-recognition in Vietnam. Currently, TCL's share of the Vietnamese color television market is nearly 20%. After its success in Vietnam, TCL established manufacturing bases for color televisions in India and Indonesia, and expanded its market throughout Southeast Asia. At the same time, TCL also set up braches in the Philippines, Indonesia, Singapore, India, Russia, Mexico and Thailand.[31]

In September 2002, TCL entered the European market by purchasing the Schneider color television production plant. TCL was able to enter the European market rapidly by continuing to use the name of Schneider for televisions produced, thus, capitalizing on brand recognition.

In May 2003, TCL entered the U.S. market by purchasing the U.S. color TV and DVD player manufacturer, Go-Video. TCL also acquired Go-Video's sales network in the transaction. TCL also formed an alliance with Phillips to export televisions from China to the U.S. That year, TCL exported 1.5 million color televisions to the United States.[32]

In November 2003, TCL entered into an important alliance. TCL and the French company, Thomson, one of the world's top 500 enterprises, signed an agreement in Guangzhou to merge their color television and the DVD divisions. This established the TCL-Thomson joint venture. TCL currently holds 67% of the stock in this venture, while Thomson holds 33%.[33] The strength of this joint venture lies in the fact that it is a manufacturer of core spare parts, its ability to keep the cost of its products low, the fact that it has multiple brands in various markets, and its sales network.

The TCL-Thomson company adopted a multi-brand strategy to enter various markets. In Asia and the emerging markets, it primarily used the TCL brand. In Europe, it primarily used the Thomson brand. In North America, it primarily used the RCA brand, and adopted the use of other brands in its possession to meet differing market demands.

In August 2004, TCL and Alcatel formed a joint venture to produce, service, develop, and sell mobile phones and other related products. On May 17, 2005, TCL officially announced that it would purchase 45% of the stock held by Alcatel in the joint venture. In effect, TCL announced that it would buy out Alcatel.[34] The communication division of TCL wanted to employ the same business strategy that TCL's color television division used. That is, they wanted to achieve a dominant position in the global mobile communication industry by using a multi-brand strategy.

In June 2005, the TCL group officially founded a Middle Eastern subsidiary in Dubai. This subsidiary's business stretches across various countries in the Middle East, including Egypt, Turkey, and even North Africa.

In 2002, China Central Television chose Li Dongsheng as one of the top ten figures in the Chinese economy in its annual award ceremony. The U.S. Fortune magazine also proclaimed Li Dongsheng as one of 2003's Asian economic leaders.[35] All of this, however, is just a preface to a series of mistakes that TCL made in its foreign acquisitions.

TCL's Purchasing Mistakes:

The German Schneider Company was considered an old brand, and it used old technology. It had also changed hands several times. TCL wanted to use this old brand to promote its high-end television in Europe. Unfortunately, the combination of the high-tech TCL and the low-tech Schneider Company produced inconsistent results.

In the TCL-Thomson joint venture, TCL was only able to use the patents, the brand, the high-end color television technology, and the marketing channels for free for two years.

When TCL purchased Alcatel mobile, it obtained the 2G, and the 2.5G patented technologies; however, it was unable to obtain the 3G technology, which promised an explosive growth opportunity. TCL's series of purchases and acquisitions were obviously not correctly choreographed.

After TCL's merger with Thomson, the resulting joint venture experienced continuous losses. Li Dongsheng at first allotted 18 months to reverse these losses. After 18 months, however, he could not turn the tide. Jack Welch, a former CEO of Thomson's television business declared in despair to Li Dongsheng that in his opinion it would be impossible for Thomson to become profitable again.[36] TCL's purchase of Thomson is, therefore, a textbook example of how not to engage in a globalization strategy. It was also a learning opportunity for TCL for which it paid a high price.

It is interesting to know that when TCL was trying to open up the Vietnam market, it incurred 1.8 billion Yuan loss during the 18-month period before it turned a profit.[37] In spite of this loss, no one seemed to pay much attention. However, when TCL entered the European and American markets, and showed initial losses, it encountered widespread questioning. When Li Dongsheng did not fulfill his original plan, and failed to turn the tide, researchers and critics came out one after another, like Monday morning quarterbacks, and criticized Li

Dongsheng and TCL's failure at internationalization. Li Dongsheng's replied to these criticisms by saying that the acquisition of Thomson and Alcatel seemed to be good opportunities.[38] He continued by saying:

> That year when we were deciding whether to go global, many different opinions were offered. Some believed we should concentrate our resources on the domestic market. I thought that both the domestic and foreign markets should be synchronized. I feared that if we tried to internationalize later, we may have had a better industrial foundation, but we may also have lost the opportunity presented. Advancement in internationalization also requires experience and time. That cannot be avoided.[39]

Another reason Li Dongsheng decided to go global was information that he gleaned from conversation with the CEO of Japan's Sony corporation, Ken Kutanagi. This CEO said that China is a very big market, which is a good thing for TCL, but also a bad thing. It is a bad thing he explained because the size and conformability of the Chinese domestic market would not give much impetus for Chinese enterprises to go global. The CEO said that Sony met this challenge a long time ago, and faced it by becoming an internationalized company, whose overseas business surpasses its domestic business. This CEO believed that Chinese enterprises should learn not only from the example of Sony, but from the example of internationalized U.S. business as well.[40]

The critics, however, say that strategic opportunism is only suitable for the survival of small companies. Mere acquisition, they say, cannot replace strategy. If a big company enters the European and American markets without an overall strategy, even if it is initially successful, it cannot bring about an overall improvement of the company's competitive ability. In addition, they maintain, the risk of failure for companies who try to enter the European and American market is exceptionally high. TCL should not have been in such a haste to expand. Unlike what Li Dongsheng maintained, his critics hold that opportunities exist all the time for companies to expand. In order to enter the overseas markets, Li Dongsheng's critics say, a company should possess both a positive attitude and a self-assured posture.

TCL's Entry into the Vietnamese Market:

TCL's first step overseas was its 1997 foray into Vietnam. TCL was planning to use Vietnam as a base from which to access the markets of Southeast Asia. The countries which comprise the Association of Southeast Asian Nations have a total population of more than 500 million. There is only a 5% customs duty on commodities entering the markets of the Association of Southeast Asian Nations from Vietnam.[41] Moreover, TCL was hopeful that it would be able to enter the European Union markets from Vietnam.

The European Union currently has set up high trade barriers against Chinese electrical appliances. By using Vietnam's membership in the Association of Southeast Asian Nations, TCL hoped that its products could enter the European market through Vietnam, thereby, avoiding the trade barriers.

Generally speaking, the Vietnamese market is quite similar to the Chinese market. This similarity greatly benefits TCL. Vietnam's political system is also quite similar to China's. The Vietnamese government and its procedures are quite similar to China's as they existed in 1980's during China's initial period of reform and opening up. The Chinese frame of mind is not dissimilar to the Vietnamese frame of mind. In addition, TCL decided that it would not invest huge amounts in Vietnam that it would keep its operation costs low, and that the risk of investing in Vietnam was small. It was because of all of these factors that TCL determined that Vietnam was a good place to experiment with foreign investment. The first difficulty that TCL faced in Vietnam was the bad reputation in Vietnam of goods made in China. In addition, in emerging markets, such as Vietnam, brand competition is quite intense. The usual pattern is that while the Japanese goods have the best reputation for quality, the South Korean products have the highest sales volume and market share. Since the Japanese and South Korean enterprises had already entered the Vietnamese market, TCL took the route of lowering its prices. Unfortunately, TCL's pricing strategy had the unintended side effect of exacerbating the already poor reputation of Chinese goods. The Vietnamese people assumed that since TCL's products were priced lower than those of its competitors', they were of inferior quality. In addition, language problems, and local communication and management all posed additional challenges to TCL.

Although TCL has made great inroads into the Vietnamese market, it cannot be said that TCL's Vietnamese journey has been a complete success. It is so because it failed to make a significant contribution towards TCL's two goals: 1) creating international brand recognition, and 2) making a significant profit from the color TV business. The Vietnamese market's scale is too small, equivalent to only one quarter of the market of the city of Guangzhou.[42] Moreover, TCL's venture into Vietnam did not enable it to enter the markets of Singapore, Malaysia, and Thailand. To enter these markets, TCL must start from scratch to establish recognition of its brand. In contrast to TCL's expectations, hardly any of its electronic appliances produced in Vietnam were exported to the countries of the Association of Southeast Asian Nations. TCL's plan to avoid trade barriers, customs duties, political issues, quotas and quantity limits was more theoretical than practical.

TCL's Russian Market:

On October 30, 2004, TCL sponsored a tour of its Shenzhen group in China for 70 Russian merchants involved in the retail sale of electrical appliances. At the conclusion of the tour, these same merchants attended a press conference about TCL's new product releases. After the press conference, these Russian merchants signed purchase agreements on the spot with TCL to sell 330,000 color televisions in Russia for a contract price of 50 million US dollars. At this event, the Russian merchants displayed enormous enthusiasm for TCL's products. To facilitate its Russian strategy, TCL invited not only these 70 merchants but also several Russian public figures to visit the Shenzhen TCL group for 5 days. TCL also went as far as chartering its own airplane to bring the Russians to Shenzhen.[43] This personalized strategy not only strengthened the Russian merchants' confidence in TCL, it also enhanced recognition of the TCL brand in Russia. All in all, the Russian dealers' visit laid a solid foundation for TCL's later smooth entry into the Russian market.

TCL's Indian Market:

Although India has a well-developed retail sales network for electrical appliances, its manufacturing industry for these same appliances is relatively weak. India's factories for electrical appliances are small scale, and of low productivity. These factories also lack adequate quality control and modern equipment. It was in view of these circumstances that in August 2000 TCL chose the Indian electrical appliance retailer, Baron International Limited, as its long-term partner to develop the Indian electrical appliance market. Baron International Limited is one of the India's largest retailers of electrical appliances.[44] Although TCL made a wise choice for a retail partner in India, it unfortunately made a poor choice for a manufacturing partner in India. The company that TCL picked as a manufacturing partner did not bargain in good faith with TCL. It was economically weak, and it dragged down the joint venture with TCL. The choice of this company as a manufacturing partner was the sole cause of TCL's poor economic performance in India. This experience made the TCL leadership aware of how important it is to choose the correct partner in a foreign venture. Of course, TCL has also had successful foreign ventures, such as in the Philippines, where, unlike in India, TCL chose an appropriate partner.[45]

The Downturn of TCL's Efforts at Internationalization:

Since TCL spent 8.2 million euros to buy the German Schneider company on October 29, 2002, it has yet to realize a profit on its investment.[46] From the time that TCL acquired Alcatel's mobile phone division in April 2005, TCL's stock has continuously dropped. TCL's joint venture with Thomson (TCL-Thomson Electronics) is problematic, since the cost of this re-organization will expend two years worth of TCL's future profit.[47] TCL's position as one of the top industries in China rests on its production of old style cathode ray tube (CRT) color televisions. Even though most experts believe that the cathode ray tube will be replaced by flat panel displays within the next 3 to 5 years, TCL-Thomson Electronics (TTE) is nevertheless gambling on the continued use of the CRT. The TTE venture is apparently bringing much uncertainty to an otherwise bright future for TCL. In addition, both Phillips and Panasonic have started to regard TCL as a strategic competitor, although they used to maintain amicable relations with TCL. In addition, the establishment of TCL-Thomson has put in jeopardy several million OEM orders for TCL to produce color televisions for companies, with which it has had working relations for many years. As for TCL–Thomson, it is somewhat premature to ask how to make it an enterprise with a worldwide presence. The most urgent question facing it at the present time is how to make it profitable. During the long and difficult period after the acquisition of Thomson, a great number of its staff left—a sure symptom of a failed merger and acquisition. Since TCL lost such a large portion of its staff, it apparently obtained nothing from its acquisitions but two names—Thomson and Alcatel.

TCL's Mistake Concerning Schneider:

TCL's Expectations for the Purchase of Schneider -

Government and financial circles in Germany showed great support for TCL's purchase of Schneider, since Germany is generally favorable to Chinese manufacturing investment project. In fact, TCL's purchase of Schneider is the fourth such investment project in Germany. After the sale, both the German Economic Minister and the governor of the state of Bavaria where Schneider is located gave their whole-hearted approval to the transaction. Schneider is an established German producer of household appliances with a 113 year history. It has 3 production centers for color televisions, and can produce them at a rate of 1 million per year.[48] In addition, it has well-developed sales and marketing channels in Europe, as well as a large portion of the European market share. TCL hoped to avoid EU trade barriers by purchasing Schneider. Starting from 2002, the European Union imposed a quota on the import of Chinese electrical appliances of 400,000 units per year.[49] In addition, the EU has attached many other conditions to the import of goods from China. Aside from hoping to avoid these trade barriers by the purchase of Schneider, TCL was expecting to make use of Schneider's preexisting market in Germany and Europe, as well as capitalizing on Schneider's brand recognition. In short, TCL was anticipating a rapid entrance into the European markets. Other factors that weight heavily in TCL's decision to purchase Schneider was that Schneider also had a foundation in the European communication and information industry. Such a foundation could facilitate the entrance of TCL's communication and information business into the European market. It was also thought that the purchase of Schneider could bring to TCL a management staff with valuable skills and experience on the international markets, as Meyer indicates that Chinese companies have a lot to gain from merging with Western firms.

Factors Working Against the Success of the Purchase -

However, at that time, Schneider's production lines had been operating at a serious loss. Schneider also had a reputation in Germany of being a somewhat old-fashioned company. Its ownership had changed hands many times, and it even declared bankruptcy on several occasions. In addition, its products were clearly inferior to those of TCL. At the present time, color televisions are very inexpensive in Germany, and the market is near saturation. Currently, there is demand in Germany for new and advanced products. Unfortunately, most Germans do not associate the Schneider name with such products. If TCL were to paste the Schneider label on its own ultra thin, and advanced television sets for sale in Germany, the Germans would not accept it. Schneider is, in fact, a brand on the decline in the European markets. Neither its assets, its brand image, nor its distribution channels could support TCL's dream of easy entrance into the markets of the European Union. After operating under the Schneider brand name in Europe for some time, TCL was faced with inevitable disappointment. Although it seemed to TCL initially that the European market was within its grasp, it turned out that very few people paid attention to—let alone bought—TCL's Schneider color televisions. Faced with such a harsh reality, Li Dongsheng had no choice but to acknowledge to the public media that it was a mistake for TCL to purchase Schneider.

Reaction to TCL's Failure –

Some people believed that TCL's purchase of Schneider was based on flawed logic. The people who believed this maintained that although TCL was buying a German television factory, that factory had in essence already gone out of business. On the other hand, despite Schneider's bankruptcies, it had a workforce, which was very responsible and devoted to the company. In fact, these workers kept the Schneider plant in sparkling condition, despite its economic condition. The critics said that if such devoted workers and management could not save Schneider, what more could TCL have done to improve the enterprise after the takeover. In other words, these critics believe that there was no room for TCL to improve the company.

Mr. Li Dongsheng acknowledged that these critics were making a reasonable assessment of the situation. He further added that when a business is purchased, all the things planned for do not occur, and all the things that are never expected take place. He gave as an example one of the unexpected problems that, unbeknownst to TCL, Schneider had withdrawn from some markets, and was engaged in legal disputes concerning the use of its brand name by local distributors. When TCL took over Schneider's markets, the first thing they had to deal with was not the markets themselves, but the residual legal issues. Li admitted that when they were evaluating Schneider project, they did not use professional consultants to do research, rather, TCL's management made the decision to purchase Schneider based nearly on their own judgment—admittedly quite risky behavior. Li went on to say that such was not the case during the mergers of TCL with Thomson and Alcatel. At those times, TCL's management made sure that extensive research into both companies was done before their purchases. In addition, he explained that Thomson's situation was completely different from that of Schneider's. While Schneider had undergone several bankruptcies, Thomson's business was always in continuous operation. The challenge remaining for TCL regarding Thomson is to make correct decisions with regard to future commercial operations, rather than having to deal with leftover economic and legal issues as was the case with Schneider.[50]

TCL's Thomson Strategy:

On October 10, 2004, the merger between TCL and Alcatel Mobile was officially announced in Beijing. During the ceremony, there was an ubiquitous presence of flowers and decorations, as well as of the flags of China and France. At the same time and in the same city, China was also conducting a grand ceremony declaring 2004 to be "The Year of French Culture." It was apparently no coincidence that these two events took place on the same day. This was the second large Chinese transaction with the French company since TCL purchased Thomson the year before. As a result of the Thomson and Alcatel transactions, TCL became a significant force in Sino-French economic relations. It was also because of these transactions that in September 2005, Li Dongsheng was awarded the French National Medical of Honor by French president Jacques Chirac.[51]

TCL acquired Thomson and Alcatel in order to gain a technological advantage. Thomson has thousands of global patents and inventions in its portfolio, while Alcatel has advanced expertise regarding 2G and 3G mobile communications technology.[52] TCL's acquisition of these two companies will improve its domestic competitive ability, while helping it to consolidate its domestic markets. TCL also gained two valuable international brand names through these acquisitions. This will help it to gain a presence in the overseas markets, and potentially helps it circumvent increasingly formidable trade barriers against Chinese goods. For example, in April 2004, the U.S. Department of Commerce imposed import duties of 24.48 percent on China's largest TV maker, Sichuan Changhong; 22.36 percent on TCL; 11.36 percent on Konka; and 4.35 percent on Xiamen Overseas Chinese Electronic Co. The Department of Commerce also placed import duties of 21.49 percent on nine other domestic TV makers including the Haier Group, Hisense Electric, Philips Consumer Electronics, Skyworth Digital Holdings, SVA Group, Starlight International Holdings and three subsidiaries of Xinghui.[53]

There had been mixed reactions towards the TCL-Thomson merger. Proponents believe that the resulting company from the merger will gain a superior position in the three big markets, Asia, Europe and America. Proponents also believe that TCL's supply of low cost labor will complement Thomson's technological superiority. TCL-Thomson, they maintain, has strong brand recognition in each of the three aforementioned markets. The result of the merger has a technical force of nearly 1,000 engineers, and entire series of products, as well as global services.[54] The proponents maintain that if both participants in the merger can fully leverage their respective advantages in both labor cost and research, it will form a powerful challenge to the leading status of Japanese and South Korean enterprises in the global electrical appliances industry. TCL's previous strategy to avoid trade barriers was to serve chiefly as an OEM supplier to foreign companies. Now that it has acquired Thomson's technology, proponents of the merger maintain that it now poses a direct threat to Japanese and South Korean enterprises.

Opponents to the merger believe that TCL should first work to improve the image of its own brand, improve its own products, and only then should enter overseas markets. They believe that TCL's current plan puts the cart before the horse—that is, TCL is entering the overseas markets before it has solidified its presence in the domestic Chinese market. This two-front strategy of TCL will inevitably put the company in an untenable position. Moreover, these same critics point to Boston Consulting Company's feasibility study on TCL's prospective purchase of Thomson, which described the prospects of the merger as far from optimistic, and fraught with risk. They also point to Thomson's losses in the European and North American markets, which in 2003 amounted to 1.7 billion US dollars.[55]

Moreover, Thomson supported trade barriers against the importation of Chinese color television sets erected by the European Union in 1998 and by the United States in 2003. What is more, Thomson was one of several European and American enterprises that demanded that Chinese enterprises pay royalties on patents related to DVDs and other television technologies.[56] At the same time, it turned out that TCL could only use Thomson's patents and brand name for two years. Consequently, after the merger, TCL did not obtain either a ready-made marketing channel for its Chinese television sets, nor did it obtain unlimited use of high-end color television production technology. All of this came as a great shock to the management of TCL.

In 2004, former Thomson CEO, Jack Welch, went to China to give a speech. Afterwards, Li Dongsheng enthusiastically asked Welch his thoughts on TCL's purchase of Thomson, as well as any suggestions he might have about a post-merger strategy for the company. Mr. Welch said quite frankly that since he had been unable to make Thomson a profitable business, he had sold it out 14 years previously. He added that since Thomson had changed hands many times in the ensuing 14 years, many other people had been unable to turn Thomson around.[57]

Li Dongsheng's Ideas:

Mr. Li has stated that it was a difficult decision whether or not TCL should merge with Thomson. He signed on Morgan Stanley and Boston as consultants, and Thomson signed on Goldman Sachs and McKinsey & Company, all of which are some of the world's top consultation companies. Li stated that Morgan Stanley's position on the merger was neutral, while the Boston company's position was negative, suggesting that TCL and Thomson not merge. Li Dongsheng has also said that Boston's negative opinion had strong effect on him. He, therefore, decided to hold many internal meetings in TCL, in which the matter was repeatedly discussed. He reiterated that it was an extremely difficult decision to make. The major factor against the merger was that some people felt that TCL would be faced with problems in consolidating the two companies. Li Dongsheng maintains that TCL decided to go forward with the merger, since they considered the chance to purchase Thomson during their period of internationalization a rare opportunity. Li Dongsheng and his staff also tried to look behind the numbers and beyond the assessment of the Boston Consulting Firm.[58]

The color television business is the major source of loss for TCL's European section. It accounted for a loss of 618 million dollars, about 83.7% of TCL's total loss for that year.[59] Li Dongsheng said that the European losses were caused by the company's inattention to that market. For a long time, TCL concentrated its efforts on reversing the losses in the North American market, to the neglect of the European market. Li went on to say that in the past year, the European market experienced great changes. In just a 2-year span, the sales of flat panel televisions have outpaced those of the CRT type televisions that TCL was manufacturing. It was TCL's inability to respond rapidly to this situation, he said, that caused TCL's European division to incur hundreds of millions of dollars in losses.[60]

It is true that since the second half of 2005, the European color television market has changed drastically, with sales of flat panel televisions far outstripping those of traditional CRT televisions. Unfortunately for TCL, the management and production structure of its Europe division was build around the manufacture of CRT products. Thus, it was completely unable to adapt to the market shift. Even before it was aware of the shift in the European market, TCL was concentrating its efforts on making its recently acquired RCA brand profitable in North America. During the first half of 2005, TCL was successful in making inroads into the North American market. It was, in fact, gaining North America when it was losing Europe. TCL also underestimated its ability to maintain a high quality workforce in its European section. It failed to realize that since the television production industry was in decline in Europe, it was in the intractable position of being unable either to attract talent or to reduce staff. The fact is that the complexity of the European market was far beyond TCL's prognostications of only a few months earlier. It even failed to foresee that such a simple process as printing a set of new handbooks for its products would require 16 different editions in as many languages to suit the European market.[61]

The Mistake of Purchsing Alcatel Mobile – Wan Mingjian's Story

To everyone's surprise, TCL, with little experience in cross-cultural mergers, and after its purchase of Thomson in 2004, went on to acquire Alcatel. This, too, turned out to be a bad choice for TCL. TCL entered into the acquisition with the hopes of gaining Alcatel's 3G technology. Unfortunately for TCL, the 3G technology was at that time owned by the Fujitsu-Alcatel joint venture.[62] What is more, TCL's newly acquired Alcatel division went on to lose more money than the ill-fated Thomson division. In addition, after TCL acquired Alcatel, it lacked a clear business strategy for the new division, TCL was, therefore, unsure of the direction to which it should steer its acquisition. TCL's acquisition of Alcatel caused great dissatisfaction in the ranks of TCL's workforce. Since TCL had to make up for the loss of millions of yuan each month because of Alcatel, TCL was forced to reduce salaries. This caused a loss in personnel for TCL with the marketing and research departments leading the exodus. At the end of 2004, even Wan Mingjian, the architect of the TCL-Alcatel merger, submitted his resignation.

Wan Mingjian was born in Yibin, a mountainous area of Sichuan province. His personality is typical of the people who come from that region. His demeanor is both haughty and hearty. Wan Mingjian strongly advocated purchasing Alcatel to make it a second feather in the cap of TCL, which was still basking in the glow of the purchase of Thomson. Li Dongsheng was not in a position to say no to Wan Mingjian, since he had a source of great success for TCL. Mr. Wan was personally responsible for 70% of TCL's annual profit.[63] TCL's management was also under great pressure from its own mobile communication's division to purchase Alcatel. This division, a source great cash flow for TCL, was arguing that since TCL had recently expanded its color television production capabilities by the acquisition of Thomson, it should do the same for the mobile communication's division by acquiring Alcatel. Mr. Wan was heard to have said after it was clear that the purchase of Alcatel was an unmitigated disaster: "It was a pity that I only had Alcatel to gamble with, otherwise I would have wagered even more."[64] This indicates that Mr. Wan's rationality was clouded by his aspirations and ambition. But perhaps Mr. Wan said these words because a manager can enjoy both fame and fortune that arises from successful wagers in business, but he himself is not personally liable for any losses when the cards turn against him.

Before the acquisition of Alcatel, Wan Mingjian was chairman of the board and CEO of TCL's mobile division. After the acquisition, Mr. Wan was the CEO of TCL-Alcatel. After it had become clear that the purchase of Alcatel was a bad decision for TCL, Li Dongsheng tried repeatedly to discuss with Mr. Wan ways of turning the situation around. In addition, TCL's board of directors suggested many different ways to Mr. Wan how he could use his personnel and marketing system. Wan Mingjian dismissed all these suggestions as being "non-professional." In June 2004, during an interview with a reporter, Wan smugly said: "If I do not produce the guiding principles for this company, it will surely go under."[65]

There are many stories circulating concerning the details of Wan Mingjian's resignation. There is even some suggestion that a faction within TCL's ranks, jealous of and threatened by Mr. Wan's power and success, laid a trap for Mr. Wan into which his own ambition led him, a trap named Alcatel. This is an indication that the strategy of Chinese companies may entail some extra-rational element. The slightest investigation would reveal that in this case the extra-rational element was jealousy. In order to eliminate a potential rival and perhaps in order to survive, Chinese managers might use any strategic move, including a purchase which is unfavorable to their own company. Wan joined the rival television maker, Changhong, after leaving TCL. Whatever be exact nature of the circumstances that surrounded Mr. Wan's departure from TCL, it is clear that he had no choice but to leave.

After Mr. Wan left TCL, Li Dongsheng stated that before TCL purchased Alcatel mobile, the TCL management looked at the question too simplistically. The TCL management thought that since Alcatel had fewer than 1,000 employees, and had no factory—just a research and marketing system, TCL could design the purchase plan itself, and, thereby, save several million euros in consultation expenses.[66] However, since TCL's management failed to foresee the problems which arose after the purchase, it saved money in the short term, but lost money in the long term. This was an expensive lesson for TCL concerning the process of internationalization.

When Mr. Wan's resignation brought great public attention to TCL, a reporter asked Li Dongsheng if Mr. Wan Mingjian left because he wasn't a team player. Li responded that when an enterprise develops past a certain stage, there should be a spirit of coordination and cooperation among the members of management, as well as a sharing of the company's internal resources. Someone who isn't a team player can hinder this kind of development. From another perspective, at one time in TCL's development, the so-called "hired gun" with little cooperative spirit was important for TCL's growth. This type of people brought with them the entrepreneurial spirit that TCL required at that time. Looking from this positive viewpoint, it was the entrepreneurial spirit that was an important factor in growth of TCL. Its importance lay in the fact that such a spirit can make an enterprise's management team take initiative, shoulder responsibility, and face competition and challenge. When an enterprise's values and culture reaches maturity, it must find a balance between the "hired gun" and team player mentalities. Li Dongsheng summed up the matter by stating that Wan Mingjian's department from TCL was direct result of less than satisfactory ratings for his performance. It was thus a normal personnel change under TCL's policies.[67]

Post-Acquisition Difficulties, Adjustments and Plans:

According to Li Dongsheng, one of the biggest tasks facing a company after it makes an acquisition is the establishment of an effective worldwide management structure. As for the merger with Thompson, jobs with the joint venture have been given to management teams from both of the companies. As for the major markets of this joint venture, Li has stated that they are China, emerging economies, Europe and the U.S. Accordingly he has set up management teams to operate these four business units. An executive committee composed of top managers at both companies has been formed at headquarters. The main responsibility of this committee is to reorganize, develop and manage the global business. The committee is considering such functional areas as sourcing, manufacturing, management of the supply chain and product research and development. It is also trying to coordinate the global use of resources. Hopefully, the committee's coordination of global resources will put these resources to their maximal use. Their objective in making this global allocation is to maximize their synergies and make the best possible use of their resources. The committee is also in the process of starting up a world-wide information management system, a financial system and a common legal system. This integration is estimated to be completed within 18 months.[68]

Li believes that the greatest challenges they are facing during this period of integration are effective communications with other companies, and the achievement of mutual understanding about business cultures and values. In order to facilitate better communications, they have held many training sessions and meetings among senior management. The hope is that such projects will enhance their integration while creating new synergies.[69]

As for TCL's strategy concerning the market in the US, they believe that it has been tough—especially for consumer electronics products—in recent years. The United States, however, is a crucial part of their global strategy, and the exploration of this market is an imperative for them. Even Thompson was not performing well in the US market in the recent past. It was losing market share and suffering losses. To counter this, two committees were created: one whose task was to contain costs, and the other whose task was to create value. The cost containment committee sets its sights on manufacturing, sourcing and supply-chain management in hopes of enhancing their competitive posture and financial position. The committee on value creation is more concerned with new products, planning and development, new markets and opportunities, and new customer resources with the hope of improving sales and marginal contribution. They are also considering avenues to improve their efficiency in the US market, including possible business restructuring and reforms.[70]

Li has indicated that TCL is not currently planning for future acquisitions. Its venture with Thompson has already required a great investment of time, resources and energy. The management of TCL has learned that they must consider several important factors before engaging in any future merger or acquisition. The first factor they must consider is whether both companies' assets complement each other. This is far more important than mere consideration of the companies' book value. The second factor is how to establish—at least in the initial stages—mechanisms for effective communications between the management teams of both companies. The third factor is the maintenance of high moral and confidence among the rank and file of both organizations. This factor is of especially great importance. Some deliverable result should be produced within the first six months after the merger to keep morale and confidence levels high. The long term objectives of the merger or joint venture need to be clearly understood. The management and employees should share these objectives in order for them to dedicate themselves to the stated goals.[71]

Introduction to Haier:

Haier's development has had three stages: 1. The first stage was the establishment of its brand name. This stage lasted approximately from 1984 to 1991. Haier_started out by acquiring the Qingdao Air Conditioning and Refrigeration Manufacturing plant. After that, Haier_took over many non-profitable companies from the provincial governments of Guangdong and Wuhan. Haier used these acquisitions to establish businesses in air conditioning, washing machines, and color televisions. 2. The second period of Haier's development was one of rapid expansion and diversification. This stage occupied the years of 1992 to 1998. During this period, Haier was engaged in many industries, including the manufacture of white, black and cream color electrical appliances, small electrical appliances, pharmaceutical goods, bio-engineering products, and was also engaged in the financial services industry. 3. Haier has been in a state of internationalization from 1999 until the present. In 2001, Haier extended its reach overseas by buying an Italian refrigerator manufacturing factory. Up until now, Haier has established 13 manufacturing factories, and 18 trade centers all over the world.[72]

Haier's globalization:

The first type of Haier's globalization was the globalization of the design of its products. At present, Haier has established 8 foreign design centers for its products for distribution mainly in the developed countries. The second type of Haier's globalization was the globalization of its purchase of materials necessary for its products. Every day Haier purchases roughly 260,000 kinds of raw materials. In order to obtain the best suppliers, Haier uses its global network for bidding and purchasing. The third type of globalization was the globalization of Haier's manufacture of its products. Haier has a total of 8 industrial complexes, two of which are foreign—one in the United States, and one in Pakistan. Of Haier's 50 factories, 13 are on foreign soil. The fourth type of Haier's globalization was globalization of sales and marketing. Haier has a total of more than 40,000 sales offices and 23 foreign sales companies involved in its chain of distribution. These offices and companies are bringing about development and innovation in Haier's global marketing. The fifth type of globalization was the globalization of funding. In 2002, Haier seized the opportunity of China's joining the WTO, and the gradual opening up of the Chinese financial industry. Haier collaborated with New York Life and the Paris Bank to establish two joint ventures. Haier, thereby, became more involved in the insurance and banking industries. Before this, the Haier group already controlled the Qingdao Commercial Bank, the Anshan Trust, and Yangtze Securities. In the next 3 years, Haier's U.S. branch will strive to have an Initial Public Offering (IPO) in New York. Haier's European branch will strive to have an IPO in Milan. Through the development of its financial services, Haier is clearly trying to integrate its industrial and financial resources. By the two prongs of industry and finance, Haier is on the fast track to internationalization.[73]

In August 2001, Haier ranked number six on Forbes magazine's list of "The Ten Largest Manufacturers of White Goods in the World." Haier has also gained the world's interest for its innovations in management and corporate culture. Harvard University, the European Industry and Commerce Institute, and the Swiss IMD International have all used case studies involving Haier in their teaching materials.[74]

Haier has successively registered its trademark in 102 countries. Haier has successively met the requirements of 8 national and regional quality testing organizations, including the UL in the U.S., and the German VDE. One after another, Haier's refrigerators, freezers, and air-conditioners have received ISO9001 certification. In the domestic Chinese market, the Haier's four main products, refrigerators, freezers, air conditioners, and washing machines have 30% of the market share. As for foreign markets, Haier products are sold in 12 out of the 15 largest European chain stores, and in 8 out of the 10 largest U.S. chain stores. These stores in the U.S. include Wal-Mart, Best Buy, Sears, Lowe's, Home Depot and Target. The world's largest department store, Macy's, also sells one of Haier's small refrigerators.[75]

Subdivisions and Market Innovations of Haier:

Haier has successfully sub-divided its market, and has adapted itself to local requirements. Because Haier was late in entering the international markets, its scale and strength was and continues to be far inferior to that of the world's famous large companies, such as Whirlpool, Electrolux, General Electric and Samsung Electronics. Therefore, from the beginning, Haier has chosen to use its products to fill up vacancies in the market left by the other companies.

For instance, when Haier first entered the U.S. market, it produced a small refrigerator for use by students in dormitories. Haier had discovered that there was a large untapped demand for such refrigerators in the U.S. market. This is because student dormitories are usually small, and such refrigerators can also serve as a small table in small quarters. It was Haier's innovation to add a folding top for the small refrigerator, as well as to add a board which can be pulled out. In this way, Haier's refrigerator could also serve as a computer desk.[76] After much development and design, Haier's small refrigerator filled the gap in the U.S. market.

Another example of Haier's catering to local (in this case American) custom is its series of Piaowei refrigerated liquor cabinets. When Haier discovered that wine was fashionable with America's bourgeois, it designed a transparent, curved liquor cabinet, that fit the demands of America's consumers. The cabinet has exquisite lines, delicate modeling, a unique function, and a computer-controlled thermostat for storing many different types of wine. In addition, Haier's designers changed a horizontal border which divided the cabinet in two into 10 horizontal and parallel steel bars. When a bottle is placed in the cabinet, these bars give it the impression of a beautiful woman resting on a comfortable bed—a design which is both practical and charming. Haier's liquor cabinet quickly became the rage of the U.S. market, and it currently holds 90% of the U.S. market share. Moreover, its price is double those of its competitors.'[77]

The design of Haier's products results from close attention to consumer demand. For example, for the American market, it specifically designed a refrigerator called "The Big General" whose outward appearance and refrigeration ability were adapted to the American usage. For the Indonesian market, it designed a single door refrigerator, that was both energy efficient and suitable for a wide range of voltages, all of which Indonesian consumers prefer. For the Pakistani market, Haier especially designed a washer that can hold 15 long gowns at one time, which is suitable for the requirements of daily life in Pakistan.[78]

Haier's U.S. Market:

Haier established its design center in Los Angeles, its trading center in New York City and its production center in South Carolina. The management structure of Haier's design, production, and sales centers is patterned on the U.S. model of business operations. Haier's manufacturing plant in South Carolina occupies 600 acres, and is Haier's largest overseas production base.[79] To all appearances, this factory looks like any other U.S. factory. All the staff are Americans with the exception of the general manager and two technical personnel who were sent from Haier's headquarters in China. The factory's management style follows that of its American counterparts. Many products which Haier sells in the U.S. are designed specifically for the American market. Haier's U.S. branch operates a customer service hotline which covers the entire country. In addition, South Carolina's Camden city named a road after Haier. Kershaw county, also located in South Carolina, awarded Haier with a prize for its contribution to the community.[80] All indicators seem to show that Haier is dedicated to establishing itself as a brand known for quality. Haier must pay a high price for this goal. Haier's labor costs at its South Caroline's refrigerator factory are 10 times what they would be in China. This obviously hurts Haier's competitive ability. What is even more to Haier's disadvantage is that the greater part of the U.S. consumer appliance manufacturing industry is located close to the Mexican border. In this way, these appliance producers can reap the benefit of the low cost of Mexican labor, while at the same time enjoying the benefits of NAFTA.

In spite of this, we cannot say that Haier is a loser in the U.S. market. Since the establishment of its first factory in the U.S. in 1999, Haier has developed rapidly. It has a 50% share of the American market for refrigerated liquor cabinet, as well as for small refrigerators.[81] Although Haier has achieved a certain degree of brand recognition in the United States, and has obtained a respectable amount of the market share, its U.S. branch continues to operate in the red. Although Haier is known in China for its successful diversification, in the U.S., Haier has nearly expanded from the refrigerator market to the washing machine and air conditioner markets. In other words, it has been restricting itself in the United States to the production of white-goods consumer appliances. It has not been successful in expanding into the markets for small electrical appliances, computers, and television sets.

Haier's Attempt to Purchase Maytag:

In June 2005, the Haier group acknowledged that it was considering buying Maytag, American third largest manufacturer of electrical appliances. On June 21st, the Maytag company announced that Haier in conjunction with Bain Capital and Blackstone Capital, two investment companies, was bidding 12.8 billion US dollars. This amount was considerably higher than that of the next largest bidder, the Ripplewood company. Haier also pledged to undertake Maytag's debts of 970 million US dollars, bring the total amount of the bid to 22.5 billion US dollars. Haier tried to keep a low profile in China concerning its bid for Maytag.[82]

It is widely surmised that Haier intended to purchase Maytag to increase its presence in the European and U.S. markets. Currently, Maytag's three largest markets are in North America, Europe and the Middle East. Haier hoped that its purchase of Maytag would greatly help Haier's internationalization. Haier was hoping to capitalize on Maytag's mature brand and sales channels, while making up for Maytag's high production costs with relatively inexpensive and plentiful Chinese labor. The large amount of money that Haier was willing to spend for Maytag was indeed a test. Market professionals had already been questioning Haier's business capacity and low profit margin when the offer was made. After Whirlpool counter attacked, Haier analyzed the situation and withdrew its bid for Maytag. This was a wise choice on the part of Haier's management.

Haier's internationalization strategy met with criticism. During the past five years, the slow pace of Haier's internationalization and its apparent difficulty in turning a profit has put Haier under much pressure. Judging from Haier's poor fiscal performance in 2004, it will be difficult for it financially to develop new markets.[83] Since TCL and Lenovo had raised the bar for internationalization through the acquisition of foreign companies, Haier, when presented with the opportunity to purchase Maytag, felt compelled to make an offer and follow the lead of TCL and Lenovo. Maytag also seemed to be an appropriate business for Haier to purchase since it would help improve Haier's overall image in the U.S., as well as promoting public perception of the quality of its product. All these factors led Haier to make its offer for Maytag.

Logic would seem to imply that when one large company purchases an even larger company, the resulting company will have a larger presence on the global market. From the long-term view, however, it is difficult to tell whether such an acquisition will have the desired result. Many mergers of large companies have in fact resulted in a whole that was less than the sum of its parts. For example, when Sony purchased Colombia Pictures, it originally planned to graft superior Japanese technology onto the American entertainment industry, however, it turned out that Sony's purchase eventually caused a loss of 2.7 billion US dollars. America Online was initially attracted to Time Warner as a source of content for its internet based network. This seemingly perfect match of companies shortly turned into a disaster for all parties.[84] When TCL purchased Thomson, a French manufacturer of televisions and DVD players, it did so with the hope of combining European technology and marketing knowledge with the low cost of Chinese manufacturing, in order to create the world's largest producer of televisions. However, even before the ink was dry on the final agreement, the resulting company was drowning in losses. These examples have led experts to conclude that in mergers and acquisitions of massive companies, the outcome is determined more by what the purchasing company can provide to the purchased company rather than *vice versa*. For example, Haier, the purchasing company, could not provide Maytag with either brand, technical, or marketing superiority—the very things that Haier was hoping to obtain in the acquisition. From its dealings with Maytag, Haier learned that in future acquisitions, it should look not only towards what it can obtain from the purchased company, but also to what it could bring to the purchased company.

The Internationalization Models of Haier and Galanz:

Galanz – The Galanz group's predecessor was the Guizhou feather production factory, a rural enterprise in the city of Shunde, in Guangdong province. In 1991, Galanz purchased equipment necessary to produce microwave ovens from the Japanese Toshiba company. In 1992, Galanz officially went into the business of producing microwave ovens. Galanz's business grew rapidly over the next ten years. In 2001, Galanz sold 12 million microwave ovens, for which it received 7.017 billion Yuan. At that time, it held 75% of the Chinese domestic market share, and 35% of the international market share.[85] The French media recently reported that Galanz was the world's largest producer of microwave ovens. Currently, the top producers of microwave ovens are in turn the Chinese Galanz company, the Japanese Sharp company, the South Korean Samsung company, the Japanese Panasonic company, American Whirlpool, U.S. GE, South Korean Samsung, South Korean Daewoo, and the Japanese Sanyo corporation. European, American, Japanese and South Korean industry experts universally agree that the world of microwave oven production belongs to Galanz.[86]

The two separate paths towards internationalization taking by Haier and Galanz respectively are typical of the path chosen by Chinese companies. On their paths towards internationalization, Haier emphasizes brand recognition, while Galanz engages in Original Design Manufacturing (ODM); Haier emphasizes diversification, Galanz specialization. While both strategies seem completely different, they have both led to astonishing successes.

It is well known that Haier was originally a state-owned enterprise, and its predecessor was the Qingdao Electric Refrigerator Plant. Galanz, however, has always been privately owned and operated. In China, Haier is considered to be the model of a state-owned enterprise. It is a shining example of Chinese business acumen. Its brilliant reputation has earned it great leeway with the government, yet it is not to say that Haier is totally unrestricted by the state. Since Galanz was created under China's policy of reform and openness, and developed under virtually private economic conditions, it, unlike Haier, is thus concerned only with pleasing the market, rather than with pleasing the state. It can follow its own path of development without interference from the state and grow, hopefully, into a worldwide industrial producer of microwave ovens.

The Strategic Difference between Brand Name and ODM Sales:

Haier is chiefly concerned with brand recognition, while Galanz has adopted the strategy of ODM production. In fact, Haier is considered to have the most regard for its brand name of any company in China. Haier's brand name consequently has the highest value of any other. Unlike Haier, Galanz adopted the ODM strategy in its internationalization process, that is, instead of placing emphasis on its own brand, it produces products for other companies to be sold under other brand names. Galanz does not hesitate to place the logos of other companies on products which Galanz itself has produced. Galanz uses its business solely for production. It leaves the job of sales and promotion to the merchants of other brands.

Galanz's ODM strategy depends on two factors: price elasticity and the economies of scale. As an example of price elasticity, in 1995, it sold 200,000 units. In 1996, it reduced its prices as much as 40%, and as a result, it sold 650,000 units, a 325% increase over the previous year's sales.[87] The reduction in price also had the effect of increasing the scope of Galanz's markets. This effect was especially noticeable in low income countries. Since Galanz's growth was still in the initial stages at that time, it did not sacrifice too much by implementing a strategy of low price and giving up its brand name. Thus, the ODM strategy became a logical choice for Galanz.

Haier's Strategy of Diversification and Galanz's Strategy of Specialization

In January 1992, Haier started to implement its strategy of diversification. It has completed production of one product, and was starting to produce another. It expanded its production line from solely the manufacture of refrigerators to the manufacture of the majority of consumer appliances. One after another Haier began producing washing machines, air conditioners and televisions. Galanz, however, concentrates only on the production of microwave ovens. Since they have developed a specialized expertise in the production of microwave ovens, it can produce them in a large scale with little difficulty. Because the microwave industry is technologically mature, price to the consumer is the only advantage one company in the industry has over another. Because China has the advantage of a cheap labor force, which will ultimately result in lower prices for consumers, many overseas brands have decided to collaborate with Galanz, and move their production lines to China. Galanz is responsible solely for production, while the overseas companies are responsible for product sales and promotion. The industrial pattern of international giants is big at both ends, the brand end and the channel of distribution end. The part devoted to manufacturing forms an—as it were—small middle section. The entire chain of production and distribution can thus be viewed as being sort of dumbbell-shaped. Glanz must be strong in the middle, the manufacturing sector. Its role in the industrial process can be viewed as being, metaphorically speaking, olive-shaped. The complementary shapes of the two sectors, the brand and channel distribution dumbbell, and the manufacturing olive, will place Galanz in the enviable position of being "workshop to the world". As a consequence, Galanz has paid a very small price to become the ODM producer and run the production lines for 48 overseas microwave oven companies, while simultaneously engaging in other business relations with more than 80 transnational enterprises.[88] Without investing so much as a penny in advertising, Galanz has brought its products into the European and American markets in vast quantities.

The cases of Haier and Galanz show that there is not just one successful road to internationalization. Each enterprise should take the path towards internationalization that is most suitable to its individual characteristics. However, when a company stays at the OEM stage, although it is engaged in exporting at trade, it is not increasing the brand recognition of its products, and it is most certainly not engaged in FDI Moreover, a company at this stage is not in the process of creating its own marketing channels. However, the creation of world-class brands in the global electrical appliance's market is the only way for the complete internationalization of Chinese electrical appliance manufacturers.

Haier v. TCL v. Hisense – A Comparison and Contrast:

- Commonalities -

Cooperation with Global Electrical Appliance Giants:

On January 8, 2002, the Haier group and Japan's Sanyo formed the Sanyo-Haier joint-stock company. This company takes the Chinese and Japanese markets as its foundation, creates a bigger market by the alliance of Haier and Sanyo, and exchanges market resources.[89] In this way, Haier smoothly entered the Japanese market, which is known for having harsh conditions for foreign companies. Haier refrigerators are sold in Japan's biggest chain store, Japan United Stores Company (JUSCO), which has more than 200 branch locations. According to the marketing plan of the JUSCO store, Haier's refrigerators will soon account for 20% of the refrigerators sold by this chain store.[90] In February 2002, Haier and the Taiwanese Shengbao group signed a cooperation agreement. In June of that same year, Haier established a joint venture with German OBI, by which the two companies will develop China's home furnishing market.[91]

Hisense chose the Japanese corporation, Sumitomo, as its partner in internationalization. On July 30, 2002, Hisense and Sumitomo officially announced their alliance, and established Hisense-Sumitomo company with headquarters in Japan. The new company is mainly engaged in the sale of Hisense electrical products in Japan. It is also using Sumitomo's international retail network to promote the sale of Hisense products in the European and American markets.[92]

TCL believes that if it acquires core technology, it will be able to grasp the initiative in its markets, and will finally become a world-class multinational corporation. To do this, however, TCL must form alliances and cooperate with the world's multinational corporations. To this end, TCL has cooperated with the Dutch Phillips company and Japan's Panasonic and Toshiba. In this way, it can allocate its resources on a global scale more judiciously, reduce cost, accelerate the development of core technology, and promote the enterprise's international competitive strength.

On April 9, 2002, the TCL group and Panasonic reached an agreement in Beijing to cooperate in the electrical appliances industry. Panasonic entered this agreement because it was in a difficult position. At the time Panasonic believed its disappointing showing in the worldwide markets was caused to a great extent by its lack of an adequate market in China. As a consequence of its small Chinese network, Panasonic's goods were only sold in the major cities of China and not the rest of the country. After analyzing situation, Panasonic came to the conclusion that if it wanted to capture the Chinese markets, it should make use of TCL's sales network in the smaller cities and towns in China. Through its cooperation with TCL, Panasonic is not only using TCL's Chinese network to expand its market, but more importantly, Panasonic is controlling its costs more efficiently, and is able to use more of its existing resources for development. TCL entered into the agreement with the belief that it would be able to make use of Panasonic's ability in research and development. TCL also hoped that its cooperation with Panasonic would bring it advanced technology, in particular, AV, DVD, SD and plasma technology. In addition, TCL expected to acquire experience in international marketing and management, as well as enjoy preferential treatment in the purchase of essential spare parts from Panasonic. With Panasonic's support, TCL not only started the Chinese domestic plasma color television market, but also has since taken the lead in reducing prices for these sets.[93]

On August 22, 2002, Phillips and TCL signed a marketing agreement. According to this agreement, TCL would be the sole agent for the sale of Phillips' color televisions in 5 provinces, namely, Guangxi, Guizhou, Jiangxi, Anhui and Shanxi.[94]

In 2003, TCL and Toshiba announced the formation of two joint ventures, both of which would be involved in the production and sales of refrigerators and washing machines. The manufacturing unit of this joint venture is controlled by Toshiba, while the sales unit is controlled by TCL. In 2004, TCL and Italy's DeLonghi together contributed 100 million dollars to set up the world's largest production center for dehumidifiers and portable air conditioners, located in Guangzhou. TCL has also engaged in ventures with companies, such as U.S. Infocus, South Korean Bhflex, and Japan's Sumitomo for the joint development of television monitors.[95]

TCL's strong point is not the establishment of joint ventures with foreign companies, but its use of foreign capital. In this way, it maintains power throughout the life of a joint venture as opposed to merely being used by foreign companies. TCL's guiding principle, when it embarks upon a joint venture, is to maintain controlling rights over the entire operation. Specifically, TCL is good at selecting joint venture targets with an appropriate scale and strength which can be helpful to TCL. It can also convince the other party to the venture to let TCL control management. For instance, TCL's strategic partners include Toshiba, which has formidable capabilities in international operations and technical research and development. Sumitomo, another of TCL's partners, has abundant capital and many years of previous cooperation with TCL. Another partner, Namtai Electronic has much experience in the design and manufacture of digital products. Kingsoft produces superior electronic products and spare parts. Hong Kong's Pentel, a subsidiary of the Dutch Phillips company, is well known for the research and manufacture of mobile electronic equipment.[96]

The Reform Concerning the Ownership of Chinese Businesses:

The property rights of all the large international companies are diverse. This multiplex structure of property rights is advantageous to the enterprise's long term development. Large enterprises such as Hisense and TCL were all initially state-owned. The enterprise and its destiny were in the hands of local government officials. Such a structure of property rights is disadvantageous to an enterprise's international development. For this reason, electrical appliance manufacturers, such as TCL and Hisense, have been diligently seeking a transformation of property rights, when it comes to the ownership of a company. TCL successfully achieved property right reform after 16 years of unremitting attempts. It is a good example for other Chinese electrical appliance manufacturers of property right transformation. Hisense is still in the process of carrying on property right reform.

TCL successfully completed its joint stock system transformation in 2002, and obtained high praise from people in all walks of life. Before TCL conducted its property right reform, the Guangdong Province Huizhou municipal government held 100% of the stockholder's rights in TCL. During the 5 year period from 1996 to 2001, TCL went about unceasingly changing its enterprise's ownership system. The percentage of state-own stock in TCL during this time dropped from 100% to 58%. At the same time, TCL's internal staff acquired 42% of the stock in the company. In 2001, with the cooperation of the Huizhou municipal government, the TCL group made further changes to its ownership structure. This led to the events of April 2002 in which TCL distributed partial ownership in its stock to five foreign companies, namely, Japan's Toshiba, the Sumitomo bank, Phillips' subsidiary Pentel, Hong Kong's Kingsoft group, and the Namtai group. Altogether these five companies owned 12.38% of TCL's stock. The Huizhou municipal government further reduced the percentage of TCL's stock that it held from 58% to 40.97%. The staff and management of TCL presently hold 25% of its stock. Other founders hold 15.65% of the stock.[97] The influx of international capital raised the performance requirements for the company's management. This influx of capital also led to a qualitative change in the entire management system. In short, by transforming its stock system and introducing new strategic investors, the TCL group transformed itself from a state-owned enterprise under the absolute control of the local authorities into a modern enterprise. Its stockholder's rights are now shared by the local government (which now has limited power over the country), corporate management, and strategic investors. This change in corporate structure went hand in hand with TCL's establishment of itself as an independent legal entity. It also guaranteed the implementation of TCL's strategy for internationalization.

Hisense is also facing the question of property right reform in its process of internationalization. Hisense believes that sole ownership by the state works against the company's adapting to the market economy, as well as its conforming to the manifold requirements of internationalization. Of all the difficulties that Chinese companies must face, the question of state ownership is by far the most difficult. If Hisense continues to be solely state-owned, its process of internationalization will lead nowhere. As early as 1994, Hisense tried to imitate the reform in ownership structure of Stone Corporation's reform of ownership structure, but failed. Hisense current has several billion yuan in assets. Since it is completely state-owned, Hisense dare not act rashly to change its property right structure.[98] If it does, its leadership could be easily charged with draining state assets. Therefore, Hisense is cautiously treading lightly on the path of property rights reform.

- Differences -

The Internationalization Process of Chinese electrical appliance enterprises generally follows one of two patterns. The first pattern is characterized by an easy start with later difficulties. This seems to be the pattern of TCL and Hisense. The other pattern, which Haier seems to have followed, is characterized by initial difficulties that gradually dissipate. A majority of China's electrical appliance manufacturers, including Hisense and TCL, usually choose developing nations as their main markets. That is, they choose the path of easy start with later difficulties in their process of globalization. That is, they start with the developing nations as their markets, and then gradually enter the markets of Europe and America. Haier, however, has chosen the opposite strategy, namely, the one characterized by initial difficulties that gradually dissipate. First, it established its prestige and created brand recognition by initially entering the European and American markets. This made it quite easy for Haier to enter the markets of the developing nations.

From the very beginning, Haier had as its goal of internationalization the markets of Europe and America, in particular, those of Germany, the U.S., and Italy. It attempted to hone its business approach by entering these mature market economies and thus gain a keen competitive advantage in these developed nations. Haier also hoped that success is these extremely difficult markets could bring further success in the markets of developing nations.

As stated earlier, Haier successively achieved 15 types of certification for its products, including the American UL, the Canadian CSA, the Australian SM, the German VDE and GS, the European Union's CE, the Japanese S-MAR, and Saudi Arabia's ASO. Among them, Japan, in order to limit the number of washing machines entering its market, formulated a military-type standard for imported washing machines that was much higher than the standard for washing machines manufactured in Japan. Haier's washing machines surpassed even this military-type standard. Among the developed nations, Germany seems to pay the most attention to the quality of imported goods. It is thus quite difficult for a foreign manufacturer to obtain German certification of quality. Haier spent a year and a half in research and development in order to attain German certification. After obtaining the long sought after certification, Haier became the first Chinese manufacturer to export refrigerators to the German market.[99]

In order to coordinate the management of Haier's transnational enterprises in the United States, Haier set up a design branch in Silicon Valley in March 1998, a design center in Boston in April 1999, a marketing center in New York City and a production center in South Carolina.[100] Therefore, Haier's people believe that the seemingly risky strategy of globalization consisting of initial difficulties that gradually dissipate in fact has the highest chance of success.

Moreover, European and American dealers and businesses have highly developed channels of distribution, and are in a position to exert great influence on other markets, in particular those of the developing nations. Therefore, Haier thinks that success in the European and American markets is critical to its overall success and is much more significant than success only in the developing nations.

Hisense's journey to internationalization began in 1988, and it followed the path characterized by an easy start with later difficulties. Hisense first entered the markets of the developing nations with relative ease, such as those of South Africa, the Middle East, South America, and Southeast Asia. After obtaining a certain market share and management experience in the process of internationalization, it then progressed to the markets of the developed countries, such as the U.S. and Europe.

Hisense believes that if an enterprise wants to maintain long-term a competitive advantage, Hisense gradually attained formidable technical expertise and a management who knew how to exploit it. In this way, Hisense has been able to produce quality products at a reasonable price and, so, to gain access to the international markets. However, Hisense believes that when it tries to enter the markets of world's most advanced nations, it will be met with difficulty, even though Hisense is at the same level of technology as the industries of these advanced nations. Therefore, Hisense has adopted the path of an easy start with later difficulties. Thus, Hisense decided to internationalize by first entering the markets of the developing nations where it could establish a good reputation for its products, brand recognition, and consumer trust. Only when it has established itself in the developing nations, will it try to enter the markets of the technologically advanced nations.

TCL proceeded to internationalize in an orderly and gradual way. It first started to expand to the Southeast Asian countries, such as Vietnam, and the Philippines, countries with which it had close cultural connections. It then gradually expanded its markets to include those of the developed countries. TCL believed that it should be initially cautious since it lacked management personnel with the knowledge of multinational and foreign trade. Therefore, it decided to start with a relatively easy market, thereby, accumulating experience which it could then leverage to enter the markets of the developed nations. In this way, TCL was hoping to avoid some of the pitfalls of internationalization. It therefore decided on a path of steady growth.

Brand Name and OEM – A Closer Look:

OEM/ODM:

At present, there are 13 famous brands of electrical appliances in the world. Japan has 6—Panasonic, Sony, Toshiba, Sanyo, Sharp and Hitachi. The U.S. has 3—GE, Whirlpool and Maytag. Europe has 2—Electrolux and Simons. South Korea has 2—LG and Samsung. These 13 occupy more than 90% of the world's market share in electrical appliances.[101] Chinese electrical appliance manufacturers, however, access the world's market mainly through OEM or ODM.

OEM, on the one hand, can help large international electrical appliance manufacturers bring new products to the market rapidly. This is a result of global economic integration, as well as of industrial division of labor. This strategy of OEM also reduces the risk of investment for the large manufacturers. On the other hand, the strategy of OEM helps to employ large segments of the Chinese workforce. It also helps Chinese enterprises to show their superiority when it comes to production costs. It, thereby, provides easy access to the international markets for the Chinese enterprises. It is also quite suitable to the present economic realities facing Chinese electrical appliance manufacturers. It is, therefore, not surprising that more and more Chinese manufacturers of electrical appliances are choosing OEM to develop their presence in the international markets. However, this is causing a reduction in the number of Chinese domestically produced brands of electrical appliances.

The strategy of OEM engages China only in production. Advances in technology, markets and capital all remain outside of China. Thus, although OEM does bring certain benefits for Chinese manufacturers of electrical appliances, it ultimately blocks the road to the complete internationalization of these same Chinese enterprises. Moreover, the profit that can be made from being an OEM manufacturer is relative merger. Regardless of what it produces, the tendency for OEM manufacturers is to produce more and more goods at lower and lower profits. Initially, TCL relied completely upon OEM as the source for its exports. When the Southeast Asian Financial Crisis erupted in 1998, TCL lost massive amounts of orders because the RMB yuan was not depreciated. Having learned such a hard lesson, TCL came to realize the importance of brand recognition and marketing networks in the process of internationalization.

In the process of internationalization of Chinese electrical appliance manufacturers, there have been two different views concerning the value of a brand name. One view is that which is held by Haier and Hisense. The goal for these enterprises is to develop world famous brand names. The other view is held by TCL and Galanz. These companies use OEM to maximize their business production capacities, as well as to bring in foreign exchange income.

When Haier exports its products, it tries to polish its brand image by maintaining a quality of goods. In fact, some have said that, to Haier, quality is more important than profit. As for exports, Haier has consistently maintained that they are for the creation and maintenance of international brand, not merely for bringing in foreign exchange.

Hisense is one of the few Chinese companies that values both advanced technology and brand recognition. The goal of Hisense's internationalization efforts is to make Hisense a world renowned brand. Hisense equipped its Chinese headquarters with world class testing and instrumentation equipment. On September 28, 2001, the Chinese government awarded Hisense with its National Quality Management prize. It received this award for its business strategy of producing high-quality goods and serving the consumer. In countries outside of China, Hisense's televisions and air conditioners have received European CE certification, American UL, FCC and FDA certification, Russian GOST certification, and Australian AS certification. In Australia, the Hisense 29-inch and 34-inch television sets met with widespread consumer approval, and also received the Australian Galaxy Energy Award.[102]

Hisense is one of the few Chinese electrical appliance manufacturers which believes that its competitive advantage will come from continuous technical research and development. Hisense also believes that its core competitive ability arises from a combination of technical and market innovation. Hisense has established technology centers, post-doctoral scientific research workstations, and laboratories, which have been ranked among the best in China. Hisense devotes 5% to 8% of its sales income annually to technological research and development.[103] Hisense has made independent innovations in the arena of air conditioning technology. For example, Hisense reduced the startup time of its air conditioners to 0.7 microsecond. Since this was much better than the 2.5 microsecond startup time for Japanese air conditioners, Hisense's innovation forced these Japanese businesses to reduce prices.[104] Hisense has broken the overseas monopoly on its core technology, and has made great contributions to the industrial development of China.

Compared with that of Haier and Hisense, TCL's process of internationalization started relatively late. As stated earlier, TCL came to realize the importance of brand recognition in the process of internationalization after the 1997 financial crisis in Southeast Asia. At present, however, TCL is using its own brand name only in the markets of Southeast Asia. When TCL first entered the European and American markets, it did so mainly through the use of OEM or ODM. Now their presence in the European and North American markets is due to their acquisition of Schneider, Thomson and RCA.

Conclusion:

Since the early 1980s, the Chinese Household electrical appliance industry has undergone rapid development. The value of the industry output was US $107.5 million in 1980. By 1999, this value had soared to US $18.75 billion. During the same time, the number manufacturers of home electrical appliances in China had grown to 2,765.

Generally speaking, China's home electrical appliance industry has entered a period of slow growth and structural adjustment since late 1990s, following a rapid growth in the 1980s and early 1990s. After a period of rapid growth in the 1980s and early 1990s, the Chinese home electrical appliance industry has still been experiencing growth (albeit a more tempered growth) and has also been undergoing structural adjustment. Supply and demand in the Chinese home electrical appliance market have become more balanced over the past few years. This market has also been expanding at a steady, but not phenomenal, rate in recent years. At the same time, this market has seen the introduction of a wide range of home electrical appliances, which have been satisfying market demand and market capacity at a variety of levels. Presently, the Chinese home electrical appliance industry produces over one hundred distinct products.[105]

The first year of China's Tenth Five-Year Plan was 2001. As part of this plan, the Chinese government has been trying to increase economic development by introducing a whole host of new plans and policies.

The Chinese home electrical appliance industry has witnessed a spate of growth recently due to the development of a residential housing industry, the development of the rural economy and the development of western China. The development of the residential housing industry has proven to be a particular boon to the home electrical appliance industry.

In general, the overall economic growth in China has continued to help provide support for the growth of the domestic home electrical appliance industry. What is more, an information-oriented home electrical appliance industry has been gathering strength in China. China's household electrical appliance industry has been reacting positively to the new opportunities presented to it by China's admission into the WTO, as well as by the increasing importance of e-commerce in that nation. This growth, however, has not been affecting all home electrical appliance products equally. Price pressures have remained intense, and market competition in this sector has been experiencing an increased ferocity. This has given rise to new patterns of competing in the Chinese home electrical appliances industry.[106]

Since China's overall economy is still in overdrive, and its prospects for continued development seem bright, it is likely that the market for home electrical appliances will continue to grow. Growth in this market will no doubt be further fueled by its current expansion from the urban market, to the rural and international markets as well. Although there will likely be steady growth in the Chinese home electrical appliance market, this growth will not be evenly distributed among all of its products.[107]

The precise set of avenues by which the government and business conduct their relations is not particularly clear. What is crystal clear, however, is the industry's growing assertiveness, which seems to be tied to the economic characteristics of the industry. The larger companies are dominating the consumer electronics market. Since this market is extremely competitive, if a company obtains any economic or policy advantage, it can potentially be quite valuable.[108] The importance of these types of advantages is illustrated by the price competition that occurred in 1998.

In August of that year, the SETC, with aid of a few firms, issued the notice "Ideas on Instituting Industry Self-Discipline Prices for Some Industrial Products." The purpose of this notice was to encourage industry members to set price floors or ceilings on twenty one different products.[109] While some firms were ardent supporters of the notice, and even helped in producing it, other firms were stridently opposed to it and worked to reduce any potential impact. The State Development and Planning Commission (SDPC), in conjunction with several economists and companies, proceeded to attack the self-discipline notice as not in keeping with China's market reforms of 1998. Although the SDPC had been a long time supporter of central planning, it was ironically in favor of anything that promoted a free—or freer—market, since the cartels lessened the SDPC's burden of carrying the administrative authority over prices. Once both sides had their say, including the firms as well as others, pricing authority was restored to the SDPC by SETC and SPDC. Also, a higher threshold was set for proving the practice of dumping.[110]

The cut-throat nature of the Chinese domestic market is a force that is driving many Chinese electronics companies to seek markets overseas. By "going global," they can escape the harsh nature of domestic markets and seek more favorable foreign markets, as well as increase profit margins, and in doing so, maintain survival.

Notes

1. Shao Xingdong, *The Research on International Operation Strategy of Chinese Family Appliance Enterprises,* Master Thesis, China Oceanic University, June 2003, p. 8.

2. Ibid.

3. Ibid. p. 9.

4. This point is expressed in Andrew J. Nathan and Bruce Gilley, *China's New Rulers: The Secret Files,* New York: The New York Review of Boks, Inc., 2003; and in Barry Naughton, "SASAC Rising," *China Leadership Monitor* No. 14, Spring, 2005.

5. This point is elaborated by Erica Downs, "The Brookings Foreign Policy Studies Energy Security Series: China," The Brookings Institution, December 2006, p. 16-24.

6. Scott Kennedy, *The Business of Lobbying in China,* Harvard University Press, 2005, p. 51-53.

7. Ibid., p. 108.

8. Ibid., p. 107.

9. Ni Renfeng, "What is Changhong thinking, what is Changhong doing?" (Changhong zai xiang shenme changhong zai zuo shenmen), *China Business* (Zhongguo jingying bao), December 1, 1998, p. 8; and Zhang Zhong, "Allow Failure: a discussion with TCL president Li Dongsheng" (Yunxu shibai – yu TCL jituan zongcai li dongsheng yidu tan), *China Business* (Zhongguo jingying bao), February 9, 1999, p. 8.

10. Kennedy, 2005, p. 108.

11. Ibid., p. 109.

12. Ibid.

13.Ibid., p. 102.

14. Ibid., P. 103.

15. Ibid., p. 102-103.

16. Ibid., p. 111.

17. Ibid., p. 114.

18. Ibid., p. 113.

19. Sun Honggang, "Will color TV prices hold another 60 days?" (Caidian jiage zai kang 60 tian?), *China Business* (Zhongguo jingying bao), December 15, 1981, p. 1.

20. Li Zhiping, "Color TV color picture tube year-end summit" (Caidian caiguan suimo fenghui), *China Business Times* (zhongguo gongshang shibao), January 13, 1999, p.2; Gao Chujiang, "Color TV's great war triggered at any moment" (Caodian dazhan yichu jifa), *China Business Times* (zhongguo gongshang shibao), January 15, 1999, p.1.

21. Kennedy, 2005, p. 114.

22. Liu Jian, "Color Tube Stoppage is set" (Caidian tingchan cheng dingju), *China Business Times* (zhongguo gongshang shibao), May 24, 1999, p.1; Zhu Yangyan, "Eight large color tube factories resume production" (ba da caiguan chang hui fu shengchan), *China Business Times* (zhongguo gongshang shibao), July 16, 1999, p.1; Zhang Chunwei, "Great Price war gunpowder completely scattered, color TV heards formed alliance yesterday" (Jiage dazhan xiaoyan sanjin caidian jutou zuotian lianmeng), *Chengdu Commercial News* (Chengdu shang bao), June 10, 2000; and Guo Aibing, "Policymaker: TV Price Floor Illegal," *China Daily,* August 11, 2000.

23. Kennedy, 2005, p. 115.

24. Li Ye, Pang Xiaoling, "TCL's Continuous Progress in its Path of Internationalization," *Enterprise Studies,* No. 5, 2006, p. 84.

25. Wang Zengtao, Zhuang Guijun, and Fan Xiufeng, "Influence Factors and Framework of Chinese Manufacturing Firms' Internationalization: TCL as a Case," *Nankai Management Comments,* Vol. 8, No. 3, 2005, p. 92.

26. Pan Zhegao, "Li Dongsheng: Internationalization to Survive," *China Electronics Newspaper,* March 9, 2004.

27. Wang Zengtao, Zhuang Guijun, and Fan Xiufeng, "Influence Factors and Framework of Chinese Manufacturing Firms' Internationalization: TCL as a Case," *Nankai Management Comments,* Vol. 8, No. 3, 2005, p. 92.

28. "IBM, Maytag, Unocal ... Who's Next in China's Sights?" *Knowledge at Wharton,* University of Pennsylvania, November 21, 2005.

29. Ibid.

30. Ibid.

31. Peng Juan, "New Perspective to Internationalization," *Enterprise Studies,* March, 2006, p. 14.

32. Ibid.

33. Ibid.

34. Ibid. p. 15.

35. Wang Yukun, "TCL's Internationalization and Li Dongsheng's Retrospection," *China Manger,* No. 146, p. 54.

36. Zheng Lei, "Internationalization, Lenovo vs. TCL," *Company Cases,* September 2006, p. 85.

37. Zhou Hao, "TCL Was Impaired in its Internationalization," *China High Technological Industry Newspaper,* April 26, 2005.

38. Zheng Lei, "Internationalization, Lenovo vs. TCL," *Company Cases,* September 2006, p. 85.

39. Wang Ruping, "TCL's Internationalization Path's Benefits and Loss", CCTV-Dialogue Program, *China Industry Newspaper,* May 19, 2005.

40. Ibid.

41. He Zhiyi, "Choice of Chinese Enterprise's Path of Internationalization," *World Economic Studies,* No. 6, 2002, p. 6.

42. Song Yonggao, "From TCL's Embarrassment in Vietnam to Comment on Chinese Brand's Internationalization," *China Information Newspaper,* January 31, 2003.

43. Jia Nan, "TCL Significantly Attempt to Enter Russian Market, New Thinking about International Development," *International Finance Newspaper,* November 2, 2004.

44. Li Ye, Pang Xiaoling, "TCL's Continuous Progress in its Path of Internationalization," *Enterprise Studies,* No. 5, 2006, p. 85.

45. Shi Lu, "TCL's Internationalization Strategy's Skillfulness," *International Commercial Newspaper,* January 20, 2003.

46. Zhong Xue, "TCL: Acquisition's Risks," *China Manufacture Industry Economic Newspaper,* December 28, 2004.

47. Ibid.

48. Wang Yukun, "TCL's Internationalization and Li Dongsheng's Retrospection," *China Manger,* No. 146, p. 54.

49. Wang Zhen, "TCL: Brand Name and Acquisition – Multiple Ways towards Internationalization," *The First Financial Daily,* May 16, 2005.

50. Wang Ruping, "TCL's Internationalization Path's Benefits and Loss", CCTV-Dialogue Program, *China Industry Newspaper,* May 19, 2005.

51. Xia Ying, "How TCL Go Global?" *Southern Weekend,* October 14, 2004.

52. Zhang Ya, "TCL's Internationalization Goes Farther and Farther," *Commercial Weekly,* November 15, 2003, p. 22-23.

53. Dai Yan, "Chinese TV Makers to Appeal US Tariffs," *China Daily,* April 14, 1004.

54. "TCL: Carrying Internationalization to the End," *Consumer Daily,* November 11, 2003.

55. Wang Yukun, "TCL's Internationalization and Li Dongsheng's Retrospection," *China Manger,* No. 146, p. 54.

56. "TCL: Carrying Internationalization to the End," *Consumer Daily,* November 11, 2003.

57. Wang Yukun, "TCL's Internationalization and Li Dongsheng's Retrospection," *China Manger,* No. 146, p. 56.

58. Wang Ruping, "TCL's Internationalization Path's Benefits and Loss", CCTV-Dialogue Program, *China Industry Newspaper,* May 19, 2005.

59. Yang Yumei, "Li Dongsheng Examined his Mistakes for TCL's Huge Losses; TCL Started to Feel the Bitterness of Internationalization," *IT Time Weekly,* September 20, 2006, p. 57.

60. Ibid., p. 56-57.

61. Ibid., P. 58.

62. Wang Yukun, "TCL's Internationalization and Li Dongsheng's Retrospection," *China Manger,* No. 146, p. 56.

63. Ibid., p. 58.

64. Ibid.

65. Ibid.

66. Ibid.

67. Zhou Tao, Liu Xuchuan, "Li Dongsheng: Comments on the Performance of TCL's Internationalization," *Economic Observation Newspaper,* April 10, 2006.

68. "TCL's Dongsheng Li: 'We Should Control and Own Our Brands,'" *Knowledge at Wharton,* Wharton School of the University of Pennsylvania, June 1, 2005.

69. Ibid.

70. Ibid.

71. Ibid.

72. Cai Jianfei, "A Research on Haier's Internationalization Strategy," *Journal of Jiangsu Polytechnic University,* Vol. 4, No. 2, June 2003, p. 11.

73. Liu Fang, "Two Ways towards Outside – Analysis of Haier and TCL's International Strategies," *China and Overseas Enterprise Cultures,* November 2004, p. 26-27.

74. Cai Jianfei, "A Research on Haier's Internationalization Strategy," *Journal of Jiangsu Polytechnic University,* Vol. 4, No. 2, June 2003, p. 11.

75. Ibid., p. 12.

76. Ibid., p. 13.

77. Huang Zhiqiang, "The Way of Haier Group to Internationalization," *Journal of Guangdong Institute of Business Administration,* Vol. 18, No. 3, June 2003, p. 28.

78. Zheng Lei, "The Core of TCL's Internationalization," *China Manager,* No. 137, p. 79-80.

79. Zhang Hanhua, "Haier's Internationalization Strategy," *Enterprise's Reform and Operation,* No. 7, 2003, p. 31.

80. Liao Qingsheng, "Examine Haier's International Acquisition Strategy," *Communication and Information Newspaper,* March 16, 2005.

81. Zhang Yue, "Lost Maytag, Haier's Internationalization Continues," *Shanghai Business,* August 2005, p. 11.

82. Yu Yu, "Haier Moves its Chess in its Internationalization – Bidding for Maytag," *Electronic Appliances,* No. 7, July 2005.

83. Xi Xiangde, "Haier Expedite its Internationalization," *Commercial Weekly*, July 5, 2005.

84. Zhang Yue, "Lost Maytag, Haier's Internationalization Continues," *Shanghai Business*, August 2005, p. 13.

85. Liu Fang, "Two Ways towards Outside – Analysis of Haier and TCL's International Strategies," *China and Overseas Enterprise Cultures*, November 2004, p. 27.

86. Ibid.

87. Long Yun, Yang Yanli, and Tang Xiaoliang, "Comparison of TCL and Galanz's Internationalization Models," *Pioneering with Science & Technology Monthly*, No. 9, 2005, p. 57.

88. Liu Fang, "Two Ways towards Outside – Analysis of Haier and TCL's International Strategies," *China and Overseas Enterprise Cultures*, November 2004, p. 28.

89. He Ping, "Haier Successfully Conducted its Internationalization Strategy," *China Reform Newspaper*, February 14, 2003.

90. Shao Xingdong, *The Research on International Operation Strategy of Chinese Family Appliance Enterprises*, Master Thesis, China Oceanic University, June 2003, p. 20.

91. He Ping, "Haier Successfully Conducted its Internationalization Strategy," *China Reform Newspaper*, February 14, 2003.

92. Shao Xingdong, *The Research on International Operation Strategy of Chinese Family Appliance Enterprises*, Master Thesis, China Oceanic University, June 2003, p. 21.

93. Ibid.

94. Ibid.

95. Wang Zhen, "TCL: Brand Name and Acquisition – Multiple Ways towards Internationalization," *The First Financial Daily*, May 16, 2005.

96. Shao Xingdong, *The Research on International Operation Strategy of Chinese Family Appliance Enterprises*, Master Thesis, China Oceanic University, June 2003, p. 24.

97. Ibid., p. 22-23.

98. Ibid., p. 24.

99. Li Chengliang, Zhang Yuqin, "Haier's Internationalization Path's Enlightenment to Chinese Enterprises' Transnational Operation," *Shanghai Business*, No. 7, July 2005, p. 56-57.

100. Li Chengliang, Zhang Yuqin, "Haier's Internationalization Path's Enlightenment to Chinese Enterprises' Transnational Operation," *Public Standards*, No. 11, 2005, p. 6.

101. Shao Xingdong, *The Research on International Operation Strategy of Chinese Family Appliance Enterprises*, Master Thesis, China Oceanic University, June 2003, p. 38.

102. Shao Xingdong, *The Research on International Operation Strategy of Chinese Family Appliance Enterprises*, Master Thesis, China Oceanic University, June 2003, p. 16.

103. Ibid., p. 30.

104. Ibid.

105. China International Economic Consultants (CIEC), "Developments and Prospects of China's Household Electrical Industry," *China Industry Sector Report*, May 15, 2001.

106. Ibid.

107. Ibid.

108. Kennedy, 2005, p. 126.

109. *China Economic and Trade Reporter* (Zhongguo jingmao daokan), September 30, 1998, p. 22; Lu Zheng, *China Industrial Development Report 1999* (Zhongguo gongye fazhan baogao 1999), p. 132-133.

110. Kennedy, 2005, p. 112; and *China Business Times* (zhongguo gongshang shibao), December 8, 1998, p.2.

CONCLUSION

Investment into China is growing rapidly, since foreign firms are looking for a piece of the potentially huge Chinese market. At the same time, China's outward investment is also experiencing rapid growth, as more and more Chinese companies are searching for overseas investment opportunities. Meanwhile, mergers and acquisitions among domestic Chinese companies are on the rise. This consolidation is increasing rapidly in part because the Chinese government is encouraging domestic companies to internationalize.

Synthesis of Outward Foreign Investment

By issuing equity and by free cash flow generation, many of China's companies now have large cash reserves which they wish to spend. Some of these companies are looking to invest in the acquisition of overseas raw materials, while others are looking to expand. Most of the money that Chinese companies will send overseas will be invested in the oil and gas, mining, high-tech, telecommunications, and manufacturing sectors. Chinese companies invested US $0.6 billion overseas in 2000. By 2003, that figure had risen to US $2.1 billion. In 2006, the amount invested by Chinese companies had increased almost twenty-seven times the 2000 amount to US $16.1 billion.[1] The Chinese Ministry of Commerce currently predicts that the amount of Chinese FDI will continue to increase at a rate of 22% for the next few years, reaching a total of US $60 billion by 2010.[2]

The Chinese government's "Going Global" strategy, which it first put forth in 2000, created the first wave of outward investment from China in the 1990s. The object of this strategy was to shore up the Chinese economy and to pave the way for future economic growth and development. This first wave of outbound investment concentrated on natural resources and infrastructure, e.g., iron and steel, oil and gas, telecommunications and transportation. External factors that contributed to this wave of investment included liberalizing changes in the regulatory environment, the return of Hong Kong to the mainland in 1997 and the Asian crisis in 1998.[3] These also resulted in some takeover opportunities for China in neighboring countries.

2003 saw the emergence of the second wave of Chinese foreign investment. This wave includes a larger range of industries, is more geographically diverse and encompasses both small and large deals. This latest wave seems to be driven as much by economic considerations as by political ones. Economic considerations for outward investment include the desire of Chinese companies to avoid being restricted by an increasingly competitive domestic market, the desire to acquire global distribution networks, and the desire to obtain technological and managerial skills. Chinese companies' wish to secure long-term supplies of raw materials and energy also plays no small role in this current round of outward FDI.

In addition to traditional large state-owned enterprises, this new wave of investments includes such new, strong national companies as Haier, Huawei, TCL, Lenovo and Pearl River Pianos. These companies now have the size, financial resources and product quality to compete in the international arena, since they all spent years involved in domestic expansion and the creation of overseas clients.[4]

At this stage, overseas investment negotiations are taking place across various economic sectors. Nevertheless, some of the largest deals currently underway still involve companies in the oil and gas, high-tech, manufacturing and telecommunications sectors. These overseas ventures are fueled by a myriad of forces, including greater support from the Chinese government, the appreciation of the Chinese yuan, and increasing forms of liquidity, such as available bank facilities.[5]

The exposition and analysis of China's outward foreign direct investment illustrates the current pattern of merchant-state dualism, which was a dominant pattern of operation from the late Qing dynasty through the Nationalist period and up to the Communist revolution. This dualism was replaced by a state-dominated singular structure, when the capitalist class was eliminated in the Maoist era. China's current economic reforms, however, are restoring merchant dynamism in post-Mao China. In the 1980s, this pattern of merchant state dualism was reflected in the double-edged foreign investment strategy—that is, the leadership was able to use its strengths to reap the benefits of investments into China while guarding against problems this inward investment might have caused.[6] Merchant-state dualism is also reflected in the fact that liberalization was uneven, and often careful and hesitant, but nevertheless undeniable. The 1990s witnessed substantial merchant autonomy, as manifested in the Chinese companies' manifold paths of influence on public policy and then President Jiang Zemin's ideology of the "The Three Represents." Nevertheless, the heavy regulation of the Chinese economy and Jiang's ideology of "The Three Stresses" clearly shows that the state still has the upper hand.

Observations of Merchant Autonomy

The continued degree of merchant autonomy in China is illustrated by the flood of overseas investments by cash-rich Chinese banks, insurers, and pension funds. Moreover, Chinese financial institutions are clearly drawing the interest of foreign buyers—testimony again to merchant autonomy in China. Foreign investors have poured increasing amounts of cash into China's "Big Four" state-owned banks, as well as set their sights on smaller banks in the major cities. China is opening up its financial industry to meet commitments it made in order to gain admittance to the WTO, as well as to strengthen its financial system as it deregulates the banking industry. This increased autonomy of Chinese merchants in the financial sector is also evidenced by the plans of the state-owned banks to open subsidiary banks in foreign countries as part of China's "Going Global" strategy. Some of these countries include the U.S., Russia, Australia and several states in the Middle East.

Furthermore, additional evidence indicates merchant autonomy in China has increased, as well as autonomy of corporate governance. Such evidence includes the appearance of new banking practices and financial services to accommodate the emergence of a new urban middle class; China's opening of its booming aviation industry to foreign investment; and corporate restructuring of the state sector.

In addition, the simplification of the domestic approval process for overseas investments also bears witness to an increase in merchant autonomy. This simplification was begun when the State Council issued its "Decision Regarding the Reform of the Regulatory Framework of Investment" in July, 2004. In essence, the State Council decision removed most of the restraints imposed on enterprises engaged in foreign investment.[7]

Prior to this reform by the state council, any outward investment by a Chinese company was subject to review and approval by the Chinese government, regardless of the volume of the investment, the industry in which the investment was to be made or how the investment was to be financed. Thanks to the reform, the regime of review only applies to investments involving the use of government funds. All other investments are subject to an approval or registration regime—both of which are much simpler. The approval regime governs all investments that fall within the Catalogue of Investments Subject to Government Approval. The registration regime will govern all other investments.[8]

The Maintenance of State Control

The Chinese government is now trying to increase the quality and not the quantity of FDI, this in spite of the fact that inward investment reached an all time high in the first half of 2006. This is a clear indication that the government still has a strong hand in maintaining control of merchants. The Ministry of Commerce and the National Development and Reform Commission have both promulgated new rules concerning foreign takeovers based on national economic security grounds. Seven industries are now considered to be strategically important and so will remain under State control: telecommunications, petroleum, defense, electricity, coal mining, civil aviation and ocean shipping.[9]

The maintenance of State control over merchants in China is also illustrated by China's setbacks in the liberalization of the press and media sector, its extensive sophisticated and broad system of Internet filtering, and its administrative measures to cool down the economy in 2004 and 2006.

What is more, the relevant PRC regulations are still very rigid in spite of the simplified approval procedures for outward FDI mentioned above. This is another indication of state control over merchants. In April 2004, the NDRC, which administers the aforesaid approval regime, issued the Tentative Administrative Rules on Approval of Offshore Investments Projects. This directive prohibits Chinese legal entities from signing any definitive, legally binding agreements regarding offshore investment projects until they have obtained an NDRC-issued approval document or registration certificate. Any PRC company that signs an agreement not conditioned on receipt of approval from the NDRC is technically in breach of the NDRC Rules.[10] This stringent requirement grants the government a great influence over outward Chinese FDI. It also creates potential obstacles for Chinese investment overseas.

The Unification of State and Merchants

A myriad of industries bear witness to the interplay and unification of state control and merchant autonomy. These industries include state-owned enterprises that have sold off non-core assets due to sustained losses. Foreign players are permitted to invest in such industries, but presently they can only hold a minority share. Examples of this foreign investment can be found in China's iron and steel industry. For example, Netherlands-based Mittal Steel has secured a 36.7% stake in Hunan Valin Iron & Steel, and Luxembourg-based steel maker Arcelor has a 38.4% interest in Laiwu Steel.[11] The activism of China Mobile on the global stage as well as the creation of four major competitors in the Chinese telecommunications industry is another testimony to the interaction of government control and corporate autonomy. This interplay between state control and merchant autonomy is also revealed in the successful governmental efforts to control overseas price negotiations in the iron ore and steel industry and in its less successful attempts to close down the domestic private steel makers to avoid economic overheating. The coexistence of state control and merchant autonomy culminates in the fact that the state and the merchants have in essence become one. This unification of state and merchants is exemplified by China's management of its trillion dollar foreign reserves.

In addition, merchant-state dualism is also reflected in the political give and take both internationally and domestically, as is illustrated by China's involvement in Africa, Latin America and the Middle East for natural resources. In this political give and take, China is willing to give up political prestige for its own economic benefits.

Joint Actions of the Merchants and the State

Large state-owned multinationals are virtually a merger of merchants and state, despite the competing national and corporate interests. This dual character of PRC companies in their outward FDI campaigns results in some shared features among them. Some of these shared features have been helpful for overseas investment, while other features have worked against it.[12]

a) Government Support

Chinese companies' overseas investments are backed by the Chinese government, at least according to some views. The reasons for this state-backed FDI are quite clear: since China's economy has been heating up, the state has placed great importance on securing natural resources abroad; the acquisition of foreign assets is in part propelled by China's surplus foreign exchange reserve; and there is a political determination to have China's largest companies grow into first-class multinationals through overseas expansion. This approach has been considerably successful in recent years in Angola, Kazakhstan, and Nigeria.

b) Financing of Overseas FDI

Although Chinese companies are somewhat affected by the rigid domestic approval regulations mentioned earlier, they are at a great advantage when it comes to financing overseas acquisitions. Of course, Chinese investors are able to raise funds from drawing against their own balance sheets. In addition, they have two other sources of funding: 1) Since the Chinese government is the ultimate shareholder of the SOEs, it has given them much support for their acquisitions. 2) Chinese policy banks have provided bridging loans that have served as a second source of funds. However, such financial subsidies can have both positive and negative effects on Chinese companies that wish to invest overseas.

c) *Political Opposition*

The dual roles of Chinese companies, as representatives of the State and of the merchants, have often caused political friction in investing in the United States or other Western countries. Examples of this are the Lenovo-IBM and CNOOC-Unocal deals. Many in the United States opposed these transactions as going against US national security interests. Opponents of the Lenovo deal argued that it would give sensitive technology to a Communist country considered by some to be a political and economic rival of the United States. The CNOOC-Unocal deal was opposed because some feared it might interfere with the energy security of the United States. This type of political opposition to Chinese economic expansion will likely continue for the foreseeable future.

d) Corporate Governance

The structure of internal corporate governance of Chinese SOEs has also proved to be troublesome for conducting overseas FDI. The Chinese government is currently trying to change the management structure of SOEs, motivated in part by the companies' listings on the Hong Kong, New York and Shanghai stock exchanges. The structural change involves implementing corporate governance standards which are similar to those of Western companies. Nevertheless, Chinese companies are quite used to a bureaucratic management system, with a handful of senior officers wielding ultimate decision making power. Such a management system can cause damage to proposed transactions, particularly when internal corporate governance issues come up at a crucial stage in the transaction process. The future will see change not only to corporate formalities and procedures, but to corporate culture as well—changes which take time.[13]

Paradoxical Policy Tradeoffs:

The hybrid relations between government and business and the embedded position of merchant groups determine that China's approach to overseas FDI under current leadership faces a series of paradoxical policy tradeoffs: between the state and the market; supply expansion and demand moderation; the government and investment companies; and foreign policy and economic need.

The State versus the Market

The Chinese government will continue to try to balance the forces of the state and the forces of the market in FDI decision-making. The current leadership of China certainly has less faith in market forces than former Premier Zhu Rongji did. Some Chinese analysts even believe that the developmental strategy of the previous leadership is partly responsible for the current increase in economic differences between the urban and rural populations. This developmental strategy, with its concomitant faith in market forces, has also been blamed for the degradation of the environment. In response to these perceived flaws in the previous administrations developmental strategy, the current administration has prescribed the "Scientific Outlook on Development," as well as the creation of a comprehensive "Harmonious Society." At the same time, the current administration is acutely aware that too much state intervention in outward FDI would make little improvement. The Chinese government will no doubt make adjustments to the foreign investment approval procedures, including liberalization. This process, however, will be gradual, and relatively insubstantial in the short term out of concern for any possible impact such changes might have on social stability.

Expansion of Supply versus Moderation of Demand

A great portion of China's outward FDI is targeted to obtaining global natural resources. This targeting no doubt affects China's behaviors on the international stage. Thus any major shift in China's approach to natural resources, the energy supply in particular, will have a considerable impact on the world market. The current leadership has recently realized that it must place greater emphasis on management of the demand side, in order to correct the bias towards the supply side expressed in previous policies.[14] This change in approach was emphasized in both the 11th Five Year Plan (2006-2010) and the 17th Party Congress. China is thus making conservation an important target for sustainable economic growth.

Government versus Investment Companies

In spite of a good amount of coordination between the government and investment companies in their overseas activities, an increase in coordination between some national investment companies and the Ministry of Foreign Affairs will probably be necessary. This Ministry is anxious to keep abreast of projects pursued by the Chinese investment companies because of the potential negative impact on Beijing's foreign policy objectives. At the same time, the Chinese national investment companies also recognize the need for greater guidance about the political and economic risks abroad, since anti-foreign nationalism defeated their bids for assets in Russia (Slavneft) and the United States (Unocal).[15]

Foreign Policy versus Economic Need

The Chinese leadership is eager to pursue investments in regions where they will not interfere with the primary foreign policy objectives of the United States. An illustration of this is China's slightly differing behavior towards Iran and the Sudan. Another illustration of how Beijing balances its need for energy and its foreign policy priorities is the Chinese government's response to the furor that erupted in the United States in 2005 with regard to CNOOC's bid for Unocal. The Chinese government was never completely enthusiastic about the bid. Thus it requested that CNOOC withdraw its offer to prevent damage to Sino-US relations. The Chinese government also did not want to see any disruption to Hu Jintao's planned visit to the United States in 2005. These actions by the Chinese government are a clear illustration of Beijing giving priority to its relationship to the United States over the acquisition of foreign oil assets by a Chinese company.[16]

The Future

This overview of Chinese outward FDI has given examples of the positive and negative factors that face Chinese companies in the process of internationalization. If Chinese companies learn from their past mistakes in transactions and reach a higher level of sophistication, their future overseas investments will likely meet with success. The future success of Chinese overseas investment will also depend on whether the government can contain the concentration of wealth and market power with apparently insufficient political reforms. China's unknown political future is as intriguing as its contemporary government-business relations, since it has a market economy running atop a stagnant communist regime. On the one hand, China needs capitalist markets to make its economy more efficient, which paradoxically jeopardizes the political foundation of the Chinese government; on the other hand, China's severe non-economic and social problems are preventing the government from fully liberalizing the economy. China is now apparently dangling between these two outcomes. Faced with such a situation, the Chinese Communist Party is trying to improve, reform and prolong its tenure. The ability to deal with the challenges of governance will attest to whether the Chinese Communist Party can retain its leadership over China's development in the 21st century.

Notes

1. PPI Trade Fact of the Week, "Chinese Direct Investment Abroad Has Grown Twenty-Fold since 2000," Progressive Policy Institute, October 24, 2007.
2. Stand & Poor's Ratings Direct, "Behind the Chinese M&A Surge," *Business Week*, July 26, 2006.
3. "IBM, Maytag, Unocal . . . Who's Next in China's Sights?" *Knowledge at Wharton*, November 21, 2005, Wharton School of the University of Pennsylvania, at http://knowledge.wharton.upenn.edu/article.cfm?articleid=1262
4. Ibid.
5. Stand & Poor's Ratings Direct, 2006.
6. Margaret Pearson, *Joint Ventures in the People's Republic of China: the Control of Foreign Direct Investment under Socialism*, Princeton, New Jersey: Princeton University Press, 1991.
7. "The Challenges Facing Outbound Chinese M&A: PRO Companies' Acquisition Campaigns Share Some Generic Features—Some of These Features have Facilitated, While Others have Militate Against, Offshore Acquisitions," *International Financial Law Review*, Vol. 24, Issue 12, December 2005.
8. Ibid.
9. UNCTAD, *World Investment Report 2007*, p. 47.
10. *International Financial Law Review*, December 2005.
11. Stand & Poor's Ratings Direct, 2006.
12. These shared features have been noted in *International Financial Law Review*, December 2005.
13. *International Financial Law Review*, December 2005.
14. Downs, December 2006, p. 49.

15. "Chinese Leaders Set Out Priorities, Citing Challenges—Communist Party Produces Ambitious List to Address Social, Economic Inequities," *Wall Street Journal*, October 12, 2005. For Hu Jintao's comments on energy conservation, see "Chinese president outlines energy conservation and development policies," *BBC Monitoring Asia Pacific*, June 29, 2005.

16. Wang Fang, Francesco Guerrera and Joe Leahy, "Beijing 'never behind' bid for Unocal" *Financial Times*, August 6, 2005.

Bibliography

Books:

Alex Pravda, Blair A. Ruble, *Trade Unions in Communist States*, Boston: Allen & Unwin, Inc., 1986.

Andrew G. Walder, *Communist Neo-Traditionalism: Work and Authority in Chinese Industry*, University of California Press, 1986.

Andrew J. Nathan, *Chinese Democracy,* New York: Alfred Knopf, 1985.

Andrew J. Nathan and Bruce Gilley, *China's New Rulers: the Secret Files,* New York: NYREV, Inc., 2003.

Arthur Lewis Rosenbaum, *State and Society in China: the Consequences of Reform*, Westview Press, 1992.

Barry Naughton, *Growing Out of the Plan: Chinese Economic Reform, 1978-1993,* Cambridge: Cambridge University Press, 1995.

Bruce J. Dickson, *Red Capitalists in China: The Party, Private Entrepreneurs, and Prospects for Political Change,* Cambridge: Cambridge University Press, 2003.

Carl J. Friedrich and Zbigniew K. Brzezinski, *Totalitarian Dictatorship and Autocracy,* New York: Praeger, 1961.

Charles E. Lindblom, *Politics and Markets: The World's Political Economic Systems,* New York: Basic Books, 1977.

Christian Henriot, *Shanghai, 1927-1937: Municipal Power, Locality, and Modernization,* translated by Noel Castelino, Berkeley: University of California Press, 1993.

Danny M. Leipziger, Vinod Thomas, *Lessons of East Asia: an Overview of Country Experience*, Washington, D.C.: The World Bank, 1993.

David S. G. Goodman, *Groups and Politics in the People's Republic of China,* Armonk, NY: M. E. Sharp, 1984.

David Lampton, *Making of Chinese Foreign and Security Policy in the ERA of Reform, 1978-2000,* CA: Stanford University Press, 2001.

David Shambaugh, *Power Shift: China and Asia's New Dynamics*, University of California Press, 2005.

David L. Wank, *Commodifying Communism: Business, Trust, and Politics in a Chinese City,* Cambridge: Cambridge University Press, 1999.

David Zweig, *Internationalizing China: Domestic Interests and Global linkages*, Ithaca and London: Cornell University Press, 2002.

David Zweig, *Freeing China's Farmers: Rural Restructuring in the Reform Era*, Armonk: NY: M. E. Sharpe, 1997.

Deborah Davis and Ezra Vogel, *Chinese Society on the Eve of Tiananmen: the Impact of Reform*, Harvard University Press, 1990.

Donald P. Green and Ian Shapiro, *Pathologies of Rational Choice Theory: A Critique of Applications in Political Science,* New Haven, Conn.: Yale University Press, 1994.

Dorothy J. Solinger, *Chinese Business under Socialism: the Politics of Domestic Commerce*, 1949-1980, University of California Press, 1984.

Dorothy J. Solinger, *State and Society in China: The Consequences of Reform,* edited by Arthur Lewis Rosenbaum, Boulder: Colorado: Westview Press, 1992.

Edward Steinfeld, *Forging Reform in China: The Fate of State-Owned Industry,* Cambridge: Cambridge University Press, 1998.

Franz Schurmann, *Ideology and Organization in Communist China,* Berkeley: University of California Press, 1968.

Frederic C. Deyo, *The Political Economy of New Asian Industrialism,* edited by Frederic Deyo, Ithaca, NY: Cornell University Press, 1987.

Frederic C. Deyo, *Manufacturing Miracles: Paths of Industrialization in Latin America and East Asia,* edited by Gary Gereffi and Donald L. Wyman, Princeton: Princeton University Press, 1990.

Garry Rodan, Kevin Hewison and Richard Robison, *Political Economy of South-East Asia: Conflicts, Crises and Change*, Oxford University Press, 2001.

Gordon White, *Riding the Tiger: The Politics of Economic Reform in Post-Mao China,* Stanford: Stanford University Press, 1993.

Gordon White, Jude Howell, and Shang Xiaoyuan, *In Search of Civil Society, Market Reform and Social Change in Contemporary China,* Oxford: Clarendon Press, 1996.

Hao Yen-ping, *The Commercial Revolution in Nineteenth-Century China: The Rise of Sino-Western Mercantile Capitalism,* Berkeley: University of California Press, 1986.

Harmon Zeigler, *Pluralism, Corporatism, and Confucianism: Political Association and Conflict Regulation in the United States, Europe, and Taiwan,* Philadelphia: Temple University Press, 1988.

Henri-Claude de Bettignies, *Business Transformation in China,* London; Boston: International Thomson Business Press, 1996.

Jacques Gernet, *Daily Life in China on the Eve of the Mongol Invasion, 1250 -1276,* Stanford: Stanford University Press, 1962.

Jeanne L. Wilson, "The People's Republic of China," *Trade Unions in Communist States,* edited by Alex Pravda and Blair A. Ruble, Boston, MA: Allen & Unwin Inc., 1986.

Jeffrey A. Frieden, *Debt, Development, and Democracy: Modern Political Economy and Latin America, 1965-1985,* Princeton, NJ: Princeton University Press, 1991.

Jiang Bolung, Zou Zhenfang, *Foreign Investment of Chinese Enterprises,* Beijing: Economic Science Press, 1996.

John H. Dunning, *International Production and the Multinational Enterprise,* London; Boston: Allen & Unwin, 1981.

John H. Dunning, Rajneesh Narula, *Foreign Direct Investment and Governments,* London; New York: Routledge, 1996.

John Gardner, *Chinese Communist Politics in Action,* edited by A. Doak Barnett, Seattle: University of Washington Press.

John Gittings, *Changing Face of China: from Mao to Market*, Oxford University Press, 2005.

Joseph Fewsmith, *Party, State, and Local Elites in Republican China: Merchant Organizations and Politics in Shanghai, 1890 -1930,* Honolulu: University of Hawaii Press, 1985.

Joseph Fewsmith, *Contemporary Chinese Politics in Historical Perspective,* edited by Brantly Womack, New York: Cambridge University Press, 1991.

Joyce K. Kallgren, *Building a Nation-State: China after Forty Years*, Institute of East Asian Studies, University of California at Berkeley, 1990.

Keith Schoppa, *Chinese Elites and Political Change: Zhejiang Province in the Early Twentieth Century,* Cambridge, MA: Harvard University Press, 1982.

K. Kojima, *Direct Foreign Investment: A Japanese Model of Multinational Business Operations,* New York: Praeger Publishing Inc., 1978.

Kokubun Ryosei, Wang Jisi, *Rise of China and a Changing East Asian Order*, Washington, D.C.: Brookings Institution Press, 2004.

Li Yiling and Cao Fengqi, *Zhongguo Qiye de Kuaguojingying (Multinational Operation of Chinese Enterprises),* Beijing: China Planning Press, 1996.

Li Yuesheng, *et al., A Practical Handbook of Overseas Investment,* Shanghai: Far East Publishing House, 1993.

Liao Kuang-sheng, *Anti-foreignism and Modernization in China, 1860-1980,* Hong Kong: Chinese University of Hong Kong Press, 1984.

Lin Wulang, *Zhongguo Xiyin Waizi yu Haiwaitouzi (Inflow and Outward FDI of China),* Taipei: Mainland Affairs Council, 1997.

Liu Yan, *Multinational Corporation and Internationalization of Chinese Enterprises* (kuaguogongsi he zhongguo qiye de guojihua), Beijing, China Trust Press, 1992.

Margaret M. Pearson, *China's New Business Elite: the Political Consequences of Economic Reform,* University of California Press, 1997.

Margaret M. Pearson, *Joint Ventures in the People's Republic of China: the Control of Foreign Direct Investment under Socialism,* Princeton, New Jersey: Princeton University Press, 1991.

Marie-Claire Bergere, *The Golden Age of the Chinese Bourgeoisie, 1911-1937,* translated by Janet Lloyd, Cambridge: Cambridge University Press, 1989.

Mark Elvin, *The Pattern of the Chinese Past: A Social and Economic Interpretation,* Stanford: Stanford University Press, 1973.

Ministry of Commerce, *China Commerce Yearbook,* 2004 – 2006.

Ministry of Foreign Trade and Economic Cooperation (MOFTEC), *Yearbook of China's Foreign Economic Relations and Trade,* 2004-2007.

Ministry of Foreign Trade and Economic Cooperation (MOFTEC), *Almanac of China's Foreign Economic Relations and Trade,* 1991-2001.

Nigel Campbell, Sylvain R. F. Plasschaert and David H. Brown, *The Changing Nature of Management in China,* Greenwich, CT: JAI Press, 1991.

N.T. Wang, *China's Modernization and Transnational Corporations,* Lexington, Mass.: Lexington Books, 1984.

Pan Ye, *Zhongguo Duiwaitouzi Fazhanzhanlue (The Strategies for China to Develop Outward FDI),* Beijing: Economic Science Press, 1998.

Peng Jiangguo, *Utilization of Foreign Capital and Overseas Investment,* Beijing: Chinese Youth Publishing House, 1993.

Philippe C. Schmitter, *The New Corporatism: Social-Political Structures in the Iberian World,* edited by Fredrick B. Pike and Thomas Stritch, Notre Dame, IN: University of Notre Dame Press, 1974.

Pierre-Richard Agenor, Marcus Miller, David Vines, and Axel Weber, *Asian Financial Crisis: Causes Contagion and Consequences*, Cambridge University Press, 1999.

Richard Suttmeier, *Citizens and Groups in Contemporary China,* edited by Victor C. Falkenheim, Ann Arbor: Center for Chinese Studies, University of Michigan, 1987.

Robert Dahl, *Who Governs?* New Haven, Conn.: Yale University Press, 1961; and C. Wright Mills, *The Power Elite,* New York: Oxford University Press, 1959.

Robert Gilpin, *Global Political Economy: Understanding the International Economic Order*, Princeton, N.J.: Princeton University Press, 2001.

Robert Gilpin, *U.S. Power and the Multinational Corporation,* New York: Basic Books, 1975.

Robert Gilpin, *The Political Economy of International Relations*, Princeton, N.J.: Princeton University Press, 1987.

Robert Wade, *Governing the Market: Economic Theory and the Role of Government in East Asian Industrialization,* Princeton: Princeton University Press, 1990.

Ronald Rogowski, *Commerce and Coalition: How Trade Affects Domestic Political Alignments,* Princeton, NJ: Princeton University Press, 1989.

Ruth McVey, *Southeast Asian Capitalists*, Ithaca, New York: Cornell University Press, 1992.

Sanjaya Lall, *Transnational Corporations and Economic Development*, United Nations, London and New York: Routledge, 1993.

Scott Kennedy, *The Business of Lobbying in China,* Cambridge, Massachusetts: Harvard University Press, 2005.

Sheng Yitang, *et al., Sino-U.S.-Euro. Trading Almanac,* New York: Sino-U.S. Information Inc., Shanghai Jiao Tong University Press, 1995.

Sherman Cochran, *Big Business in China: Sino-Foreign Rivalry in the Cigarette Industry, 1890-1930,* Cambridge, MA: Harvard University Press, 1980.

S.H. Hymer, *The International Operations of National Firms: A Study of Direct Foreign Investment,* Ph.D. Thesis, M.I.T., Cambridge, Mass.: MIT Press, 1976.

Steve Chan, East *Asian Dynamism: Growth, Order, and Security in the Pacific Region,* Westview Press, 1990.

Su Dongsui, *International Management and Operations Forum and Collection* (guoji kuanli yu yunxing lunji), Shanghai, World Economic Literature Publishing House, 2000.

Susan Mann, *Local Merchants and the Chinese Bureaucracy, 1750-1950,* Stanford: Stanford University Press, 1987.

Susan L. Shirk, *The Political Logic of Economic Reform in China,* Berkeley: University of California Press, 1993.

Theodore H. Moran, *Foreign Direct Investment and Development*, Washington, DC: Institute for International Economics, 1998.

Theodore H. Moran, *Governments and Transnational Corporations,* London; New York: Routledge, 1993

Theodore H. Moran, *Multinational Corporations: the Political Economy of Foreign Direct Investment*, Lexington, Mass.: Lexington Books, 1985.

Thomas B. Gold, *Building a Nation-State: China After Forty Years,* edited by Joyce K. Kallgren, Berkeley, California: University of California Press, 1990.

Thomas N. Thompson, *China's Nationalization of Foreign Firms: The Politics of Hostage Capitalism, 1949-1957,* Baltimore: School of Law, University of Baltimore, 1979.

Tian Hung-mao, *The Great Transition: Political and Social Change in the Republic of China,* Stanford: Hoover Institution Press, 1989.

Tony Saich, *Governance and Politics of China,* New York: Palgrave MacMillan, 2004.

Tuan Yunceng, *Zhongguo Qiye Kuaguojingying ye Zanlue (China's Multinational Operation and Strategy),* Beijing: China Development Press, 1995.

United Nations Conference on Trade and Development (UNCTAD), *World Investment Report 2007*

United Nations Conference on Trade and Development (UNCTAD), *World Investment Report 2006*

Valerie Bunce and John M. Echols III, *Soviet Politics in the Brezhnev Era,* edited b Donald R. Kelley, New York: Praeger, 1980.

Victor C. Falkenheim, *Citizens and Groups in Contemporary China,* Ann Arbor: Center for Chinese Studies, University of Michigan, 1987.

Vivienne Shue, *Reach of the State: Sketches of the Chinese Body Politic*, Stanford, California: Stanford University Press, 1998.
Wang Hongying, *Weak State, Strong Networks,* Oxford: Oxford University Press, 2002.
Wellington Chan, *Merchants, Mandarins and Modern Enterprise in Late Ching China,* Cambridge, MA: Harvard University Press, 1977.
William Rowe, *Hankow, Commerce and Society in a Chinese City, 1796-1889,* Stanford: Stanford University Press, 1984.
Willy Kraus, *Private Business in China: Revival between Ideology and Pragmatism,* translated by Eric Holz, Honolulu: University of Hawaii Press, 1991.
Wlodzimierz Brus, *Pluralism in the Soviet Union: Essays in Honor of H. Gordon Skilling,* edited by Susan Gross Solomon, New York: St. Martin's Press, 1983.
World Bank, *East Asian Miracle: Economic Growth and Public Policy*, Oxford University Press, 1993.
World Bank 2000, *East Asia: Recovery and Beyond*, Washington, D.C.: the World Bank, 2000.
Yao Yang and Yin He, "Chinese Outward Investing Firms: A Study for FIAS/IFC/MIGA," Beijing: China Center for Economic Research, Peking University, 2005.
Yasheng Huang, *Selling China: Foreign Direct Investment during the Reform Era*, Cambridge University Press, 2003.
Yin Ziqing, *Zhongguo Duiwai Jingji Maoyi Gaige 20 Nian (Twenty Years of Reforms of Chinese Foreign Economy and Trade),* Henan: Zhongzhou Press, 1998.
Zhang Jing, *Fatuanzhuyi* (Corporatism), Beijing: China Social Sciences Press, 1998.

Journals:

Academy of Management Review, Academy of Management
American Political Science Review, American Political Science Association.
Asian Survey, Berkeley, California: University of California Press, *etc.*
Beijing Review, Beijing: Beijing Review Press.
Business Week, New York: McGraw Hill.
China Leadership Monitor, Hoover Institute, Stanford University Press.
China Quarterly, London, UK: University of London, Contemporary China Institute.
China Business Review, Washington, D.C.: National Council for US-China Trade.
China Economic Review, Greenwich, Connecticut: JAI Press.
East European Politics and Society, American Council of Learned Societies.
Europe-Asia Studies, Taylor & Francis, Ltd., UK.
Journal of Comparative Economics, Thomson Scientific.
Journal of Political Economy, Chicago: University of Chicago Press.
Journal of Economic Surveys, Avon, England: Tieto.
Journal of International Business Studies, Newark, N.J.: Academy of International Business and Rutgers Graduate School of Business Administration, *etc.*
Journal of Economic Studies, Aberdeen, Scotland: Department of Economics, University of Aberdeen.
Journal of International Economics, Amsterdam, North-Holland.
Strategic Management Journal, Chichester; New York: Wiley.
Telos, Telos Press.
The Australian Journal of Chinese Affairs, Contemporary China Center, Australian National University
Theory and Society, Springer.
Transnational Corporations, United Nations: Centre on Transnational Corporations.

World Economy, London: Basil Blackwell for the Trade Policy Research Centre, *etc.*
Caimao Yanjiu (Finance and Trade Research), Anhui: Anhui Institute Finance & Trade.
Gaige (Reform), Chongqing: China International Book Publishing, Inc.
Geological Bulletin of China (dizhi tongbao), China Academic Journals.
Guoji Maoyi Wenti (International Trade Journal), Beijing: International Business and Economics Press.
Guoji Jingji Hezuo (International Economic Cooperation), Beijing: International Economic Cooperation Magazine Press.
International Financial Law Review, London: Euromoney Publications Ltd.
Journal of China National Land Resources Economic Study Institute (zhongguo guotuziyuan jingjiyanjiusuo qikan), China Academic Journals.
Journal of Institutional and Theoretical Economics, Mohr Siebeck, Germany.
Jingji Kexue (Economic Science); Beijing: Beijing University Press.
Touzu Yanjiu (Investment Research); Beijing: China Investment Association and China Construction Bank Publishing House.
Transnational Corporations (kuaguo gongsi), China Academic Journals.
Productivity Studies (*shengchanli yangyu*), China Academic Journals.

Newspapers & Dissertations:

Financial Times, London, U. K. : MacRae, Curtice & Co.
Wall Street Journal, New York, N.Y. : Dow Jones.
Barron's, Chicopee, Mass. : Dow Jones & Co.
China Economic Times, a comprehensive daily newspaper of Development Research Center of the State Council, Beijing, China.
Economy Daily, China's leading business newspaper founded in early 1980s.
People's Daily (renmin ribao), Central Committee of the Communist Party of China, Beijing, China.
PPI Trade Fact of the Week, Progressive Policy Institute.
Reference News (*cankao xiaoxi*), Xinhua News Agency.
Wen Hui Bao, Wenhui-Xinmin United Press Group.
Jiang Qunying, *Research on the Current Situation and Countermeasures of Foreign Direct Investment of Chinese Enterprises* (zhongguo qiye duiwai zhijietouzi de xianzhuang he duice yanjiu), Doctoral Dissertation, Fu Dan University, 2003.
Wang Yan, *Testifying Analysis of China's Outward Foreign Direct Investment* (zhongguo duiwai zhijietouzi de shizhengfenyi), Master Thesis, Foreign Economic Trade University, China, 2006.
Yang Lan, *China Telecom Group Corporation – International Development Strategy Analysis* (zhongguo dianxin jituangongsi – guojihua fazhan zhanlue tantao), Master Thesis, Jinan University, May 2003.
Zhou Lina, *A Study on Internationalization of Telecommunication Industry – Internationalization Strategy of Telecommunication Industry in China* (dianxin chanye guojihua fazhanyanju – jianlun zhongguo dianxin Chanye guojihua zhanlue), Mater Thesis, Harbin Engineering University, February 2002.
Zhu Wenming, *China's Foreign Direct Investment Studies – Based on the Economic Globalization's Analysis and Strategy* (zhongguo duiwai zhijietouzi yanjiu – jingji uanqiuhua fenxi he zhanlue), Doctoral Dissertation, China's Academy of Social Science, 2001.